SOCIAL ENTREPRENEURSHIP INTRAPRENEURSHIP AND SOCIAL VALUE CREATION

Relevance for Contemporary Social Work Practice

Edited by Monica Nandan, Tricia B. Bent-Goodley, and Gokul Mandayam

NASW PRESS

National Association of Social Workers
Washington, DC

Kathryn Conley Wehrmann, PhD, MPH, ACSW, *President*
Angelo McClain, PhD, LCSW, *Chief Executive Officer*

Cheryl Y. Bradley, *Publisher*
Stella Donovan, *Acquisitions Editor*
Julie Gutin, *Project Manager*
Julie Palmer-Hoffman, *Copyeditor*
Julie Kimmel, *Proofreader*
Lori Holtzinger, Zinger Indexing, *Indexer*

Cover by Ashley Slade
Interior design, composition, and eBook conversion by Rick Soldin
Printed and bound by P. A. Hutchison

First impression: April 2019

© 2019 by the NASW Press

Library of Congress Cataloging-in-Publication Data

Names: Nandan, Monica, author. | Bent- Goodley, Tricia B., author. | Mandayam, Gokul, author.
Title: Social entrepreneurship, intrapreneurship and social value creation : relevance for contemporary social work practice / Monica Nandan, Tricia Bent-Goodley, and Gokul Mandayam.
Description: Washington, DC : NASW Press, [2019] | Includes bibliographical references and index.
Identifiers: LCCN 2018052626 | ISBN 9780871015389 (pbk.) | ISBN 9780871015396 (eBook)
Subjects: LCSH: Social service. | Social entrepreneurship. | Social service--Practice.
Classification: LCC HV40 .N2546 2019 | DDC 361.3/2--dc23 LC record available at https://lccn.loc.gov/2018052626

Printed in the United States of America

Contents

Part I
Intersection of Social Work Practice with Social Entrepreneurship, Social Intrapreneurship, and Social Innovation

Part II
Global Examples of Social Entrepreneurship, Social Intrapreneurship, Social Innovation, and Social Value Creation: Relevance for Social Work Practice

Foreword

Darrell P. Wheeler

At the core of most, if not all, social work efforts is a deep desire to improve well-being, particularly of vulnerable populations. Of equal significance is the desire to correct social, political, and economic ills that negatively affect the most marginalized in our society. The determination to help correct such seemingly intractable problems is a signature for the social work experience and our enduring professional impact in an often chaotic and, at times, downright hostile social environment. This passion for assisting others and bringing about social change is laudable, but in and of itself it is likely insufficient to produce or sustain needed changes.

The history of our professional efforts reinforces the need for contemporary approaches to our practices that build on our core strengths, use new technologies to understand the world as it exists today, and provide pathways to solving the problems we face. The proposition poised by Nandan, Bent-Goodley, and Mandayam in *Social Entrepreneurship, Intrapreneurship, and Social Value Creation: Relevance for Contemporary Social Work Practice* is simple: Social work does matter, particularly when we ourselves make the work we do relevant and sustainable. By shifting social innovation, entrepreneurship, and value chain approaches from a business-only model to the core of social work practice, the authors of the chapters in this volume celebrate what we do in these frontier spaces and share important ways of sustaining these efforts. This unique text explores the world through a social work lens, unapologetically lauding the strengths our profession brings to addressing complex problems of a 21st-century global landscape. The leap into this discussion is greatly facilitated by an in-depth examination of the foundational elements of entrepreneurial approaches that are innovative and provide added social value. They critically challenge the framework that social good and innovation and entrepreneurialism are incompatible. In this era of rapid systemic changes fueled by technological innovations and greater consolidation of wealth and resources in the hands of the elite few and corporations, the opposite is true. This text celebrates social work innovators and entrepreneurs who use their passion to help.

The relationships among mission, revenue, and social work practice are clearly delineated as essential to contemporary professional practice and future relevancy. Although intended for a social work audience, this text bridges disciplines and offers critical pathways to speaking to colleagues in other fields with clarity and conviction about the historical and future contributions of social work to addressing complex societal problems and enhancing social value creation.

Social Entrepreneurship, Intrapreneurship, and Social Value Creation: Relevance for Contemporary Social Work Practice should become a required reading for students and a frequently referenced resource for seasoned practitioners. This book challenges us to pursue our mission of creating empowering environments and producing social value while considering the environmental and financial components of sustainable approaches to creating social good. Creating a direct, intentional link and path between our commitment to social value and social justice is not antithetical to being innovative, entrepreneurial, and fiscally astute. Accolades to the editors and authors for challenging our thinking and celebrating our contributions.

Darrell P. Wheeler, PhD, MPH, ACSW
Provost and senior vice president
for academic affairs, Iona College,
New Rochelle, New York

Acknowledgments

Thank you to the NASW Press publications team, who have been so supportive throughout this process. We appreciate you. Also, thank you to those social work pioneers who advanced this work through their innovation and entrepreneurial spirit before we had a language for it.

Editing the various versions of the book chapters would have been almost impossible without the meticulousness, industriousness, positive spirit, and unrelenting passion of our graduate research assistant, Mrs. Karen Ake, MSW student at Kennesaw State University. With contributors from different parts of the world, writing in different styles and format, it was necessary to streamline and refine the final product, and Karen was enormously helpful in that endeavor. One may say that as a result of formatting the chapters, Karen has turned into a professional APA formatter. She never once expressed frustration or demonstrated fatigue from last-minute edits. She appeared to effortlessly juggle planning her daughter's wedding, attending to final exams and projects in the MSW program, and meeting the manuscript's submission deadline. We cannot thank her enough and wish her daughter and son-in-law the very best. Karen will graduate from the MSW program at Kennesaw State University in 2019. We wish her well in her professional career and personal life.

We would also like to express our gratitude to Ms. Ashley Price, our graduate research assistant during the early stages of manuscript preparation. Her efforts to understand the concept of social entrepreneurship, identify articles from various sources, and read and analyze the same were very valuable. Ashley graduated from the MSW Program at Kennesaw State University in May 2018. We wish her well in her professional career and personal life.

Prologue

This book has been long in the making. The idea of social work entrepreneurship or social workers' engaging in entrepreneurship has been viewed as antithetical to social work ethics by some practitioners and academicians. However, the significance of the social work entrepreneurship process is gradually being embraced and is growing in stature within the profession and schools of social work. Historically, social workers have practiced or participated in social innovation and entrepreneurship—more intuitively and organically than through formal training—while addressing complex, recalcitrant social issues. Social workers have a long history of innovation that promotes social justice, social enterprises, and change for the common good. Because social workers have to focus on the interrelationships between individual empowerment and community development, social entrepreneurship, intrapreneurship, and value creation strategies can greatly assist in these endeavors. The human services management competencies in executive leadership, resource development, strategic management, and community collaboration prepare and predispose social workers for social entrepreneurship, innovation, intrapreneurship, and value creation. Consequently, in today's dynamic and global context, it is vital that we more formally prepare social work students and practitioners to engage in innovation, entrepreneurship, and social value creation as ethical social work practice. This edited volume will benefit social workers interested in learning more about how to respond to local, national, and global issues; practice within different forms of organizational structures; initiate broad system-level change; and advance social justice.

As the concept of social entrepreneurship has grown within business and nonprofit literature, there is an increased awareness of the important and unique roles that social workers can play in this arena. Hence, more than a dozen social work academic programs offer minors, concentrations, and courses on social innovation and social entrepreneurship. Social entrepreneurship promotes innovation and adaptable, yet scalable, strategic responses to complex social and human problems. The unique contribution of this book is that it describes the concepts and principles of social entrepreneurship, social intrapreneurship, social innovation, and social value creation as they relate to social work practice. It explores connections between social work practice, social entrepreneurship, social intrapreneurship, social innovation, and social value creation nationally and internationally and how core social work values are related to these perspectives, strategies, and areas of practice. In essence, the book highlights the critical and ethical role of social workers in advancing innovative practices for promoting social change to transform and address endemic economic and social issues.

The book is divided into two parts: The first part of the book provides conceptual definitions and principles of social entrepreneurship, social intrapreneurship, social innovation, and social value creation as they relate to social work practice and ethics. The second part of the book provides examples from across the globe of either how social workers themselves engaged in social entrepreneurship, intrapreneurship, and innovation or how they partnered with, promoted, or perceived social entrepreneurship through a social work lens.

Part I

Chapter 1, "Social Entrepreneurship, Social Intrapreneurship, Social Innovation, and Social Value Creation: An Overview and Implications for Social Work," provides an overview and detailed explanation of each of the concepts. The authors discuss the important role that social workers play, and can play, in each of these areas of practice and their relationships with social work values and ethics.

Chapter 2, "Innovation and Creativity in Nonprofits," examines how innovation and creativity in nonprofits inform social work practice. The author provides details on how social work nonprofit managers and administrators can create and benefit from environments that support idea generation, innovation, and creativity to address social and organizational challenges.

Chapter 3, "Social Innovation and Social Work Practice," explores the interconnection between innovation, design thinking, and social work practice. The authors provide details on how to implement innovations in social work practice with illustrations from across the globe that have been successful. They emphasize that social work curricula should incorporate new ways of working with individuals, communities, and organizations; different types of financial resources for socially innovative work; and different organizational forms.

Chapter 4, "Financial Inclusion and Social Entrepreneurship," examines financial inclusion as a form of social work intervention and its implications for social work entrepreneurship. The author provides details on how financial inclusion interventions with vulnerable population groups assist in providing livelihood opportunities, building assets, and bridging the gap between poor households and formal financial services. It is emphasized that these socially innovative strategies and interventions are essential for social workers for promoting social justice.

Chapter 5, "Macro Practice and Its Relationship to Social Innovation," explores opportunities and connections between these two important concepts as a part of ethical social work practice. In describing the social innovation process, the author provides illustrations of how macro social workers can participate in each step of the innovation process. She also describes the process of moving from idea generation to creating social impact. Finally, she builds a case for incorporating more social innovation and entrepreneurship content into contemporary macro practice courses to make them more relevant in a global context.

Part II

Chapter 6, "Child Helpline International: From Social Work Field Action Project to an International Social Entrepreneurial Venture," describes how one social entrepreneurial venture scaled from a single city and country, through networks, collaborations, and partnerships, into an international venture that generated social value for various stakeholders across the world.

Chapter 7, "Community Development, Empowerment, and Social Entrepreneurship by 'Thankyou': An Australian Example," describes a social entrepreneurship case related to community development and empowerment of vulnerable populations, from a social work ecosystem's perspective. Using a case example of a social entrepreneurship venture from Australia, the author emphasizes how social entrepreneurship is an important form of social work practice at micro, mezzo, and macro levels for addressing the problem of poverty and associated issues, such as water crises and child and maternal health.

Chapter 8, "Innovation in a Chinese Social Work Context," provides an example of implementing and sustaining innovation, while transferring the innovation to a new international context. Here the authors describe the process of developing and evaluating a Chinese version of a family group conferencing intervention to address the issue of child neglect in a small community. This social worker–led initiative is particularly relevant for international social workers considering scaling successful innovative interventions across the globe.

Chapter 9, "Innovative Practices in Financial Inclusion and Asset Building: Relevance for Social Work Practice," describes different types of FinTech products and services relevant for building assets and financial security for economically disadvantaged populations. The author demonstrates the importance of social work practitioners engaging with, or participating in designing, innovative products and services for promoting social change and social justice. The chapter concludes with implications for social work practice and education as it pertains to asset development and financial security.

Chapter 10, "Social Entrepreneurship: Case of Livelihoods and Economic Development in an Urban Environment in India," describes a social entrepreneurship case that addresses a challenging issue of sustainable livelihood in India, from the perspective of social work practice. The chapter describes the social entrepreneurial approach used by an organization's founder; the parallels with social work practice and values; and the impact of this approach for addressing empowerment, sustainable livelihood, and economic development in a poor urban community.

Chapter 11, "Social Work Entrepreneurship: Case Examples in Homelessness and Mental Health in the United States," illuminates the social work entrepreneurship experiences of two social workers who addressed issues of homelessness and mental health. In this chapter, the authors describe their journey of identifying complex social issues, designing innovative approaches to address them, and sustaining the innovation through different types of organizational structures. These cases clearly demonstrate that social workers can be natural social innovators, entrepreneurs, intrapreneurs, and value creators while promoting social justice.

Chapter 12, "Social Entrepreneurship: A Zanzibari Example," presents a case of Zanzibari women's engagement in social entrepreneurship for community building, economic independence, and innovation. The chapter describes how social workers can promote, partner with, and sustain social entrepreneurship endeavors for supporting sustainable and transformative practices within communities.

Finally, Chapter 13, "Self-Help Groups as Social Enterprises: Citizen-Driven Social Entrepreneurship in India," provides examples of social entrepreneurial initiatives, through self-help groups, led by Muslim women who had minimal education and were living below the poverty line in a rural community. The author shares these examples of ordinary citizens who are leading social entrepreneurial efforts in their communities and using strategies often practiced by community social workers. She recommends strategies for social workers to partner with and promote such initiatives as clinical, administrative, and community practice social workers.

We hope that readers will engage with, and embrace, the efforts and perspectives of social work entrepreneurs.

PART I

Intersection of Social Work Practice
with Social Entrepreneurship, Social
Intrapreneurship, and Social Innovation

1

Social Entrepreneurship, Social Intrapreneurship, Social Innovation, and Social Value Creation: An Overview and Implications for Social Work

Monica Nandan, Tricia B. Bent-Goodley, Gokul Mandayam, and Archana Singh

Discussions of social entrepreneurship, intrapreneurship, and innovation in social work have been gradually increasing in recent years (Bent-Goodley, 2001; Berzin, Pitt-Catsouphes, & Gaitan-Rossi, 2015, 2016; Germak & Singh, 2009; Gummer, 2001; Jaskyte & Dressler, 2005; Nandan, London, & Bent-Goodley, 2015; Nandan & Scott, 2013; Savaya, Packer, Stange, & Namir, 2008). Social workers employed in various fields of practice and at different systemic levels are realizing the importance of entrepreneurial thinking and of creating shared economic and social value (Singh, 2016). Ironically, the "social" in social entrepreneurship, social intrapreneurship, social innovation, and social value creation has seldom engaged the social work profession. Though social workers are the most visible professionals occupying a realm that has been challenged by contemporary changes in the political, economic, and social landscapes, the discipline has not had a strong presence in the social enterprise movement (Neal, 2015). Over the last three decades, since Bill Drayton coined the term "social entrepreneur" (Davis, 2002), social workers have been slow to embrace the concept. It is important to remember social work's entrepreneurial endeavors throughout history, such as settlement houses and charity organization societies. Similarly, through policy advocacy, social workers spearheaded or promoted policy entrepreneurship (for example, during the War on Poverty and the New Deal era). In our opinion, social workers are important stewards of social entrepreneurship—as promoters, pioneers, and partners.

Social entrepreneurship and social work are compatible in terms of both skills and values and complement each other (Neal, 2015). Social entrepreneurship and intrapreneurship processes entail using skills, practices, and behaviors that often resonate with social work practice at the micro, mezzo, and macro levels. For instance, problem assessment, working closely with

3

various stakeholders, tapping social networks, mobilizing community and individual resources, and creating social value as a result of the innovative intervention are illustrations of parallels between social work practice and social entrepreneurship and intrapreneurship. Social workers are some of the best-prepared professionals to act in response to the world's social problems (Germak & Singh, 2009). Social workers play a decisive role in economic and social development not only in developing countries but in developed countries as well (Singh, 2016). "Social work and SE [social entrepreneurship], combined together, could potentially emerge as an effective tool to solve the world's complex social problems innovatively" (Singh, 2016, p. 31). With rapidly increasing social service needs and an ever-changing context, there is all the more need for linking social work practice with innovative approaches that are efficient and effective solutions for contemporary social problems. Given the potential of social entrepreneurship to augment social work practice, empower clients, provide alternative funding sources, and offer insulation from disruption of essential services, it is evident that social entrepreneurship dovetails with social work values of service, social justice, and competence (Neal, 2015).

Businesses too have taken a keen interest in the field of social entrepreneurship. Health, education, and employment goals are perceived by business as encouraging national investments in human resources from both demand and supply perspectives (Hopkins, 2016). Through corporate social responsibility (CSR) initiatives, businesses are focusing on shared value creation (Porter & Kramer, 2002; Rahdari, Sepasi, & Moradi, 2016). Corporations can conduct business in a way that produces not only economic value but also social value by addressing society's challenges and contributing to sustainable development (Rahdari et al., 2016). Baron (2005) made a case that social entrepreneurs can take strategic CSR activities beyond profit maximization to create social good. Actually, "socially responsible companies are those whose primary goal is profit; and, for most of them, their socially responsible behavior is motivated by the belief that it will improve the bottom line" (Dorado, 2006, p. 322). By embracing the principles of sustainable development and harnessing the benefits of shared value approaches focused on people, businesses have taken a significant leap with intersectoral collaboration by moving beyond the traditional confines of charity and philanthropy (Hopkins, 2016). More than 148 institutions of higher learning in the United States were offering courses related to social entrepreneurship, as reported by Kim and Leu (2011), though most of these courses appear to have been situated in business or public administration programs.

Although the social work profession has been slow to embrace social work entrepreneurial perspectives (Nandan & Scott, 2013), social workers are educated as social change agents for creating "something with nothing." These characteristics align with social work entrepreneurial thinking. "Social workers involved in community development initiatives with impoverished communities have been strong advocates of social enterprise . . . though, on the whole, it has been a marginal theme in professional social work" (Gray, Healy, & Crofts, 2003, pp. 141–142). Unfortunately, some practitioners and educators believe that social work entrepreneurship could conflict with the profession's code of ethics (Germak & Singh, 2009; Gray & Crofts, 2008). The popular view that social work and business disciplines are incompatible on various grounds fails to recognize the contextual reality in which social work- ers are increasingly expected to navigate issues such as service administration, reimbursement, and alternative sources of funding (Mirabito, 2012; cf. Neal, 2015). Notwithstanding this perspective, social workers across the globe are initiating or promoting social enterprises, social businesses, nonprofit organi- zations, or socially intrapreneurial projects—as is evidenced in this book—for creating innovative individual, family, and community-level changes. They are combining social work skills with business models to create social entre- preneurial ventures, corporate sector service organizations, and private prac- tices that create social value (Dale, 2012). Thus, social work entrepreneurial thinking has, in many ways, already been used within the profession without fully understanding or maximizing the knowledge and skill set related to social entrepreneurship.

Furthermore, one of the 10 imperatives for the next decade adopted by the Social Work Congress in 2010 was to infuse new models related to sustainable organizations and leadership into social work education and practice (Dale, 2012). In addition, the Grand Challenges for Social Work (Uehara et al., 2013) and the new United Nations Sustainable Development Goals (United Nations Development Programme, n.d.) are a clarion call to the profession to more actively engage with the concepts of social entrepreneurship, intrapreneur- ship, innovation, social enterprise, and shared value creation. "The scale, com- plexity, and interrelatedness of social problems—from poverty and dramatic inequality to the sustainability of health and human service infrastructures across the globe—demand problem-solving skill and collaboration at levels perhaps unprecedented in our history" (Uehara et al., 2013, p. 165).

Social entrepreneurs create local opportunities for social, physical, and economic sustainable development (Seelos & Mair, 2005). Konda, Starc, and Rodica (2015) observed the positive impact of social entrepreneurs in address- ing several UN sustainable goals—for example, in health care, education, social inclusion, employment—in Slovenia. They concluded that partnerships across sectors assisted social entrepreneurs in designing innovative solu- tions to address the aforementioned goals. Evidence was provided, and the case was built, for social entrepreneurship strategies that can transform the economy toward achievement of sustainable development (İyigün, 2015; Roy & Tripathi, 2015). Spearheading or contributing to sustainable development and environmental justice are social work's ethical responsibilities. Thus, it behooves the social work field to be ethically responsible by actively partaking in the discourse on social entrepreneurship as a viable strategy for addressing social problems (Neal, 2015).

Against this brief background, this chapter provides an overview of the changing social environment and describes social innovation, social work entrepreneurship, social intrapreneurship, social enterprise, and SV creation both within and outside the social work profession. This chapter also provides historical and contemporary approaches to social work entrepreneurship and concludes with an ethical rationale for the profession's engagement with these concepts and incorporation of these strategies within the curriculum.

Changing Social Environments Call for Innovative Thinking

Changing dynamics, increasing complexity of social issues, and the evolving nature of the funding environment have created a space where social work entrepreneurship is needed to advance practice and create social impact (Nandan & Scott, 2013). Complex and dynamic social issues also require new assessment lenses and newer intervention approaches, because traditional approaches may be inappropriate or not helpful in addressing the issues. The relatively limited and recent interest in social work entrepreneurship within the profession is partially related to several social, political, and economic factors, such as the devolution of public services, economic recession, reliance on diverse revenue streams in nonprofit organizations, and questionable effectiveness of the social welfare system (Nandan & Scott, 2013; Singh, 2016). Interestingly, "in response to the changing political and economic context, human service agencies are being forced or encouraged to adapt their governance and management to emphasize performance, innovation and flexibility" (Smith, 2015, p. 407). It is therefore not surprising that traditional funding sources are drying up, leaving many nonprofit agencies with fewer avenues for generating revenues to address ceaseless increases in service demand. Internationally, nongovernmental organizations and developmental organizations are having low levels of sustainable social impact (Rahdari et al., 2016). Social workers have been innovative and creative in building and sustaining institutions and programs that are "moving the needle." Perhaps unconsciously, they have been socially innovative, entrepreneurial, and intrapreneurial while creating social value as illuminated by Nandan and Scott (2013), who stated that social entrepreneurs "address social issues in new ways by thinking beyond conventional solutions and designing truly innovative, proactive, sustainable solutions for some of society's most vexing problems" (p. 262).

Historically, social work administrators and community planners have often utilized entrepreneurial thinking to advance their agencies and programs and ensure their sustainability, while creating the desired social impact. Today, one may propose that to sustain oneself within a social work organization, social work intrapreneurial and innovative thinking is almost a necessity.

Neal (2015) highlighted that the social work profession needs to willingly accept entrepreneurial strategies in two specific ways: (1) social work agencies should engage more with social enterprise organizations and associations, and (2) social work programs should include within their curriculum at least one course on social entrepreneurship with interdisciplinary content to get a better grasp of cross-sector collaborative approaches for creating entrepreneurial solutions to solve social problems. In addition, Zhu, Rooney, and Phillips (2016) proposed a curriculum matrix that enables students to acquire the necessary knowledge and skills for balancing the tension between addressing social welfare through social entrepreneurship while ensuring financial viability of the innovative idea.

Against this context and curriculum proposal, the next section defines the key concepts and explains the principles of social innovation, social entrepreneurship, social intrapreneurship, and social value creation.

Defining Social Innovation, Social Entrepreneurship, Social Intrapreneurship, Social Enterprise, and Social Value Creation

Before going into detail about each of the concepts, we would like to clarify that social innovation and social value creation are important components of social work entrepreneurship and intrapreneurship processes; social entrepreneurs and intrapreneurs are persons who possess specific qualities, perspectives, and predispositions that enable them to succeed in these roles (Singh, 2016). These individuals initiate the innovative change process while taking calculated risks (Bacq & Janssen, 2011), or they could be following the principle of affordable loss as explained by Sarasvathy (2001). Social enterprises are organizational vehicles or conduits—in the commercial, public, nonprofit, or civil society sectors—that are created by social entrepreneurs, or that employ intrapreneurs, for implementing socially innovative initiatives (Konda et al., 2015).

Social Innovation (SI)

Within the current dynamic political, social, and economic global context, SI is almost a necessity for professional and organizational survival and for creating sustainable solutions with lasting social impact (Salamon, Geller, & Mengel, 2010). The future of global society appears to lie in SI (Konda et al., 2015, p. 219). SI is broader than social entrepreneurship and has been used in multiple contexts. SI can take various forms in the context of sustainable business models (Hockerts & Wustenhagen, 2010; cited in Boon & Ludeke-Freund, 2013). These include (1) product and process innovations with a social purpose; and (2) innovation related to the scope of entrepreneurial, intra-preneurial, or managerial activities, such as initiating and developing social enterprises and organization-based internal activities. In a qualitative study of human service leaders' understanding and perceptions of the meaning of SI, Berzin et al. (2015) discovered that SI reflected four themes: innovative solutions, business and social enterprise, partnerships, and technology. SI goes through a development cycle of generating ideas from the bottom, developing and testing of the idea, accumulating empirically supported ideas, enabling the ideas through building synergies between unrelated systems, testing these synergies, building capacity, and finally supporting changes in structural frameworks (cf. Konda et al., 2015, p. 219).

Thus, social entrepreneurship is clearly one form or manifestation of SI. According to Dees (1998), SI is central to social entrepreneurship and argu-ably even to social intrapreneurship. SI entails implementing novel solutions that enhance individual and community welfare as compared with the status quo (H. P. Young, 2011). Some authors assert that social entrepreneurship is an "innovative, social value creating activity" (J. E. Austin, Stevenson, & Wei-Skillern, 2006, p. 1) and that social entrepreneurs are social innovators who drive social change (Mair & Marti, 2006). "Innovation in the social sphere means accomplishing more with less, working together, leveraging resources, sharing data and creating models for change that are sustainable" (Nandan, London, & Bent-Goodley, 2015, p. 42). SI encompasses imple-mentation of new and improved ideas, processes, products, and services (Baregheh, Rowley, & Sambrook, 2009) that ultimately improve quality of life (Pol & Ville, 2009). Successful corporations, too, have figured out that for sustainable long-term growth and development, investment in SI is key (Konda et al., 2015).

Through innovation, social workers can build and strengthen capacity, improve processes, create new avenues for organizational and social change, develop new streams of revenue and staffing, and build coalitions that create sustainability and have potential for continued growth. Thus, SI can be used anywhere in the process of social value creation. Berzin and Pitt-Catsouphes (2015) indicated that SI could include a shift in resource development strategies within a human service organization, new organizational structures, organizational policy innovations, or changes in service delivery processes (Pitt-Catsouphes & Berzin, 2015). In our opinion, incorporating social work perspectives into designing socially innovative solutions could greatly enable professionals to emphasize social justice for addressing social problems. In a study by Pitt-Catsouphes and Berzin (2015), respondents indicated that social workers needed to be involved in SI leadership as SI enables the adoption of new approaches to address problems of disenfranchised populations and ensure social justice. Given the increasing importance that innovation plays in the conceptualization and funding environment for solutions to address unfulfilled social needs, the concept of SI is being thoroughly examined by social work academicians, practitioners, and funders (Berzin et al., 2015).

Social Entrepreneurship (SE)

Providing social services is not the same as creating and implementing a social entrepreneurial venture or initiating a social intrapreneurial program. Existing social services may appease social issues while social entrepreneurs attempt to alleviate social issues and transform society and communities in the process. Social entrepreneurial thinking necessitates bringing together a wide range of stakeholders and organizational representatives to tackle the core of complex social and community issues (Fawcett & South, 2005). "As traditional approaches to addressing society's ills have failed, social entrepreneurship is seen as a way to leverage resources, enhance effectiveness through innovative partnerships, raise levels of performance and accountability, and ultimately achieve sustainable impact" (Wei-Skillern, 2010, p. 1).

A myriad of definitions and conceptualizations of SE and social entrepreneurs exist in the literature (see, for example, Dacin, Dacin, & Matear, 2010; Dees, 1998; Short, Moss, & Lumpkin, 2009). After extensively reviewing the literature, Choi and Majumdar (2013) proposed that SE is actually a cluster of subconcepts—social value creation, social entrepreneur, SE organization, market orientation, and SI. Except for social value creation, which is a necessary condition for SE, the other four subconcepts exist at varying levels in an SE endeavor. Improving livelihood of individuals could be the end result or an integral condition of social value creation through an SE process (Seelos & Mair, 2005). Thus, finding a universally accepted definition of SE is hardly possible. Nandan and Scott (2013) identified five definitions of social entrepreneurs that resonate with social work practice and values, two of which are noted as follows:

- Light (2006) defined a social entrepreneur as "an individual, group, network, organization, or alliance of organizations that seeks sustainable, large-scale change through pattern-breaking ideas in what governments, nonprofits, and businesses do to address significant social problems" (p. 50).
- The Skoll Foundation (cf. Dacin et al., 2010) views social entrepreneurs as transformational change agents who "pioneer innovative and systemic approaches for meeting the needs of the marginalized—the disadvantaged and the disenfranchised—populations that lack the financial means or political clout to achieve lasting benefits on their own" (p. 41).

Social entrepreneurs are influenced both by activities that help society and have a nonmonetary focus and by their own closeness to the social problem they are attempting to address (Radhari et al., 2016). SE too has been conceptualized and defined in many different ways, two of which follow:

- J. E. Austin, Stevenson, and Wei-Skillern (2006) defined SE as "innovative, social value creating activity that can occur within or across the non-profit, business or government sectors" (p. 371).
- Zahra, Gedajlovic, Neubaum, and Shulman (2009) (cf. Shepherd & Patzelt, 2011) defined SE as "activities and processes undertaken to discover, define and exploit opportunities in order to enhance social wealth by creating new ventures or managing existing organizations in an innovative manner" (p. 143).

SE can be best understood as a multidimensional and dynamic construct moving across various intersection points between the public, private, and social sectors; therefore, social entrepreneurs can design for-profit, not-for-profit, and hybrid organizations to implement their innovative strategies (Nicholls, 2006).

Social work entrepreneurship has been defined as "the creation of institutions through entrepreneurial thinking that are guided by social work ethics and based on the integration of social service, business and public relation skills" (Bent-Goodley, 2002, p. 291). In other words, social work ethics guide entrepreneurship and innovation and shape responses of practitioners and organizations for addressing social issues (Nandan, Nandan, & London, 2015). SI is an important component for social work agencies using the entrepreneurship framework for retooling their practices through establishment of strategic relationships with for-profit business organizations and public-sector agencies (Berzin et al., 2015). Social work entrepreneurs create new ventures, solutions, and interventions to advance social change. Thus, SE is not an alternative to existing social work practice but is a much-needed perspective and set of behaviors for effectively carrying out the profession's mission.

Social Intrapreneurship (SIn)

The term "social intrapreneurship" is more common in the business literature than in the social science context. SIn is a process used to create innovative, sustainable change within existing organizations. A social intrapreneur is "[a] person who focuses on innovation and creativity and who transforms a dream or an idea into a profitable venture, by operating within the organizational environment" (Carland & Carland, 2007, p. 84). Social intrapreneurs are change agents within organizations who recognize opportunities in seemingly unimportant events (Brunaker & Kurvinen, 2006). More specifically, social work intrapreneurship focuses on the ability to proactively create change within organizations by recognizing new opportunities and taking calculated risks for sustaining innovative ideas and organizations (Nandan, London, & Bent-Goodley, 2015; Nandan, Mandayam, Collard, & Tchouta, 2016).

Corporations, too, through CSR initiatives, are internally promoting social intrapreneurs. "Corporate social entrepreneurship" (CSE) is a process aimed at enabling business to develop advanced and powerful forms of CSR (J. E. Austin & Reficco, 2009). J. E. Austin, Leonard, Reficco, and Wei-Skillern (2006) defined CSE as "the process of extending the firm's domain of competence and corresponding opportunity set through innovative leveraging of resources, both within and outside its direct control, aimed at the simultaneous creation of economic and social value" (p. 170). Forward-thinking corporations are recognizing and supporting their social intrapreneurs, which ultimately help them retain talent and also fulfill society's expectations related to their social responsibility (Santos & Williams, 2013).

Social Value (SV) and SV Creation

SV can be created through various professional social work approaches, CSR, and welfare programs designed and implemented by government and civil society. SV is intrinsically linked to the concept of SE, and SV creation is the main distinctive feature of SE (Narangajavana, Gonzalez-Cruz, Garrigos-Simon, & Cruz-Ros, 2016). The core mission of SE and social enterprises is to benefit society and create SV (Defourny & Nyssens, 2010). The latent drive for SE is the creation of SV as opposed to shareholder wealth, which is achieved through innovative ways and not through replication of existing enterprises or practice (J. E. Austin, Leonard, et al., 2006). Despite disagreement on the universal definition of SE, there seems to be consensus on the notion of "social value" as being central to SE (Choi & Majumdar, 2013).

However, SE-based academic research does not usually offer a definition of SV, especially the way it is conceptualized and described through broad generic statements (Narangajavana et al., 2016). Moreover, the concept of value itself is not clear in the literature (Singh, 2016), probably owing to the multidisciplinary perspectives on the concept (Lepak, Smith, & Taylor, 2007). In addition, *value creation* refers to both the content—that is, what is value, who values what, and where value resides—and the process of new value creation—that is, how value is generated (Lepak et al., 2007).

As a result, the term "value" takes on different meanings across disciplines. For example, philosophers and ethicists study the values held by an individual or groups of individuals, such as a society (Haksever, Chaganti, & Cook, 2004). They deal with the principles or values that should guide human behavior and try to separate the rights from wrongs. Social work is also not value-free. Values constitute "a basis of identification and responsibility for all social workers—wherever they practice, whatever purposes they may serve, whatever functions they perform, whatever methods they employ, and whatever clientele they work with" (Levy, 1973, p. 35). Values are central guiding principles for the social work profession and are reflected in the moral conundrums of practice (Bisman, 2004), conceived along three basic dimensions (Levy, 1973). These are preferred conceptions of people, preferred outcomes for people, and preferred instrumentalities for dealing with people. Unlike ethicists and social workers, economists and engineers are interested in the value of things (Haksever et al., 2004). Taking this point further, from a strategic point of the view, Haksever et al. (2004) defined value "as the capacity of a good, service, or activity to satisfy a need or provide a benefit to a person or legal entity" (p. 292). This definition of value is clearly broader than the traditional definition used by some economists. It includes any type of good, service, or act that satisfies a need or provides a benefit, which may be tangible or intangible, including those that positively contribute to quality of life, knowledge, prestige, safety, physical and financial security, as well as providing nutrition, shelter, transportation, and income. It is obvious that when the "content" of value varies across disciplines, the "process of value creation" will also differ. Thus, value creation should be studied for a particular functional area or from a particular perspective.

In addition, value creation and value capture should be viewed as distinct processes, but most often the process of value creation is confused or confounded with the process of value capture or value retention (Lepak et al., 2007). The individual, organization, or society—that is, the source of value creation—is not the one that always captures or retains the value the most, because there are various stakeholders for whom value can be created. For example, in the context of charitable organizations, Polonsky and Grau (2008) defined "social value" as the total social impact a charitable organization has on all its stakeholders (donors, employees, volunteers, other charities and nonprofits, clients, and society in general). It also depends on the intended target of value creation (Lepak et al., 2007).

In the context of SE, social enterprises create value for all the stakeholders (beneficiaries, funders, investors, employees, suppliers, and so on), which can be negotiated among the stakeholders (R. Young, 2006). The main purpose of a social enterprise is to create SV irrespective of whether the value is generated within an organization or outside of it (J. E. Austin, Stevenson, & Wei-Skillern, 2006). However, beneficiaries are always the intended targets of value creation in SE. The primary mission of SE is to create SV for clients—those who receive the value created (Lepoutre, Justo, Terjesen, & Bosma, 2013). Thus, Singh (2016) restricted the concept of SV to the total impact that a social entrepreneur has on the beneficiaries (individual, community, or society as a whole) and provided two perspectives on SV. From the perspective of social entrepreneurs,

> social value creation is about bringing the desired social change or creating social impact/social outcomes, through a resolution of social problems/issues. These "social changes" or "social impacts/outcomes" include a range of impacts such as increasing awareness, empowering the beneficiaries, creating and providing socio-economic benefits to them, impacting their lives, bringing a change in their perception, attitudes, behaviour and finally, changes in norms. These changes occur at the institutional, individual, community, state, and international levels. (Singh, 2016, pp. 109–110)

The beneficiaries perceived "value" in getting various kinds of benefits created for them by social entrepreneurs and in the various positive changes and impacts in their lives brought about because of these benefits. These positive changes or impacts in their lives were both direct and indirect. Direct changes or impacts refer to getting direct benefits, opportunities, and improved capability in various forms, such as increased confidence, self-respect, income, and knowledge; and indirect impacts or changes refer to the changes or impacts beneficiaries felt in their lives as a result of the direct changes, such as their improved ability to fulfill the needs of their family members and the improved standard of living of their family. They secured opportunities in various fields, and their capability increased in various dimensions, such as their ability to earn a livelihood and fulfill the needs of family members (Singh, 2016, p. 114). R. Young (2006), too, mentioned that social entrepreneurs create SV that benefits people whose urgent needs and reasonable needs are not being met by other means.

The *values of social work* also focus on the mission of creating *social value*, which drives the process of *social value creation* in social work. Bisman (2004) rightly said, "Values and mission are central to the profession; without them there is no social work" (p. 120). The actions of social workers must promote "social change, problem-solving in human relationships and the empowerment and liberation of people to enhance well-being" (British Association of Social Workers, 2002). Employing evidence-based methods of social work practice, social work professionals aim to create social values and bring about intended social change. It is clear that, similar to the field of SE, the concepts of SV and SV creation are equally important in the field of social work. Thus, Singh's (2016) conceptualization of *social value* and *social value creation* can be used to understand these concepts within the social work context.

In addition, it is difficult to find a single indicator to measure the contributions made by SE because SV is complex, multidimensional, and contextual in nature (Weerawardena & Mort, 2006). Measurement of SV deals with understanding what value is created and for whom (Clark & Brennan, 2016; Neck, Brush, & Allen, 2009). Thus, social enterprises must identify their own metrics (financial and nonfinancial) of success based on mission, industry, area, and intended social impact (Clark & Brennan, 2016; Neck et al., 2009).

Skills

Social work values and skills are coveted credentials for being in the social enterprise space (Neal, 2015). The core skills for SI, SE, SIn, and SV creation include but are not limited to administrative and management skills; social, strategic, and community planning; financial management and development; organizing and coalition building; emotional intelligence; community development; policy advocacy; policy analysis and formation; and the ability to engage different public and social media platforms (London & Morfopoulos, 2010; Nandan, London, & Blum, 2014). As one delves deeper into these concepts, an argument can be made that social work entrepreneurship, intrapreneurship, innovation, and SV creation warrant their own focus within social work academic programs (Bent-Goodley, 2002; Nandan et al., 2014; Singh, 2016; Tropman & Morningstar, 1989).

The social work profession has the ability to make a unique contribution to the teaching and practice of social work entrepreneurship, intrapreneurship, and innovation (Pitt-Catsouphes & Berzin, 2015; Singh, 2016). The nuanced thinking of the social work entrepreneur certainly fits under macro practice; however, it is often taught neither in the classroom nor through field education. It could also be argued that such content should not be limited to macro practitioners but is also relevant to clinical practitioners who open private practices and work within communities to advance change. Social workers are change agents at all systemic levels and are key players in creating SV for individuals, families, and communities. Given social workers' strong adherence and commitment to values and ethics, as social innovators, entrepreneurs, and intrapreneurs, they can advocate, more strongly, for creating empowering opportunities for marginalized populations—SV creation aligned with the mission of the profession (Neal, 2015).

In essence, social work entrepreneurship, intrapreneurship, innovation, and SV creation are important perspectives and strategies for all fields of social work practice and at all systems of intervention. As state and federal governments continue to scale back public financing, and as private philanthropists ask for accountable social investments, social entrepreneurial and social intrapreneurial thinking is essential for social change agents like social workers to remain relevant, viable, and sustainable (Nandan & Scott, 2013).

Social Work Entrepreneurship in Action

Although we are witnessing some growth in the literature on social work entrepreneurship within social work, social work entrepreneurship, intrapreneurship, and SV creation and innovation have had a long history in the profession. The profession, in many ways, began with an entrepreneurial spirit that created large SV and has been sustained as a result. However, the idea of social work entrepreneurship has been met with some resistance (Bent-Goodley, 2002). For some, the idea of being entrepreneurial appears to be contradictory to helping professionals, advocates, and change agents (Germak & Singh, 2009). Some view social work entrepreneurship as only a for-profit business venture (Gray & Crofts, 2008). The scarcity of social work perspectives in SI literature overtly condones the rich history of innovations in social service organizations (Berzin et al., 2015). Long before William Drayton used the term "social entrepreneurship" some 30 years ago (Davis, 2002), early social work pioneers were implementing social work entrepreneurship and innovation to address larger, broader societal and local issues and adding to SV. Settlement houses were largely built on the premise of entrepreneurial thinking. For example, Jane Addams, a social work pioneer, created Hull House in 1889 as a way to provide supports and services to newly arrived European immigrants in Chicago (Lundblad, 1995). By its second year of services, Hull House was serving over 2,000 people per week. It eventually had over 13 locations. Although it started with a focus on addressing primarily individual and familial concerns, Hull House was later recognized for addressing environmental concerns, poverty, health, employment, and other social issues—SV creation activities.

During the same period, Ida B. Wells-Barnett established the Negro Fellowship League. The league was established to provide reentry services, such as opportunities to find jobs and housing, promotion of literacy, and reintegration back into the community for African American men returning home from jail or prison (Bent-Goodley, 2001). The NFL later also worked with the community to build sustainable efforts to help the men engage in voter participation and take a more active role in addressing social and civic issues within the community—SV creation activities.

Social work administrators used entrepreneurial thinking to fuel their organizations toward sustainable and impactful change, even before the profession recognized it as being entrepreneurial (Hoefer, 1993; Menefee, 1997; Tropman & Morningstar, 1989). As an example, the National Center for Children and Families (NCCF) was founded in 1915 to provide services to children who were homeless in Washington, DC (NCCF, 2016). NCCF now serves over 4,000 children and families in the Washington, DC, area. Born as a small nonprofit organization, as an orphanage providing social services for children who desperately needed them, NCCF eventually evolved into an important institution for planning and delivering much-needed social services to vulnerable children, youths, and families from diverse backgrounds. Black Family Development, Incorporated (BFDI), is another organization that has acquired sustainability through an intrapreneurial focus (BFDI, 2016). BFDI was founded in 1978 to help abused and neglected children in Detroit, Michigan. BFDI was born out of a community development project focusing on child abuse and neglect. Over time it has expanded its capacity and infrastructure to meet the increasing demand for family counseling and child welfare advocacy services in the community. Both NCCF and BFDI had to shift their foci and design innovative solutions to remain relevant and sustain themselves through political and social changes, fluctuations in public and private funding, and evolving social challenges within the communities that they serve while staying true to their mission.

During the last quarter of the 19th century, with the birth and growth of charity organization societies (COS), influential business leaders tried to bring more efficiency and effectiveness into the operations of these organizations. Training programs were established around the country to train charity investigators, who were later identified as "social workers." Mary Richmond, a recognized advocate for administration of charity societies, was invited to serve as a "staff of the newly created Russell Sage Foundation" and lead the Charity Organization Department within the foundation (D. M. Austin, 2000, p. 32). She helped streamline practices within COS and scale the new innovative practice of relief distribution, operating as a social intrapreneur.

More recently, Rebecca Kousky, a social worker and founder of Nest, has established a nonprofit organization that helps women artisans in developing countries by providing them with microloans and also markets in the United States. The Nest collaborative connects U.S. designers with more than 2,000 artisans from across the globe who have skills but need employment or a sustainable living wage (Dale, 2012). This is just one of several examples from around the world.

Social work entrepreneurship and innovation are not limited to the United States. For example, an Ashoka fellow—who is also a community practice social worker—cofounded the Bharatiya Muslim Mahila Andolan, a nonprofit organization in Mumbai, India, that organizes Muslim women in the country to collectively overcome sociocultural limitations in exercising their citizenship. Social workers have been called to bring their intersectional knowledge of business and social work practice coupled with the profession's code of ethics to the global stage (Casimir & Samuel, 2015). Not only can social workers grow these social enterprises across the globe; they are called to also document and uplift existing entrepreneurial practices around the world (Foy, 2013). These illustrations illuminate social work entrepreneurship, intrapreneurship, innovation, and SV creation. With a focused intent on growing the number of social workers in each of these areas, the profession can advance and sustain itself while addressing the social, political, and economic issues in which it is deeply invested.

Social Entrepreneurship, Intrapreneurship, Innovation, Value Creation, and the Code of Ethics

Neal (2015) builds a case for social workers' involvement in social enterprises as a means of addressing social problems. Social work entrepreneurship, intrapreneurship, SV creation, and SI are not only in compliance with the social work code of ethics but are also encouraged in many ways by this code. Social workers are bound by the National Association of Social Workers (NASW) *Code of Ethics*, which emphasizes six core principles of service, social justice, dignity and worth of the person, human relationships, integrity, and competence (NASW, 2017). Within the code, social workers are also called to engage in very specific acts that support these core areas. Section 3.07 of the code, entitled "Administration," calls on social workers to build organizations that advocate for resource allocation that is rooted in fairness and equity and to create environments that social workers can optimally engage in practice. Section 6.01 of the code, entitled "Social Welfare," calls on social workers to engage in practice that benefits the general welfare of society. It calls on social workers to act as tools of change and to ensure that they are working to benefit the common good and to advance the needs of those who are vulnerable and oppressed in particular—another form of SV creation. Section 6.04 of the *Code,* entitled "Social and Political Action," promotes the notion that social workers work toward ensuring equal access to resources and opportunities, promote social justice, and safeguard protections for the vulnerable. Each of these components of the code is propelling contemporary social workers to think and behave differently to create sustainable social change, that is, to use SI, SE, and SIn perspectives for creating social change. Social entrepreneurs work for social well-being by helping marginalized and disadvantaged people to enhance their capabilities, access basic human needs, and become contributing members of society (Singh, 2016). By employing these perspectives and strategies, social workers can continue advancing the goals of the profession within the guidelines of the *Code of Ethics*.

Zhu et al. (2016) presented a teaching model—a curriculum matrix—to assist fledgling social entrepreneurs in balancing the tension between social and commercial outcomes or logic. The curriculum matrix aims to incorporate values, ethics, and problem solving into practice. Zhu et al. (2016) proposed that students need to

> empirically define the situation they face, state and compare the merits of differing values, state the principle that each value honors (social or commercial), consider and compare other ethical values, decide to whom they are being loyal, evaluate the presence of others deserving loyalty, select a course of action embracing the most important values, principles, loyalties, and evaluate the impact of the decision. (pp. 617–618)

Through their teaching model, they proposed integrating, in a coherent fashion, disparate commercial and social logics through behavioral, sociological, and cognitive frameworks.

Conclusion

The roots of social work are in innovative and entrepreneurial thinking. The pioneers of the profession had to creatively address complex social and economic challenges while being financially sustainable. In recent decades, social workers have been called on to think creatively, seek diverse funding, mobilize social capital, and collaboratively deliver innovative and sustainable solutions to recalcitrant social issues. Social workers are poised to contribute to make significant advancements in social entrepreneurship, intrapreneurship, innovation, and SV creation. By intently harnessing these strategies and perspectives, the profession can grow its impact in local communities around the world. Not only is the profession capable of incorporating these strategies, it has been doing so since the turn of the 20th century.

The historic Wingspread meeting of the leading organizations within the social work profession and the 2010 Social Work Congress developed imperatives that speak to the thesis of this chapter:

> infusing models of sustainable business and management practice in social work education and practice . . . clarifying and articulating the unique skills, scope of practice and value added of social work to prospective social work students . . . empirically demonstrating to prospective recruits the value of social work profession in both social and economic terms. (Williams, 2015, p. 68)

In addition, social work entrepreneurship, intrapreneurship, and innovation are important processes for mobilizing the profession as it embarks on addressing the 12 Grand Challenges for Social Work over the next two decades: healthy development of youths, closing the health gap, stopping family violence, advancing productive lives of individuals, eradicating social isolation, ending homelessness, creating social responses to the changing environment, promoting just decarceration, building financial capacity of community members, reducing extreme economic inequality, tapping technology for promoting social good, and achieving economic and political justice (American Academy of Social Work and Social Welfare, 2018). Finally, in addition to the existing practices, the social work profession may need other tool kits to systemically attend to the United Nations Sustainable Development Goals (United Nations Development Programme, n.d.). Social work entrepreneurship creates an opportunity for the profession.

References

American Academy of Social Work and Social Welfare. (2018). *12 challenges.* Retrieved from http://aaswsw.org/grand-challenges-initiative/12-challenges/

Austin, D. M. (2000). Social work and social welfare administration: A historical perspective. In R. J. Patti (Ed.), *The handbook of social welfare management* (pp. 27–54). Thousand Oaks, CA: Sage Publications.

Austin, J. E., Leonard, H. B., Reficco, E., & Wei-Skillern, J. (2006). Social entrepreneurship: It is for corporations, too. In A. Nicholls (Ed.), *Social entrepreneurship: New models of sustainable change* (pp. 169–180). New York: Oxford University Press.

Austin, J. E., & Reficco, E. (2009, March 3). *Corporate social entrepreneurship* (Working Paper No. 09-101). Retrieved from http://www.hbs.edu/faculty/Publication%20Files/09-101.pdf

Austin, J. E., Stevenson, H., & Wei-Skillern, J. (2006). Social and commercial entrepreneurship: Same, different, or both? *Entrepreneurship Theory and Practice, 30*(1), 1–22. doi:10.1111/j.1540-6520.2006.00107.x

Bacq, S., & Janssen, F. (2011). The multiple faces of social entrepreneurship: A review of definitional issues based on geographical and thematic criteria. *Entrepreneurship & Regional Development, 23*, 373–403. doi:10.1080/08985626 .2011.577242

Baregheh, A., Rowley, J., & Sambrook, S. (2009). Towards a multidisciplinary definition of innovation. *Management Decision, 47*, 1323–1339. doi:10.1108/00251740910984578

Baron, D. P. (2005). *Corporate social responsibility and social entrepreneurship* (Working paper). Retrieved from https://www.gsb.stanford.edu/ faculty-research/working-papers/corporate-social-responsibility-social -entrepreneurship

Bent-Goodley, T. B. (2001). Ida B. Wells-Barnett: An uncompromising style. In I. B. Carlton-LaNey (Ed.), *African American leadership: An empowerment tradition in social work history* (pp. 87–98). Washington, DC: NASW Press.

Bent-Goodley, T. B. (2002). Defining and conceptualizing social work entrepreneurship. *Journal of Social Work Education, 38*, 291–302. doi:10.1080/1043779 7.2002.10779098

Berzin, S. C., & Pitt-Catsouphes, M. (2015). Social innovation from the inside: Considering the intrapreneurship path. *Social Work, 60*, 360–362. doi:10. 1093/sw/swv026

Berzin, S. C., Pitt-Catsouphes, M., & Gaitan-Rossi, P. (2015). Defining our own future: Human service leaders on innovation. *Human Services Organizations: Management, Leadership & Governance, 39*, 412–425. doi:10.1080/23303 131.2015.1060914

Berzin, S. C., Pitt-Catsouphes, M., & Gaitan-Rossi, P. (2016). Innovation and sustainability: An exploratory study of intrapreneurship among human service organizations. *Human Service Organization: Management, Leadership & Governance, 40*(5), 1–13. doi:10.1080/23303131.2016.1184207

Bisman, C. (2004). Social work values: The moral core of the profession. *British Journal of Social Work, 34*, 109–123. doi:10.1093/bjsw/bch008

Black Family Development, Inc. (2016). *About* [Web page]. Retrieved from http://blackfamilydevelopment.org/index.php/home/about

Boon, F., & Ludeke-Freund, F. (2013). Business models for sustainable innovation: State of the art steps towards a research agenda. *Journal of Cleaner Production, 45*, 9–19. doi:10.1016/j.jclepro.2012.07.007

British Association of Social Workers. (2002). *The code of ethics for social work.* Brighton, UK: Author.

Brunaker, S., & Kurvinen, J. (2006). Intrapreneurship, local initiatives in orga-nizational change processes. *Leadership and Organization Development Journal, 27*, 118–132. doi:10.1108/01437730610646624

Carland, J. C., & Carland, J. W. (2007). Intrapreneurship: A requisite for suc-cess. *Entrepreneurial Executive, 12*, 83–94. doi:10.1080/23303131.2014.955236

Casimir, A., & Samuel, E. (2015). Social work and the challenge of entrepre-neurship in Africa. *Open Journal of Political Science, 5*, 155–165. doi:10.4236/ojps.2015.52017

Choi, N., & Majumdar, S. (2013). Social entrepreneurship as an essentially contested concept: Opening a new avenue for systematic future research. *Journal of Business Venturing, 29*, 363–376. doi:10.1016/j.jbusvent.2013.05.001

Clark, C., & Brennan, L. (2016). Social entrepreneurship: A global model for evaluating long-term impact. *International Journal of Entrepreneurship, 20*(1), 1–15. Retrieved from http://www.alliedacademies.org/articles/ijevol20no 12016.pdf#page=5

Dacin, P. A., Dacin, M. T., & Matear, M. (2010). Social entrepreneurship: Why we don't need a new theory and how we move forward from here. *Academy of Management Perspectives, 24*(3), 37–57. doi:10.5465/AMP.2010.52842950

Dale, M. (2012, January). Social work takes on business. *NASW News, 57*(1). Retrieved from http://www.socialworkblog.org/nasw-news-article/2012/01/social-work-takes-on-business/

Davis, S. (2002). *Social entrepreneurship: Towards an entrepreneurial culture for social and economic development.* Arlington, VA: Ashoka.

Dees, J. G. (1998, October 31). *The meaning of "social entrepreneurship."* Retrieved from https://entrepreneurship.duke.edu/news-item/the-meaning-of-social -entrepreneurship/

Defourny, J., & Nyssens, M. (2010). Conceptions of social enterprise and social entre-preneurship in Europe and the United States: Convergences and divergences. *Journal of Social Entrepreneurship, 1*(1), 32–53. doi:10.1080/19420670903442053

Dorado, S. (2006). Social entrepreneurial ventures: Different values so differ-ent processes of creation, no? *Journal of Developmental Entrepreneurship, 11*, 319–343. doi:10.1142/S1084946706000453

Fawcett, B., & South, J. (2005). Community involvement and primary care trusts: The case for social entrepreneurship. *Critical Public Health, 15*(2), 191–204. doi:10.1080/09581590500144660

Foy, R. D. (2013). Utilizing the social learning theory as a new paradigm to evaluate the International Labour Organization (ILO) assessment of sup-port for growth-oriented women entrepreneurs in Uganda. *Journal of Afri-can Studies and Development, 5*, 27–32. doi:10.5897/JASD11.023

Germak, A. J., & Singh, K. K. (2009). Social entrepreneurship: Changing the way social workers do business. *Administration in Social Work, 34*(1), 79–95. doi:10.1080/03643100903432974

Gray, M., & Crofts, P. (2008). Social development and its relevance to Australian social work. *Australian Social Work, 61*(1), 88–103. doi:10.1080/0312407070 1818757

Gray, M., Healy, K., & Crofts, P. (2003). Social enterprise: Is it the business of social work? *Australian Social Work, 56*(2), 141–164. doi:10.1046/j.0312 -407X.2003.00060.x

Gummer, B. (2001). Innovate or die: The necessity for change in contemporary organizations. *Administration in Social Work, 25*(3), 65–84. doi:10.1300/ J147v25n03_05

Haksever, C., Chaganti, R., & Cook, R. G. (2004). A model of value creation: Strategic view. *Journal of Business Ethics, 49*, 291–305. doi:10.1023/B:BUSI .0000017968.21563.05

Hockerts, K., & Wustenhagen, R. (2010). Greening Goliaths versus emerging Davids—Theorizing about the role of incumbents and new entrants in sustainable entrepreneurship. *Journal of Business Venturing, 25*, 481–492. doi: 10.1016/j.jbusvent.2009.07.005

Hoefer, R. (1993). A matter of degree: Job skills for human service administrators. *Administration in Social Work, 27*, 1–20. doi:10.1300/J147v17n03_01

Hopkins, M. (2016). *Corporate social responsibility (CSR) and the United Nations sustainable development goals (SDG): The role of the private sector.* Retrieved from https://www.csrfi.com/wp-content/uploads/2013/10/CSR-and-the-United-Nations-SDGs.pdf

İyigün, N. Ö. (2015). What could entrepreneurship do for sustainable development? A corporate social responsibility-based approach. *Procedia—Social and Behavioral Sciences, 195* (World Conference on Technology, Innovation and Entrepreneurship), 1226–1231. Retrieved from https://ac.els-cdn.com/ S1877042815037325/1-s2.0-S1877042815037325-main.pdf?_tid=27b670bf-93e8-42eb-ab6a-b57a1a2ce4de&acdnat=1539375494_dd6deab202b6ad32b 799c48ccee29742

Jaskyte, K., & Dressler, W. W. (2005). Organizational culture and innovation in nonprofit human service organizations. *Administration in Social Work, 29*(2), 23–41. doi:10.1300/J147v29n02_03

Kim, M., & Leu, J. (2011). The field of social entrepreneurship education: From the second wave of growth to a third wave of innovation. In U. Ashoka & D. Brock (Eds.), *Social entrepreneurship education resource handbook* (pp. 8–9). Washington, DC: Ashoka U.

Konda, I., Starc, J., & Rodica, B. (2015). Social challenges are opportunities for sustainable development: Tracing impacts of social entrepreneurship through innovations and value creation. *Economic Themes, 53*, 215–233. doi:10.1515/ethemes-2015-0012

Lepak, D. P., Smith, K. G., & Taylor, M. S. (2007). Value creation and value capture: A multilevel perspective. *Academy of Management Review, 32*(1), 180–194. doi:10.5465/AMR.2007.23464011

Lepoutre, J., Justo, R., Terjesen, S., & Bosma, N. (2013). Designing a global standardized methodology for measuring social entrepreneurship activity: The global entrepreneurship monitor social entrepreneurship study. *Small Business Economics, 40*, 693–714. doi:10.1007/s11187-011-9398-4

Levy, C. S. (1973). The value base of social work. *Journal of Education for Social Work, 9*(1), 34–42. doi:10.1080/00220612.1973.10671941

Light, P. C. (2006). Reshaping social entrepreneurship. *Stanford Social Innovation Review, 4*(3), 47–51. Retrieved from http://www.nyu.edu/social-entrepreneurship/news_events_resources/pdf/paul_light.pdf

London, M., & Morfopoulos, R. G. (2010). *Social entrepreneurship: How to start successful corporate social responsibility and community-based initiatives for advocacy and change.* New York: Routledge.

Lundblad, K. S. (1995). Jane Addams and social reform: A role model for the 1990s. *Social Work, 40*, 661–669. Retrieved from http://www.vonsteuben.org/ourpages/auto/2015/3/20/54841189/Addams.pdf

Mair, J., & Marti, I. (2006). Social entrepreneurship research: A source of explanation, prediction and delight. *Journal of World Business, 41*(1), 36–44. doi:10.1016/j.jwb.2005.09.002

Menefee, D. (1997). Strategic administration of nonprofit human service organizations: A model for executive success in turbulent times. *Administration in Social Work, 21*, 1–19. doi:10.1300/J147v21n02_01

Mirabito, D. M. (2012). Educating a new generation of social workers: Challenges and skills needed for contemporary agency-based practice. *Clinical Social Work Journal, 40*, 245–254. doi:10.1007/s10615-011-0378-6

Nandan, M., London, M., & Bent-Goodley, T. (2015). Social workers as social change agents: Social innovation, social intrapreneurship and social entrepreneurship. *Human Service Organizations, Management, Leadership and Governance, 39*, 38–56. doi:10.1080/23303131.2014.955236

Nandan, M., London, M., & Blum, T. (2014). Community practice social entrepreneurship: An interdisciplinary approach to graduate education. *International Journal of Social Entrepreneurship and Innovation, 3*, 51–70. doi:10.1504/IJSEI.2014.064106

Nandan, M., Mandayam, G., Collard, C., & Tchouta, R. (2016). An examination of community practice social workers as social intrapreneurs or social entrepreneurs. *International Journal of Social Entrepreneurship and Innovation, 4*, 114–133. doi:10.1504/IJSEI.2016.076686

Nandan, M., Nandan, S., & London, M. (2015). Catalysts and agents of social change: Imperatives for social innovations. In J. Wallace (Ed.), *Social change perspectives, challenges and implications for the future* (pp. 19–40). New York: Nova Publishers.

Nandan, M., & Scott, P. (2013). Social entrepreneurship and social work: The need for a transdisciplinary education model. *Administration in Social Work, 37*, 257–271. doi:10.1080/03643107.2012.684428

Narangajavana, Y., Gonzalez-Cruz, T., Garrigos-Simon, F. J., & Cruz-Ros, S. (2016). Measuring social entrepreneurship and social value with leakage: Definition, analysis and policies for the hospitality industry. *International Entrepreneurship and Management Journal, 12*, 911–934. doi:10.1007/s11365-016-0396-5

National Association of Social Workers. (2017). *Code of ethics of the National Association of Social Workers.* Washington, DC: Author.

National Center for Children and Families. (2016). *National Center for Children and Families: About us* [Web page]. Retrieved from http://www.nccf-cares.org/our-history/

Neal, A. A. (2015). The intersection of social work and social enterprise. *Journal of Social Work Values & Ethics, 12*(2), 1–9. Retrieved from http://jswve.org/download/2015-2/Fall%202015-Full%20issue-JSWVE-12-2.pdf

Neck, H., Brush, C., & Allen, E. (2009). The landscape of social entrepreneurship. *Business Horizons, 52*, 13–19. doi:10.1016/j.bushor.2008.09.002

Nicholls, A. (2006). Introduction. In A. Nicholls (Ed.), *Social entrepreneurship: New models of sustainable change* (pp. 1–35). New York: Oxford University Press.

Pitt-Catsouphes, M., & Berzin, S. C. (2015). Teaching note—Incorporating social innovation content into macro social work education. *Journal of Social Work Education, 51*, 407–416. doi:10.1080/10437797.2015.1012947

Pol, E., & Ville, S. (2009). Social innovation: Buzz word or enduring term? *Journal of Socio-Economics, 38*, 878–885. doi:10.1016/j.socec.2009.02.011

Polonsky, M. J., & Grau, S. L. (2008). Evaluating the social value of charitable organizations: A conceptual foundation. *Journal of Macromarketing, 28*, 130–140. doi:10.1177/0276146708314585

Porter, M. E., & Kramer, M. R. (2002). The competitive advantage of corporate philanthropy. *Harvard Business Review, 80*, 56–68. Retrieved from https://sharedvalue.org/sites/default/files/resource-files/Competitive_Advantage.pdf

Rahdari, A., Sepasi, S., & Moradi, M. (2016). Achieving sustainability through Schumpeterian social entrepreneurship: The role of social enterprises. *Journal of Cleaner Production, 137*, 347–360. doi:10.1016/j.jclepro.2016.06.159

Roy, R., & Tripathi, V. (2015). Social entrepreneurship for sustainable economic development: A need to increase workforce participation. *Global Journal of Enterprise Information System, 7*(2), 106. doi:10.18311/gjeis/2015/2972

Salamon, L. M., Geller, S. L., & Mengel, K. L. (2010). Nonprofits, innovation, and performance measurement: Separating fact from fiction. *Listening Post Project, 17*, 1–25. Retrieved from http://ccss.jhu.edu/wp-content/uploads/downloads/2011/09/LP_Communique 17_2010.pdf

Santos, F., & Williams, J. (2013, November 7). The rise of the social intrapreneur. *INSEAD Knowledge.* Retrieved from https://knowledge.insead.edu/responsibility/the-rise-of-the-social-intrapreneur-2961#t4GdebtdvLLcy0X3.99

Sarasvathy, S. D. (2001). Causation and effectuation: Toward a theoretical shift from economic inevitability to entrepreneurial contingency. *Academy of Management Review, 26*, 243–263. doi:10.2307/259121

Savaya, R., Packer, P., Stange, D., & Namir, O. (2008). Social entrepreneurship: Capacity building among workers in public human service agencies. *Administration in Social Work, 32*(4), 65–86. doi:10.1080/03643100802293840

Seelos, C., & Mair, J. (2005). *Sustainable development: How social entrepreneurs make it happen* (IESE Business School Working Paper No. 611). Retrieved from https://ssrn.com/abstract=876404

Shepherd, D. A., & Patzelt, H. (2011). The new field of sustainable entrepreneurship: Studying entrepreneurial action linking "what is to be sustained" with "what is to be developed." *Entrepreneurship Theory and Practice, 35*(1), 137–163. doi:10.1111/j.1540-6520.2010.00426.x

Short, J. C., Moss, T. W., & Lumpkin, G. T. (2009). Research in social entrepreneurship: Past contributions and future opportunities. *Strategic Entrepreneurship Journal, 3*, 161–194. doi:10.1002/sej.69

Singh, A. (2016). *The process of social value creation: A multiple-case study on social entrepreneurs in India.* New Delhi, India: Springer.

Smith, S. R. (2015). Managing human service organizations in the 21st century. *Human Service Organizations: Management, Leadership, & Governance, 39*, 401–411. doi:10.1080/23303131.2015.1087783

Tropman, J. E., & Morningstar, G. (1989). *Entrepreneurial systems for the 1990s: Their creation, structure, and management.* New York: Quorum Books.

Uehara, E., Flynn, M., Fong, R., Brekke, J., Barth, R. P., Coulton, C., et al. (2013). Grand challenges for social work. *Journal of the Society for Social Work & Research, 4*, 165–170. doi:10.5243/jsswr.2013.11

United Nations Development Programme. (n.d.). *United Nations Sustainable Development Goals.* Retrieved from http://www.undp.org/content/dam/undp/library/corporate/brochure/SDGs_Booklet_Web_En.pdf

Weerawardena, J., & Mort, G. S. (2006). Investigating social entrepreneurship: A multidimensional model. *Journal of World Business, 41,* 21–35. doi:10.1016/j .jwb.2005.09.001

Wei-Skillern, J. (2010). Networks as a type of social entrepreneurship to advance population health. *Preventing Chronic Disease, 7*(6), A120. Retrieved from http://www.cdc.gov/pcd/issues/2010/nov/10_0082.htm

Williams, J. H. (2015). Unification, crafting imperatives, and defining a profession. *Social Work Research, 39,* 67–69. doi:10.1093/swr/svv008.

Young, H. P. (2011). The dynamics of social innovation. *Proceedings of the National Academy of Sciences of the United States of America, 108,* 2185–2291. doi:10.1073/pnas.1100973108

Young, R. (2006). For what it is worth: Social value and the future of social entrepreneurship. In A. Nicholls (Ed.), *Social entrepreneurship: New models of sustainable social change* (1st ed., pp. 56–73). New York: Oxford University Press. doi:10.5465/amle.2013.0263

Zahra, S. A., Gedajlovic, E., Neubaum, D. O., & Shulman, J. M. (2009). A typology of social entrepreneurs: Motives, search processes and ethical challenges. *Journal of Business Venturing, 24,* 519–532. doi:10.1016/j.jbusvent. 2008.04.007

Zhu, Y., Rooney, D., & Phillips, N. (2016). Practice-based wisdom theory for integrating institutional logics: A new model for social entrepreneurship learning and education. *Academy of Management Learning & Education, 15,* 607–625. doi:10.5465/amle.2013.0263

2

Innovation and Creativity in Nonprofits

Kristina Jaskyte Bahr

The field of social work is guided by the National Association of Social Workers (NASW) *Code of Ethics*, and one of its ethical standards speaks to social work managers' ethical responsibility to the broader society. This code states that social workers promote social change with and on behalf of individuals, families, groups, organizations, and communities. In addition, social workers "seek to promote the responsiveness of organizations, communities, and other social institutions to individuals' needs and social problems" (NASW, 2017, p. 1). Fundamental to the success of social work is awareness and understanding of forces in the environment that create and contribute to social problems.

To be successful in those efforts—promoting change, promoting organizations' responsiveness, and understanding the external environment—social work managers have to possess numerous competencies. Initiation and facilitation of innovation process is one such competency that is included on the list of human services management competencies (Hassan & Wimpfheimer, 2015) and is regarded as essential for social work managers (Berzin, 2012). Unfortunately, "To a large extent . . . social work organizations with deep knowledge about a range of social issues have not found a seat at the social innovation table" (Berzin & Pitt-Catsouphes, 2015, p. 360).

Because one way to lead social innovation is through social intrapreneurship, or design and implementation of innovation within an existing organization (Pitt-Catsouphes & Berzin, 2015), it is essential that social work managers have knowledge and skills needed for successful facilitation of innovation in their organizations. Although the social innovation literature has focused primarily on creation of new entrepreneurial efforts and organizations (Berzin & Pitt-Catsouphes, 2015), it is important that social work managers know how to capitalize on the creative capacities of their employees to develop, support, and scale innovations internally. A guidebook for human services professionals titled *Human Services Management Competencies* includes specific skills necessary for initiating and facilitating innovative change processes: helping employees with implementing innovation and supporting risk taking, supporting innovative practices with a goal of improving program services and addressing program-related issues, and keeping up with trends and shifts in the environment that call for innovative response (Hassan & Wimpfheimer, 2015).

Unfortunately, the practice settings where social workers are employed are often seen as barriers to innovation development, diffusion, and adoption. To infuse innovation, organizations would have to change organizational policies and procedures, structure, and culture (Traube, Begun, Okpych, & Choy-Brown, 2017). Having a good understanding of how innovation happens is critical for facilitating innovation process successfully. The purpose of this chapter is to provide an overview of the innovation process and different factors influencing it. Possessing this knowledge is key for social work managers, because the innovation process entails two subprocesses, each influenced by a different set of factors. Not knowing what those factors are and not being prepared to address their impact on the process might result in failed innovation efforts.

Innovation Process

In this chapter, *innovation* is defined as a process during which ideas are transformed into outputs that add value for the customers. Although innovation can occur at the individual, group, and organizational levels, the focus of this chapter is solely on organizational innovation. The innovation process encompasses two subprocesses. The first one is the generation of ideas that are appropriate, useful, and actionable (O'Sullivan & Dooley, 2009). Although employees might share their ideas with their colleagues, it is only when those ideas are implemented in the organization that they are considered innovation. Thus, the second subprocess is transforming ideas, or coming up with practical applications for ideas and choosing ones that deliver desired results. Interpreting and evaluating ideas, experimenting and consensus building, and formalization and routinization constitute major steps in this innovation subprocess (Seelos & Mair, 2012).

The ideas generated during the first subprocess will vary in levels of creativity (West, 2002). Some ideas will be created internally and will be novel (developed as a result of a creativity process), and some will be accessed from the external environment, that is, borrowed or adapted (see Figure 2.1). Anderson, Potocnik, and Zhou (2014) proposed that "ideas can be assessed on a continuum in terms of novelty and radicalness and . . . that innovation may also include absolutely novel and radical ideas as well as ideas that are less novel and more incremental" (p. 1299). Although coming up with something

FIGURE 2.1 Innovation Process

IDEA GENERATION	IDEA TRANSFORMATION
Subprocess	Subprocess
CREATIVITY	**ORIGINAL INNOVATION**
generation of novel and potentially useful ideas	*Radical/Incremental*
ACCESSING EXTERNAL IDEAS	**BORROWED/ADAPTED INNOVATION**
Radical/Incremental	*Radical/Incremental*

entirely new might appear very appealing, in reality both—novel and radical as well as borrowed and incremental ideas—will be important and desirable.

The mix of creativity (generation of novel ideas) and innovation (idea implementation) will depend on the organization's needs at different times. Being able to balance creativity and innovation is critical for any organization (Ross & Segal, 2002). Ross and Segal's (2002) typology of organizations in terms of creativity and innovation is useful for understanding an organization's current position with regard to its competition and deciding which direction it wants to take. Creativity and innovation are placed on two axes, the intersection of which forms nine different organizational types. The organizations that are suggested to fail are the ones that have low or medium creativity and low innovation. Those organizations need most help with identifying good ideas and working through the process to develop and support them. The organizations that have high creativity and low or medium innovation are called indulgers and wasters. There is no lack of creativity there, but ideas do not get implemented. Those organizations that have low or medium creativity and medium innovations are called followers and cruisers. Organizations that implement programs developed by other organizations are called copiers. These organizations can borrow best practices from other organizations and adapt other people's ideas. Although those organizations can do well for a while, they will not gain an edge unless they start capitalizing on employees' creativity. The most ideal scenario is when an organization is high on creativity and innovation. This type of an organization is called a winner. Winners are systematic about both creativity and innovation (Ross & Segal, 2002).

To develop a breakthrough response to major challenges that their organizations face, social work managers have to understand that both organizations and employees need to be creative and innovative. Kasper and Clohesy (2008) suggested that innovation management can be a rational process

> with its own distinct set of processes, practices, and tools. . . . Systematic innovation requires well-managed and repeatable process, to move an organization beyond dependence on the lightning-strike of sporadic innovations and to create a more constant and dependable flow of new ideas. (pp. 6–7)

To make innovation happen more reliably, social work managers will have to make sure that innovation works as a disciplined process, recognizing that predictors of idea generation and idea implementation will differ (Zhou & Hoever, 2014). The sections that follow focus on the two subprocesses and their predictors.

Figure 2.2 shows innovation as a process encompassing two subprocesses: (1) idea generation and (2) idea implementation and transformation. Contextual and personal factors are identified for each subprocess, along with moderators that influence whether creative ideas are converted into innovation. A reader can see that although creativity is seen as the first step of innovation, it is not necessarily the only source of ideas. New ideas and practices can also be accessed from the external environment. The assumption underlying this model is that as long as an organization intentionally introduces a new idea and that idea is transformed into innovation, the organization is said to engage in innovation.

The Idea Generation Subprocess

Creativity is often seen as the first step in the innovation process. Although most of the research has defined creativity as an outcome, creativity in this chapter is defined as the process leading to the generation of ideas that are novel and useful (West, 2002). Those ideas can pertain to services provision, organizational structures, staffing strategies, service delivery, target markets, work procedures, products, revenue generation, and so on, and can vary in the degree to which they are creative. Unsworth (2001) proposed that creativity can be open or closed. Open creativity includes ideas that are discovered by the employees internally, whereas closed creativity includes ideas that are presented to employees (this distinction between internally generated novel ideas and externally accessed ideas is made clear in Figures 2.1 and 2.2). In addition to varying in their levels of creativity, ideas can differ in their levels of radicalness. Ideas that constitute a significant departure from the status quo are radical, whereas ideas that suggest some changes in existing order are incremental (George, 2007).

FIGURE 2.2 Individual, Organizational, and Environment Factors Related to Innovation Subprocesses

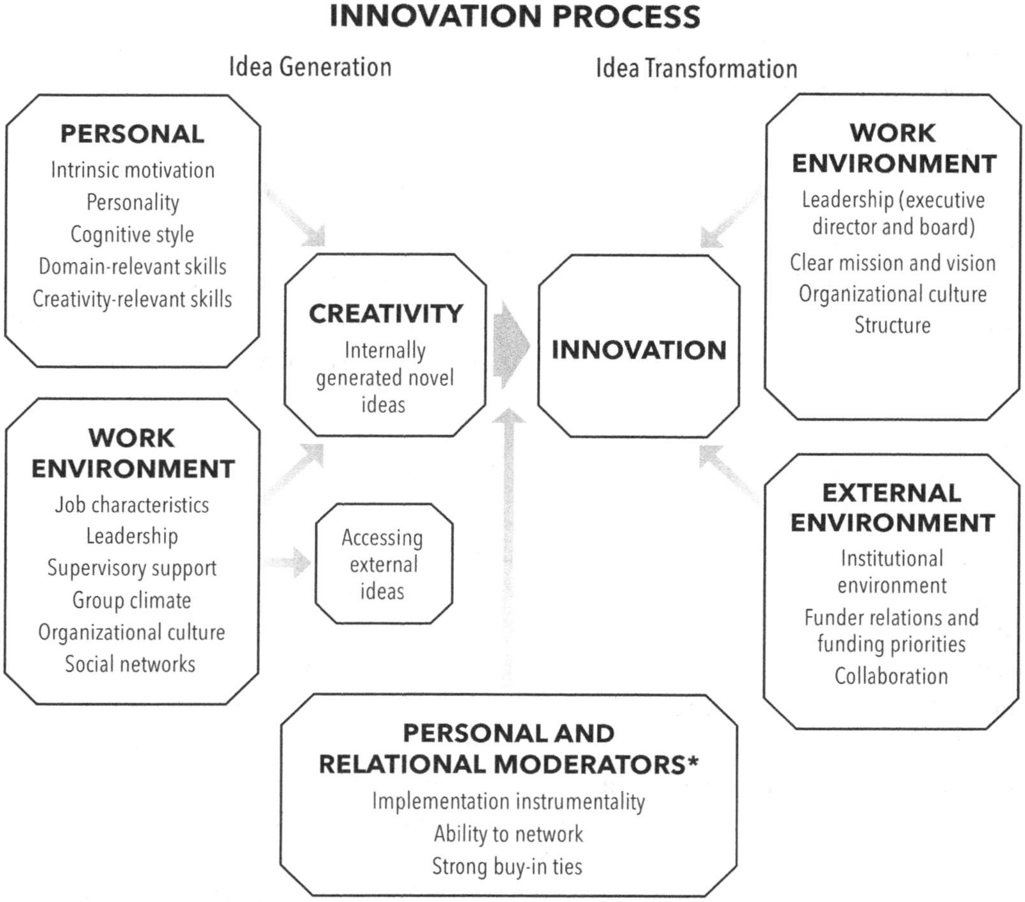

INNOVATION PROCESS

Idea Generation   Idea Transformation

PERSONAL
Intrinsic motivation
Personality
Cognitive style
Domain-relevant skills
Creativity-relevant skills

CREATIVITY
Internally generated novel ideas

INNOVATION

WORK ENVIRONMENT
Leadership (executive director and board)
Clear mission and vision
Organizational culture
Structure

WORK ENVIRONMENT
Job characteristics
Leadership
Supervisory support
Group climate
Organizational culture
Social networks

Accessing external ideas

EXTERNAL ENVIRONMENT
Institutional environment
Funder relations and funding priorities
Collaboration

PERSONAL AND RELATIONAL MODERATORS*
Implementation instrumentality
Ability to network
Strong buy-in ties

*These factors will serve as moderators between creativity and innovation.

According to Sawyer (2012), creativity takes place over time. He identified eight stages that individuals go through: find and formulate the problem, acquire knowledge relevant to the problem, seek a broad range of information related to the problem, take time for incubation, generate a large variety of ideas, combine ideas in unexpected ways, select the best ideas, and externalize the idea by using materials and representations. Amabile and Pillemer (2012) identified five stages of the creativity process: problem or task identification, preparation (gathering information to prepare to undertake the task), response generation (producing solutions or responses to the problem), response validation (evaluating novelty and usefulness of responses or solutions), and outcome (communicating the outcome). Knowing that creativity results from many different mental processes is critical for social work managers and administrators because they are able to facilitate them. According to the

Human Service Management Competencies, a capable manager "Recognizes the value of optimizing the human potential of staff . . . and develops healthy and productive practices that develop staff in all ways" (Hassan & Wimpfheimer, 2015, p. 4). These skills are especially relevant for social work managers seeking to capitalize on employee creativity.

Factors Influencing Idea Generation

As social work managers seek to optimize employees' creative potential and implement practices that help them develop in meaningful ways, it is important that managers are familiar with the most influential models of creativity, which include personal factors as well as work environment factors that either enhance or restrict employee creativity (Amabile, 1996; Woodman, Sawyer, & Griffin, 1993). Among personal factors believed to be related to employee creativity are knowledge and abilities (Anderson et al., 2014; Zhou & Hoever, 2014), creative-thinking and domain-specific skills (Amabile, 1997), personality (openness to experience, proactive personality, positive affect; Feist, 1999), cognitive style (adaptor versus innovator; Kirton, 1994), and self-concepts and identity (creative self-efficacy). Task motivation (intrinsic motivation) is seen as critical for creativity to occur. Employees with creative potential may not actually produce creative ideas if they are not willing or able to engage in creative activities. Skills that are relevant to the process of fostering creativity that social work managers should possess are designing and managing "the workplace to ensure a positive and supportive culture and climate for staff" and developing "healthy and productive practices that develop staff in all ways" (Hassan & Wimpfheimer, 2015, p. 10). As social work managers seek to encourage employee creativity, they should be mindful of numerous work environment factors that can enhance or restrict creative performance by promoting or diminishing intrinsic motivation (Zhou & Shalley, 2003).

Amabile (1997) identified the following work environment factors that affect employee creativity: organizational motivation to innovate, resources (time, personnel, resources), and managerial practices (enabling challenging work and providing encouragement). Numerous organizational scholars have made arguments for the importance of organizational culture in fostering employee creativity and have identified organizational values and norms involved in promoting creativity (Martins & Terblanche, 2003). According to Giugni (2004), key components of organizational culture are freedom to explore a variety of possibilities for thought and action, encouragement to generate and develop ideas, recognition for creativity, and the organization's desire to make creativity part of its functioning. Drawing on the results of two studies, Amabile, Conti, Coon, Lazenby, and Herron (1996) suggested that values placed on creativity—risk taking, pride in employees and enthusiasm about their capabilities, and future-oriented strategy—influence employee creativity. Koberg and Chusmir (1987) similarly argued that cultures placing value on risk taking, results orientation, creativity, stimulation, challenge, and enterprise encourage creativity because they are dynamic and exciting. O'Reilly and Tushman (1997) suggested a number of norms that should stimulate creativity. The first set of norms is related to two factors stimulating creativity: support for risk taking and change and tolerance for mistakes.

In their discussions of work environments supportive of creativity, some scholars have emphasized the importance of leadership, arguing that support for creativity has to come from the highest organizational levels (Giugni, 2004; Proehl, 2001). Jung (2000) suggested that leaders can create work environments and conditions in which employees have opportunities to get involved in creative efforts. Leaders may increase the possibility of creative output by setting clear and engaging directions; leading by example; serving as mentors and coaches; providing necessary resources; and creating appropriate organizational structure, climate, culture, and human resource practices (Shalley & Gilson, 2004). Furthermore, leaders' behaviors may influence employees' perceptions of their work environments, which, in turn, can affect their creativity (Amabile, Schatzel, Moneta, & Kramer, 2004). In particular, such behaviors as monitoring, encouraging employees to express their opinions, providing timely and constructive feedback, providing freedom and autonomy, providing high levels of social support, expressing concern for employees' feelings, balancing employees' freedom and responsibility, being noncontrolling, recognizing good work, and facilitating skill development have been suggested to influence work environments toward greater creativity (Amabile, 1998; Amabile et al., 2004; Carson & Carson, 1993; Cummings & Oldham, 1997; Deci & Ryan, 1987; West, 1989). In summary, knowing what values and norms encourage creativity and innovation is essential for social work managers, as they are responsible for establishing and maintaining organizational culture and designing and managing the workplace to ensure positive and supportive culture and climate for employees (Hassan & Wimpfheimer, 2015).

The role of supervisors in creating a work context that is supportive of creativity has also been discussed. Effectively communicating and interacting with work groups, setting clear goals, showing confidence in a group, and being open to new ideas were identified as positive supervisory behaviors in the componential theory of creativity (Amabile, 1997). George and Zhou (2007) identified interactional justice and cognitive trust as two ways in which supervisors can provide a supportive environment. When interactional justice is high—that is, when employees are treated with dignity and respect and when employees feel like their supervisors are professional, knowledgeable, and devoted—employees may be more likely to take risks and offer creative ideas. In another study, supervisors' expectations for creativity had a positive effect on employee creativity (Tierney & Farmer, 2004). When employees perceived that creativity was expected, their creative self-efficacy increased. Because social work managers are in a position to engage and empower their employees (Hassan & Wimpfheimer, 2015), they should acknowledge that supervisors can play a significant role in that process.

Because the work group appears to have a social influence on individual creativity, it is important to account for its possible effects on employee creativity (Woodman et al., 1993). King and Anderson (1995) suggested that enhancing the creativity of individual employees is not sufficient for fostering innovation. Innovation is a social process that involves interaction and exchanges within and among work groups, and therefore these processes can positively or negatively affect organizational innovativeness and creativity. Groups can influence members to conform to their values and to comply with their rules and expectations. Conversely, if risk taking, experimentation, freedom, and innovation are the predominant work group values, they can encourage and stimulate creativity. In his theory of group innovation, West (1989) proposed that a work group climate with emphasis placed on the quality of decision making and task performance and employees feeling safe to propose and develop new ideas, will be conducive to group creativity.

Contemporary research has also sought to understand the role of individuals' social networks in influencing their creativity. Effects of a small-world network structure, which has a short path length and is highly locally clustered, and weak network ties seem to have a differential impact on creativity. Uzzi and Spiro (2005) suggested that up to a certain point, a small-world network can be beneficial for creativity because it can help spread information and material across clusters, but it becomes detrimental when small worldliness increases and starts having a homogenizing effect. In that case, it becomes difficult to come up with ideas that are novel and represent the departure from an existing order. Essentially, those networks that promote the sharing of heterogeneous information and perspective will have a positive impact on creativity (Uzzi & Spiro, 2005). The value of networks and partnerships is reflected in the guide for human service professionals, *Human Services Management Competencies*. To be successful managers, social workers are expected to be competent in building relationships with complementary agencies, institutions, and community groups and in using collaborative teams to share intervention strategies and adjust intervention processes, offering staff an opportunity to learn from experts (Hassan & Wimpfheimer, 2015). Social work managers should consider the importance of individual networks for encouraging employee creativity.

Finally, a number of studies offer empirical support for the effect of job characteristics on creativity. According to Cummings and Oldham (1997), complex jobs should contribute to employee creativity. Having autonomy to decide how and when to do their jobs, needing to use a variety of skills, seeing the significance of the jobs' outcomes, and receiving feedback from the job itself should encourage employees to be more creative (Cummings & Oldham, 1997). Other researchers similarly found that when employees have complex jobs characterized by high autonomy, skill variety, feedback, freedom, and challenging work, their creativity should be enhanced (Amabile & Gryskiewicz, 1989; Hatcher, Ross, & Collins, 1989). Because social work managers are in a position to empower and engage employees, as well as promote healthy and productive practices that develop employees in all ways (Hassan & Wimpfheimer, 2015), they should consider job redesign as one strategy for encouraging creativity.

The Idea Transformation Subprocess

The second subprocess entails idea transformation into innovation. As innovation has been linked to a number of work environment and external environment factors, it is important that social work managers know what those factors are and how they can affect innovation to successfully facilitate the innovation process.

Work Environment Factors and Idea Transformation. In her model of innovation in human service organizations, Jaskyte (2009) included four major internal contextual factors: organizational culture (culture strength, values, and structure), vision and mission, leadership and the board, and organizational structure (formalization, centralization, size, and specialization). Light (1998) similarly identified four factors that affect innovation in nonprofit and government organizations: internal structure, leadership, internal management systems, and the external environment in which an organization functions.

Organizational culture has received significant attention as a factor that has a major impact on innovation. For many years, homogeneity of organizational values was seen as essential for becoming an excellent company (Denison, 1990; Pervaiz, 1998). This is changing as researchers are increasingly recognizing the heterogeneous nature of organizational culture and argue that strong cultures are problematic for innovations (Jaskyte & Dressler, 2005). Organizations with strong cultures might have difficulties in implementing new ways of functioning, in responding to changes in the external environment, and in generating new solutions to the problems that arise (Nemeth, 1997; Trice, 1993). Collins and Porras (1994) noted that innovation requires an organizational culture that is entirely opposite to a strong predictable culture, which emphasizes adherence to organizational expectations.

Numerous researchers have identified the organizational values, norms, and beliefs that characterize an innovative organization. These include working in collaboration with others, team orientation, creativity and innovation, risk taking, experimentation, flexibility, respect for individuals, tolerance, being supportive, taking initiative, sharing information freely, external orientation, future orientation, tolerance of mistakes, lack of stability, and people orientation (Amabile, 1997; Dellana & Hauser, 2000; Hurley & Hult, 1998; Jaskyte & Dressler, 2005; Kitchell, 1995; Russell, 1990).

Although values, norms, and beliefs characterizing innovative organizations are numerous, Jaskyte and Dressler (2005) suggested that the combination of cultural consensus and values, norms, or beliefs that are being shared is important to consider. Their results showed that the higher the cultural consensus on such values as stability, security, low level of conflict, predictability, rule orientation, team orientation, and working in collaboration with others was, the less innovative the organization ended up being.

Another major factor repeatedly suggested to affect innovation is leadership (Jaskyte, 2004; Osborne, 1998). Because leadership is seen as the most critical and overarching competency that is most directly related to organizational success (Hassan & Wimpfheimer, 2015), it is critical that social workers be knowledgeable about the role leaders play in the innovation process. In addition, as social work managers are expected to use different leadership styles, it is helpful for them to know what leadership style is most conductive to innovation.

Leaders can serve as role models throughout the innovation process, make explicit and instill values and norms that support innovation, create organizational structures needed to support innovation through its different stages, design a reward and incentive system for innovative idea generation and implementation, direct resources and energy toward implementing new programs, and lend power and legitimation to innovative activities (Hasenfeld, 1983; Peters & Waterman, 1982; Van de Ven, 1986). Many authors identify transformational leadership as an ideal leadership style for promoting innovation (Howell & Higgins, 1990; Jaskyte, 2011). Transformational leaders use charisma, individualized consideration, inspiration, and intellectual stimulation to encourage creativity and enhance employees' capacity to innovate.

While focusing on executive directors as leaders, researchers have failed to recognize that the leadership of a nonprofit organization lies not just with the executive director but also with the board and its chair (Jaskyte & Holland, 2015). Because social work managers are expected to work together with board members to position and change the organization to make sure that it succeeds in the ever-changing environment, as well as to demonstrate "the ability to assemble a leadership team of individuals whose skills and abilities supplement one's own" (Hassan & Wimpfheimer, 2015, p. 4), understanding the board's role in facilitating innovation can be especially valuable.

Deschamps and Nelson (2014) identified five areas of governance that have potential to affect innovation: strategy review (participation in strategy discussions), risk management (explicitly managing the innovation portfolio and following new and immerging trends in the environment), auditing (reviewing the organization's innovative performance), auditing management's innovation performance, and chief executive officer (CEO) and top management nomination (appointing an innovation-oriented CEO).

Boards can also create a culture conducive to innovation, set goals and priorities for innovation, provide freedom to come up with new ideas, encourage innovation, and approve innovative proposals (Daft, 1978). In addition, members of the board can contribute to the acquisition of needed resources. They can bring different linkages and resources to the board, all of which are needed to foster and support innovation. This role encompasses a number of activities, such as linking the organization to important entities and stakeholders, providing expertise, administering advice and counsel, building external relations, bolstering the public image of the organization, and helping the organization formulate strategy (Hillman & Dalziel, 2003; Miller-Millesen, 2003). Members of the board can also work together with the executive director and other stakeholders to understand the environment in which the organization functions, stay informed about and present new issues and opportunities faced by the organization, invite questions and feedback from stakeholders, and shed new light on problems and opportunities (Chait, Ryan, & Taylor, 2005).

An organization's vision and mission statements guide its strategic direction—what programs and services are being provided, what programs are to be grown and cut back, and which relationships with organizations and individuals are being pursued (Sullivan-Mort & Weerawardena, 2006). McDonald (2007) suggested that having a clear mission will help an organization focus on supportive innovations and resist mission drift. The author goes on to describe mechanisms through which mission clarity can contribute to an organization's innovative capacity: generating ideas that are in line with an organization's goals and objectives, lowering barriers to communicating and evaluating new ideas because those new ideas will be based on a common mission, decreasing levels of resistance to innovation during the innovation process because of the stakeholders' commitment to mission, and lowering levels of resistance to idea formalization and diffusion. Understanding the mission's centrality in the innovation process is important for social work managers who are expected to know how to create a mission statement, ensure that programs align with the overall mission, and review the mission to ensure its relevance to the current situation (Hassan & Wimpfheimer, 2015).

Finally, among the structural factors affecting innovation are specialization (the range of occupational specialties), centralization (the degree to which power and control is concentrated in the hands of a few individuals—which has a negative effect), formalization (the degree to which an organization emphasizes rules and regulations—which has a negative effect), and size (which can have either a positive or negative effect) (Damanpour, 1991; Kimberly, 1981; West, Smith, Feng, & Lawthom, 1998; Zaltman, Duncan, & Holbeck, 1973).

External Environment Factors and Idea Transformation. To facilitate the innovative process, social workers should stay current on trends in the environment and identify gaps that call for an innovative response (Hassan & Wimpfheimer, 2015). Knowing what external factors can have a significant impact on an organization's innovation is critical for successfully facilitating the innovation process. Seelos, Mair, Battilana, and Dacin (2011) argued that innovation depends on "a number of cognitive, normative, and regulative institutions that shape their task environment" (p. 21). The institutional environment can encourage or constrain the actions of organizations by dictating priorities for innovative actions, influencing how resources get distributed, and specifying legitimate actions and outcomes (Mair & Marti, 2009).

When discussing funder relations as an external factor influencing innovation, it is important to consider who has control over funds and the conditions under which funds are made available. Stone, Bigelow, and Crittenden (1999), after reviewing nonprofit strategy literature, found that innovations in nonprofits were driven by funders' requirements, more so than by actual desire to satisfy customers' needs. More current literature points to the powerful role foundations can play in encouraging and supporting innovation. Foundations can use their capital to support introducing and testing ideas proposed by social work entrepreneurs. They can risk investing in the areas where a return on investment is uncertain (Hammack & Anheier, 2013; Payton, 1983). Foundations can also act as social entrepreneurs that can foresee and address the problems that other organizations are not interested or able to address (Hammack & Anheier, 2013). In addition, foundations can serve as conveners of individuals, groups, and organizations that are interested in innovation and change across sectors, regions, and communities. Finally, foundations can influence the culture of the nonprofit sector through the choice of programs that they fund, the approval of particular organizational characteristics that get reinforced through awardee selection processes, and requirements for matching funds (Froelich, 1999). The two factors combined—institutional environment and funder relations—influence a field in which organizations function, making competition for resources and the search for their legitimacy and place in a larger system a part of those organizations' reality.

Collaboration has been suggested as one way to address the challenges that competition brings about. Among the numerous benefits of collaboration are improved efficiency and effectiveness; participation in organizational networks, which can result in increased capacity for innovation; and joint learning and sharing of resources, which can contribute to innovation capacity building (Powell & Grodal, 2006). Vernis, Iglesias, Sanz, and Sanz-Carranza (2006) provided a list of other benefits, such as increased impact and reach of programs, increased negotiating power for future engagements, improved ability to adjust to the environment, enhanced resource optimization, and improved overall social positioning of the nonprofit sector.

The importance of collaboration is clearly reflected in the guide for human services professionals, *Human Service Management Competencies* (Hassan & Wimpfheimer, 2015). Social work managers should be competent in building relationships with complementary agencies, institutions, and community groups. Establishing partnerships, collaborating with other organizations, identifying opportunities for partnerships, and effectively managing policy advocacy coalitions are all skills needed for successful management of human service organizations (Hassan & Wimpfheimer, 2015).

Moderators of the Creativity–Innovation Link

At this point, a reader has a good understanding of the two innovation subprocesses and their determinants. It is important to reemphasize that generation of creative ideas does not guarantee their implementation. In fact, a number of authors argue that the production of ideas is more prevalent than their transformation into actual innovations (West, 2002). Therefore, it is important to consider a number of factors that might influence this idea transformation into innovation. Baer (2012) was among the first researchers to argue that idea implementation is not guaranteed and to identify a set of moderators that influence the relation between creativity and idea implementation. According to him, implementation instrumentality, or the extent to which employees expect positive desirable outcomes to be associated with implementation of their ideas, is likely to serve as an important moderator. Expecting positive outcomes (performance improvements, image gains, and so on) can serve as a powerful motivator for innovative behavior and can be an intrinsic motivator because implementation instrumentality focuses on idea implementation specifically (Baer, 2012). The second important moderator is networking ability. Social work managers and employees have to be skilled in development and use of social networks to successfully mobilize support and advocacy needed to improve the chances of their idea being implemented. Baer (2012) noted that those moderators will be more important when creativity is high—that is, when the idea is a significant departure from dominant ways of doing things. The opposition to an idea that is of low creativity will not be nearly as strong and will require less effort to transform it into innovation. Conversely, as creativity increases, so will the importance of implementation instrumentality and networking ability. The last moderator is strong social ties. Strong social ties to others might allow successful implementation of ideas within an organization. This moderator in combination with implementation instrumentality will affect idea implementation (Baer, 2012).

Conclusion

As human service organizations are facing numerous challenges, it is important that social work managers know how to make innovation happen more reliably. Information provided in this chapter should help social work managers make innovation a well-managed, disciplined, and repeatable process. Having a good understanding of the innovation process and its determinants should help social work managers not only assess the areas in which their organizations are lacking but come up with ideas for making needed changes to facilitate creativity and innovation processes.

References

Amabile, T. M. (1996). *Creativity in context*. Boulder, CO: Westview Press.

Amabile, T. M. (1997). Motivating creativity in organizations: On doing what you love and loving what you do. *California Management Review, 40*, 39–58. doi:10.2307/41165921

Amabile, T. M. (1998, September/October). How to kill creativity? *Harvard Business Review*, pp. 76–87. doi:10.4135/9781446213704.n2

Amabile, T. M., Conti, R., Coon, H., Lazenby, J., & Herron, M. (1996). Assessing the work environment for creativity. *Academy of Management Journal, 39*, 1154–1184. doi:10.2307/256995

Amabile, T. M., & Gryskiewicz, N. D. (1989). The Creative Environment Scales: Work environment inventory. *Creativity Research Journal, 2*, 231–253. doi:10.1080/10400418909534321

Amabile, T. M., & Pillemer, J. (2012). Perspectives on the social psychology of creativity. *Journal of Creative Behavior, 46*(1), 3–15. doi:10.1002/jocb.001

Amabile, T. M., Schatzel, E. A., Moneta, G. B., & Kramer, S. J. (2004). Leader behaviors and the work environment for creativity: Perceived leader support. *Leadership Quarterly, 15*, 5–32. doi:10.1016/j.leaqua.2003.12.003

Anderson, N., Potocnik, K., & Zhou, J. (2014). Innovation and creativity in organizations: A state-of-the-science review, prospective commentary, and guiding framework. *Journal of Management, 40*, 1297–1333. doi:10.1177/0149206314527128

Baer, M. (2012). Putting creativity to work: The implementation of creative ideas in organizations. *Academy of Management Journal, 55*, 1102–1119. doi:10.5465/amj.2009.0470

Berzin, S. C. (2012). Where is social work in the social entrepreneurship movement? [Commentary]. *Social Work, 57*, 185–188. doi:10.1093/sw/sws004

Berzin, S. C., & Pitt-Catsouphes, M. (2015). Social innovation from the inside: Considering the "intrapreneurship" path [Commentary]. *Social Work, 60*, 360–362. doi:10.1093/sw/swv026

Carson, P. P., & Carson, K. D. (1993). Managing creativity enhancement through goal-setting and feedback. *Journal of Creative Behavior, 27*, 36–45. doi:10.1002/j.2162-6057.1993.tb01385.x

Chait, R. P., Ryan, W. P., & Taylor, B. E. (2005). *Governance as leadership: Reframing the work of nonprofit boards*. Hoboken, NJ: John Wiley & Sons.

Collins, J. C., & Porras, J. I. (1994). *Built to last*. New York: HarperCollins.

Cummings, A., & Oldham, G. R. (1997). Enhancing creativity: Managing work contexts for the high potential employee. *California Management Review, 40*(1), 22–38. doi:10.2307/41165920

Daft, R. L. (1978). A dual core model of organizational innovation. *Academy of Management Journal, 21*, 193–210. doi:10.2307/255754

Damanpour, F. (1991). Organizational innovation: A meta-analysis of effects of determinants and moderators. *Academy of Management Journal, 34*, 555–590. doi:10.1093/acrefore/9780190224851.013.19

Deci, E. L., & Ryan, R. M. (1987). The support of autonomy and the control of behavior. *Journal of Personality and Social Psychology, 53*, 1024–1037. doi:10.1037/0022-3514.53.6.1024

Dellana, S. A., & Hauser, R. D. (2000). Corporate culture's impact on a strategic approach to quality. *Mid-American Journal of Business, 15*(1), 9–20. Retrieved from https://pdfs.semanticscholar.org/4574/97f1607bbb8755bd1f409342d545e6272205.pdf#page=9

Denison, D. R. (1990). *Corporate culture and organizational effectiveness*. New York: John Wiley & Sons.

Deschamps, J., & Nelson, B. (2014). Governing innovation in practice: The role of the board of directors. In *Innovation governance: How top management organizes and mobilizes for innovation* (pp. 31–47). Somerset, UK: Jossey-Bass.

Feist, G. J. (1999). The influence of personality on artistic and scientific creativity. In R. Sternberg (Ed.), *Handbook of creativity* (pp. 272–296). New York: Cambridge University Press.

Froelich, K. A. (1999). Diversification of revenue strategies: Evolving resource dependence in nonprofit organizations. *Nonprofit and Voluntary Sector Quarterly, 28*, 246–268. doi:10.1177/0899764099283002

George, J. M. (2007). Creativity in organizations. *Academy of Management Annals, 1*, 439–477. doi:10.1080/078559814

George, J. M., & Zhou, J. (2007). Dual tuning in a supportive context: Joint contributions of positive mood, negative mood, and supervisory behaviors to employee creativity. *Academy of Management Journal, 50*, 605–622. doi:10.5465/AMJ.2007.25525934

Giugni, S. (2004). Nurturing imagination: Fostering creativity in your organization. In C. Barker & R. Coy (Eds.), *Innovation and imagination at work* (pp. 63–97). Sydney, Australia: McGraw-Hill.

Hammack, H. K., & Anheier, H. K. (2013). *A versatile American institution: The changing ideas and realities of philanthropic foundations.* Washington, DC: Brookings Institution Press.

Hasenfeld, Y. (1983). *Human service organizations.* Englewood Cliffs, NJ: Prentice Hall.

Hassan, A., & Wimpfheimer, S. (2015). *Human services management competencies.* Retrieved from https://socialworkmanager.org/wp-content/uploads/2016/01/Competency-Brochure-4-19-15-With-Forms.pdf

Hatcher, L., Ross, T. L., & Collins, D. (1989). Prosocial behavior, job complexity, and suggestion contribution under gainsharing plans. *Journal of Applied Behavioral Science, 25*, 231–248. doi:10.1177/0021886389253002

Hillman, A. J., & Dalziel, T. (2003). Boards of directors and firm performance: Integrating agency and resource dependence perspectives. *Academy of Management Review, 28*, 383–396. doi:10.2307/30040728

Howell, J. M., & Higgins, C. A. (1990). Champions of technological innovation. *Administrative Science Quarterly, 35*, 317–341. doi:10.2307/2393393

Hurley, R. F., & Hult, T. M. (1998). Innovation, market orientation, and organizational learning: An integration and empirical examination. *Journal of Marketing, 62*(3), 42–54. doi:10.2307/1251742

Jaskyte, K. (2004). Transformational leadership, organizational culture and innovativeness in nonprofit organizations. *Nonprofit Management and Leadership, 15*, 153–168. doi:10.1002/nml.59

Jaskyte, K. (2009). Innovation in human service organizations. In Y. Hasenfeld (Ed.), *Human services as complex organizations* (pp. 481–503). Newbury Park, CA: Sage Publications.

Jaskyte, K. (2011). Predictors of administrative and technological innovations in nonprofit organizations. *Public Administration Review, 71*(1), 77–86. doi:10.1111/j.1540-6210.2010.02308.x

Jaskyte, K., & Dressler, W. (2005). Organizational culture and innovation in nonprofit human service organizations. *Administration in Social Work, 29*(2), 23–41. doi:10.1300/J147v29n02_03

Jaskyte, K., & Holland, T. (2015). Nonprofit boards: Problems and opportunities [Guest editorial]. *Human Services Organizations: Leadership, Management and Governance, 39,* 163–166. doi:10.1080/23303131.2015.1035612

Jung, D. I. (2000). Transformational and transactional leadership and their effects on creativity in groups. *Creativity Research Journal, 13,* 185–195. doi:10.1207/S15326934CRJ1302_6

Kasper, G., & Clohesy, S. (2008). *Intentional innovation: How getting more systematic about innovation could improve philanthropy and increase social impact.* Retrieved from https://www.wkkf.org/resource-directory/resource/2008/09/intentional-innovation-full-report

Kimberly, J. R. (1981). Managerial innovation. In P. C. Nystrom & W. H. Starbuck (Eds.), *Handbook of organizational design* (pp. 84–104). Oxford, UK: Oxford University Press.

King, N., & Anderson, N. (1995). *Innovation and change in organizations.* New York: Routledge.

Kirton, M. J. (1994). *Adaptors and innovators: Styles of creativity and problem solving* (2nd ed.). New York: Routledge.

Kitchell, S. (1995). Corporate culture, environmental adaptation, and innovation adoption: A qualitative/quantitative approach. *Journal of the Academy of Marketing Science, 23,* 195–206. doi:10.1177/0092070395233004

Koberg, C. S., & Chusmir, L. H. (1987). Organizational culture relationships with creativity and other job-related variables. *Journal of Business Research, 15,* 397–409. doi:10.1016/0148-2963(87)90009-9

Light, C. P. (1998). *Sustaining innovation: Creating nonprofit and government organizations that innovate naturally.* San Francisco: Jossey-Bass.

Mair, J., & Marti, I. (2009). Entrepreneurship in and around institutional voids: A case study from Bangladesh. *Journal of Business Venturing, 24,* 419–435. doi:10.1016/j.jbusvent.2008.04.006

Martins, E. C., & Terblanche, F. (2003). Building organizational culture that stimulates creativity and innovation. *European Journal of Innovation Management, 6*(1), 64–74. doi:10.1108/14601060310456337

McDonald, R. E. (2007). An investigation of innovation in nonprofit organizations: The role of organizational mission. *Nonprofit and Voluntary Sector Quarterly, 36,* 256–281. doi:10.1177/0899764006295996

Miller-Millesen, J. L. (2003). Understanding the behavior of nonprofit boards of directors: A theory-based approach. *Nonprofit and Voluntary Sector Quarterly, 32*, 521–547. doi:10.1177/0899764003257463

National Association of Social Workers. (2017). *Code of ethics of the National Association of Social Workers.* Washington, DC: Author.

Nemeth, C. J. (1997). Managing innovation: When less is more. *California Management Review, 40*(1), 59–74. doi:10.2307/41165922

O'Reilly, A. A., & Tushman, M. L. (1997). Using culture for strategic advantage: Promoting innovation through social control. In M. L. Tushman, & P. Anderson (Eds.), *Managing strategic innovation and change: A collection of readings* (pp. 200–216). New York: Oxford University Press.

Osborne, S. P. (1998). Naming the beast: Defining and classifying service innovations in social policy. *Human Relations, 51*, 1133–1155. doi:10.1177/001872679805100902

O'Sullivan, D., & Dooley, L. (2009). Defining innovation. In D. O'Sullivan & L. Dooley (Eds.), *Applying innovation* (pp. 3–33). Thousand Oaks, CA: Sage Publications.

Payton, R. (1983). Philanthropic values. In *Working papers for Spring Research Forum: Since the Filer Commission* (pp. 41–87). Washington, DC: Independent Sector.

Pervaiz, K. A. (1998). Culture and climate for innovation. *European Journal of Innovation Management, 1*(1), 30–47. doi:10.1108/14601069810199131

Peters, T. J., & Waterman, R. H., Jr. (1982). *In search of excellence: Lessons from America's best-run companies.* New York: Warner Books.

Pitt-Catsouphes, M., & Berzin, S. C. (2015). Teaching note: Incorporating social innovation content into macro social work education. *Journal of Social Work Education, 51*, 407–416. doi:10.1080/10437797.2015.1012947

Powell, W., & Grodal, S. (2006). Networks of innovators. In R. R. Nelson, D. C. Mowery, & J. Fagerberg (Eds.), *The Oxford handbook of innovation* (pp. 56–85). Oxford, UK: Oxford University Press.

Proehl, R. A. (2001). *Organizational change in the human services.* doi:10.4135/9781452231228

Ross, B., & Segal, C. (2002). *Breakthrough thinking for nonprofit organizations: Creative strategies for extraordinary results.* San Francisco: Jossey-Bass.

Russell, R. D. (1990). Innovation in organizations: Toward an integrated model. *Review of Business, 12*(2), 19–47.

Sawyer, K. (2012). Extending sociocultural theory to group creativity. *Vocations and Learning, 5*(1), 59–75. doi:10.1007/s12186-011-9066-5

Seelos, C., & Mair, J. (2012). *What determines the capacity for continuous innovation in social sector organizations?* Retrieved from http://www.christianseelos.com/capacity-for-continuous-innovation_PACS_31Jan2012_Final.pdf

Seelos, C., Mair, J., Battilana, J., & Dacin, M.T. (2011). The embeddedness of social entrepreneurship: Understanding variation across local communities. In M. Lounsbury, (Ed.), *Research in the sociology of organizations* (vol. 33, pp. 333–363). Bingley, UK: Emerald Publishing.

Shalley, C. E., & Gilson, L. L. (2004). What leaders need to know: A review of social and contextual factors that can foster or hinder creativity. *Leadership Quarterly, 15*, 33–53. doi:10.1016/j.leaqua.2003.12.004

Stone, M. M., Bigelow, B., & Crittenden, W. (1999). Research on strategic management in nonprofit organizations: Synthesis, analysis, and future directions. *Administration & Society, 31*, 378–423.

Sullivan-Mort, G., & Weerawardena, J. (2006). Networking capability and international entrepreneurship: How networks function in Australian-born global firms. *International Marketing Review, 23*, 549–572. doi:10.1108/02651330610703445

Tierney, P., & Farmer, S. M. (2004). The Pygmalion process and employee creativity. *Journal of Management, 30*, 413–432. doi:10.1016/j.jm.2002.12.001

Traube, D. E., Begun, S., Okpych, N., & Choy-Brown, M. (2017). Catalyzing innovation in social work practice. *Research on Social Work Practice, 27*, 134–138. doi:10.1177/1049731516659140

Trice, H. M. (1993). *Occupational subcultures in the workplace*. Ithaca, NY: ILR Press.

Unsworth, K. (2001). Unpacking creativity. *Academy of Management Review, 26*, 289–297. doi:10.2307/259123

Uzzi, B., & Spiro, J. (2005). Collaboration and creativity: The small world problem. *American Journal of Sociology, 111*, 447–504. doi:10.1086/432782

Van de Ven, A. H. (1986). Central problems in the management of innovation. *Management Science, 32*, 509–607. doi:10.1287/mnsc.32.5.590

Vernis, A., Iglesias, M., Sanz, B., & Sanz-Carranza, A. (2006). *Nonprofit organizations: Challenges and collaboration*. New York: Palgrave Macmillan.

West, M. A. (1989). Innovation amongst health care professionals. *Social Behavior, 4*, 173–184.

West, M. A. (2002). Sparkling fountains or stagnant ponds: An integrative model of creativity and innovation in work groups. *Applied Psychology: An International Review, 51*, 355–424. doi:10.1111/1464-0597.00951

West, M. A., Smith, H., Feng, W. L., & Lawthom, R. (1998). Research excellence and departmental climate in British universities. *Journal of Occupational and Organizational Psychology, 71*, 261–281. doi:10.1111/j.2044-8325.1998.tb00676.x

Woodman, R. W., Sawyer, J. E., & Griffin, R. W. (1993). Toward a theory of organizational creativity. *Academy of Management Review, 18*, 293–321. doi:10.5465/AMR.1993.3997517

Zaltman, G., Duncan, R., & Holbeck, J. (1973). *Innovations and organizations*. New York: John Wiley & Sons.

Zhou, J., & Hoever, I. J. (2014). Research on workplace creativity: A review and redirection. *Annual Review of Organizational Psychology and Organizational Behavior, 1*, 333–359. doi:10.1146/annurev-orgpsych-031413-091226

Zhou, J., & Shalley, C. E. (2003). Research on employee creativity: A critical review and directions for future research. *Research in Personnel and Human Resource Management, 22*, 165–217. doi:10.1016/S0742-7301(03)22004-1

3

Social Innovation and Social Work Practice

James M. Mandiberg, Joshua P. H. Livingston, and Joe Silva

Social workers have initiated or contributed to social innovations but most often have not conceptualized their efforts in this way. For example, settlement houses were a new approach in support of poor and immigrant communities in the late 19th century. Today, such efforts resulting in a social movement may be labeled as social innovation and scaling. In 1968, John Durand converted the Occupational Training Center of Christ Child School in St. Paul, Minnesota, to a supported work program and a short time later created an early affirmative business, Minnesota Diversified Industries. Today affirmative businesses are called work integration social enterprises, or WISEs (Warner & Mandiberg, 2006). In the late 1940s, a group of people recently discharged from Rockland State Hospital in New York who met together for mutual support hired a Michigan social worker, John Beard, to help them design a more viable program. Together they created one of the most internationally replicated mental health models, Fountain House. Even today Fountain House's socially innovative mutual support model is quite different from current mental health services (Doyle, Lanoil, & Dudek, 2013).

In its simplest form, social innovation means a novel approach to a vexing social problem. However, it is not that simple. "Novel" could mean an alternative way of conceptualizing or defining an issue, a different way of using resources, new outcome expectations for service users, borrowing an old idea or model from another country or another client population, or numerous other ways of making something novel. In addition, the term "innovation" can refer to both a process, as in a novel way of doing things, and an outcome, as in something achieved that is very different from the usual (Phills, Deiglmeier, & Miller, 2008).

This chapter provides an introduction to social innovation. In the course of reviewing the ways in which social innovation is approached by social workers and other social service providers, the chapter looks at how social innovations created by social workers often differ from those created by non–social workers and some of the reasons for the differences. The chapter also looks at issues of scale, incorporation options for social innovations in the United States, the different ways that social innovations are funded or capitalized, and some of the approaches to social innovation from outside social work that could inform social workers' efforts. A short introduction to design thinking is also included. Design thinking is an approach to dealing with the kinds of seemingly intractable problems that social workers often face. The chapter ends with some examples of social innovations and a discussion of the importance of social innovation for social work. The chapter also includes mention of the ethical issues that may arise for social workers engaged in social innovation and notes how social work's ethical and professional norms provide guidance for dealing with these issues.

Examining Innovation Frameworks: Logic, Impact, and Scale

The world of business has become focused on innovation. The business environment is changing so fast that if organizations do not innovate constantly, they are at risk of falling behind. Joseph Schumpeter, one of the founders of the study of entrepreneurship and innovation economics, wrote that "creative destruction is the essential fact about capitalism" (1942, p. 83). Schumpeter's core idea was that capitalism advances and stays vital when new products, services, and technologies replace old ones. One of the most influential current thinkers about business innovation, Clayton Christensen, has promoted the idea that disruptive innovation determines progress in the current market and into the future (Christensen, 1997; Christensen, Baumann, Ruggles, & Sadtler, 2006). Christensen distinguished between sustaining and disruptive innovations. Sustaining innovations allow existing firms to maintain their market positions by making evolutionary improvements to products and services that meet current customer expectations. Disruptive innovations, conversely, create new market demand, oftentimes for products and services that customers did not know they wanted, or needed, because these products and services never existed before.

Although creative destruction and disruptive innovation are innovation concepts pertaining to the for-profit sector, social innovations can occur in any one or in any combination of the three sectors—for-profit, nonprofit, and public. When they occur in combinations of sectors, we often refer to them as "hybrid." For example, iDE, a nonprofit-sector nongovernmental organization (NGO) founded by Paul Polak, a psychiatrist and the former director of Southwest Denver Mental Health Center, has had a large-scale impact on subsistence-level farm families in South Asia, Southeast Asia, Africa, and South America. iDE designs technologies that substantially increase farm yields and, as a result, farmers' incomes. iDE's social innovations include redesigning irrigation technologies to be very low cost, manufacturing the irrigation technologies in local communities to build their economies, and selling the technologies to farmers at a low and affordable cost rather than the more typical NGO approach of giving them away. By selling the irrigation technologies at an affordable cost, the farmers are more invested in using and maintaining them, which owing to their simple design are easy for the farmers to repair. iDE's innovations are a hybrid of social innovations—the organization is a nonprofit that uses the market to create social value. Farm families that were dependent on rain for a single growing season can now produce two to three harvests by using iDE's treadle pumps and drip irrigation systems (Polak, 2008).

The brief example of iDE highlights some important issues that exist in many but not all social innovations. First, Polak was an outsider to the world of international development. He came from the world of social services. Innovations in general, and social innovations as well, often come from those who are from outside the field in which they are innovating. They are not constrained by inheriting the beliefs and models that led to the current way of doing things. Rather, they may be able to bring fresh perspectives to the issue, allowing them to come up with ideas that may seem discordant to those already in the field. Social innovators often challenge deeply held beliefs, and some of those already in the field may find the ideas unacceptable.

Second, one way that iDE measures its success is by social impact. Traditional for-profit enterprises are said to have single bottom lines. Traditional for-profit businesses measure their success in the form of profits they generate, often calculated as return on investment (ROI). Social ventures, created by social workers to provide services, have not relied on a single measure of success for all such activity. In the late 1990s, there was a great deal of interest in the concept of a social return on investment (SROI) measure, first proposed by the social innovation intermediary organization REDF. SROI was appealing because it held the promise of a methodology, similar to for-profit ROI, for measuring value as social impact. Although the concept of SROI is still of interest, and different SROI methodologies have been developed, REDF itself found the approach to be very time and resource consuming and has stopped using it (Javits, 2008). iDE uses a simpler approach. It set the target of $10.00 in added income or savings for iDE clients for every dollar invested in working with its clients (iDE Global, n.d.). Although different methodologies are used, all social innovations desire and warrant measurable social impacts.

Third, iDE is deeply concerned with issues of scale. iDE focuses on social innovations that have the potential to improve the lives of millions of people. However, when one considers issues of scale, there is no single right answer. Traditional ideas of scale are scaling up and scaling out. Scaling up is growing larger, making more of something, and having a broad impact from a single source. The idea that to be successful an organization needs to grow larger and benefit from economies of scale follows this line of thinking. Scaling out is replicating multiple examples of the same thing, which we often call dissemination. Social workers are often asked or required to replicate evidence-based interventions in different locations or with different population segments—an example of scaling out. And when this diffusion is done with fidelity, it is an example of scaling out without adaptation to local conditions or context.

Scaling deep, a concept proposed by Taylor, Dees, and Emerson (2002), focuses on strongly embedding the social innovation in the community or communities of concern. A social innovation that is scaled deep may not have broad social impact but has significant impact on the community of concern. Scaling deep is thoroughly consistent with social work values and practices. Our person-in-environment perspective requires us in clinical, community, and organizational practices to consider the relationship of the person, community, or organization with whom we work with the environment in which they are embedded. Another idea of scale is right scaling. Right scaling considers how economically sustainable a social innovation is in a particular community. It looks to match the size of the social innovation with the size of the supporting community. Right scaling also is in line with social work practice and values. Social workers involved with community development will recognize right scaling as responsible community development practice because the social innovation is not extended beyond the needs and abilities of the community. Evaluating the effectiveness and appropriateness of scaling entails examining the number of people affected in scaling up and out, how people and communities are affected in scaling deep, and right scaling to ensure that the social innovation is appropriate for the community.

Social Innovation and Human Service Organizations: Comparing Approaches

Society turns to the social work profession to address difficult social, emotional, and material problems. Social workers are naturally motivated and inspired for social innovation by their direct experience with social service users. Social workers and many of the people they work with are confronted by seemingly intractable problems of poverty, disability, stigma and discrimination, social and economic exclusion, directly experienced and historical trauma, lack of affordable housing, poor education, and so many other individual and collective disadvantages. Social workers and their clients directly experience the significant and unintended consequences of overly simplistic social policies, funding cuts, and the oftentimes underperforming intervention technologies available to address these issues.

Although there is high motivation for social workers to create social innovations, they work in policy and organizational environments—called institutional environments—that may actively or inherently oppose innovation, especially innovation that appears to be very different from the way human services have been organized or conceptualized in the past. Institutional environments are significantly regulated or influenced by institutional actors such as governmental authorities, funders, regulators, licensing bodies, professional groups, and advocates. Organizations in institutional environments are successful when they conform to the expectations of these institutional actors and run the risk of failure when they do not (DiMaggio & Powell, 1983). Imagine a situation in which a social service organization informs its funder that it does not want to implement the evidence-based practice required by its contract; that it cannot meet licensing regulations because it is doing something innovative that is not allowed by the license; or that it wants to use professional staff in new ways.

Contrast this example with for-profit businesses that exist in a market environment, where customers decide who and what is successful. These organizations succeed by standing out and offering a product or service that is of better quality, has unique and different features, is cheaper, or is marketed and advertised more effectively. The business that takes innovative risks may fail if the investors, other stakeholders, or customers do not trust or buy the innovation. Similarly, a social service organization that innovates beyond what the institutional actors expect or require could fail. Fear of failure is a major hazard and deterrent when trying something new. Social innovators need to be willing to risk failure and also risk loss of resources, reputation, and social or political capital. Assessing the risk tolerance of a social service organization that is thinking about social innovation is essential. The loss of funds in a failed social innovation may put social service organizations and their clients at risk. Conversely, many social service interventions underperform and without innovation will continue to do so.

Assessing the risk of an innovation is an important ethical concern for professional social workers. Ethical considerations include asking the following questions: (1) Who will benefit if the innovation is successful, and who will suffer if it is not? (2) Does the innovation contribute to or counter social inequality? and (3) Does the social innovation principally meet the needs of service users, or are only other interests favored? These types of concerns, and the fiduciary responsibility of not using funding for very risky ventures, especially in nonprofit organizations, need to be considered when social workers engage in social innovation. In addition, when initiating any kind of change in social services, it is important to consider how the change process may undermine the stability of service users. As in other instances of ethical dilemmas, social work's code of ethics is a helpful guide.

"How Do We Pay for It?": Traditional and Nontraditional Tactics

Pursuing social innovation within a funded social service organization carries special considerations. Innovations in business use funds from investors who realize that there is some risk to their investment and potential ROI. Today, funding for social services in the United States primarily comes from government contracts and third-party insurance reimbursements, and to lesser extents from private fundraising and foundations. Government agencies that contract for services and third-party reimbursors are purchasing specific services that are most often established interventions, not new social innovations. In fundraising, donors who contribute to social service organizations typically donate to an organization's general appeal for funds. When donating to a general appeal, donors may not expect that their contributions will fund risky ventures. Donations for social innovations are often procured through targeted appeals to donors who are interested in the social innovation or through special project appeals in which the riskiness of the social innovation is specified.

Traditionally, public agencies or nonprofit organizations provide social services in the United States. Public agencies and divisions of local, state, and federal government may have restrictions for use of funds that affect social innovations. Similarly, nonprofits approved as 501(c)(3) tax-exempt organizations by the U.S. Internal Revenue Service also have restrictions on how they may use funds. For example, although nonprofit organizations may make a "profit," or what in nonprofit accounting is called a surplus, generating a profit is not allowed to be the principal activity of the organization. Similarly, because 501(c)(3) nonprofits serve the public interest, donors are prohibited from profiting from the activities of nonprofit organizations. These restrictions on public and nonprofit organizations limit how they are able to fund social innovations.

Funding of social innovations in social work has typically occurred through foundations, targeted fundraising appeals, the single-minded focus of an innovator, and modifications to existing funded services that do not contravene contractual obligations. Foundations traditionally have been willing to take some risks in developing social innovations. This may occur when a foundation becomes especially interested in a new or difficult-to-address social issue or when a social innovator approaches a receptive foundation with a new and interesting idea. In these instances, foundations may fund a pilot project to test the feasibility of the innovation. Pilot projects of this sort evolve in their development as they experiment and test feasibility.

At the street level (Lipsky, 2010), a social worker may have a novel idea of how to modify an intervention or, authorized or not, may try something new with service users. Social workers attempting social innovation of this latter type need to be careful that their modification to services does not violate any contractual obligations or place them in an ethically compromised position with their clients, such as a dual relationship. An example of an ethically compromising social innovation is one that involves and could place at risk the financial assets of a client. This latter kind of social innovation may raise ethical concerns for professional social workers, who are wise to consult the National Association of Social Workers (2017) *Code of Ethics* and fellow professional social workers about such ventures.

More recently, other forms of funding have also become available for social innovations. Social venture funders have grown since the 1990s, when many young technology entrepreneurs suddenly found themselves wealthy and wanting to use some of their new wealth to contribute to their communities. For example, in 1997, technology entrepreneurs in Seattle created Social Venture Partners (SVP) to fund social innovations affecting social and environmental conditions. SVP, itself a social innovation, has scaled, and today there are over forty cities worldwide with SVP activities involving over 3,200 participants (Seattle, 2011).

New fundraising approaches, such as crowdfunding, are also used to fund social ventures. Crowdfunding occurs when those looking to fund a project, such as a social innovation, raise small amounts of money from many donors, typically through crowdfunding Internet sites. These sites do not pass along the raised funds until the project accrues its proposed amount. There are different types of crowdfunding, sometimes restricted by how the social venture is incorporated. Typical models include crowdfunding with no expectation of any return to the donor, often used by nonprofit ventures; crowdfunding with expectations of receiving a product once it is produced; and crowdfunding with expectations of some financial return, which can include interest on the investment or an equity share in the venture. The last type is available only for one of the many for-profit incorporated forms of social innovations.

Crowdfunding sites, themselves entrepreneurial ventures, go in and out of business. Not all crowdfunding sites welcome social innovations; purely profit-seeking ventures and innovations dominate the crowdfunding world. A current crowdfunding site that is specifically for social ventures is startsome good.com. StartSomeGood is for social purpose innovations and encourages tax-exempt nonprofits to highlight this focus to potential donors. The site also offers advice, and even a course, on how to crowdfund effectively. The crowdfunding site Kiva follows a different model. At kiva.org contributors choose a person or a project to make a loan to, in $25 increments. Once the loan is paid back through Kiva, the contributor may choose a new person or project or choose to have their contribution returned to him or her. Kiva facilitates these loans internationally to those who are financially excluded and unable to receive other forms of nonexploitative loans. Kiva-facilitated loans are similarly available in the United States but are also available to social innovators with concrete social impact objectives. A third site is causevox.com. Causevox provides a sophisticated platform and support for various types of crowdfunding. Although it is focused on social ventures, Causevox hosts crowdfunding campaigns for nonprofits, NGOs, and for-profit organizations pursuing social innovations.

Before concluding this section, we need to mention self-funding of needs as another common approach to funding social ventures. Similar to entrepreneurs in general, many social innovators start their work by using their own funds or by borrowing against their own credit sources. Often social innovators are so passionate about their ideas that initially funding them in this way is an acceptable calculated risk.

Organizing a Social Innovation

This chapter began with a discussion of an organization, iDE, that practices hybrid social innovations through a nonprofit organization but uses the market for creating social impact. Social innovations can occur within different incorporated entities. Some social innovations begin as the work of a few people unconcerned about how to structure the innovation in the future. Once an innovation catches attention and has traction and some preliminary impact, early innovators must consider best ways to sustain and perhaps grow the effort. Agency-based social workers are most familiar with working under the auspices of a nonprofit organization. Contract and grant-funded nonprofit social service agencies assist people and communities in need and often pursue incremental innovations. At the same time, as discussed earlier, they are often constrained by their institutional environments from pursuing social innovations that are fundamentally different from normative models, at least in the programs already funded through existing contracts.

Agency-based social workers who want to pursue social innovations within their current agencies need to discuss their plans with the agency's executives, including the fiscal officer, as some innovations can complicate the tax-exempt and legal status of the organization. The socially innovative social worker pursuing this form of social intrapreneurship (Berzin & Camarena, 2018; Nandan, Mandayam, Collard, & Tchouta, 2016) may also need to educate her or his organization's managers about the variety of social innovations and their benefits to service users. There are some ways for a parent nonprofit organization to engage in social innovation that may not be concordant with the entity's current activities, without undue risk. For example, a nonprofit may own a for-profit limited liability corporation (LLC) for a market-involved social innovation without putting the parent nonprofit's assets in jeopardy. Similarly, it may be possible for one nonprofit to spin off a second nonprofit. An attorney should always be consulted about the options for complex organizational structures.

There are various ways that those who are interested in building social innovation capacity within a social service organization can proceed. Organizations, including social service agencies, tend to adopt a consistent strategic position relative to innovation and change. Some organizational cultures and managers are comfortable with initiating innovation, some with adopting innovation after it has been created by others, and some are most comfortable with maintaining traditional approaches or the status quo. It is important to know the organizational culture and position of its managers concerning change before engaging in social innovation within an agency. At the same time, it is important to be clear about what changes are feasible and what changes might affect the funding and stability of the organization.

A culture of innovation needs to be promoted and modeled by leadership within the organization. Organizations that encourage innovation within existing services, or intrapreneurship, adopt various ways to promote it. This includes pushing some important decision making from the top levels down to line levels; creating processes within the organization for innovation, such as establishing a fund for innovative projects; collectively recognizing innovative initiative; and creating competitive processes within the organization for innovative ideas. As in all organizational change, the reputation of the innovator, within and outside the organization, is critical in gaining support and achieving success.

Independent social workers, and those who want to work outside an existing agency structure, have many options about what organizational form to use for their social innovations. Many may be most familiar with nonprofit organizations and so may assume that is the correct form. If the social innovation is market involved, one or another for-profit incorporation form may be more appropriate. Nonprofits may make a surplus. If, however, the surplus is inconsistent with the original articles of incorporation of the nonprofit, the organization may be required to pay Unrelated Business Income Taxes (often referred to by the abbreviation UBIT) on the surplus. In those instances, the social innovator may want to consider one of several for-profit forms of organizing. Again, an attorney familiar with these issues should always be consulted.

A social entrepreneur may choose not to incorporate but to function as a sole proprietorship initially or for a longer term. The hazard in doing this is that the personal assets of the innovators, such as real property and bank accounts, are at risk if the innovation loses money or is subject to legal actions against it. Until recently, many social innovators choosing to incorporate as a for-profit used the LLC form mentioned earlier. An LLC separates the innovator's personal property from the business property, thus protecting the personal property.

Recently, several social purpose for-profit incorporation forms have been created. These are referred to as hybrid incorporation forms and as double-bottom-line businesses because they have objectives in two sectors. Hybrid organizations that have additional environmental objectives are called triple-bottom-line businesses. In the United States, states are responsible for establishing incorporation forms. As a result, each state may have somewhat different incorporation forms or different requirements and specifications. This is also true of hybrid incorporation forms. However, there are some hybrid incorporation forms that have been adopted by multiple states. These new forms include the low-profit limited liability corporation (L3C), the benefit corporation, the social purpose corporation, and some other variants (Lane, 2011; Tyler, Adsher, Garman, & Luppino, 2015). Most states have adopted only one of these new hybrid organization models, although some states have adopted more than one. Because adoptions and revisions to these models occur often, social work social innovators should research the forms available in their states, territory, and tribal lands.

Each of the hybrid models are written to take advantage of different opportunities. Foundations are limited in making grants to only 501(c)(3) nonprofit and public organizations. Social purpose businesses incorporated as for-profits may not receive grants from foundations. However, a foundation may make a program-related investment (PRI) in a social purpose for-profit through, for example, an interest-bearing loan. The L3C was written to make it attractive for foundations to fund social innovations through PRIs. Social investors may need some form of assurance that their social investment is in an organization that adheres to sound business, ethical, and socially responsible practices. The benefit corporation incorporation form requires that businesses clearly state these principles in their incorporation papers and have a credible independent external evaluation of whether they are meeting the principles. B-Corp is the most used external evaluator, and B-Corp certification has become an important quality seal in attracting both investors and customers. The managers and owners of traditional businesses are constrained to make profit-maximizing decisions. The social purpose corporation allows managers and owners to include social or environmental considerations into their decision making.

The choice of incorporation form is a strategic one. In many instances, a specific social innovation legitimately could be incorporated as a 501(c)(3) nonprofit or any one of the several hybrid corporations. The decision is influenced by the advantages and disadvantages of the incorporation forms themselves and the mission and needs of the social innovation. For example, if the social innovation requires grant funding from a foundation or is depending on tax-deductible donations, it must incorporate as a 501(c)(3) nonprofit. If, conversely, the organization is interested in attracting funds from social investors, these investors may be more familiar with one of the for-profit hybrid forms, for instance, a social innovation incorporated as a social purpose business. Because social work social innovators are most often more familiar with their innovation than they are with the subtleties of incorporation, it would be important to consult with attorneys and certified public accountants in making these decisions.

Methods to Engage in Social Innovation

Though there is no single way to approach social innovation, there are some common approaches. Two such approaches are bottom-up and top-down ideas, designs, and plans of social innovations. People who have direct experience with the condition or issue being addressed by social innovation often develop and design bottom-up ways of addressing it. That direct experience may be living with or in the condition or being in a helping role for those who are living with or in it. Social workers and other social service workers are an example of the latter. Social workers are charged by society to directly assist people with social, economic, physical, educational, and psychological needs. Their bottom-up approaches to social innovation come from the direct experience of what has worked and not worked in the lives of those they assist and what the personal and cultural values are that may make one solution successful and another not. Top-down social innovation solutions start with a desire to help and an idea, rather than lived experience. This has led to inappropriate or early scaling of untested innovations and innovations that are not respectful of local values and customs.

Both bottom-up and top-down methods have advantages and disadvantages. Two cases may highlight some of the risks of a top-down approach. There are various anti-malaria social innovation campaigns, some of which distribute free nets to people in affected areas. The nets are impregnated with insecticides to further their effectiveness. The idea was that readily available and free nets would encourage people to use them. However, many people who received the nets had different priorities than preventing malaria and had other ideas about how else to use the nets. Gettleman (2015) found that in some communities the nets were used for fishing in rivers and lakes, because obtaining food may be a more pressing issue than preventing malaria for some. A problem with using the nets for fishing is that the insecticide on them poisoned some of the breeding grounds of the fish people were catching, killing fish populations. Nets were also balled up by children and used as soccer balls and goal nets. A bottom-up approach may have prevented this circumstance. Bottom-up planning always involves the users of the innovation in the innovation planning process, which would have informed the planners about other critical needs in the community, including ones that may undercut the social innovation's impact.

In 1994, a businessman in South Africa conceived an innovative idea of attaching a water pump to a children's playground merry-go-round for communities dependent on ground water and traditional manual hand pumps. His idea, called the Playpump, was that children playing with the merry-go-round could pump water as they played into an elevated water tower for storage. The community could then draw from the stored water in the tower, which would get replenished each time children were at play. In addition, he thought he could finance the maintenance of the pump system by selling advertising on the four sides of the water tower. It was an attractive social innovation that included a market mechanism for funding the maintenance. The idea got a lot of attention and led to a $60 million public–private partnership through the U.S. President's Emergency Fund for AIDS Relief. The partnership included $10 million in contributions from the U.S. government, endorsements from George and Laura Bush and the Clinton Foundation, fundraising by the rapper Jay-Z, and other forms of support (Chambers, 2009). The social innovator was encouraged to scale up, which he did with the resources from these various supporters. The excitement around this innovation was captured in a 2005 Frontline story (keepitcampaign, 2009).

Five years later, the project was a failure, as reported in a follow-up Frontline story (Frontline World, 2010). Children in many locations did not play at the merry-go-round as often as expected, and many grew uninterested in it. That left the women of the village to spin the merry-go-round, which many found difficult, sometimes owing to their age or physical condition. The old hand pump was easier for adults to use. The Playpumps often broke and did not pump water into the water towers, and advertisers were uninterested in many instances in advertising on them. The project was largely abandoned and disavowed by those who had been so enthusiastic. Again, a more bottom-up approach may have avoided this unfortunate outcome and waste of resources.

However, not all social innovations that start with a conceptual idea result in failures. An example is Lavamae.org. Lava Mae was started in 2013 by Doniece Sandoval, a marketing executive in San Francisco who had a totally unconventional idea concerning an aspect of homelessness. Although she had witnessed neighbors become homeless because of sharp increases in housing costs, she had little other experience of homelessness. She read in the newspaper that the San Francisco public transportation company, MUNI, was soliciting ideas for what to do with retired buses. She wondered if a municipal bus could be converted into mobile shower facilities for people who are homeless.

In large part, the hard work that it took to accomplish the goal was completed through Doniece's sheer force of will and her ability to promote her idea to others, including MUNI. Instead of appealing to traditional funders, she raised money for converting the buses on the crowdfunding site IndieGoGo. Each bus has two showers, including toilets and a high-capacity tankless demand hot water heater. Because carrying the water needed on a bus would be unstable, the buses use fire hydrants as their water sources. People who are homeless get 15 to 20 minutes of alone time in the shower, clean towels and toiletries to use, and a hygiene kit when they leave. Lava Mae has expanded its fleet of mobile showers to include showers in converted trailers. Having a dignified and private way to keep clean does more than help with hygiene. It restores dignity, a core value in the NASW (2017) *Code of Ethics*, and creates new possibilities for individuals.

Considering the Design Thinking Paradigm

There are various ways to plan a bottom-up social innovation. iDE, the NGO that was discussed at the beginning of this chapter, designs radically affordable water irrigation technologies for farmers earning $1 and $2 a day in developing economies. iDE's founder, Paul Polak, always begins by talking to the people iDE intends to work with and asking them what they believe they need. Only after he and other employees at iDE have talked with potential consumers will iDE begin focusing on potential solutions (Polak & Warwick, 2013). It is important to note at least two issues in this very bottom-up approach to social innovation. First, iDE always starts by asking potential users what they think they need. This is a value that many social workers would agree with but one that is not always practiced. Second, iDE is focused on design. Design thinking is very different from the typical linear approach to addressing social issues that often is followed by social workers in social services.

Social services have come to be dominated by linear approaches to planning services, approaches that purport to lead to desired outcomes. A good example of this is the ubiquitous logic model that is used in social service planning. Logic models identify a small set of outcome objectives and impacts and then create a linear picture of the inputs needed, the activities that will be used, the outputs to be achieved, and their expected outcomes and impacts. To conceptualize such a model, the planner must strip away the complexity that is present in all social problems to be able to focus on a simple enough version of the problem to fit into the logic model schema. Resulting program models also reflect this simplified linear vision, typically resulting from using a top-down approach to social service planning. The view from the top often obscures the "messiness" on the ground. The results are often a mismatch between the complexity of the conditions and lives of social service users and the overly simple and prescriptive models that are created to address complex needs (Westley, Zimmerman, & Patton, 2007).

Design thinking follows a completely different path. In a 1982 article, Nigel Cross outlined some of the elements of design thinking. Cross cited studies by Lawson (1979, 2006), who used problem-solving exercises to compare graduate architecture students and graduate science students. Lawson found that the two groups used very different strategies. The science students looked for rules they could apply to complete the exercise, whereas the architecture students, trained in design, looked for various solutions and then decided on the most appropriate one. That is, the scientists used a problem-focused strategy, and the architects used a solution-focused strategy. In a follow-up experiment, Lawson (2006) used the same research with younger children and found no clear and consistent differences among them. This implies that design thinking and analytic thinking are learned strategies to problem solving.

Cross (1982) and others have noted that a feature of design thinking is to come up with many possible solutions and choose from them after trying them out. This is known as rapid prototyping. Rapid prototyping involves developing quick and inexpensive prototypes of the design solutions and letting potential users experience them to see how well they work. This helps developers decide whether to modify the existing prototype or turn to a different prototype solution. Horst Rittel (in Churchman, 1967) and later Rittel and Webber (1973) first described *wicked problems*. "Wicked" refers to how difficult some problems are to solve, not implying moral judgment. Many have subsequently described the features of wicked problems. Synthesizing the thoughts of Rittel and Webber (1973), Conklin (2006), and others, we can define wicked problems as sharing the following features:

- There is not one best way to formulate a wicked problem. The problem may not be well understood until a solution is developed because the solution helps to define the problem.
- Solutions to wicked problems are good or bad, not true or false, right or wrong.
- We may not know when or if we have solved a wicked problem, as there is no definitive test of the solution.
- Wicked problems are often tightly coupled to other problems, and the solution may reveal those other problems.

Social workers may find this brief list to be familiar. These professionals are asked to address social, personal, and interpersonal problems that are often very difficult to resolve—intractable in nature. Often, because of their complexities, these problems are difficult to define and understand. Unfortunately, the simple solutions that social workers may use, or are asked to use, do not solve the problem, solve a part of the problem, or create new problems. Many of the problems that social work addresses look like "wicked problems," which raises the issue of whether these professionals have been using the problem-focused approach when they should be using a solution-focused approach.

Design thinking can be learned. University-based social innovation programs, such as the D School at Stanford University, and design companies that have embraced social design, such as IDEO, have developed effective social design training approaches. IDEO's Human Centered Design is, perhaps, the most influential and accessible of these trainings, including online manuals and training modules. Another useful approach is frog's (n.d.) Collective Action Toolkit.

Design thinking is nonreductionist and embraces complexity. Traditional planning in social services aims for consensus on a singular vision. In contrast, those using design thinking often purposively upset emerging consensus on singular visions by inviting people from fundamentally different backgrounds and training to participate in the process or purposely introduce dissonant examples, issues, and factors. Although all planning contains elements of creativity and rationality, often design thinking favors a creative solution, whereas linear processes favor a rational solution.

Examples of Social Innovation in Social Services

Thus far, brief examples of successful social innovation have been presented from international development (iDE), on the challenges of homelessness (Lava Mae), from social venture funding (Social Venture Partners), and from innovative funding methods (crowdfunding). In addition, problematic top-down social innovations related to mosquito net distribution and clean water sourcing were also described. In this section, some additional examples will illustrate the range of social issues in which social workers are regularly involved and can be innovative—in the areas of homelessness, job creation, and incarceration.

Dignity Village in Portland, Oregon, is a community of residents with histories of homelessness who came together for mutual protection and support; the community has been stable since 2001. The village's governance structure is democratic, and it is incorporated as a 501(c)(3) nonprofit organization to qualify to rent land from the City of Portland. This self-organized community has a contract with the city as a transitional facility, but the core residents have permanent membership and housing at Dignity Village. The community's housing has progressed from tents to semi-permanent housing cobbled together from street-gathered, recycled, and donated materials, to various solutions for more permanent structures, such as straw-bale construction.

This example of a bottom-up social innovation also has used bottom-up approaches to scale out its methods. Early in its evolution, Dignity Village created a Web site that in part had a central information exchange site for other self-organized encampments—an expression of self-determination by people who were homeless. The Web site allowed its members to build solidarity between encampments through information and strategy exchange. In addition, Dignity Village put information on its Web site about how to successfully re-create similar encampments in other locations. That information is now on a separate Web site (http://www.tentcitiestoolkit.org/index.html), hosted by a media group.

Another example of a bottom-up social innovation involving homelessness is the Mad Housers of Atlanta. The Mad Housers precut material for small plywood huts, transport the unassembled precut huts to unused land in the Atlanta area where they assemble the huts and then turn over the hut's keys to a person who is homeless. The organization does not seek permission from the landowner to place a hut but will move it if requested. The Mad Housers, incorporated as a 501(c)(3) in 1988, started when a group of Georgia Tech engineering students began talking about whether there was an engineering approach to house people who were homeless—whom they passed daily on their way to classes. Initially, they designed and built plywood huts in each other's driveways and garages. In addition to core members of the organization, the Mad Housers have many volunteers who work with them, including school and church groups and others concerned with issues of social justice. Similar to Dignity Village, the Mad Housers have, for many years, included advice and blueprints on its Web site for others who wish to replicate the model. These two examples of scaling out while scaling deep demonstrate how to use existing approaches for social justice, which clearly resonates with social work values.

REDF, formerly the Roberts Enterprise Development Fund, is an intermediary organization in San Francisco that funds and assists in job-creating social enterprises for social service populations. It is itself a social innovation and an example of an expanding infrastructure that supports social innovation and social enterprise. REDF began in 1997 when the Homeless Economic Development Fund (HEDF), also funded by the Roberts family, completed its operations. HEDF identified a need for social enterprises that would create jobs. Since then, REDF has been a leader in initiating social enterprise models focused on job creation and other supportive approaches that generate SROI. Initially, REDF focused its investment and incubation within the San Francisco Bay Area, and now its initiatives are national. REDF has been a federal Social Innovation Fund recipient since 2010 and has been a leader in the Social

Enterprise Alliance (SEA), the U.S. trade organization for social enterprises. REDF founded the SEA-related project SE4Jobs, an effort to promote job-creating social enterprises nationally (REDF, n.d.).

Social innovation incubators and accelerators are also part of the expanding infrastructure. Incubators typically work with those who have beginning ideas and need assistance in formalizing and initially launching them. Accelerators typically work with already founded social innovations and social enterprises and help them achieve social impact and economic viability. These incubators and accelerators provide workspace and equipment, technical expertise, assistance with project and organizational development, and in some instances funding in a cooperative environment, where participants are encouraged to support each other in their separate endeavors.

Social tech incubators like Sidewalk Labs (Alphabet) and Blue Ridge Labs (Robin Hood Foundation) in New York City focus on technology-related social innovations. They draw together teams composed of subject experts, designers, product managers, and engineers to explore ways to use technology to help underserved populations. Sidewalk Labs facilitates "smart cities" by deploying technology to address urban issues (crowding, congestion, health care disparities), many of which fall within social workers' bailiwick. Blue Ridge Labs creates products and services for underserved and underresourced people, which can then be scaled with the assistance of the lab. For example, Good Call is a service that notifies a person's support network if he or she has been arrested in the Bronx, New York. Innovations like this are simple, in that they aim to resolve or prevent social issues (such as mass incarceration) by automating a part of the process. In this case, when individuals are arrested, their one phone call will notify the Bronx Defenders' office as well as anyone whom users have designated as a part of their support system during their initial signup with Good Call. This innovation facilitates due process.

Another kind of social innovation incubator assists people with workforce disadvantages to pursue self-employment by helping them start small businesses. An example of inclusive entrepreneurship is Start-up NY (Shaheen, 2016), which helps people with various physical, psychiatric, and developmental disabilities start small businesses by coordinating existing small business development resources. A stand-alone model, the Enterprise People, was created in Madison, Wisconsin, to assist people in mental health recovery to start small businesses (Mandiberg & Edwards, 2016). One of its innovations was to classify clinical issues—which many would see as obviating small business ownership—as concrete business planning issues, which could be accommodated when they arise.

A third example is Rise Asset Development in Toronto, Canada. Rise Asset Development combines business incubation for people with psychiatric disabilities with a robust source of capital for starting small businesses. It provides incubation for entrepreneurs who live in poverty and have a disability and who often may not have access to traditional sources of capital for business development.

The last example concerns a community development social innovation approach for socially and economically excluded populations, such as individuals in mental health recovery. James Mandiberg, a social worker, and Dick Warner, a psychiatrist, and their collaborators designed the approach based on their work with people with serious mental health conditions (SMHCs). The major conceptual innovation is to perceive people with SMHCs as their own *identity community*, rather than as dysfunctional individual members of the broad community. Because all communities have economies that can be built up, so too can the community identity of people in mental health recovery (Mandiberg, 2010, 2012). Their work has created various community and economic development models building identity community infrastructure in housing, a business development model, business incubation, banking, and others (Mandiberg & Telles, 1990; Mandiberg & Warner, 2012, 2013; Warner & Mandiberg, 2013).

Some people trained in other fields, such as business, are beginning to think like social workers. Social workers can welcome this as an opportunity to work with new collaborators or see it as a challenge to traditional social work. The work of Transformative Consumer Research (TCR) is an example. TCR views market interactions as a major part of contemporary life and explores ways to improve the outcomes of these interactions for the benefit of consumers, especially poor consumers (Blocker et al., 2013). The work of Madhu Viswanathan, a business professor at the University of Illinois, is an example. His work focuses on subsistence marketplaces and the hazards consumers confront in those environments. Among other social innovations, his work addresses the abuses people who are illiterate or marginally literate face in marketplace interactions (Viswanathan & Sridharan, 2009; Viswanathan, Sridharan, Gau, & Ritchie, 2009). Viswanathan and his collaborators have developed innovative ways of increasing the marketplace literacy of poor consumers, reducing the power inequalities in market interactions.

Implications for the Future of Social Work Teaching and Practice

Social workers have always been socially innovative because of the nature of the social problems they have addressed within resource-restrained environments. Society has tasked social work to address intractable or wicked problems, which requires creativity and innovation. Social workers have actively involved community members and potential beneficiaries for co-creating solutions. Unfortunately, however, many social workers are employed in environments that do not support or nurture innovation. The imperative from funders to (1) adopt single forms of intervention versus a robust toolkit of interventions; (2) favor incremental "sustaining" innovations rather than new "disruptive" innovations; (3) become increasingly more specialized in their skills and practices; and (4) overuse linear thinking stifles innovation among social workers. Professions can become innovation-averse as they establish or reinforce their legitimacy and effectiveness.

All social innovators need some guidance for their creativity. This includes processes, such as design thinking, and advice from diverse and bottom-up participants. The NASW (2017) *Code of Ethics* can guide social innovations that are within the realm of social work's professional values. Social innovation is something that may need to be learned. Unfortunately, most schools of social work primarily focus on well-established practices, with very few schools and programs offering courses on creativity and innovation in practice; moreover, such courses, when they exist, are most often offered as electives and not as part of the core curriculum.

Incorporating social innovation into practice courses early in the training and experience of social workers can offset social workers' default tendency to rely only on existing interventions and path-dependent approaches. A social innovation perspective provides the profession with more opportunities to be agile and responsive to communities and populations that may not always benefit from traditional social service programming. Moreover, social innovation requires involving innovation beneficiaries for designing and developing, and often implementing, the innovative initiatives. This approach is quite different from how most social work interventions are designed and delivered today—service users are expected to comply with, not participate in co-creating, the innovative interventions.

An orientation toward social innovation also allows the profession to expand its practice and knowledge base. Social services have become overly reliant on welfare state contracts and reimbursements. Although it is helpful to have public funding that supports social services, the restrictive nature of that support and its anti-innovation tendencies have limited the ways social work and social services can be responsive to evolving and complex social problems and needs. The restrictive nature of support limits the kinds of organizations that can provide social services. A social innovation orientation and approach could allow the profession to rethink how services should be developed, delivered, and organized. Social innovation is especially important for addressing the Grand Challenges identified by the American Academy of Social Work and Social Welfare (n.d.). Social workers should consider initiating and leading hybrid forms of incorporations; using cooperative and mutual support structures; using market mechanisms where appropriate; collaborating with professions from the hard sciences such as engineering; and, again, involving service recipients more actively in addressing the Grand Challenges. Social workers should participate in, and partner with, innovation incubators, accelerators, and other collaborative efforts that are constantly developing and testing ideas that address complex problems. Through these partnerships, social workers can share important and often unique points of view, skill sets, knowledge bases, and experiences for social innovation and, in doing so, reinforce the value of social work.

Conclusion

Social innovation is in the DNA of social work. Engaging in social innovation ensures social work's relevance for the future. Interactions and interventions with individuals, communities, and organizations naturally lead social workers to explore more effective ways to create meaningful sustainable impact. The nature of social workers' relationships with beneficiaries enables professionals to engage in a participatory bottom-up process of innovation. Social workers invite various kinds of input for addressing issues—a strategy consistent with design thinking. Nonetheless, social workers do need formal exposure to design thinking to generate greater participation in social innovations. With social workers participating in the social innovation process, chances of the innovation adhering to the core values of the profession are high: among them, social justice, equality, social and economic inclusion, and dismantling oppression.

Social workers do need to gain additional skills, knowledge, and comfort with (1) new ways of working with individuals, communities, and organizations; (2) different types of financial resources for socially innovative work; and (3) different organizational forms. In addition, social workers need to carve out new collaborations for concurrently addressing social, economic, and environmental justice. If social workers execute these recommendations, they will have more flexibility and diversity in their career options and broader impact.

References

American Academy of Social Work and Social Welfare. (n.d.). *Grand challenges for social work.* Retrieved from http://aaswsw.org/grand-challenges-initiative/

Berzin, S., & Camarena, H. (2018). *Innovation from within: Redefining how nonprofits solve problems.* New York: Oxford University Press.

Blocker, C. P., Ruth, J. A., Sridharan, S., Beckwith, C., Ekici, A., Goudie-Hutton, M., et al. (2013). Understanding poverty and promoting poverty alleviation through transformative consumer research. *Journal of Business Research, 66*, 1195–1202. doi:10.1016/j.jbusres.2012.08.012

Chambers, A. (2009, November 24). Africa's not-so-magic roundabout. *Guardian.* Retrieved from https://www.theguardian.com/commentisfree/2009/nov/24/africa-charity-water-pumps-roundabouts

Christensen, C. M. (1997). *The innovator's dilemma: When new technologies cause great firms to fail.* Boston: Harvard Business Review Press.

Christensen, C. M., Baumann, H., Ruggles, R., & Sadtler, T. M. (2006). Disruptive innovation for social change. *Harvard Business Review, 84*(12), 94–101.

Churchman, C. W. (1967). Guest editorial: Wicked problems. *Management Science, 14*(4), B141–B142.

Conklin, J. (2006). *Dialogue mapping: Building shared understanding of wicked problems.* Chichester, UK: John Wiley & Sons.

Cross, N. (1982). Designerly ways of knowing. *Design Studies, 3*, 221–227. doi:10.1016/0142-694X(82)90040-0

DiMaggio, P., & Powell, W. W. (1983). The iron cage revisited: Collective rationality and institutional isomorphism in organizational fields. *American Sociological Review, 48*, 147–160. doi:10.2307/2095101

Doyle, A., Lanoil, J., & Dudek, K. (2013). *Fountain House: Creating community in mental health practice.* New York: Columbia University Press.

frog. (n.d.). *The collective action toolkit puts design-thinking tools into the hands of local change agents to transform communities.* Retrieved from https://www.frogdesign.com/work/frog-collective-action-toolkit

Frontline World. (2010). Troubled water [Video file]. Retrieved from http://www.pbs.org/frontlineworld/stories/southernafrica904/video_index.html

Gettleman, J. (2015, January 25). Meant to keep malaria out, mosquito nets are used to haul fish in. *New York Times.* Retrieved from https://www.nytimes.com/2015/01/25/world/africa/mosquito-nets-for-malaria-spawn-new-epidemic-overfishing.html

iDE Global. (n.d.). *Our promise of 10:1.* Retrieved from https://www.ideglobal.org/story/measurement-and-evaluation

Javits, C. I. (2008). *REDF's current approach to SROI.* San Francisco: REDF. Retrieved from http://redf.org/app/uploads/2013/10/REDFs-Current-Approach-to-SROI-Opinion-Paper-2008.pdf

keepitcampaign. (2009, November 14). PBS Frontline World View: Play pump [Video file]. Retrieved from https://www.youtube.com/watch?v=wrmQ9s2t1Jw

Lane, M. J. (2011). *Social enterprise: Empowering mission-driven entrepreneurs.* Chicago: American Bar Association Press.

Lawson, B. R. (1979). Cognitive strategies in architectural design. *Ergonomics, 22*(1), 59–68. doi:10.1080/00140137908924589

Lawson, B. R. (2006). *How designers think: The design process demystified.* New York: Routledge.

Lipsky, M. (2010). *Street-level bureaucracy: Dilemmas of the individual in public services* (30th anniversary expanded ed.). New York: Russell Sage Foundation

Mandiberg, J. M. (2010). Another way: Enclave communities for people with mental illness. *American Journal of Orthopsychiatry, 80,* 167–173. doi:10.1111/j.1939-0025.2010.01020.x

Mandiberg, J. M. (2012). The failure of social inclusion: An alternative approach through community development. *Psychiatric Services, 63,* 458–460. doi:10.1176/appi.ps.201100367

Mandiberg, J. M., & Edwards, M. (2016). Business incubation for people with severe mental illness histories: The experience of one model. *Journal of Policy Practice, 15*(1/2), 82–101. doi:10.1080/15588742.2016.1109964

Mandiberg, J. M., & Telles, L. (1990). The Santa Clara County Clustered Apartment Project. *Psychosocial Rehabilitation Journal, 14,* 21–28. doi:10.1037/h0099448

Mandiberg, J. M., & Warner, R. (2012). Business development and marketing within communities of social service clients. *Journal of Business Research, 65,* 1736–1742. doi:10.1016/j.jbusres.2012.02.015

Mandiberg, J. M., & Warner, R. (2013). Is mainstreaming always the answer? The social and economic development of service user communities. *Psychiatrist, 37,* 153–155. doi:10.1192/pb.bp.112.040659

Nandan, M., Mandayam, G., Collard, C. S., & Tchouta, R. (2016). An examination of macro practice social workers as social intrapreneurs or social entrepreneurs. *International Journal of Social Entrepreneurship and Innovation, 4,* 114–133. doi:10.1504/IJSEI.2016.076686

National Association of Social Workers. (2017). *Code of ethics of the National Association of Social Workers.* Washington, DC: Author.

Phills, J. A., Deiglmeier, K., & Miller, D. T. (2008). Rediscovering social innovation. *Stanford Social Innovation Review, 6*(4), 34–43.

Polak, P. (2008). *Out of poverty.* San Francisco: Berrett-Koehler Publishers.

Polak, P., & Warwick, M. (2013). *The business solution to poverty: Designing products and services for three billion new customers.* San Francisco: Berrett-Koehler Publishers.

REDF. (n.d.). *SE4Jobs.* Retrieved from http://redf.org/se4jobs/

Rittel, H.W.J., & Webber, M. M. (1973). Dilemmas in a general theory of planning. *Policy Sciences, 4,* 155–169. doi:10.1007/BF01405730

Schumpeter, J. (1942). *Capitalism, socialism, and democracy.* New York: Harper & Bros.

Seattle. (2011, June 29). How it all started [Blog post]. Retrieved from http://www.socialventurepartners.org/2011/06/29/how-it-all-started/

Shaheen, G. E. (2016). Inclusive entrepreneurship: A process for improving self-employment for people with disabilities. *Journal of Policy Practice, 15*(1–2), 58–81. Retrieved from https://doi.org/10.1080/15588742.2016.1109963

Taylor, M., Dees, G., & Emerson, J. (2002). The question of scale: Finding an appropriate strategy for building on your success. In G. Dees, J. Emerson, & P. Economy (Eds.), *Strategic tools for social entrepreneurs: Enhancing the performance of your enterprising nonprofit* (pp. 235–264). New York: John Wiley & Sons.

Tyler, J., Adsher, E., Garman, K., & Luppino, A. (2015). Producing better mileage: Advancing the design and usefulness of hybrid vehicles for social purpose ventures. *Quinnipiac Law Review, 33*, 237–337.

Viswanathan, M., & Sridharan, S. (2009). From subsistence marketplaces to sustainable marketplaces: A bottom-up perspective on the role of business in poverty alleviation. *Ivey Business Journal, 73*(2), 1–15.

Viswanathan, M., Sridharan, S., Gau, R., & Ritchie, R. (2009). Designing marketplace literacy education in resource-constrained contexts: Implications for public policy and marketing. *Journal of Public Policy & Marketing, 28*(1), 85–94. doi:10.1509/jppm.28.1.85

Warner, R., & Mandiberg, J. (2006). An update on affirmative businesses or social firms for people with mental illness. *Psychiatric Services, 57*, 1488–1492. doi:10.1176/ps.2006.57.10.1488

Warner, R., & Mandiberg, J. M. (2013). Social networks, support and early psychosis: Mutual support within service-user communities. *Epidemiology and Psychiatric Sciences, 22*, 151–154. doi:10.1017/S2045796012000686

Westley, F., Zimmerman, B., & Patton, M. (2007). *Getting to maybe: How the world is changed*. Toronto: Vintage Canada.

4

Financial Inclusion and Social Entrepreneurship

Mathieu R. Despard

Financial markets and institutions have increased in power and dominance over the last several years, driving much of the global economy (Dore, 2008; Krippner, 2005). Financial services are ubiquitous to participation in a market economy, allowing households to conduct everyday transactions, track spending, manage resources, cope with unexpected emergencies, make large purchases, save, and invest (Ladha, Asrow, Parker, Rhyne, & Kelly, 2017). Financial services also offer tools for economic mobility, enabling individuals to start businesses, pay for college, and buy homes. In emerging market economies, financial services are critical for supporting sustainable livelihoods and small enterprise development.

To navigate increasingly complex financial services systems, individuals need to be financially capable—to have financial knowledge and skills and access to financial products and services (Sherraden, 2013). The World Bank defines financial inclusion as "access to useful and affordable financial products and services," particularly among "disadvantaged and low-income segments of society" (2017b). Financial inclusion promotes shared prosperity—economic equity that supports economic growth—poverty reduction, and financial health (Ladha et al., 2017; World Bank, 2014).

Yet half of the world's population lacks a bank account (World Bank, 2014). Even in the United States, which boasts a sophisticated and well-capitalized financial services system, millions of households are un- or underbanked—especially economically vulnerable households (Federal Deposit Insurance Corporation [FDIC], 2016). Many financial products and services are not affordable, nor do they meet the needs of low-income households. Only 9 percent of over 1,600 bank branches surveyed offered basic checking accounts that met Bank On National Account Standards for safety and affordability (Friedline, Despard, Eastlund, & Schuetz, 2017).

Financial Inclusion and Social Justice

Financial inclusion is an issue of social justice for social workers, who "strive to ensure access to needed information, services, and resources; equality of opportunity; and meaningful participation in decision making for all people" (NASW, 2015, p. 5). "Build Financial Capability for All" is one of the 12 Grand Challenges enumerated by the Academy of Social Work and Social Welfare. This challenge includes a call for "access to basic financial services and asset-building programs" and "voice in design of suitable financial products and services, and a way to influence decisions of consumer protection organizations and financial regulators" (Sherraden et al., 2015, pp. 10–11).

Social workers are well prepared to promote financial inclusion for three key reasons. First, social workers are familiar with the economic circumstances and challenges of lower-income households and individuals experiencing challenges such as serious mental illness (Cuddeback, Blank Wilson, Despard, Tomar, & Chowa, 2016) and intimate partner violence (Postmus, Hetling, & Hoge, 2015; Sanders, 2013). This understanding can unlock new ideas for financial inclusion among underserved groups. Second, social work practice is guided by the person-in-environment perspective, which is highly useful in understanding how individuals interact with financial services systems nested in larger social, cultural, and economic contexts. Third, social workers understand how systems can exclude and marginalize people and are adept at identifying ways to promote social inclusion through collaborative efforts at the local level and advocacy for changes in public policies.

Financial Inclusion as an International Policy Goal

Governments around the world have embraced financial inclusion as a policy goal (Arun & Kamath, 2015). The G20 launched the Global Partnership for Financial Inclusion (GPFI) to implement a financial inclusion action plan to support development of national financial inclusion policies among member countries (GPFI, 2014). Many countries outside the G20 have also made financial inclusion an important policy goal. As of 2015, 31 mostly low- and lower-middle-income countries, including Belarus, Indonesia, Malawi, and Peru, had a national financial inclusion strategy (NFIS), while an additional 27 countries were developing an NFIS (Alliance for Financial Inclusion, 2015).

However, national financial inclusion goals and strategies reflect market failure; the private sector has fallen short of ensuring access to and use of safe and affordable financial services for all households, especially low-income households. Thus, financial inclusion can be construed as an opportunity for social entrepreneurs to correct market failures (Austin, Stevenson, &

Wei-Skillern, 2006; Dees, 1998) as well as public policies that have resulted in economic exclusion. This chapter describes financial services systems, financial inclusion and exclusion, and how social workers can apply social entrepreneurship methods to promote financial inclusion. The focus is primarily on financial inclusion in the United States, though issues and examples from other countries are also offered.

The Financial Services Landscape

Social workers need to understand the financial services systems that they wish to disrupt and transform using social entrepreneurial strategies. These systems include formal, alternative or informal, and mobile financial services and many actors other than banks.

Formal Financial Services

Formal financial services include products and services offered by government-regulated and government-insured banks, credit unions, and financial services and investment firms, including checking and savings accounts, debit, prepaid debit, and credit cards, loans, and retirement and investment accounts and services. The number of bank branches in the world grew by 13 percent from 2000 to 2015, including 8 percent in low- and middle-income countries. Yet in high-income countries, branches declined by 20 percent (World Bank, 2017a). The number of banks in the United States declined greatly from the mid-1980s to the middle of the first decade of 2000s as a result of deregulation, globalization, and technological advances (Jones & Critchfield, 2005). The number of banks continues to decline each year, though at a slower rate compared with prior years (FDIC, 2017). The three largest banks—Bank of America, JPMorgan Chase, and Wells Fargo—alone hold roughly a third of the market share of deposits, reflecting consolidation of the banking industry over the last several years (FDIC, 2012).

Credit unions are nonprofit financial institutions that comprise a much smaller U.S. market share than banks and are owned by members who join based on employment, geographic location, or group membership requirements (MyCreditUnion.gov, n.d.; Schenk, 2012). Community development credit unions, community development financial institutions (CDFIs), and community development banks, loan funds, and venture capital funds are organized to serve low- and moderate-income households and communities (Opportunity Finance Network [OFN], 2017). In addition to a commitment to offering safe and affordable financial products and services, CDFIs play an important role in financing small businesses and nonprofits and in developing commercial real estate and affordable housing in economically distressed neighborhoods (OFN, 2017).

Historically, laws to establish financial services regulation and consumer protections have been passed in the United States in response to major economic events, market failures, and discriminatory practices. Most of the current regulatory system was established following the Great Depression, which was caused in part by bank failures resulting from risky business ventures and investments. The Community Reinvestment Act (CRA) of 1977 was passed in response to redlining—lending practices that discriminated against African Americans and other racial and ethnic minorities. Federal agencies conduct CRA examinations to determine the extent to which banks are meeting the credit needs of the entire community. The Dodd–Frank Wall Street Reform and Consumer Protection Act of 2010 introduced new regulations of the largest banks to prevent another major financial crisis as occurred in 2008. The Consumer Financial Protection Bureau was formed as a result of the Dodd–Frank Wall Street Reform and Consumer Protection Act of 2010 to hold banks and other financial institutions directly accountable for practices that harm consumers, leading to a $100 million fine against Wells Fargo for opening bank accounts without consumers' authorization.

Governmental ownership, regulation, and oversight of formal financial services varies widely in other countries and changes over time. For example, from 1999 to 2011, Venezuela, Turkey, and Bangladesh imposed the greatest changes in bank capital requirements, while the United Kingdom, Mexico, and Austria made the greatest changes in loosening these requirements. Bank assets as a percentage of gross domestic product, market consolidation of assets, and supervisors per bank also vary widely across countries (Barth, Caprio, & Levine, 2013).

Alternative and Informal Financial Services

Alternative financial services (AFS) in the United States are offered largely absent government regulation and oversight, including transaction services like check cashing, bill pay services, and remittances, as well as payday, auto title, pawn, and refund anticipation loans. These services can be found in stand-alone "money" stores or in convenience, grocery, and liquor stores and other retail outlets (FDIC, 2016). Informal financial services refer to unregulated or loosely regulated products and services offered by firms, organizations, and self-organized mutual assistance groups in response to the demand for transfers and credit to support income-generating activities and livelihoods, particularly in lower-income regions of the world (McKernan, Pitt, & Moskowitz, 2005; Seibel, 2014). Examples include rotating savings and credit associations (ROSCAs), village savings and loan associations (VSLAs), lending circles, deposit collectors, and microfinance.

Though not regulated formally by a central bank or other agency, informal financial services are governed by long-held customs and social norms and processes (Seibel, 2014). For example, Susu collection is a traditional and ancient financial service in West Africa (mostly Ghana) that enables households to save a small amount every day to accumulate savings (Aryeetey & Steel, 1995). Lending circles, ROSCAs, and VSLAs incorporate social norms and interactions to ensure members make contributions or repay their loans.

Mobile Financial Services

Mobile or digital financial services refer to banks and credit unions' online and mobile banking platforms and cashless digital payment platforms such as M-PESA—used by over two-thirds of Kenyan adults—PayPal, Google Wallet, and Apple Pay, which facilitate retail transactions and person-to-person money transfers. Mobile financial services also include Internet-only banks, online independent bill-paying services, and companies that develop and market personal finance apps aimed at helping consumers achieve their financial goals. Collectively, these efforts are also referred to as financial technology, or "FinTech," and have the potential to promote financial inclusion if innovation and access to technology is geared more toward underserved consumers, and regulations are updated to protect consumers (Gorham & Dorrance, 2017).

Financial Services and Inclusion: Complex Adaptive Systems

Measured as use of formal financial services, financial inclusion varies widely across countries and regions, as well as within countries, on the basis of household characteristics. Large majorities of individuals in the Global South lack bank accounts while the opposite is true for the Global North. For example, 95 percent of individuals in the eurozone have a bank account compared with 18 percent in sub-Saharan Africa (World Bank, 2015). Yet there are also important between-country differences within regions to note. For example, Kenya has made tremendous strides in financial inclusion since the middle of the first decade of the 21st century compared with many other countries in sub-Saharan Africa and ranks first in financial inclusion among a group of 21 emerging economies (Villasenor, West, & Lewis, 2015).

Within-country differences are also important to note. Only 7 percent of U.S. households were unbanked in 2015. However, 20 percent were considered underbanked—that is, they held a checking or savings account yet used AFS such as check cashing and payday loans (FDIC, 2016). Moreover, bank account usage in the United States is lower among racial and ethnic minorities, female-headed households, young people, lower-income persons, and immigrants (FDIC, 2016; Paulson & Rhine, 2008; Rao & Malapit, 2014; Rhine, Di, Greene, & Perlmeter, 2016). For example, 18 percent of black households are unbanked compared with only 3 percent of white households (FDIC, 2016).

To promote financial inclusion, it is important to understand variation in the use of financial services. Physical proximity is one factor. The number of bank branches per 100,000 adults is positively associated with rates of bank account ownership across regions and countries (World Bank, 2015). Proximity to bank branches (Goodstein & Rhine, 2017) and to AFS providers (Bhutta, Skiba, & Tobacman, 2015; Friedline & Kepple, 2017) is associated with the use of these financial service providers. Individuals in Malawi and Uganda who live far away from bank branches were less likely than others to use bank accounts (Dupas, Karlan, Robinson, & Ubfal, 2016).

The availability of financial services is affected by market conditions, population growth, consumer preferences, and government regulation. Despard and Friedline (2017) found that the density of bank and credit union branches is much higher in the Midwest and Northeast United States, where the population is shrinking, than in the South and West, where the population is growing. The availability of AFS such as check cashing and payday loans increased dramatically in the 1990s and first decade of the 21st century in the United States in response to regulatory changes that promoted market consolidation of banks and branch closings (Negro, Visentin, & Swaminathan, 2014), though several states have banned or restricted these loans (Gross, Hogarth, Manohar, & Gallegos, 2012).

Financial product and service features also affect use. Bank fees may be too high or households may lack enough slack in their budgets to justify using accounts (Dupas et al., 2016; FDIC, 2016; Parrish & Frank, 2011). Overdraft fees—fees assessed when an account holder writes a check or conducts a debit transaction for an amount that exceeds the balance in her or his account—are especially odious. Fusaro (2008) found that the median implicit interest rate on these fees was 4,000 percent. Repeated account overdrafts are a reason why people become involuntarily unbanked (Campbell, Jerez, & Tufano, 2012). Customers' banking histories—including overdrafts—are recorded by Chex-Systems, Inc., which maintains a database that can be used by banks to block opening an account at another bank.

Households that have difficulty meeting basic needs are at very high risk of incurring, yet are the least able to afford, these fees. It is hardly surprising that lower-income consumers who get hit by overdraft fees would be reluctant to own a bank account. Bank policies concerning minimum account balances and documentation requirements (Beck, Demirgüç-Kunt, & Martinez Peria, 2008) and a lack of transparency concerning fees and customer protections (Realini & Mehta, 2015; Servon, 2017) create additional barriers.

Use of financial services also has psychological, social, and cultural dimensions. Studies from several countries (Chowa & Despard, 2013; Kim, LaTaillade, & Kim, 2011; Ssewamala, Karimli, Chang-Keun, & Ismayilova, 2010; Webley & Nyhus, 2006) indicate that youth and young adults' knowledge, attitudes, and skills related to using financial services are influenced by familial relationships through both instruction and modeling (Gudmunson & Danes, 2011). Servon (2017) found that check cashing store customers preferred these stores over banks because of the transparency of prices and better customer service. Mobile financial services are seen as superior to banks in enabling customers the ability to control their finances, giving customers access to funds, and providing convenience (Burhouse, Navarro, & Osaki 2016).

Lack of trust and familiarity with banks is a key reason why people are unbanked. Low- and moderate-income consumers are more comfortable with employees of AFS providers because they speak their languages and dress similarly, while banks feel unwelcoming and intimidating (Rengert & Rhine, 2016). These findings suggest a social element to use of financial services, consistent with the popularity of informal services such as lending circles, savings clubs, and money guards.

Age and life stage also explain use of financial services. In their early working years, younger people have greater needs for transaction-related services and access to credit for student and car loans, whereas their use of retirement savings products is much lower compared with that of older people (Lusardi, Mitchell, & Curto, 2010). Bank account ownership in the United States is positively associated with age (FDIC, 2016), while ownership of smartphones and use of mobile banking is negatively associated with age (Burhouse et al., 2016). Also, households cycle in and out of bank account ownership as their financial circumstances change (FDIC, 2016; Rhine et al., 2016).

Use of different types of financial services is not mutually exclusive, boundaries across types of financial services are permeable, and financial services evolve over time. Some U.S. households have bank accounts but also use alternative products and services like check cashing and payday loans (FDIC, 2016) and turn to informal services such as money guards and savings clubs (Morduch, Ogen, & Schneider, 2014). Banks in the United States have recently begun offering services such as check cashing and bill payments to customers without bank accounts—services typically offered by AFS providers. Similarly, banks and credit unions are experimenting with new physical locations—limited service branches in grocery stores and other retail locations, kiosks, and automated micro-branches. Anticipating new federal regulations, payday lenders in the United States have recently shifted away from lump sum to installment repayment products.

Kenya's M-PESA mobile finance system, which was launched in 2007 by Safaricom, a major mobile network provider, is used widely as an alternative to banks. The success of M-PESA is attributed to the market dominance of Safaricom, government regulations allowing mobile providers to provide financial services, lack of trust in banks related to postelection ethnic violence in 2007–2008, and the high cost of other payment and money transfer services (Rosengard, 2016).

In Ghana, Susu collection is a long-standing cultural tradition to enable households to save (Aryeetey & Steel, 1995), though this system is adapting. Susu companies have fallen under increased regulation and oversight by Ghana's central bank and have partnered with banks to implement new digital services (Michaels, 2012).

Formal and informal financial institutions partner in Africa, Asia, and Latin America to reach rural households (Pagura & Kirsten, 2006). In the United States, payday lenders, which offer very high-interest short-term loans, are financed by large banks (Connor & Skomarovsky, 2010). Microfinance was initiated in the 1970s by nongovernmental organizations (NGOs) in postwar Bangladesh (Hulme & Moore, 2007) and in Indonesia as government-subsidized credit schemes to support poor rice farmers (Robinson, 2001). Yet crises such as the thousands of suicides among borrowers in the Indian state of Andhra Pradesh in 2010 attributed to unchecked industry growth and commercialization (Mader, 2013) have led to calls for increased regulation and monitoring of microfinance institutions (Pouchous, 2012).

The previous examples illustrate how the use of financial services is affected by a set of individual, social, and environmental factors that interact and change over time—consistent with social work's person-in-environment perspective. Thus, financial inclusion can be thought of as affected by the behavior of financial services as complex adaptive systems—a set of dynamic and evolving interactions among individual and institutional actors with different interests and perspectives within a larger political, cultural, and social context (Auspos & Cabaj, 2014).

Financial services evolve over time and cross categorical boundaries. The idea that households are either "banked" or "unbanked" is a misnomer, and defining financial inclusion as use of formal financial services is insufficient. Instead, as the World Bank (2017b) argued, financial inclusion should be construed as whether households have access to and use safe and affordable financial services that meet their needs over the life course. This definition implies that the services households use to meet their needs will vary based on context, life stage, and members' goals and preferences—ideas consistent with social work's person-in-environment perspective and the ethical principle of self-determination.

Financial Services and Household Economic Well-Being

Social entrepreneurs seek to develop innovative solutions to social problems. Lack of financial inclusion alone is not a problem; it is a problem only insofar as it negatively affects quality of life. Thus, it is important to consider the evidence concerning the relationship between use of financial services and financial and other outcomes.

Access to and use of financial services affects whether households, which are defined as an individual or group of people who live together and share material resources and obligations, are able to consistently meet basic needs, cope with financial emergencies, and build assets to unlock new opportunities and meet needs during retirement. Using bank products and services supports a range of household needs—securely depositing funds, paying bills, accessing credit, building assets, and earning interest (Birkenmaier & Fu, 2015; FDIC, 2016).

Most evidence concerning the relationship between use of financial services and household financial security comes from the United States. Having a bank account is associated with the ability to meet basic needs (Grinstein-Weiss, Perantie, Oliphant, deRuyter, & Despard, 2016; Sullivan, Turner, & Danziger, 2008). For instance, Friedline and Kepple (2017) found that low-income households had a 5 percent higher probability of being able to pay monthly bills for each additional bank or credit union branch they had in their community. Having a bank account can make it easier to conduct transactions via debit cards and online bill pay to ensure bills are paid on time. Accounts also make it easier to track income and expenses to help households manage their budgets.

Bank account ownership also helps households save money (Fitzpatrick, 2015; Friedline, Johnson, & Hughes, 2014; Manturuk, Dorrance, & Halladay, 2015). Evidence from studies of matched savings and child development accounts in the United States indicate that lower-income households save money when granted access to accounts, support, and incentives (Grinstein-Weiss, Wagner, & Ssewamala, 2006; Huang, Nam, Sherraden, & Clancy, 2015; Manturuk et al., 2015; Nam, Kim, Clancy, Zager, & Sherraden, 2013; Sherraden, Schreiner, & Beverly, 2003). Having savings helps smooth consumption (Carroll & Samwick, 1998), reduces risk for material hardship (Gjertson, 2016), lowers financial strain (Rothwell & Han, 2010), and is especially important to help people cope with unexpected dips in income and expenses (Lambert, 2008; Larrimore, Dodini, & Thomas, 2016; Morduch & Schneider, 2017; Pew Charitable Trusts, 2017).

Use of AFS such as check cashing and payday loans is associated with being unbanked (Despard, Perantie, Luo, Oliphant, & Grinstein-Weiss, 2015) and having lower income (Despard, Grinstein-Weiss, Ren, Guo, & Raghavan, 2016; FDIC, 2016). AFS use is positively associated with material hardship (Despard et al., 2015) and negatively associated with establishing credit (Lim et al., 2014; Lusardi & de Bassa Scheresberg, 2013; Pew Charitable Trusts, 2012).

Although transaction-based AFS such as check cashing and bill payments are viewed favorably by consumers as an alternative to owning a checking account (Rengert & Rhine, 2016; Servon, 2017), credit-based AFS—especially payday loans—are viewed as predatory and unaffordable. Payday loans charge triple-digit interest rates and can trap individuals in debt through repeated loan rollovers. Over two-thirds of borrowers use these loans to meet basic needs and make credit card payments and remain indebted for an average of five months (Pew Charitable Trusts, 2012). However, studies on the effects of payday loans have produced mixed results concerning bankruptcy risk (Skiba & Tobacman, 2011), credit scores and delinquencies (Agarwal, Skiba, & Tobacman, 2009; Bhutta, 2014), and foreclosures (Morse, 2011).

Evidence from studies in other countries supports the importance of access to both formal and informal financial services regarding financial outcomes, yet evidence concerning impacts on other outcomes is mixed. In a randomized evaluation of microcredit programs in India, Banerjee, Duflo, Glennerster, and Kinnan (2015) found positive impacts on micro-enterprise investment by, and consumption of, consumer goods, yet no impacts related to consumption, health, children's education, or women's empowerment. Similarly, access to free bank accounts with no minimum monthly balance requirements in Malawi, Uganda, and Chile was not associated with improved savings, business investment, health, or education outcomes (Dupas et al., 2016). Ghanaian youth randomly assigned to receive free savings accounts had no better financial capability, education, psychosocial, or health outcomes compared with youth who were not offered these accounts (Chowa et al., 2015).

However, in granting individuals and households access to bank accounts, product features may affect outcomes. Individuals in the Philippines randomly assigned to receive commitment savings products—savers commit to setting aside a certain amount of money on a regular basis and have restricted access to their funds—had much higher savings balances than a control group (Ashraf, Karlan, & Yin, 2006).

Use of VSLAs has been found to have positive impacts on meals consumed, household expenditures, and number of rooms in northern Malawi (Ksoll, Lilleør, Lønborg, & Rasmussen, 2016) and on coping with drought shocks, savings, access to credit, women's empowerment, and business activity in Ghana, Malawi, and Uganda (Karlan et al., 2012). Abubakari, Sadik, and Keisan (2014) found a positive association between VSLA participation and child nutrition and health outcomes in Ghana. A field experiment in Afghanistan found positive effects on savings behavior by enrolling employees in automatic payroll deductions (Blumenstock, Callen, & Ghani, 2016).

Evidence from the selected studies cited earlier suggest that access to formal financial services is associated with positive household financial outcomes in the United States, whereas access to informal or less formal financial services is associated with positive household financial and other outcomes in emerging economies in other parts of the world. Thus, context is important. In the United States, exclusion from formal financial services may consign low-income households to fringe economies where opportunities for economic mobility are absent. Yet in emerging economies where formal financial services are less available and accessible to poorer households, informal services fill an important gap.

Social Entrepreneurship and Financial Inclusion

Social entrepreneurship is construed as the application of market principles and business practices to solve social problems (Dees, 1998; Martin & Osberg, 2007) and advance innovative and sustainable social change solutions (Light, 2006) in which financial returns are secondary (Mair & Marti, 2006). Financial services represent a "stable equilibrium that causes the neglect, marginalization, or suffering of a segment of humanity" that social entrepreneurs want to disrupt (Martin & Osberg, 2007, p. 39). Business as usual in financial services means that low-income and other vulnerable households lack access to safe and affordable financial products and services that they need to make ends meet. The social entrepreneurial challenge thus is to disrupt this pattern of financial exclusion.

A key reason why the goal of financial inclusion remains unfulfilled is that products and services offered by banks do not meet the needs of financially excluded households. Traditional banking products for lower-income households are generally unprofitable for banks and are a poor match for problems such as having little income to pay for financial services and income and expense volatility (Cohen et al., 2015). In many emerging economies, banks simply lack the capital and capacity to establish the market presence to ensure financial inclusion, which leaves the task of financial inclusion up to NGOs, as has been the case with microfinance institutions.

Therefore, social work entrepreneurs must decide how to intervene in the face of both types of market failure. This can occur through two main strategies: product innovation and cross-sector partnerships. Social workers' familiarity with the needs and circumstances of low-income and other vulnerable households and their ethical commitment to confront economic exclusion can inform product innovation. Social work's long history in organizing communities positions the professional well in facilitating efforts to promote financial inclusion. Numerous examples of these strategies in action, as well as roles social workers can place, are described in chapter 9.

Product Innovation and the Role of Social Workers

Product innovation refers to the process of designing and testing financial products and services that can better meet the needs of financially excluded households. Social workers can embrace the challenge of developing products and services that meet a range of household needs related to conducting transactions, accessing credit, and saving and investing across the life course. To meet this challenge, social workers should engage in design thinking informed by behavioral economics and seek opportunities to leverage technology.

Design Thinking and Behavioral Science. Design thinking refers to a process of inspiration, ideation, and implementation of solutions to problems during which the prospective end user of the solution is at the center of all design decisions. Designers seek to understand customer needs, preferences, and motivations and deliberately elicit diverse perspectives to develop new ideas and approaches for solving a problem, and feedback from prospective end users is sought during prototyping and implementation (Brown & Wyatt, 2010; Siota, Klueter, Staib, Taylor, & Ania, 2017).

Design thinking is a natural outgrowth of the social work principle of starting where the client is and client-centered practice. Using participatory community assessment methods, social workers can engage financially excluded individuals to understand the financial products and services they want and would likely use, paying close attention to issues of cost and the customer experience. Social workers are well attuned to the financial challenges and day-to-day struggles marginalized people experience, which yields important insights that social workers can introduce to local banks and credit unions to inform product and service design. Yet social workers also need to consider what products and services are financially sustainable from the financial institution perspective. Drivers of low profitability for banks among consumers include low and unstable account balances, high use of in-person services, and small loans (Cohen et al., 2015).

An example of design thinking in action is the Center for Financial Services Innovation, which hosts the Financial Solutions Lab to encourage nonprofits, FinTech start-ups, and financial institutions to develop and test new products and services aimed at improving household financial health. Internationally, organizations such as Innovations for Poverty Action, Ideas 42, and the Abdul Latif Jameel Poverty Action Lab work with NGOs and other organizations to design and test financial service innovations.

Design thinking is enhanced if behavioral science guides the ideation phase so that products and services are designed to help overcome behavioral barriers to positive financial behaviors, such as overvaluing consumption relative to saving (Benhabib, Bisin, & Schotter, 2010), procrastination, and limited attention to financial decisions (Johnson et al., 2012). Product and service features guided by behavioral science include automated savings, savings reminders, tools for tracking financial goals, commitment devices such as self-imposed account withdrawal restrictions, and visual account tools to mirror mental accounting processes (Cohen et al., 2015).

FinTech and the Role of Technology. Technology has the potential to help banks reach financially excluded households (Burhouse et al., 2016; Gorham & Dorrance, 2017; Realini & Mehta, 2015), such as through the fast-growing FinTech industry—companies and businesses dedicated to using technology to create new and better financial products and services. Technology is a particularly important driver of financial inclusion given the lack of physical bank branches in rural areas across the globe. The widespread dissemination and adoption of the M-PESA digital finance platform in Kenya (Rosengard, 2016) illustrates how technology can be leveraged to promote financial inclusion. A range of FinTech innovations have proliferated rapidly in the United States and other countries recently—mobile banking, video chat with bank tellers, online lending platforms, digital wallets, mobile and peer-to-peer payment and lending systems, remote deposit capture, prepaid debit cards, automated savings programs, mobile financial management apps, and more. Harnessed effectively, these innovations may be an important tool for meeting one of the social work Grand Challenges to "build financial capability for all" (Sherraden et al., 2015).

Yet there are some reasons why technology may fall short of full financial inclusion. Mobile and smartphone ownership is lower among unbanked households, and these households often use cash to conduct transactions (Burhouse, Homer, Osaki, & Bachman, 2014). Lower-income households are less likely than higher-income households to use mobile banking (Despard & Friedline, 2017) and prefer using cash for a wider range of transactions (Bennett, Conover, O'Brien, & Advincula, 2014). Financially excluded households across the globe are also more likely to be employed informally and to be paid in cash (Smith Nightingale & Wandner, 2011; Lahaye, Abell, & Hoover, 2017).

Also, digital access itself is not universal. Rural areas in nearly all countries lack sufficient cellular coverage and broadband access. Even within urban areas in the United States, low-income areas have less coverage than more affluent areas (Koutroumpis & Leiponen, 2016). Thus, the global digital divide constrains the potential of mobile technologies to promote financial inclusion. More broadly, the digital divide is a form of social exclusion that social workers should address by increasing access to information technology in excluded households (Steyaert & Gould, 2009). Social workers are well accustomed to ensuring that individuals have the access to resources they need—food, transportation, health care, and so on. In an age in which so many transactions are electronic (for example, applying for a job, paying bills, accessing children's school assignments), digital access is a basic need that social workers can help fulfill.

Another limitation of FinTech is that most start-up companies wish to sell new products and services to banks and employers to enhance the customer experience of the financially included, not to reach the financially excluded. That is, unless it can create new efficiencies to lower costs for banks to provide the financial products and services financially excluded households want, technology by itself is insufficient to ensure financial inclusion. Still, social workers need to understand these new technologies and partner with FinTech entrepreneurs and companies to identify new opportunities to reach the financially excluded.

Cross-Sector Partnerships

Financial exclusion is a complex problem unlikely to be solved by financial institutions alone. Cross-sector partnerships to promote financial inclusion are important for three reasons: banks have the capital and market presence in most economies to promote financial inclusion, nonprofits and NGOs have a track record of reaching the financially excluded with innovative solutions (Karlan, 2014), and governments can pass laws and implement regulations that facilitate or hinder financial inclusion. Thus, financial inclusion will not be achieved unless these three sectors work together. This represents an important opportunity for social workers to play facilitative, brokering, and negotiating roles in promoting inclusive social and economic development (Weil, Gamble, & Ohmer, 2013).

For example, nonprofit Self-Help's Community Advantage Program (CAP) purchases mortgages made by banks to lower-income and higher-credit-risk borrowers and sells these loans on the secondary market to Fannie Mae (a government-sponsored enterprise), which holds these mortgages or packages them in mortgage-backed securities to be sold to investors. A loan loss reserve fund is financed by the Ford Foundation. CAP allows banks to then initiate additional mortgages, expanding homeownership opportunities for lower-income borrowers and communities (Center for Community Capital, n.d.). Minnesota-based Sunrise Banks is a certified B Corporation, a company certified to use business methods to solve social and environmental challenges (https://www.bcorporation.net). Sunrise Banks provides short-term employee loans in partnership with Employee Loan Solutions, a for-profit FinTech start-up, as an alternative to expensive payday and auto title loans. For these types of market interventions, social workers can play an important advocacy role, such as advocating for increased federal funding for CDFIs and state and federal financial service regulations that enable new products that benefit financially excluded households to come on market.

Public–private partnerships characterize large-scale efforts to promote financial inclusion. For example, the Central Bank of Kenya has partnered with Financial Sector Deepening, an NGO, to develop and support financial service innovations and monitor progress in increasing access to and use of financial services. In the United States, Cities for Financial Empowerment supports a national coalition of local "Bank On" coalitions of banks, local governments, and nonprofit organizations to provide safe and affordable basic banking products and services to financially excluded households.

Social workers play important community practice roles as resource brokers, facilitators, and coalition builders (Gamble & Weil, 2013) that can support cross-sector partnerships to promote financial inclusion and asset building. For example, while working for a community action agency, I formed a partnership of banks, credit unions, community housing development organizations, a credit counseling agency, a community college, local government, a small business development center, and a local United Way chapter to implement an individual development account (IDA) program. The IDA program helped lower-income people buy homes, start businesses, and receive postsecondary education.

Role of Public Policies

As described earlier, product innovation fueled by design thinking and technology and cross-sector partnerships are key strategies for social work entrepreneurs to use and support to promote financial inclusion. Yet laws and regulations are needed to ensure that new financial products and services do not harm consumers. For example, the payday loan industry in the United States grew rapidly in the late 1990s and early part of the 21st century, ushering in an era of small-dollar credit innovation that includes auto title, pawn, and refund anticipation loans. Subsequently, several states have either banned or restricted payday and other, similar types of loans. The Consumer Financial Protection Bureau announced new regulations in 2017 greatly restricting consumer loans with terms of 45 days or less.

Laws and regulations are also needed to provide the enabling context for cross-sector financial inclusion partnerships (Lahaye et al., 2017). For example, banks have made strides in mortgage lending to minority and lower-income households yet are restricted from selling these loans on the secondary market—hence the need for Self-Help's CAP program described earlier. Social workers need to understand the financial services innovation and regulatory landscape and to partner with consumer advocacy groups such as the

Consumer Federation of America to advocate for laws and regulations that enable cross-sector partnerships that generate new products and services that meet the needs of financially excluded households.

Promises and Limitations of Financial Inclusion

This chapter describes financial inclusion as an important public policy goal and issue in the context of social workers' ethical obligation to promote social and economic justice. Social workers should and can play important roles to create an economy that works for all, not just some, as embodied in the American Academy of Social Work and Social Welfare's goal of "Financial Capability for All," one of its Grand Challenges (Sherraden et al., 2015).

Social workers can promote financial inclusion at all levels of practice. At the micro level, social workers can increase their own financial knowledge and literacy so that they can offer sound information, referrals, and counseling to clients regarding financial products and services. To accomplish this, social workers can pursue additional training, such as through the Center for Financial Social Work or the Association for Financial Counseling and Planning Education (Despard & Chowa, 2013). Social workers can also advocate within their own agencies to form partnerships with banks, credit unions, and credit counseling agencies to make it easier for clients to access financial products and services.

At the mezzo practice level, social workers can play important roles in forming community coalitions and cross-sector partnerships to promote financial inclusion. Examples include the Cities for Financial Empowerment Fund's Bank On initiative; Money Smart KC, supported by the Federal Reserve Bank of Kansas City; local America Saves campaigns; and asset-building coalitions through United Way chapters and local governmental agencies.

At the macro practice level, social workers can play an important role in organizing grassroots support for state and federal policies that promote financial inclusion and consumer protections. This can be accomplished by working with state asset-building coalitions and forming connections with national organizations such as Prosperity Now and the Consumer Federation of America.

Still, social workers should also acknowledge the limitations of financial inclusion in promoting the social and economic well-being of individuals, households, and communities. Access to and use of safe and affordable financial services should be viewed as a necessary but insufficient condition for economic justice and well-being. Ultimately, the success of financial inclusion should be judged in terms of what financial products and services do to help households achieve their goals. Even the best-designed safe and affordable products and services will do nothing for households with a persistent lack of sufficient income to meet basic needs (Cohen et al., 2015). What good are safe and affordable financial products and services if the lowest-paid employees in a community cannot afford basic needs such as housing and food? Thus, financial inclusion should be subsumed under a broader goal of economic justice and reducing economic inequality.

References

Abubakari, A., Sadik, B. B., & Keisan, Y. (2014). Impact of village savings and loans associations on the nutritional status of under-five children: A case study in the Sissala West district of Upper West Region. *Pakistan Journal of Nutrition, 13*, 390–396. doi:10.3923/pjn.2014.390.396

Agarwal, S., Skiba, P. M., & Tobacman, J. (2009). *Payday loans and credit cards: New liquidity and credit scoring puzzles?* (National Bureau of Economic Research No. w14659). Retrieved from http://www.nber.org/papers/w14659

Alliance for Financial Inclusion. (2015). *National financial inclusion strategies: Current state of practice.* Retrieved from http://www.afi-global.org/sites/default/files/publications/fisplg-state_of_practice.pdf

Arun, T., & Kamath, R. (2015). Financial inclusion: Policies and practices. *IIMB Management Review, 27*, 267–287. doi:10.1016/j.iimb.2015.09.004

Aryeetey, E., & Steel, W. F. (1995). Savings collectors and financial intermediation in Ghana. *Savings and Development, 19*, 191–212. Retrieved from http://www.jstor.org/stable/25830413

Ashraf, N., Karlan, D., & Yin, W. (2006). Tying Odysseus to the mast: Evidence from a commitment savings product in the Philippines. *Quarterly Journal of Economics, 121*, 635–672. doi:10.1162/qjec.2006.121.2.635

Auspos, P., & Cabaj, M. (2014). Applying a complexity lens to long-standing issues in community change. In *Complexity and community change* (pp. 32–55). Washington, DC: Aspen Institute.

Austin, J., Stevenson, H., & Wei-Skillern, J. (2006). Social and commercial entrepreneurship: Same, different, or both? *Entrepreneurship Theory and Practice, 30*, 1–22. doi:10.1108/17576381311329661

Banerjee, A., Duflo, E., Glennerster, R., & Kinnan, C. (2015). The miracle of microfinance? Evidence from a randomized evaluation. *American Economic Journal: Applied Economics, 7*(1), 22–53. doi:10.1257/app.20130533

Barth, J. R., Caprio, G., Jr., & Levine, R. (2013). Bank regulation and supervision in 180 countries from 1999 to 2011. *Journal of Financial Economic Policy, 5*, 111–219. doi:10.1108/17576381311329661

Beck, T., Demirgüç-Kunt, A., & Martinez Peria, M. S. (2008). Banking services for everyone? Barriers to bank access and use around the world. *World Bank Economic Review, 22*, 397–430. doi:10.1093/wber/lhn020

Benhabib, J., Bisin, A., & Schotter, A. (2010). Present-bias, quasi-hyperbolic dis-
counting, and fixed costs. *Games and Economic Behavior, 69*, 205–223. doi:10.
1016/j.geb.2009.11.003

Bennett, B., Conover, D., O'Brien, S., & Advincula, R. (2014). *Cash continues
to play a key role in consumer spending: Evidence from the Diary of Consumer
Payment Choice.* San Francisco: Federal Reserve Bank of San Francisco.
Retrieved from http://www.frbsf.org/cash/files/FedNotes_Evidence_from_
DCPC.pdf

Bhutta, N. (2014). Payday loans and consumer financial health. *Journal of Banking & Finance, 47*, 230–242. doi:10.1016/j.jbankfin.2014.04.024

Bhutta, N., Skiba, P., & Tobacman, J. (2015). Payday loan choices and consequences. *Journal of Money, Credit and Banking, 47*, 223–260. doi:10.1111/
jmcb.12175

Birkenmaier, J., & Fu, Q. (2015). The association of alternative financial services usage and financial access: Evidence from the national financial capability study. *Journal of Family and Economic Issues, 37*(3), 1–11. doi:10.1007/
s10834-015-9463-2

Blumenstock, J., Callen, M., & Ghani, T. (2016, April 9). *Mobile-izing savings with
automatic contributions: Experimental evidence on dynamic inconsistency and the
default effect in Afghanistan* (Working paper). Retrieved from http://www
.poverty-action.org/sites/default/files/publications/mobile-izing-savings.pdf

Brown, T., & Wyatt, J. (2010). Design thinking for social innovation. *Development Outreach, 12*, 29–43. doi:10.1596/1020-797X_12_1_29

Burhouse, S., Homer, M., Osaki, Y., & Bachman, M. (2014). *Assessing the economic inclusion potential of mobile financial services.* Washington, DC: Federal
Deposit Insurance Corporation. Retrieved from https://www.fdic.gov/
consumers/community/mobile/mobile-financial-services.pdf

Burhouse, S., Navarro, B., & Osaki, Y. (2016). *Opportunities for mobile financial
services to engage underserved consumers: Qualitative research findings.* Washington, DC: Federal Deposit Insurance Corporation. Retrieved from https://
www.fdic.gov/consumers/community/mobile/mfs_qualitative_research_
report.pdf

Campbell, D., Jerez, A. M., & Tufano, P. (2012). Bouncing out of the banking
system: An empirical analysis of involuntary bank account closures. *Journal of Banking & Finance, 36*, 1224–1235. doi:10.1016/j.jbankfin.2011.11.014

Carroll, C. D., & Samwick, A. A. (1998). How important is precautionary saving?
Review of Economics and Statistics, 80, 410–419. doi:10.1162/003465398557645

Center for Community Capital. (n.d.). *Self-Help's Community Advantage Program*
(Regaining the Dream: Case Studies in Sustainable Low-Income Mortgage
Lending). Chapel Hill: University of North Carolina. Retrieved from http://
ccc.sites.unc.edu/files/2013/02/Self-HelpCaseStudy.pdf

Chowa, G. A., & Despard, M. (2013). The influence of parental financial socialization on youth's financial behavior: Evidence from Ghana. *Journal of Family and Economic Issues, 35*, 376–389. doi:10.1007/s10834-013-9377-9

Chowa, G., Masa, R., Ansong, D., Despard, M., Wu, S., Hughes, D., et al. (2015). *Impacts of financial inclusion on youth development: Findings from the Ghana YouthSave Experiment* (CSD Research Report No. 15-35). St. Louis: Washington University in St. Louis, Center for Social Development. Retrieved from http://csd.wustl.edu/Publications/Documents/RR15-35.pdf

Cohen, N., Davis, K., Tantia, P., Wright, J., Chandrasekhar, C., & Spence, T. (2015). *Reimagining financial inclusion* (Report by Oliver Wyman and Ideas42). Retrieved from http://www.ideas42.org/wp-content/uploads/2015/11/Reimagining-Financial-Inclusion-Final-Web-1.pdf

Connor, K., & Skomarovsky, M. (2010). *The predators' creditors: How the biggest banks are bankrolling the payday loan industry* (National People's Action and Public Accountability Initiative report). Retrieved from http://public-accountability.org/wp-content/uploads/2011/09/payday-final-091410.pdf

Cuddeback, G., Blank Wilson, A., Despard, M., Tomar, N., & Chowa, G. (2016). Financial insecurity and risk experiences of justice involved persons with severe mental illnesses. *Social Work in Mental Health, 15*, 615–631. doi:10.1080/15332985.2016.1267069

Dees, J. G. (1998). *The meaning of social entrepreneurship.* Kansas City, MO, and Palo Alto, CA: Kauffman Foundation and Stanford University. Retrieved from http://community-wealth.org/sites/clone.community-wealth.org/files/downloads/paper-dees.pdf

Despard, M., & Chowa, G.A.N. (2013). Training social workers in personal finance: An exploratory study. *Journal of Social Work Education, 49*, 689–700. doi:10.1080/ 10437797.2013.812895

Despard, M., & Friedline, T. (2017). *Do metropolitan areas have equal access to banking? A geographic investigation of financial services availability.* Lawrence: University of Kansas, Center on Assets, Education, & Inclusion. doi:10.13140/RG.2.2.35411.78881

Despard, M., R., Grinstein-Weiss, M., Ren, C., Guo, S., & Raghavan, R. (2016). Effects of a tax-time savings intervention on use of alternative financial services among lower-income households. *Journal of Consumer Affairs, 51*, 355–379. doi:0.1111/joca.12138

Despard, M. R., Perantie, D. C., Luo, L., Oliphant, J., & Grinstein-Weiss, M. (2015). *Use of alternative financial services in low- and moderate-income households: Evidence from Refund to Savings* (CSD Research Brief No. 15-57). St. Louis: Washington University in St. Louis, Center for Social Development. Retrieved from http://csd.wustl.edu/Publications/Documents/RB15-57.pdf

Dore, R. (2008). Financialization of the global economy. *Industrial and Corporate Change, 17*(6), 1097–1112. doi:10.1093/icc/dtn041

Dupas, P., Karlan, D., Robinson, J., & Ubfal, D. (2016). *Banking the unbanked? Evidence from three countries* (Working paper). Retrieved from http://www.poverty-action.org/sites/default/files/publications/3countrysavings.pdf

Federal Deposit Insurance Corporation. (2012). *FDIC community banking study.* Washington, DC: Author. Retrieved from https://www.fdic.gov/regulations/resources/cbi/report/cbi-full.pdf

Federal Deposit Insurance Corporation. (2016). *2015 FDIC National Survey of Unbanked and Underbanked Households.* Washington, DC: Author. Retrieved from https://www.fdic.gov/householdsurvey/2015/2015report.pdf

Federal Deposit Insurance Corporation. (2017). *Statistics at a glance.* Retrieved from https://www.fdic.gov/bank/statistical/stats/2017mar/fdic.pdf

Fitzpatrick, K. (2015). Does "banking the unbanked" help families to save? Evidence from the United Kingdom. *Journal of Consumer Affairs, 49*, 223–249. doi:10.1111/joca.12055

Friedline, T., Despard, M., Eastlund, R., & Schuetz, N. (2017). *Are banks' entry-level checking accounts safe and affordable? Comparing a stratified random sample of banks to safety and affordability guidelines.* Lawrence: University of Kansas, Center on Assets, Education, & Inclusion.

Friedline, T., Johnson, P., & Hughes, R. (2014). Toward healthy balance sheets: Are savings accounts a gateway to young adults' asset diversification and accumulation? *Federal Reserve Bank of St. Louis Review, 96*, 359–389.

Friedline, T., & Kepple, N. (2017). Does community access to alternative financial services relate to individuals' use of these services? Beyond individual explanations. *Journal of Consumer Policy, 40*(1), 51–79. doi:10.1007/s10603-016-9331-y

Fusaro, M. A. (2008). Hidden consumer loans: An analysis of implicit interest rates on bounced checks. *Journal of Family and Economic Issues, 29*, 251–263. doi:10.1007/s10834-008-9101-3

Gamble, D. N., & Weil, M. (2013). Community practice interventions. In *Encyclopedia of social work.* Retrieved from http://socialwork.oxfordre.com/view/10.1093/acrefore/9780199975839.001.0001/acrefore-9780199975839-e-532

Gjertson, L. (2016). Emergency saving and household hardship. *Journal of Family and Economic Issues, 37*, 1–17. doi:10.1007/s10834-014-9434-z

Global Partnership for Financial Inclusion. (2014). *2014 financial inclusion action plan.* Retrieved from http://www.gpfi.org/sites/default/files/documents/G20%20Financial%20Inclusion%20Action%20Plan.docx.pdf

Goodstein, R. M., & Rhine, S. L. (2017). The effects of bank and nonbank provider locations on household use of financial transaction services. *Journal of Banking & Finance, 78*, 91–107. doi:10.1016/j.jbankfin.2017.01.016

Gorham, L., & Dorrance, J. (2017). *Catalyzing inclusion: Financial technology and the underserved.* Chapel Hill: Center for Community Capital, University of North Carolina at Chapel Hill. Retrieved from https://communitycapital .unc.edu/files/2017/10/CCC-FinTech-Report-2017-1.pdf

Grinstein-Weiss, M., Perantie, D. C., Oliphant, J. E., deRuyter, A., & Despard, M. R. (2016). *Characteristics and hardships associated with bank account ownership among Refund to Savings participants* (CSD Research Brief No. 16-09). St. Louis: Washington University in St. Louis, Center for Social Development. Retrieved from http://csd.wustl.edu/Publications/Documents/RB16-09.pdf

Grinstein-Weiss, M., Wagner, K., & Ssewamala, F. M. (2006). Saving and asset accumulation among low-income families with children in IDAs. *Children and Youth Services Review, 28,* 193–211. doi:10.1016/j.childyouth.2005.03.005

Gross, M. B., Hogarth, J. M., Manohar, A., & Gallegos, S. (2012). Who uses alternative financial services, and why? *Consumer Interests Annual, 58,* 2012–2057.

Gudmunson, C. G., & Danes, S. M. (2011). Family financial socialization: Theory and critical review. *Journal of Family Economic Issues, 32,* 644–667. doi: 10.1007/s10834-011-9275-y

Huang, J., Nam, Y., Sherraden, M., & Clancy, M. (2015). Financial capability and asset accumulation for children's education: Evidence from an experiment of child development accounts. *Journal of Consumer Affairs, 49*(1), 127–155. doi:10.1111/joca.12054

Hulme, D., & Moore, K. (2007). Why has microfinance been a policy success in Bangladesh? In A. Bebbington & W. McCourt (Eds.), *Development success: Statecraft in the South* (pp. 105–139). London: Palgrave Macmillan UK.

Johnson, E. J., Shu, S. B., Dellaert, B. G., Fox, C., Goldstein, D. G., Häubl, G., et al. (2012). Beyond nudges: Tools of a choice architecture. *Marketing Letters, 23,* 487–504. doi:10.1007/s11002-012-9186-1

Jones, K. D., & Critchfield, T. (2005). Consolidation in the U.S. banking industry: Is the long, strange trip about to end. *FDIC Banking Review, 17*(4), 31–61. Retrieved from https://www.fdic.gov/bank/analytical/banking/2006jan/ article2/article2.pdf

Karlan, D. (2014). The next stage of financial inclusion. *Stanford Social Innovation Review, 12*(4), 43–49.

Karlan, D., Thuysbaert, B., Udry, C., Cupito, E., Naimpally, R., Salgado, E., & Savonitto, B. (2012). *Impact assessment of savings groups: Findings from three randomized evaluations of CARE village savings and loan associations programs in Ghana, Malawi and Uganda, final report.* New Haven, CT: Innovations for Poverty Action. Retrieved from http://www.poverty-action.org/printpdf/6221

Kim, J., LaTaillade, J., & Kim, H. (2011). Family processes and adolescents' financial behaviors. *Journal of Family and Economic Issues, 32,* 668–679. doi:10.1007/s10834-011-9270-3

Koutroumpis, P., & Leiponen, A. (2016). Crowdsourcing mobile coverage. *Telecommunications Policy, 40,* 532–544. doi:10.1016/j.telpol.2016.02.005

Krippner, G. R. (2005). The financialization of the American economy. *Socio-Economic Review, 3,* 173–208. doi:10.1093/SER/mwi008

Ksoll, C., Lilleør, H. B., Lønborg, J. H., & Rasmussen, O. D. (2016). Impact of village savings and loan associations: Evidence from a cluster randomized trial. *Journal of Development Economics, 120,* 70–85. doi:10.1016/j.jdeveco.2015.12.003

Ladha, T., Asrow, K., Parker, S., Rhyne, E., & Kelly, S. (2017). *Beyond financial inclusion: Financial health as a global framework* (Report of the Center for Financial Services Innovation in partnership with the Center for Financial Inclusion at Accion). Retrieved from http://www.centerforfinancial inclusion.org/storage/documents/FinHealthGlobal-FINAL.2017.04.11.pdf

Lahaye, E., Abell, T. E., & Hoover, J. K. (2017). *Vision of the future: Financial inclusion 2025* (CGAP Focus Note No. 107). Washington, DC: Consultative Group to Assist the Poor. Retrieved from http://www.cgap.org/sites/default/files/Focus-Note-Vision-of-the-Future-Jun-2017_0.pdf

Lambert, S. J. (2008). Passing the buck: Labor flexibility practices that transfer risk onto hourly workers. *Human Relations, 61,* 1203–1227. doi:10.1177/0018726708094910

Larrimore, J., Dodini, S., & Thomas, L. (2016). *Report on the economic well-being of U.S. households in 2015* (Board of Governors of the Federal Reserve System Report). Retrieved from https://www.federalreserve.gov/2015-report-economic-well-being-us-households-201605.pdf

Light, P. C. (2006). Reshaping social entrepreneurship. *Stanford Social Innovation Review, 4*(3), 47–51. Retrieved from http://www.nyu.edu/social-entre preneurship/news_events_resources/pdf/paul_light.pdf

Lim, Y., Bickham, T., Broussard, J. A., Dinecola, C. M., Gregory, A., & Weber, B. E. (2014). The role of middle-class status in payday loan borrowing: A multivariate approach. *Social Work, 59,* 329–337. doi:10.1093/sw/swu033

Lusardi, A., & de Bassa Scheresberg, C. (2013). *Financial literacy and high-cost borrowing in the United States* (Working Paper No. 18969). Retrieved from http://www.nber.org/papers/w18969.pdf

Lusardi, A., Mitchell, O. S., & Curto, V. (2010). Financial literacy among the young. *Journal of Consumer Affairs, 44,* 358–380. doi:10.1111/j.1745-6606.2010.01173.x

Mader, P. (2013). Rise and fall of microfinance in India: The Andhra Pradesh crisis in perspective. *Strategic Change, 22*(1–2), 47–66. doi:10.1002/jsc.1921

Mair, J., & Marti, I. (2006). Social entrepreneurship research: A source of explanation, prediction, and delight. *Journal of World Business, 41*(1), 36–44. doi:10.1016/j.jwb.2005.09.002

Manturuk, K., Dorrance, J., & Halladay, J. (2015). Building emergency savings through "impulse saving." In J. Michael Collins (Ed.), *A fragile balance: Emergency savings and liquid resources for low-income consumers* (pp. 125–140). New York: Palgrave Macmillan.

Martin, R. L., & Osberg, S. (2007). Social entrepreneurship: The case for definition. *Stanford Social Innovation Review, 5*(2), 28–39. Retrieved from http://www.ngobiz.org/picture/File/Social%20Enterpeuneur-The%20Case%20of%20Definition.pdf

McKernan, S. M., Pitt, M. M., & Moskowitz, D. (2005). *Use of the formal and informal financial sectors: Does gender matter?* (Working Paper No. 3491). Retrieved from http://www.urban.org/sites/default/files/publication/51806/411160-Use-of-the-Formal-and-Informal-Financial-Sectors-Does-Gender-Matter-.PDF

Michaels, L. (2012, October 1). Delivering technology solutions to Susu collectors [Blog post]. Retrieved from http://www.cgap.org/blog/delivering-technology-solutions-susu-collectors

Morduch, J., Ogden, T., & Schneider, R. (2014). *An invisible finance sector: How households use financial tools of their own making* (U.S. Financial Diaries Issue Brief). New York: Financial Access Initiative at New York University. Retrieved from http://www.usfinancialdiaries.org/issue3-informal

Morduch, J., & Schneider, R. (2017). *The financial diaries: How Americans cope in a world of uncertainty*. Princeton, NJ: Princeton University Press.

Morse, A. (2011). Payday lenders: Heroes or villains? *Journal of Financial Economics, 102*(1), 28–44. doi:10.1016/j.jfineco.2011.03.022

MyCreditUnion.gov. (n.d.). *Learn about credit unions.* Retrieved from https://www.mycreditunion.gov/about-credit-unions/Pages/default.aspx

Nam, Y., Kim, Y., Clancy, M., Zager, R., & Sherraden, M. (2013). Do Child Development Accounts promote account holding, saving, and asset accumulation for children's future? Evidence from a statewide randomized experiment. *Journal of Policy Analysis and Management, 32*(1), 6–33. doi:10.1002/pam.21652

National Association of Social Workers. (2017). *Code of ethics of the National Association of Social Workers.* Washington, DC: Author.

Negro, G., Visentin, F., & Swaminathan, A. (2014). Resource partitioning and the organizational dynamics of "fringe banking." *American Sociological Review, 79*, 680–704. doi:10.1177/0003122414537644

Opportunity Finance Network. (2017). *What is a CDFI?* Retrieved from https://ofn.org/what-cdfi

Pagura, M., & Kirsten, M. (2006). Formal–informal financial linkages: Lessons from developing countries. *Small Enterprise Development, 17*(1), 16–29. Retrieved from http://www.ruralfinanceandinvestment.org/sites/default/files/1151488968730_Financial_linkages_study_synthesis_short.pdf

Parrish, L., & Frank, J. (2011). An analysis of bank overdraft fees: Pricing, market structure and regulation. *Journal of Economic Issues, 45*, 353–362. doi:10.2753/JEI0021-3624450212

Paulson, A., & Rhine, S.L.W. (2008). The financial assimilation of an immigrant group: Evidence on the use of checking and savings accounts and currency exchanges. *Journal of Family and Economic Issues, 29*, 264–278. doi:10.1007/s10834-008-9097-8

Pew Charitable Trusts. (2012). *Payday lending in America: Who borrows, where they borrow, and why.* Washington, DC: Author. Retrieved from http://www.pewtrusts.org/~/media/legacy/uploadedfiles/pcs_assets/2012/PewPaydayLendingReportpdf.pdf

Pew Charitable Trusts. (2017). *Are American families becoming more financially resilient? Changing household balance sheets and the effects of financial shocks* [Issue brief]. Retrieved from http://www.pewtrusts.org/~/media/assets/2017/04/financialshocks_brief.pdf

Postmus, J. L., Hetling, A., & Hoge, G. L. (2015). Evaluating a financial education curriculum as an intervention to improve financial behaviors and financial well-being of survivors of domestic violence: Results from a longitudinal randomized controlled study. *Journal of Consumer Affairs, 49*, 250–266. doi:10.1111/joca.12057

Pouchous, A. (2012). *The regulation and supervision of microfinance: Main issues and progress* [TKN report]. Retrieved from http://www.iisd.org/pdf/2012/regulation_supervision_microfinance.pdf

Rao, S., & Malapit, H. J. L. (2014). Gender, household structure and financial participation in the United States. *Journal of Family and Economic Issues, 36*, 606–620. doi:10.1007/s10834-014-9426-z

Realini, C., & Mehta, K. (2015). *Financial inclusion at the bottom of the pyramid.* Victoria, British Columbia, Canada: FriesenPress.

Rengert, K. M., & Rhine, S.L.W. (2016). *Bank efforts to serve unbanked and underbanked consumers: Qualitative research.* Washington, DC: Federal Deposit Insurance Corporation. Retrieved from https://www.fdic.gov/consumers/community/research/QualitativeResearch_May2016.pdf

Rhine, S. L., Di, W., Greene, W. H., & Perlmeter, E. (2016). Savings account ownership during the great recession. *Journal of Family and Economic Issues, 37*, 333–348. doi:10.1007/s10834-016-9489-0

Robinson, M. (2001). *The microfinance revolution: Sustainable finance for the poor.* Retrieved from https://openknowledge.worldbank.org/handle/10986/28956

Rosengard, J. K. (2016). *A quantum leap over high hurdles to financial inclusion: The mobile banking revolution in Kenya* (Working Paper No. 2015-005). Retrieved from http://ash.harvard.edu/files/ash/files/swift-institute_financial-inclusion_final-1_2.pdf

Rothwell, D. W., & Han, C. K. (2010). Exploring the relationship between assets and family stress among low-income families. *Family Relations, 59,* 396–407. doi:10.1111/j.1741-3729.2010.00611.x

Sanders, C. K. (2013). Financial capability among survivors of domestic violence. In J. Birkenmaier, M. Sherraden, & J. Curley (Eds.), *Financial capability and asset development: Research, education, policy, and practice* (pp. 85–107). New York: Oxford University Press.

Schenk, M. (2012). *Commercial banks and credit unions: Facts, fallacies, and recent trends.* Washington, DC: Credit Union National Association. Retrieved from https://www.cuna.org/Research-And-Strategy/DownLoads/combanks_cus/

Seibel, H. D. (2014, July 1). The continued relevance of informal finance in development. *World Politics Review.* Retrieved from http://www.world politicsreview.com/articles/13891/the-continued-relevance-of-informal-fi nance-in-development

Servon, L. (2017). *The unbanking of America: How the new middle class survives.* Boston: Houghton Mifflin Harcourt.

Sherraden, M., Schreiner, M., & Beverly, S. (2003). Income, institutions, and saving performance in individual development accounts. *Economic Development Quarterly, 17*(1), 95–112. doi:10.1177/0891242402239200

Sherraden, M. S. (2013). Building blocks of financial capability. In J. Birkenmaier, M. S. Sherraden, & J. Curley (Eds.), Financial capability and asset development: Research, education, policy, and practice (pp. 3–43). New York: Oxford University Press.

Sherraden, M. S., Huang, J., Frey, J. J., Birkenmaier, J., Callahan, C., Clancy, M. M., & Sherraden, M. (2015). *Financial capability and asset building for all* (Working Paper No. 13). Retrieved from http://aaswsw.org/wp-content/uploads/2016/01/WP13-with-cover.pdf

Siota, J., Klueter, T., Staib, D., Taylor, S., & Ania, I. (2017). *Design thinking: The new DNA of the financial sector* [Report by IESE Business School University of Navarra and Oliver Wyman]. Retrieved from http://www.iese.edu/research/pdfs/ST-0441-E.pdf

Skiba, P. M., & Tobacman, J. (2011). *Do payday loans cause bankruptcy?* (Vanderbilt Law and Economics Research Paper No. 11-13). Retrieved from http://papers.ssrn.com/sol3/papers.cfm?abstract_id=1266215

Smith Nightingale, D., & Wandner, S. A. (2011). *Informal and nonstandard employment in the United States: Implications for low-income working families* (Brief No. 20). Washington, DC: Urban Institute. Retrieved from https://www.nacha.org/news/new-nacha-survey-showsadoption-and-awareness-direct-deposit-ach-continues-build

Ssewamala, F., Karimli, L., Chang-Keun, H., & Ismayilova, L. (2010). Social capital, savings, and educational performance of orphaned adolescents in sub-Saharan Africa. *Children and Youth Services Review, 32,* 1704–1710. doi:10.1016/j.childyouth.2010.07.013

Steyaert, J., & Gould, N. (2009). Social work and the changing face of the digital divide. *British Journal of Social Work, 39,* 740–753. doi:10.1093/bjsw/bcp022

Sullivan, J. X., Turner, L., & Danziger, S. (2008). The relationship between income and material hardship. *Journal of Policy Analysis and Management, 27*(1), 63–81. doi:10.1002/pam.20307

Villasenor, J. D., West, D. M., & Lewis, R. J. (2015). *The 2015 Brookings Financial and Digital Inclusion Project report: Measuring progress on financial access and usage.* Washington, DC: Center for Technology Innovation at Brookings. Retrieved from https://www.brookings.edu/wp-content/uploads/2016/06/fdip2015.pdf

Webley, P., & Nyhus, E. K. (2006). Parents' influence on children's future orientation and saving. *Journal of Economic Psychology, 27,* 140–164. doi:10.1016/j.joep.2005.06.016

Weil, M., Gamble, D. N., & Ohmer, M. L. (2013). Evolution, models, and the changing context of community practice. In M. Weil, M. Reisch, & M. L. Ohmer (Eds.), *The handbook of community practice* (2nd ed., pp. 117–149). Los Angeles: Sage Publications.

World Bank. (2014). *Financial inclusion: Global financial development report 2014.* Retrieved from http://siteresources.worldbank.org/EXTGLOBALFINRE PORT/Resources/8816096-1361888425203/9062080-1364927957721/GFDR-2014_Complete_Report.pdf

World Bank. (2015). *The little data book on financial development 2015/16.* Retrieved from https://openknowledge.worldbank.org/bitstream/handle/10986/22553/9781464805547.pdf

World Bank. (2017a). *Commercial bank branches (per 100,000 adults).* Retrieved from http://data.worldbank.org/indicator/FB.CBK.BRCH.P5?end=2015&start=2001

World Bank. (2017b, April 5). *Financial inclusion: Overview.* Retrieved from http://www.worldbank.org/en/topic/financialinclusion/overview

5

Macro Practice and Its Relationship
to Social Innovation

Stephanie Cosner Berzin

Macro social work practice involves work with large groups, communities, and institutions to intervene on the systems level. Although macro social work has often been considered through lenses that include community organizing, policy reform, administration, nonprofit leadership, research, and social planning, changes to the social sector require new consideration of how social work macro practice relates to social innovation and related concepts. Social innovation, as an umbrella term, speaks to pathways and processes that allow for social problems to be solved in new and more effective or efficient ways (Berzin & Camarena, 2018). To accomplish this requires multiple pathways that can include social entrepreneurship, social intrapreneurship, or social enterprise. For macro social workers, these new approaches are important given challenges to the existing social sector, which include widening social disparities, fundamental shifts in socioeconomic and political opportunities (Johansen, 2009), and declining funding, even with post-recession recovery (Husch, 2011; Lawrence & Mukai, 2011). Macro social workers solve systemic problems by building and leading organizations that respond to social issues. The social innovation process is relatively new for macro social workers—hence, it is critical to build skill for implenting this process.

Defining Social Innovation

Social innovation has been lauded as an approach that reimagines solutions to social problems. Although literature on social innovation often focuses solely on the definition as an outcome, some definitions incorporate ideas of enhancing society's capacity and collaboration (Rüedel & Lurtz, 2012). Almost all share a common theme about transformational responses to social problems. Although many definitions are rooted outside social work, the following is a definition based in social work concepts and values:

> Social innovation is an umbrella term that encompasses multiple pathways and processes that address the root causes of social injustices. The solutions are more effective, efficient, and/or sustainable—socially, economically and environmentally—than previous solutions and are a result of collaboration with diverse stakeholders. (Berzin & Camarena, 2018, p. 5)

In this definition, social innovation is both a process and an outcome. This focus on process is critical as the field imagines the role for macro practitioners in the "doing" of social innovation work. There is a need to reimagine social innovation by using transdisciplinary approaches and considering multiple pathways toward innovation (Berzin & Pitt-Catsouphes, 2015; Nandan & Scott, 2012).

Social innovation is sometimes considered as analogous to social entrepreneurship, though a broader definition includes two distinct approaches: social entrepreneurship and social intrapreneurship (Berzin & Camarena, 2018; Berzin & Pitt-Catsouphes, 2015; Germak & Singh, 2010). The current literature on, and media attention to, social innovation has focused almost exclusively on social entrepreneurship as the primary path to innovation. Although no single definition exists, social entrepreneurship definitions almost universally espouse an individual (or small group) pursuit of social mission (Dacin, Dacin, & Matear, 2010). Choi and Majumdar (2014) focused on the creation of social value as a prerequisite to social entrepreneurship specifically. Most definitions of social innovation and social entrepreneurship focus on characteristics of individual social entrepreneurs (see Choi & Majumdar, 2014), their operating sector, the specific processes and resources used by the entrepreneur, and the missions and outcomes associated with these activities. This individualistic approach promotes a concept of emergent "heroes" who can "save the world" (Dacin, Dacin, & Tracey, 2011) and neglects the capacity and promise of work from existing organizations.

An expanded paradigm of social innovation includes complementary paths that celebrate both the promise of entrepreneurs with their individual pursuit of new organizations for social mission and the potential for innovation among larger groups of stakeholders and organizations. More recent work has begun to acknowledge social intrapreneurship as a potential path to social innovation (Berzin & Pitt-Catsouphes, 2015; Kistruck & Beamish, 2010; Nandan, London, & Bent-Goodley, 2015). Intrapreneurship, as originally conceptualized, refers to the work of individuals who take the risk and responsibility for developing new ideas, projects, products, or services within existing organizations (Pinchot & Pellman, 1999). Social intrapreneurship occurs when innovation work is done within existing organizations for the purpose of social good. Specifically, it refers to the use of entrepreneurial principles—that is, risk taking, innovative approaches, change orientation, and sustainable business models—within existing institutions for the purpose of solving or responding to social problems (Berzin & Camarena, 2018). Intrapreneurship is particularly relevant for social work as it leverages the field's extant leadership and commitment to human service management. Macro social workers have been engaged in human service management and service delivery for decades. The expertise that comes from these positions includes deep understanding of social problems, strong connections to community, content knowledge about past policy and interventions, and knowledge and commitment to the population. Using this expertise supports the ability of existing organizations to innovate and create effective solutions to social problems (Berzin & Pitt-Catsouphes, 2015). Further, existing organizations bring the promise of scale, sustainability, leadership diffusion, existing social capital, and existing infrastructure to social innovation.

Whereas social entrepreneurship and social intrapreneurship represent two complementary paths to implement social innovation, other conceptualizations focus on the type of outcome that emerges with innovation. Social innovation can take many forms, which can include technology-based innovations, programs, products, changes in service or process, and new policies.

Social enterprise is an approach to social innovation that has received significant attention in recent years. Social enterprise refers to the use of business models or practices to solve social problems (Berzin & Camarena, 2018). A whole organization may function as a social enterprise, or one component of an organization may use this approach. Common approaches to social enterprise include

- earned income
- social business
- creating jobs for hard-to-employ populations (that is, using the business as an employment and/or training opportunity)

Social enterprises can function using a variety of legal classifications. Low-profit limited liability companies (L3Cs) represent a particular legal classification of social enterprises designed to blend business and social purpose. They must be organized for a social purpose with profit as a secondary aim. L3Cs are eligible for both general investments and program-related investments. They are required to pay taxes and are able to distribute excess profit back to owners and investors. Benefit corporations are another legal classification of social enterprise. In this case, the primary function of the benefit corporation must be to achieve a public benefit (social, environmental, and so forth), and the company's fiduciary interests must be redefined to include the interests of the company and shareholders, as well as the nonfinancial interests of the public and social good (Clark & Vranka, 2013). Benefit corporations must submit a public annual report documenting their performance on social and environmental outcomes to maintain this specific status. Social enterprise mechanisms have become an important part of the human service landscape as agencies are trying to compete for scarce resources and consider revenue diversification. Each of these approaches to social innovation provides new avenues for social work macro practitioners.

Social Innovation Concepts and Macro Social Work

As macro practice incorporates concepts from social innovation, the field of innovation can also learn from macro social work practice. Although social innovation, social entrepreneurship, social intrapreneurship, and social enterprise represent different ideas, they share common themes that can enhance practice (Nandan, London, & Blum, 2014).

Social innovation and related concepts share a commitment to extensive engagement with the consumers and beneficiaries. Much like social work language around client empowerment and client-centered practice, innovation work is concerned with putting the client or user's needs at the forefront. Innovation requires engaging the client or end user at each point in developing, testing, implementing, and sustaining innovation.

One of the primary ways that innovators work with both problems and solutions is through a focus on visible and tangible activities. Using a variety of communication tools like drawings, photos, video, and models adds to one's ability to understand an issue and supports solution development. Nonverbal communication tools spark creativity and open participation to a wider range of people. For example, in one of my projects with the Center for Social Innovation at Boston College, working cross-culturally with youths whose parents were incarcerated, social workers used drawing and games to elicit responses about programmatic needs before developing recommendations.

Social entrepreneurs work by getting out physically to particular spaces, building models, and testing ideas with tangible, visible approaches. Social work macro practitioners can augment practice by using these approaches. In my own experience with the Center for Social Innovation at Boston College, macro social workers developing programs to support disconnected youths went into the youths' neighborhoods and spent time at a night school, talking to youths, teachers, and staff. The social workers were working to understand the youth experience by physically spending time in that space and learning from the experience. In another example, social workers in an adult day health center built solutions to support clients with early-stage Alzheimer's disease by developing online support services for clients. Rather than launching the Web site immediately, the social workers used an iterative process with clients with Alzheimer's disease to model, refine, and eventually develop the site.

Building on tangible activities and nonverbal communication strategies, innovators also make heavy use of technology. Technology can be an outcome of innovation and can also be a part of the process. There is an inextricable link between innovation and technology. Technology can be used to engage a much wider range of people through crowdsourcing or virtual approaches; to collect different types of data than what would otherwise be available, including the use of sensors, GPS data, and biomarkers; and to communicate in different ways through such resources as on-demand communication, virtual interactions, and social media. In one example, a peer-delivered HIV prevention program was administered using closed Facebook groups (Young et al., 2014). Technology has the potential to radically alter social work practice and support innovation (Goldkind & Wolf, 2015).

Social innovation and related concepts also call on expertise and process strategies from across domains. The application of social entrepreneurship (and social intrapreneurship) principles supports nonprofit organizations in providing services and weathering economic scarcity (Stecker, 2014). Social enterprise uses business skills to solve social problems. This requires macro social workers to incorporate skills from other disciplines. Skills that support design thinking and business acumen may be borrowed from the fields of management and design. Process approaches may be learned from engineering, while technical skills coming out of computer science can support macro social workers. Entrepreneurial and intrapreneurial approaches understand that collaboration and cross-disciplinary perspectives are required to solve the most difficult problems. Macro practitioners need to both enhance interdisciplinary skill sets and consider collaboration as an imperative (Nandan & Scott, 2012).

Last, considering innovation concepts, a focus on risk and experimentation is paramount. Innovation is built on the premise of testing new ideas with the potential for failure. This does not come easy to the social sector, as failure carries potential risks that affect real people and problems and consumes already scarce economic and other resources. Building social work's capacity for experimentation and failure requires not only shifting mind-set and culture but initiating and promoting funding resources that allow such activities.

Although social innovation concepts can enhance skills and practices within macro practice, it is important to acknowledge that as the social innovation field develops, there is tremendous opportunity to infuse important tenets of social work into innovation practice. Early leadership in social innovation came from schools of management, design, engineering, and public policy generating dialogue congruent with the training of these fields (Brock & Steiner, 2009; Mirabella & Young, 2012). Macro practitioners are uniquely positioned to augment existing social innovation thinking with their deep understanding of social problems, community partnership and coalition building, and management and leadership of existing agencies (Nandan, London, & Blum, 2014).

Social work's rich history in understanding and solving complex social problems can support existing work in social innovation. The outcome focus often seen in social innovation and social entrepreneurship work (see Dacin et al., 2011; Rüedel & Lurtz, 2012) contrasts with social work's approach. Social work focuses on outcome but also remains committed to understanding root cause and unintended consequences. Critical gains can be made for developing innovative solutions by investing in understanding, framing, and reframing social problems. In addition, as innovation work values community engagement and community adoption of innovation (Shaw & Carter, 2007), social workers bring crucial expertise in these areas (Nandan, London, & Blum, 2014). Perhaps one of the most significant contributions to social innovation is macro social work's experience in, and leadership of, existing social service organizations. Much of the work on social entrepreneurship is particularly concerned with leadership (Dacin et al., 2011). Macro social workers have long been in leadership positions within social and human service organizations. Macro social workers can bring consumer perspectives, assessment skills, community organizing, and planning and development skills to social innovation. This experience, coupled with existence of social capital and agency resources, can support the development and implementation of innovation efforts. Intrapreneurial efforts depend on initiatives of employees within existing agencies, and human service organizations are well poised to engage in these efforts (Berzin & Pitt-Catsouphes, 2015). Essentially, macro social workers' expertise and human capital can be leveraged for social innovation.

Social Innovation Processes and Macro Practice

In addition to broad tenets of social work that can support social innovation, specific social work practice models can be linked to social innovation processes. Social innovation and related concepts can be compared and connected to more traditional social work practices and used to expand or enhance them. Social innovation processes vary, but many use a framework with the following components (Berzin & Camarena, 2018; Berzin & Pitt-Catsouphes, 2014; Murray, Caulier-Grice, & Mulgan, 2010):

- Problem identification
- Response generation
- Prototyping
- Implementation
- Assessment and systemic change

Each phase in the social innovation process can be linked to social work macro practice methods such as community planning, program design, community development, policy practice, administration, and social planning. These methods can be integrated with and enhanced by social innovation processes.

Problem Identification

In both social entrepreneurship and intrapreneurship approaches, innovation typically begins with some type of prompt or inspiration. This phase is concerned with identifying and understanding a problem. Social work has a long history of understanding and assessing social problems. Traditional social work macro approaches rely heavily on community needs assessment. Extending traditional assessment to rely on innovation approaches might include strategies such as rapid assessment and response, review of extremes, positive deviance, and future search. Participatory methods, which support social work's client-empowerment perspectives and innovation's user-led design approach, could include the following tactics: participatory 3-D modeling, participatory rural appraisal, or community-based systems dynamics. Immersive approaches such as observation and ethnography could be borrowed from other fields. From the business sector, the ability to understand complex issues could come from competitive analysis, benchmarking, market research, and feedback systems. Technology-based approaches, including user-centered data and data analytics, support problem identification, mapping, and understanding. Future-oriented approaches, including scenario building, forecasting, Delphi, and simulation, could also deepen understanding of social issues. All of these methods can be used to further support problem identification, mapping, and understanding.

As an example, imagine a group of macro social workers working on programming related to a low-income neighborhood with limited affordable, healthy food options. Traditional approaches might include community surveys, interviews with key informants, and mapping of existing resources. Through innovation techniques, the group might use participatory 3-D modeling approaches, adding consumer perspectives to mapping; ethnographic or visiting approaches that place the social workers into the neighborhood context; and benchmarking, which creates comparisons to other low-income neighborhoods that have more robust offerings.

Response Generation

After investing time to understand a particular social issue, efforts are directed toward consideration of a range of solutions. Program planning approaches often include crafting program goals and objectives, designing the approach, and perhaps developing logic models. Traditional activities might include program team meetings, brainstorming, literature review, reviewing best practice examples, consulting clinical experts, and examining evidence-based practices. In the most inclusive examples, organizations solicit client input as program decisions are made.

Building on these competencies, open innovation strategies could allow a wider range of participants to generate solutions (Chesbrough, 2003). Open innovation strategies allow for external ideas to be brought into the decision-making process rather than relying solely on internal input. A wide range of open innovation strategies have been suggested. They may include engaging broad groups of citizens through media, idea banks, competitions and challenges, and open forums (Murray et al., 2010). Technology allows crowdsourcing at new levels; people from across the globe can contribute solutions and codesign and cocreate them as well. User- or client-centered approaches can also be used to engage end users in significant ways for program planning and design.

Consider city officials working with a human service agency to reduce violence in a particular neighborhood. Social workers would certainly look to past examples, existing literature, and community partners for solutions. Innovative approaches would expand response generation and perhaps include an open call or competition for ideas from the broader public or a crowdsourcing approach that allowed many people to provide input and ideas and cocreate neighborhood solutions.

Prototyping

Prototyping phases, often a cornerstone of innovation approaches, focus on testing and refining solutions. In more traditional planning approaches, solutions are often developed during a pilot phase. Piloting requires significant investment and typically a complete or at least partial rollout of the intended solution. The pilot might involve small groups or subgroups of the larger population that the innovation intends to benefit. Pilots often involve data collection to assess effectiveness and prove the concept. One could argue that randomized controlled trials are a form of prototyping in which solutions are tested before being implemented with larger populations (Murray et al., 2010). Social work relies heavily on evidence-based approaches, incorporating research, practice wisdom, experience, and client perspectives into program planning and development (Gilgun, 2005).

Innovation-oriented approaches, by contrast, often depend on ideation and prototyping phases. Ideation and prototyping typically involve generating and testing incomplete solutions or models for feedback (Brown, 2009).

Rapid prototyping, born out of the design field, is an iterative approach that allows for feedback and refinement as the solution is being developed in a time-limited or brief period. Different than a process evaluation, this approach allows the developer to receive continuous feedback for refining the solution. The prototype can be a simple mock-up or a small-scale working model that allows for quick and easy modifications (Berzin & Camarena, 2018). The rapid approach is appropriate for receiving continual feedback and for adapting quickly, before investing in development. Prototyping, as an extension of traditional social work methods, allows design, testing, and refinement before implementation and scaling of programs and services, when appropriate.

In traditional macro social work approaches, a program is often built in a pilot phase to test its elements and determine effectiveness. Consider an example in which an agency working with families that are homeless wanted to design a mobile technology application for providing housing-related resources and services to its clients. Rather than building the app and testing it with small numbers of families (that is, a pilot), the social workers could use a prototyping approach. In this case, they might start with sketches of the app that loosely represent the intention and bring these to users and staff for feedback. The group might then build out the framework, technical specifications, sample content, and sample layouts for the app and take these to different stakeholders for feedback. In the next iteration, parts of the app might be built and rolled out to the end user but with room for feedback and improvement. These iterative processes allow feedback throughout the process and constant refinement of the solution.

Implementation

Following the conception and development of an innovative idea, the process requires substantial investment for its implementation and sustainability. Macro social work brings significant expertise in program implementation and the administration of program, policy, and community-based initiatives. To supplement macro social work expertise, many argue for the inclusion of management, innovation, or entrepreneurial skills (Dart, 2004; Nandan & Scott, 2012). Further, given the changing complexities of the social sector, social work managers need to be positioned to operate across sectors and provide leadership that supports public, private, and nonprofit work (Watson & Hegar, 2013).

Part of the role of implementation and sustaining change relates to financial considerations. Although social work is adept at securing and maintaining resources, even during scarce times, innovation warrants expanded approaches. Moving beyond traditional sources of funding, like grants, government contracts, and charitable giving, innovators can use social enterprise models to consider business approaches for sustainability. Further, macro social workers can access financial support through crowdfunding and social venture philanthropy. Social impact bonds, also called pay-for-success bonds, are another financial tool for implementing new ideas (Palandjian, 2011). Social impact bonds provide a financing mechanism between the government, a social sector agency, and private investors. Socially motivated investors raise capital to put toward an innovation or effective social program run by a social sector agency. The government agrees to pay out the bond if the program is able to effectively achieve a predetermined socially beneficial outcome. These approaches for sustainability require different skills and knowledge than traditional macro social work. Macro social workers need to understand different organizational models that allow for hybrid structures, blurred boundaries between nonprofit and for-profit entities, and cross-sector relationships. Expanded preparation for macro practice will require fluency with these approaches.

In the realm of financial considerations, macro social workers are adept at raising funds through private philanthropy, government contracts, and grants. Consider a situation in which resources are scarce, and a large population of youths is aging out of the foster care system, where government support has been discontinued. An innovative solution by an organization I worked with was the development of a social enterprise that employed former foster youths, helped them develop professional skills, and also generated revenues to support the program.

Assessment and Systemic Change

The final stage in program and social planning approaches aligns with the last phase of innovation, in which assessment, scaling, and systemic change are primary goals. Although planning is not always a linear process, these tasks naturally follow full implementation. Again, macro social work practitioners bring significant expertise. Social work programs use scaling and replication to expand successful programs and reach wider populations. Moving toward large-scale, systemic change has always been a primary focus for macro practitioners. This may involve going from singular, localized programs to large-scale, national programs or using policy mechanisms to bring about broad social change. Where innovation and social intra-/entrepreneurship expand current practice is in thinking about diffusing the demand and knowledge about innovation to a wider audience (see Murray et al., 2010). Berzin and Camarena (2018) argued for the need to incorporate innovation as a critical component of the social sector and develop sector capacity to engage in innovation on an ongoing basis. Changes in the social sector would require shifts in funding models, philanthropic support for innovation activities, and leadership development.

Models and practices of innovation can be intimately tied to traditional social work practice. An expanded framework makes use of these complementary practices and embeds whatever practices are needed for effective, sustainable change. When schools of social work develop such models, innovations can support systemic change in the social sector.

Moving from Ideas to Social Impact

Examining social innovation frameworks and practices helps support macro social work practice. Whereas these represent opportunities for skill development and expanding traditional macro practice activities, more concrete steps help the field of social work develop practitioners for innovation and move innovative ideas toward impact. The conceptual approach to social innovation presented here suggests both entrepreneurial and intrapreneurial paths.

To develop entrepreneurial social workers requires cultivating individuals with the characteristics to pursue risk taking and change. Social entrepreneurial qualities include being innovative; taking initiative; having persistence, creativity, a penchant for problem solving, a commitment to vision, and an ability to overcome challenges to reach that vision; and being a change agent (Abu-Saifan, 2012). Although distinct challenges exist to educate social entrepreneurs (Tracey & Phillips, 2007), the social work field can develop opportunities that support creative thinking (Nandan & Scott, 2012). Pedagogical models that emphasize case approaches and experiential learning have been used for this type of education (Brock & Steiner, 2009).

Particularly in the intrapreneurial space, social work managers and leaders can help create the environment and support for innovation to flourish (Berzin & Camarena, 2018). Organizations can create physical space and provide opportunities for interactions that support creativity. Allowing time and incentives for innovation work can fundamentally alter staff commitment to these activities. Developing unlikely collaborations and interdisciplinary approaches or using diverse team structures also promotes intrapreneurial work.

In both the entrepreneurial and intrapreneurial paths to innovation, developing a skill set and the "big idea" are just the beginning. In entrepreneurship, writing a formal business plan that defines mission, opportunity, value proposition, product or service details, competitive analysis, management and staff, and projected financial structure are important steps. Even for a nonprofit approach, the preparation of a business plan or comparable document (see Wolk & Kreitz, 2008) helps outline key features. Validating the idea through market research and early experimentation helps prove the idea's value. Building a team and identifying appropriate collaborators are important. Finally, identifying funding sources (which may include crowdfunding sites) and developing a pitch to seek resources are significant steps as the social entrepreneur begins implementing the idea or solution.

In the intrapreneurial path, the steps to implementation and social impact rely more heavily on the integration of the idea into the broader organizational context (Berzin & Camarena, 2018). Engaging with agency leadership and connecting to the agency board are critical steps to ensure appropriate buy-in. Linking the innovation to the agency mission and primary agency functions are imperative to its adoption. It can be important to consider how current agency infrastructure and resources might support the idea, while also considering new opportunities for funding. In intrapreneurship, the key factors for success are finding synergy between the idea and the agency mission and finding people to both champion the idea and help with development and implementation. Developing creative ideas is an important part of innovation, but getting the right support and resources behind the idea is crucial for moving to implementation and eventually having the desired social impact.

Social Innovation and Social Work Values: Convergence or Conflict?

As the social work profession builds on its understanding of social innovation and layers social work values on the conceptual underpinnings of social innovation, it becomes clear that innovation is not only an option but an imperative for the profession. Many fear that innovation represents an abandoning of social work values or a conflict with ethical considerations (Germak & Singh, 2010). If social innovation is viewed solely as an extension of business practices in the social sector or as the commodification of social services, this conflict would be unavoidable (Germak & Singh, 2010). If an agency determines the need for substance abuse services for its clients and cannot meet the demand with existing resources, a social enterprise model might be instituted (for example, using a fee-for-service approach for some clients, launching an unrelated business to generate revenue). The agency is then beholden to its NASW value around commitment to the client by providing services where none exist, while simultaneously balancing its sustainability needs.

Clearly, there are many aspects of social work services and delivery that do little to produce financial gain. If the rubric for assessing added value in social work was assigned merely to those endeavors that provide the greatest economic value, the social sector would lose many of its most important services. Hence, social innovation, as articulated earlier, is about using the best resources and most effective, efficient means to respond to social problems.

If the social innovation definition incorporates social justice, then it is deeply aligned with the NASW (2017) *Code of Ethics*. Values related to human dignity, solidarity, partnership, integrity, and cultural competence promote a reciprocal relationship with vulnerable populations and value self-determination. These values, more implicit than explicit in the literature, will bolster social innovation, social entrepreneurship, and social intrapreneurship.

The *Code of Ethics* outlines six broad ethical principles, many of which are aligned with social innovation. The first goal outlined in the code speaks to social work's commitment to help people and ameliorate social problems. This is, in fact, the purpose of social innovation. It is designed to support individuals and communities in need and to address endemic social, economic, and environmental issues in new ways.

Considering the ethical principle around challenging social injustice, the social innovation process can focus on issues of poverty, discrimination, and injustice. The social entrepreneurship and social intrapreneurship perspectives provide new strategies for combatting oppression and promoting equity. Social workers can champion the incorporation of social justice principles into the social innovation, entrepreneurship, and intrapreneurship dialogues across the world. In other words, social work can ensure that innovation occurs on behalf of the most vulnerable. This may be implied within social entrepreneurship and social intrapreneurship processes; however, social workers can make that explicit.

The principle of competence requires social workers to continue expanding their professional knowledge and apply them in practice. This principle asks the social work profession to continue to improve its knowledge base related to service development and delivery—the crux of social innovation. It is about building on what one knows and improving it for better, more effective, and more efficient solutions. In addition, this value calls on the field of social innovation to acknowledge the profound expertise that social work brings to solving complex social problems. Leveraging the capacity and expertise of individuals, community members, professionals, and organizations, macro social workers have the potential to solve problems through a range of creative solutions.

The NASW (2017) *Code of Ethics* also places tremendous value on the centrality of human relationships and the importance of partnership. The process of social intrapreneurship and social entrepreneurship requires commitment to reciprocal relationships. In the Young Foundation's definition of social innovation, social innovations create new relationships or collaborations (Social Innovation Exchange & Young Foundation, 2010). In social innovation, social embeddedness has a dual meaning for the term "social"—implying both a social purpose and the importance of relationships and interaction (Berzin & Camarena, 2018). Within social entrepreneurship process, social relationships and user input are often at the forefront. Innovators value local relationships during the development and implementation of innovation efforts (Shaw & Carter, 2007). Social work values community-driven engagement and brings the imperative of expertise into community work (Nandan, London, & Blum, 2014). In addition, embedding empathy into social innovation provides an important pathway for reciprocal relationships. Within social work, empathy is deeply tied to the importance of reciprocal relationships (Gerdes & Segal, 2011).

The ethical principle tied to dignity and worth values self-determination and client input. Social innovation processes incorporate user input and user-led approaches. This value placed on user opinions and contributions is in accordance with social work's commitment to valuing individuals.

Each of these NASW principles is integral to social innovation. With macro social workers engaged in social innovation research, there is greater opportunity for aligning the profession's values and social innovation process and outcomes. As social workers expand the conceptualization of social innovation, social entrepreneurship, social intrapreneurship, and social enterprise, they can ensure incorporating principles of social and environmental justice.

Social Innovation as Part of the Future of Macro Practice

Looking forward, social workers can not only illuminate the social innovation concept and process but also strategically incorporate social innovation into the field of macro practice. McBeath (2016) outlined 10 recommendations for reenvisioning macro social work practice as a response to the challenges faced by the profession. He, like others, is concerned with the disinvestment in macro social work and the significant need for the profession to respond to social injustice at a systemic level. Though social work has historically been represented by two complementary branches of macro and micro work, Rothman (2013) pointed out inequity in the field's attention to macro social work and the growing imbalance in the profession. Rothman (2013) found a decline in macro content in MSW programs, and in 2016, only 10.3 percent of MSW students self-identified as macro practitioners (Council on Social Work Education, 2016). These trends are alarming and in contrast to the understanding that solving complex social problems requires sustained innovative interventions and systemic changes.

Social entrepreneurs are known to be agents of change, as are macro practice social workers. Macro social workers are specifically trained to engage in system-changing, large-scale shifts for supporting vulnerable populations. Increasing the quality and supply of macro social workers, as McBeath (2016) argued, is critical for sustaining the macro practice workforce. Social innovation, entrepreneurship, and intrapreneurship perspectives can augment the preparation of this workforce. These perspectives can strengthen the quality and quantity of the macro practice workforce by preparing graduates to work across sectors; leverage multiple approaches for program planning, development, and implementation; and garner traditional and nontraditional resources. Equipping social work macro practitioners with social entrepreneurship, social intrapreneurship, and social innovation skills will allow them to remain competitive and more effectively solve complex social problems. In addition, such development can potentially draw students into the profession. Social innovation provides an opportunity to engage today's social work students with new paradigms that are having a dramatic impact on the social sector. Finally, social innovation can strengthen the reimaging of macro social work practice and also expand its scope.

References

Abu-Saifan, S. (2012, February). Social entrepreneurship: Definitions and boundaries. *Technology Innovation Management Review*, pp. 22–27. Retrieved from https://doaj.org/article/13c56d9474d44cadaaac9a6065234c77

Berzin, S. C., & Camarena, H. (2018). *Innovation from within: Redefining how nonprofits solve problems*. New York: Oxford University Press.

Berzin, S. C., & Pitt-Catsouphes, M. (2014). A social work approach to social innovation. *International Journal of Innovation, Creativity and Change, 1*(4), 7–18.

Berzin, S. C., & Pitt-Catsouphes, M. (2015). Social innovation from the inside: Considering the intrapreneurship path [Commentary]. *Social Work, 60,* 360–362. doi:10.1093/sw/swv026

Brock, D., & Steiner, S. (2009). Social entrepreneurship education: Is it achieving the desired aims? *SSRN*. doi:10.2139/ssrn.1344419

Brown, T. (2009). *Change by design: How design thinking transforms organizations and inspires innovation*. New York: HarperCollins.

Chesbrough, H. W. (2003). The era of open innovation. *MIT Sloan Management Review: Sloan Select Collection, 44*(3), 35–47.

Choi, N., & Majumdar, S. (2014). Social entrepreneurship as an essentially contested concept: Opening a new avenue for systematic future research. *Journal of Business Venturing, 29,* 363–376. doi:10.1016/j.jbusvent.2013.05.001

Clark, W. H., & Vranka, L. (2013, January 8). *The need and rationale for the benefit corporation: Why it is the legal form that best addresses the needs of social entrepreneurs, investors, and ultimately, the public.* Retrieved from http://benefitcorp.net/sites/default/files/Benefit_Corporation_White_Paper.pdf

Council on Social Work Education. (2016). *Statistics on social work education in the United States.* Alexandria, VA: Author.

Dacin, M. T., Dacin, P. A., & Matear, M. (2010). Do we need a theory of social entrepreneurship? *Academy of Management Perspectives, 24*(3), 37–57.

Dacin, M. T., Dacin, P. A., & Tracey, P. (2011). Social entrepreneurship: A critique and future directions. *Organization Science, 22,* 1203–1213. doi:10.1287/orsc.1100.0620

Dart, R. (2004). Being business-like in a nonprofit organization: A grounded and inductive typology. *Nonprofit and Voluntary Sector Quarterly, 33,* 290–310. doi:10.1177/0899764004263522

Gerdes, K. E., & Segal, E. (2011). Importance of empathy for social work practice: Integrating new science. *Social Work, 56,* 141–148. doi:10.1093/sw/56.2.141

Germak, A., & Singh, K. K. (2010). Social entrepreneurship: Changing the way social workers do business. *Administration in Social Work, 34*(1), 79–95. doi:10.1080/03643100903432974

Gilgun, J.F. (2005). The four cornerstones of evidence-based practice in social work. *Research on Social Work Practice, 15,* 52–61. doi:10.1177/1049731504269581

Goldkind, L., & Wolf, L. (2015). A digital environment approach: Four technologies that will disrupt social work practice [Commentary]. *Social Work, 60,* 85–87. doi:10.1093/sw/swu045

Husch, B. (2011). *The Fiscal Survey of States: National Governors Association and the National Association of State Budget Officers.* Retrieved from https://www.nga.org/files/live/sites/NGA/files/pdf/FSS1111.PDF

Johansen, B. (2009). *Leaders make the future: Ten new leadership skills for an uncertain world.* San Francisco: Berrett-Koehler Publishers.

Kistruck, G. M., & Beamish, P. W. (2010). The interplay of form, structure, and embeddedness in social intrapreneurship. *Entrepreneurship Theory and Practice, 34,* 735–761. doi:10.1111/j.1540-6520.2010.00371.x

Lawrence, S., & Mukai, R. (2011). *Foundation growth and giving estimates.* Retrieved from http://foundationcenter.issuelab.org/resources/13532/13532.pdf

McBeath, B. (2016). Re-envisioning macro social work practice. *Families in Society, 97,* 5–14. doi:10.1606/1044-3894.2016.97.9

Mirabella, R., & Young, D. R. (2012). The development of education for social entrepreneurship and nonprofit management: Diverging or converging paths? *Nonprofit Management & Leadership, 23*(1), 43–57. doi:10.1002/nml.21049

Murray, R., Caulier-Grice, J., & Mulgan, G. (2010). *The open book of social innovation.* London: Young Foundation.

Nandan, M., London, M., & Bent-Goodley, T. (2015). Social workers as social change agents: Social innovation, social intrapreneurship, and social entrepreneurship. *Human Service Organizations: Management, Leadership & Governance, 39*(1), 38–56.

Nandan, M., London, M., & Blum, T. C. (2014). Community practice social entrepreneurship: An interdisciplinary approach to graduate education. *International Journal of Social Entrepreneurship and Innovation, 3*(1), 51–70. doi:10.1504/IJSEI.2014.06410

Nandan, M., & Scott, P. (2012). Social entrepreneurship and social work: The need for a transdisciplinary education model. *Administration in Social Work, 37*, 257–271. Retrieved from http://www.tandfonline.com/doi/abs/10.1080/03643107.2012.684428

National Association of Social Workers. (2017). *Code of ethics of the National Association of Social Workers*. Washington, DC: Author.

Palandjian, T. (2011). Social impact bonds: A new way to scale nonprofit success. *Root Cause Online*. Retrieved from http://rootcause.org/blog/social-impact-bonds-a-new-way-scale-nonprofit-success?A=SearchResult&SearchID=2522274&ObjectID=4801598&ObjectType=35

Pinchot, G., & Pellman, R. (1999). *Intrapreneuring in action. A handbook for business innovation*. San Francisco: Berrett-Koehler Publishers.

Rothman, J. (2013). *Education for macro intervention: A survey of problems and prospects*. Retrieved from https://www.acosa.org/joomla/pdf/Rothman ReportRevisedJune2013.pdf

Rüedel, D., & Lurtz, K. (2012). *Mapping the various meanings of social innovation: Towards a differentiated understanding of an emerging concept*. Oestrich-Winkel, Germany: EBS Business School Research Paper Series.

Shaw, E., & Carter, S. (2007). Social entrepreneurship: Theoretical antecedents and empirical analysis of entrepreneurial processes and outcomes. *Journal of Small Business and Enterprise Development, 14*, 418–434. doi:10.1108/14626000 710773529

Social Innovation Exchange & the Young Foundation. (2010). *Study on social innovation*. Retrieved from https://www.youngfoundation.org/wp-content/uploads/2012/10/Study-on-Social-Innovation-for-the-Bureau-of-European-Policy-Advisors-March-2010.pdf

Stecker, M. J. (2014). Revolutionizing the nonprofit sector through social entrepreneurship. *Journal of Economic Issues, 48*, 349–358. doi:10.2753/JEI0021-36 24480208

Tracey, P., & Phillips, N. (2007). The distinctive challenge of education social entrepreneurs: A postscript and rejoinder to the special issue on entrepreneurship education. *Academy of Management Learning & Education, 6*, 264–271. doi:10.5465/AMLE.2007.25223465

Watson, L. D., & Hegar, R. L. (2013). The tri-sector environment of social work administration: Applying theoretical orientations. *Administration in Social Work, 37,* 215–226. doi:10.1080/03643107.2012.676609

Wolk, A., & Kreitz, K. (2008). *Business planning for enduring social impact: A how-to guide.* Cambridge, MA: Root Cause.

Young, S. D., Holloway, I., Jaganath, D., Rice, E., Westmoreland, D., & Coates, T. (2014). Project HOPE: Online social network changes in an HIV prevention randomized controlled trial for African American and Latino men who have sex with men. *American Journal of Public Health, 104,* 1707–1712. doi:10.2105/AJPH.2014.301992

PART II

Global Examples of Social Entrepreneurship, Social Intrapreneurship, Social Innovation, and Social Value Creation: Relevance for Social Work Practice

6

Child Helpline International: From Social Work Field Action Project to an International Social Entrepreneurial Venture

Jeroo Billimoria

This chapter provides a brief summary of the challenges experienced by "street children" and describes the formation of a social entrepreneurial venture initiated by social workers and policy entrepreneurs for scaling efforts at an international level. More specifically, this chapter describes a case of a social entrepreneurial process and evolution of the venture, which began as an experimental project for social work students following dialogues with a few individual street children and has now grown into a network of organizations that support over 20 million children every year. Social work and social entrepreneurship skills and principles will be applied to the case description in this chapter.

Scope of the Problem

The terms "children of the street" and "street children" are often used by social workers, nongovernmental organizations (NGOs), and international agencies like the United Nations Children's Fund (UNICEF) to refer to those who live on the street, as opposed to those who work on the streets and return home at some point (Glauser, 2015). Street children are also categorized as children who are less than 18 years of age, who spend all or most of their time on the street, who maintain minimal or no contact with their families, and who "lack supervision, protection or guidance, which makes them vulnerable to [a] wide range of health and psychological hazards" (United Nations Office for Drug Control and Crime Prevention [ODCCP], n.d., p. 7). These children are often subjected to family violence, drugs, police brutality, public stigmatization, detention, structural violence, and natural disasters, and they bear the consequences of civil war and crisis in regions like Iraq (de Benitez, 2007).

A study by Mathur, Rathore, and Mathur (2009) depicted the intensity and type of abuse experienced by street children in the Indian city of Jaipur. Of the 200 street children interviewed, almost 62 percent experienced moderate levels of general, health, verbal, physical, and psychological abuse, and almost 38 percent reported several levels of abuse in these categories. Gender differences existed, where boys were abused significantly more often and more severely than girls, especially related to "overall" and health abuse. Age, income, and multitype maltreatment and neglect were correlated with abuse of street children. Blaming poverty alone for maltreatment of children is a simplistic explanation. There are several causes for children ending up on the streets to fend for themselves (Dressler, 2007). A study conducted in Cairo and Alexandria reported that many Egyptian families who were economically marginalized demonstrated strong tendencies of becoming seriously dysfunctional and would place their children in circumstances that resulted in them leaving their homes and being subjected to the hazards of the street milieu (ODCCP, n.d.).

The *State of the World's Street Children: Violence* reported that street children are subjected to multiple abuses—unfortunately, many by governments across the world—that their experiences are strikingly similar across the globe, that integrated prevention and protection services need to be developed, and that civil society efforts are gradually integrating services for children, families, and communities to reduce risk for street children (de Benitez, 2007). Social workers have a long tradition of being involved with child welfare, working and advocating for children and their families to ensure their safety and well-being. Consequently, it is very important for social workers and social entrepreneurs to listen and effectively respond to the concerns expressed by children on the streets. With the appropriate responses from national child protection systems, children can be in safe environments to learn and grow into productive individuals (de Benitez, 2007).

Childline India: A Case Study

Problem Identification and Opportunity Recognition

The initial idea of a uniform, toll-free number for children in India emerged in dialogue between street children in Mumbai, academics from the Tata Institute of Social Sciences (TISS), and social workers working with this group of children in the early 1990s. At the time, TISS had several action-based programs providing real-life experiences for the students, and Childline was one of TISS's experimental projects. The street children expressed a need for a service where they could access peer support around the clock, regardless of the nature of the issue. Existing services, friends, or family members did not offer the consistency and emergency support necessary. The suggested service would be a peer-led phone and outreach service through which street children could access emergency support and advice. Given the daily challenges faced by street children, accessibility was key. The service had to be available around the clock and be free of charge. Because many street children moved from one city to another, it was also important that there was a uniform number to call regardless of the child's location. The street children also defined the target group for the service and the issues the service should address.

Social work skills and values related to scientific inquiry, research-informed practice, critical thinking, engagement with diversity, the advance of human rights and social justice, application of knowledge of human behavior in different social contexts to guide assessment and interventions, and resourceful responsiveness to evolving community and social contexts all were visibly at play at this stage of the process (Council on Social Work Education, 2015). This experimentation vividly demonstrates Kotter's statement that for innovation to occur, social work practitioners have to "leave their comfort zones, experiment, and try new ideas" (as cited in Robbins, 2013, p. 3). Social entrepreneurs identify a situation as an opportunity when they perceive that with their abilities and resources they can have a positive impact on the context and address a social issue (Cajaiba-Santana, 2010). In this case, the TISS academicians, social work students, and the street children all recognized that the contextual elements were favorable for them to innovate (McKendall & Wagner, 1997); further, in this instance, the opportunities were indeed "communally and relationally constituted" (Cajaiba-Santana, 2010, p. 96). The key players during the opportunity recognition phase identified the social problem, shared the same with others within the network, were very socially aware, and displayed an entrepreneurial mind-set (Żur, 2015).

Assessment and Innovation

Initially, it proved difficult to convince stakeholders about the necessity for this particular type of service. To provide evidence of the necessity for street children to access this type of support, a participatory study was conducted in which street children surveyed their peers through pictograms. They were also taught how to analyze the collected data and present it in an effort to advocate for children's rights. During several dialogues with the children, it became apparent and was decided that the Department of Telecommunications should be approached. As India had ratified the UN Convention on the Rights of the Child (UNCRC) in 1990, the director and vice chancellor of TISS, Armaity S. Desai, wrote a letter to the Department of Telecommunications (Maharashtra Telephone Nigam Limited) to argue that the department was obliged to provide a toll-free number for children as part of India's commitment to protecting children's rights under the UNCRC. After a year, this resulted in the toll-free number 1098 designated for vulnerable children, initially within Mumbai.

Network and Collective Impact

The results of the participatory study also indicated that the support needs of the street children were too widespread for just one organization to address. A young person suggested involving organizations and individuals in Mumbai who already worked to support street children. These organizations were mapped by students from TISS and were approached to join the network, which would form the initial Childline. The resulting initial network consisted of an academic organization (the Department of Family and Child Welfare at TISS), NGOs working with children, other networks, and the children themselves. In 1996, the social entrepreneurship venture Childline India was launched in Mumbai. As Tan (2012) has recommended, social workers of the future need to be social visionaries with an entrepreneurial spirit to create a better world for all. Undoubtedly, social workers and the TISS academic community were visionaries in designing the cross-sector alliance that helped with addressing a highly complex social problem by creating social impact (Bahar, 2017).

The social entrepreneurship process involves mobilizing partners and stakeholders from various sectors to address a social cause (Leadbeater, 1997). The social entrepreneur acts as a bridge or a tie between various players in a network and also between networks. Involving beneficiaries in the network greatly enhances their well-being and also the social entrepreneur's ability to cocreate sustainable solutions (Hervieux & Turcotte, 2010). In Mumbai, social innovation and entrepreneurship occurred within a network of a plethora of actors and institutions working collaboratively (Rao-Nicholson, Vorley, & Kahn, 2017).

Growth and Challenges

After Childline India was launched and began its growth trajectory, the resources and services at hand soon became insufficient to sustain the growth. Apart from the small set of organizations that formed the initial core network, no new organizations volunteered to support Childline. For Childline to continue, key personnel from TISS advocated to the Ministry of Social Justice and Empowerment to support and assume responsibility for Childline. In June 1998, the Ministry of Social Justice and Empowerment organized a workshop to determine the need for a national phone service for children. It was decided that the ministry would support the replication of Childline in phases.

Childline adopted a multisectoral approach to networking and partnerships. Children and young people with experience living on the streets would raise awareness and provide peer-to-peer support. Organizations and agencies working with children were able to provide professional knowledge and resources. However, because children come into contact with a range of different agencies in society, a broader approach was deemed necessary to improve the lives of vulnerable children. This multisectoral approach was referred to as "allied systems" and included the police, health care agencies, the juvenile justice system, the educational system, the transport system, the labor system, and elected representatives of the community (Childline India Foundation, 2001). Each of these systems would have a clearly defined role but share the vision and mission of Childline. The allied systems also included the corporate sector and media. The approach to the corporate sector was to build partnerships rather than donor relations, making sure the corporate world acknowledged and understood the importance of children's rights (Childline India Foundation, 2002). Partnering with the media was also an important approach in terms of reaching out to children, raising awareness, and advocating for the rights of children. In 2001, the successful working model of Childline India was ready to be shared.

> Social work [was] in a unique position to share its professional and scientific wisdom and inform social innovation. Considering social innovation usually entails involvement of multiple stakeholders and key players from different disciplines, social work [in this situation played] a pivotal role as mediator in bringing all parties to the table to develop the best solutions. (Bahar, 2017, p. 133)

Childline expanded to other cities and districts through a social franchise model with partnership at its core. Interprofessional and interorganizational collaboration and advocacy were important social work skills that were apparent and used at this stage (Council on Social Work Education, 2015), as was the value of promoting social justice. The networking and mobilizing strategies often used by social entrepreneurs (Leadbeater, 1997) were also evident at this stage of growth and scaling.

Concept of Child Helpline

For readers unfamiliar with the concept, a child helpline is an organization that offers support and advice through phone services, digital means, drop boxes in schools, postal services, radio, and mobile outreach. In countries where child protection systems are more fragile, child helplines can provide services such as shelter, education, and legal services. A child helpline should be toll-free, have a short number that is easy to remember, and stay open around the clock. Child helplines fulfill a child's fundamental right to be heard. Through data collected on contacts, child helplines can help to reveal trends on issues facing children and young people. It is important to realize that many child helplines, in particular in developing countries, have not received much academic attention. By writing this chapter, particularly for a social work entrepreneurship audience, I hope to inspire academicians and social work practitioners to effectively use these repositories of data—coming directly from millions of children all over the world—for research and for innovative solutions.

Child Helpline International: Scaling for Social Justice

In August 2001, Childline India Foundation organized the International Consultation for Child Helplines in Pune, in partnership with the Government of India and Childline UK. The event was supported by Ashoka Innovators for the Public, the British High Commission, the International Forum for Child Welfare, Plan International, Save the Children UK, and UNICEF (Childline India Foundation, 2002). Representatives from child helplines discussed the need for a "help desk" to support existing child helplines and establish new ones. It was evident through networking that there was an ever-increasing need for the development of child helplines. As a social work entrepreneur, I was asked to take on strategic planning and consensus building among the helplines, which resulted in the birth of Child Helpline International—officially launched during an international consultation in Amsterdam in 2003. In 2004, Child Helpline International, a nonprofit collective impact organization, had 46 members; in 2017, it had 181 members in 147 countries. In its first year of operation, there was a steep increase in membership requests from child helplines in developing countries, contradicting the notion that child helplines were a service predominantly for industrial countries (Child Helpline International, 2004).

As the NASW (2017) *Code of Ethics* states, "Social workers promote social justice and social change with and on behalf of clients" (p. 1). Furthermore, social workers' primary goals are to address needs and social problems, while preserving the dignity and worth of individuals (NASW, 2017). These values were exemplified by members of Child Helpline International, which adopted a bottom-up approach to decision making. Members would be involved in decisions, and the organization would act on the needs of children as expressed via child helplines. Principles of community organizing and planning were clearly used; these included balancing process and product of organizing and planning, utilizing the complex values displayed during organizing in a sociopolitical context, making a case, knowing who holds different types of power, and recognizing and responding to opposition to change (Mizrahi, 2014).

The initial strategic goals included establishing child helplines in each part of the world, providing knowledge sharing and support for child helplines, establishing minimum quality standards for child helplines, partnering with the telecommunications sector, and collecting annual data to advocate for children's rights. The strategic goals were all under the umbrella of reaching out to the maximum number of vulnerable children and young people possible. The collective expertise of the Child Helpline International members in starting and scaling up child helplines also led to collaborations with NGOs to start child helplines in a range of developing countries. These scaling efforts not only resonate with social work values but also with social work competencies related to intervening with organizations and communities, locally, nationally, and internationally for advancing human rights (Council on Social Work Education, 2015; NASW, 2017).

Scaling Process and Trends

Child Helpline International works with stakeholders and partners at local, regional, and national levels to ensure that all children in all countries have access to a national, toll-free child helpline that is open around the clock (Child Helpline International, 2016). Child Helpline International arranges international and regional consultations for child helplines and peer exchanges, offers opportunities for capacity building and training, provides support and advice for child helplines, and monitors standards for child helplines globally. Child Helpline International also annually collects and analyzes data from the member child helplines, providing statistics on the number of calls, reasons why children call, and case studies.

Between 2004 and 2014, members of Child Helpline International received over 126 million contacts from children, young people, and concerned adults (Child Helpline International, 2014b). However, only 41 million of these contacts were answered, largely owing to a lack of financial and human resources. The greatest number of contacts were received in Europe (46 percent), followed by Asia Pacific (31 percent), Africa (14 percent), the Americas and Caribbean (7 percent), and the Middle East and North Africa (MENA) (2 percent). Most of the children who contact child helplines are between the ages of 10 and 18 years and usually do so via telephone, even though digital forms of communications have become increasingly common.

Globally, the top four reasons to contact a child helpline are abuse and violence (17 percent), peer relationships (17 percent), psychosocial and mental health (16 percent), and family relationships (15 percent). Other reasons include sexuality and sexual awareness (13 percent); school-related issues (6 percent); issues related to homelessness, runaways, and basic needs (5 percent); physical health (3 percent); legal matters (3 percent); substance use and abuse (2 percent); commercial exploitation (1 percent); issues related to HIV/AIDS-infected or HIV/AIDS-affected children (1 percent); and discrimination (1 percent) (Child Helpline International, 2014b). Through the global child helpline data, trends can be distinguished. For example, immediate or extended family members commit 50 percent of all abuse and violence cases reported. There has been a steep rise in calls about child custody and child support and about teachers committing a large number of abuse and violence transgressions in schools. It may surprise some readers to learn that there has been a large increase in contacts regarding issues related to psychosocial and mental health in countries with a high human development index (HDI). The HDI is a composite index of a country's average life expectancy, education levels, and per capita income (United Nations Development Programme, 2016).

Relationships, Collaborations, and Advocacy for Global Scaling

Building and maintaining human relationships with stakeholders, complementary organizations and institutions, and community groups is a significant social work management competency (Hassen & Wimpfheimer, 2015). Building these relationships can strengthen social capital, which can be leveraged to coproduce solutions for endemic social problems (Gittell & Vidal, 1998). An NASW policy statement for social workers in the child welfare system encourages the funding of programs that prevent child maltreatment and also the integration of programs and funding streams to maximize collaborations between different systems, such as child welfare, domestic violence, substance abuse, and public health, to name a few (NASW, n.d.). The NASW (2017) *Code of Ethics* encourages social workers to advocate for resources that effectively meet their clients' needs. These competencies, principles for advocacy, and values are evident in the scaling of Child Helpline International.

Just as Childline India brokered a partnership with the Department of Telecommunications, Child Helpline International had to approach similar international actors. These included the International Telecommunications Union and several international actors in the private sector, the United Nations, and the Committee on the Rights of Child.

Partnership with International Telecommunications Union

At the International Consultation in 2003, the member child helplines drafted a letter to the International Telecommunications Union (ITU), requesting its support for child helplines. In 2004, Child Helpline International identified that there was little focus on children in the ITU Draft Declaration of Principles and Plan of Action and presented recommendations to include children and child helplines. In the following years, Child Helpline International attended several large-scale meetings within the context of ITU, such as the World Telecommunication Development Conference (WTDC) and the World Summit on the Information Society, to advocate for the allocation of a short, toll-free number for child helplines. The advocacy efforts were reflected in the Tunis Agenda and Tunis Commitment of 2005.

That same year, a memorandum of understanding was signed to explore the opportunities to build a global network of child helplines and promote children's access to information and communication technology (ICT). Most significantly, the Dutch delegation at the WTDC, which included representatives from Child Helpline International, presented Resolution 38, which for the first time would enable the ITU to provide funds for children's programs. Child Helpline International joined an ITU study group that sought to discuss the potential of one global number for child helplines, an idea that was dismissed a few years later in favor of regionally harmonized numbers. The partnership with the ITU anchored the cause of Child Helpline International within the United Nations, which facilitated advocacy efforts for local child helplines with their local providers and governments. The NASW (2017) *Code of Ethics* strongly encourages social workers to advocate for changes in policy and legislation to improve social and environmental conditions to promote social justice. In the case of Child Helpline International, social work entrepreneurs continuously initiated or participated in policy advocacy and policy entrepreneurship efforts on behalf of vulnerable children. Policy entrepreneurs were catalysts and drivers of policy change processes (Mintrom & Norman, 2009).

Partnerships with the Private Sector

Simultaneously, Child Helpline International has cultivated relationships with the private ICT sector. Before the start of Child Helpline International, some child helplines already had working relationships with telecom providers, so it was relevant to identify relationships that already existed and build on these to reach consensus on a regional and international level. In 2014, through the Free Our Voices campaign, Child Helpline International succeeded in signing a memorandum of understanding with the Global System Mobile Association (GSMA) that was endorsed by 25 mobile operators connected to GSMA. Child Helpline International and GSMA are now working together to advocate for mobile operators to support or extend children's confidential access to child helplines toll-free around the clock (GSMA, 2015). GSMA's recommendations to its members is to waive costs for both children and child helplines, raise awareness, help with analysis of future use of technology, and promote knowledge exchange to make sure technology is safe for children.

Relationship with the United Nations

In 2004, Child Helpline International collaborated with the United Nations Study on Violence Against Children (UNVAC) (United Nations Office of the High Commissioner on Human Rights, n.d.). The member child helplines attended regional sessions to submit and discuss data contributions for the study. The results of the study were published in 2006 and contained recommendations to all member states to have child helplines as part of their child protection system. Since then, Child Helpline International has published an annual report on violence against children based on child helpline data and developed a working relationship with the UN special representative of the secretary general on violence against children, Marta Santos Pais (she is now a special adviser to the Child Helpline International's Advisory Board). Pais (2010) has on several occasions highlighted the importance of child helplines in eradicating violence against children. In 2014, the UN Global Survey on Violence Against Children was launched, and child helplines were described as an important support mechanism for young people in crisis. The partnership with UNVAC has been significant in establishing the status of child helplines within child protection systems.

Advocacy of the Committee on the Rights of the Child

The Committee on the Rights of the Child (CRC, 2006) monitors the implementation of the UNCRC in nations that have ratified the convention. Apart from the reports from respective governments, civil society organizations can also submit alternative reports. This monitoring process results in Concluding Observations, which contain the committee's concerns and recommendations. At the first International Consultation of Child Helplines, the members of Child Helpline International drafted a letter to the CRC and the ITU, which urged them to recognize child helplines as an integral part of child protection systems. By invitation from Child Helpline International, the then-chair of the CRC committee, Jaap Doek, visited Childline India to understand how child helplines protect and support children. This resulted in a recommendation from Doek to the CRC to promote children's access to a child helpline.

As a result of the advocacy work, Child Helpline International and its members started to submit alternative reports about child helplines and child protection. A review of this work was done in 2014, showing that the UN Committee on the Rights of the Child mentioned child helplines in 90 out of 129 Concluding Observations (Child Helpline International, 2014a). The review indicated that it was more likely for a country to establish or scale up a child helpline if this was explicitly mentioned in the Concluding Observations. It is hard to establish the exact impact the alternative reports created by Child Helpline International had on the UN committee's suggestion, but before 2004 there was no organization specifically targeting the development of this child protection mechanism, and it was an insignificant item on the global agenda. These efforts speak to the ethical principles of service and social justice that guide social workers (NASW, 2017).

Impact of Child Helpline International

This international social entrepreneurial venture, based on extensive networks and collaborations, has benefited not only the street children and other vulnerable groups of children directly but also service providers and academicians. It has added to a network of data collection on a population segment that is hard to locate, and it has assisted with the passage of an international resolution to protect the exploitation of children online.

Social entrepreneurs create social value through the social changes they initiate and implement (Nicholls, 2006). Child Helpline International has had widespread social impact as evidenced by the social change it has created globally. Specifically, the helpline network has affected the way stakeholders in different societies across the world engage with, and respond to, the issue of child maltreatment and protection. Child helplines refer children to other services, inform them about their rights, guide them through child protection systems, and initiate policies to address their needs. Using their social capital, helplines are building a solution that adds social value in terms of creating a positive impact on children, caregivers, and community members alike (Acs, Boardman, & McNeely, 2011). The social value of protecting children from violence was the driving force behind this venture, which was scaled internationally to benefit communities across cultures and continents. The network of helplines is an innovative way to address the problem of violence against children, and by being effective and sustainable, it has created social value in communities across the world (Auerswald, 2009). More practical examples of added social value and social impact will be illustrated in the following sections.

Data and Violence

Eradicating violence against children is a top priority for the global collective of child helplines, but there is still a long way to go. According to the World Health Organization (2014) *Global Status Report on Violence Prevention*, there are large gaps in data regarding nonfatal violence affecting children, which undermines violence prevention efforts. Most instances of violence against children do not come to the attention of authorities and service providers, and only half of the 133 countries surveyed reported conducting population-based surveys on child maltreatment, gang violence, and youths. Child helpline data collection therefore is essential in preventing and eradicating violence against children.

ICT Sector and Child Online Protection

An unforeseen positive outcome of the aforementioned partnerships was the development of joint efforts in protecting children online—an issue that is growing in prevalence and relevance internationally. At the International Consultation of Child Helplines 2008 in Jordan, the topic of children at risk online was discussed, as calls about this had started to reach the child helplines. A trend could be detected, and Child Helpline International joined ITU's child online protection initiative (COPI) in 2009. In 2014, ITU Resolution 67 included child helplines as actors in protecting children online. As a result of the engagement with COPI, representatives of Child Helpline International were invited to speak at the First African Child Online Protection summit. In 2016, ITU and Child Helpline International launched the campaign "Partnering to Protect Children and Youth," which aims to showcase how ITU member states, regulators, industry, and academia are strengthening the work of national child helplines, while fostering awareness and collaboration on Child Online Protection (ITU, 2016).

The same year, Child Helpline International and GSMA organized a multisectoral workshop in London on the role of child helplines and the way different actors can support each other in protecting children online. This resulted in a series of publications on how to tackle child online exploitation. The work on protecting children online continued when 25 child helplines from Child Helpline International and UNICEF Global joined a partnership called Leadership in Empowering and Activating Child Helplines to Protect Children Online, as part of the global #WeProtect program. The project sought to map the knowledge and capacity of child helplines to respond to issues on child online protection and support the development of this capacity. In the MENA region, Zain Group in partnership with Child Helpline International ran a media campaign across eight markets to raise awareness of the negative effects of child abuse, including television and print advertisements and in social media.

Two regional examples from Child Helpline International members demonstrate the regional impact. The first is the launch of child helplines in the MENA region as there were no child helpline services there before the founding of

Child Helpline International; and the second is the development of child help-lines in Europe, the progress and outcomes of which have been evaluated.

Development of Child Helplines in MENA

In 2016, mobile operator Zain Group ran a media campaign across its markets in the MENA region to raise awareness of the negative effects of child abuse. It also presented several child protection initiatives and highlighted the role of ICT in supporting child helplines. This exemplifies the success of the development of child helplines in the MENA region, where there were no child helplines when Child Helpline International was founded. Today, Child Helpline International has 20 child helpline members in 16 countries in the MENA region (https://www.childhelplineinternational.org/child-help lines/child-helpline-network/). This development started in 2003, when representatives from Jordan attended the International Consultation for Child Helplines in Amsterdam.

Child Helpline International then joined a partnership with UNICEF to establish child helplines in the region. Building on existing relations with Jordan since the International Consultation, Child Helpline International was invited by UNICEF to speak about the role of child helplines in preventing child abuse and child trafficking at the first Arab International Society for the Prevention of Child Abuse and Neglect conference, held in Jordan in 2006. In addition to representation from the Jordan River Foundation, interest in starting a child helpline was expressed by Yemen, Syria, Lebanon, Egypt, and Palestine.

In 2006, Child Helpline International received a grant from the Arab Gulf Programme for United Nations Development Organizations to support the start of child helplines in the MENA region. In 2007, the Ministry of Social Affairs from Saudi Arabia visited the Swiss member child helpline, as part of the planning process to start a child helpline in Saudi Arabia. The UK Muslim Youth Helpline hosted the Social Support Centre team working in Abu Dhabi, United Arab Emirates, to help the latter gain the necessary knowledge needed to establish a child helpline.

As part of the work to establish child helplines in the MENA region, the 2008 International Consultation for child helplines was held in Jordan. Among other things, this resulted in important partnerships with the League of Arab States, UNICEF MENA, and the MENA Child Protection Initiative. As a result of the partnership with the League of Arab States, Child Helpline International was invited to make a presentation at the Child Rights Committee at the League of Arab States in 2012. Between 2006 and 2011, Child Helpline International also sent alternative reports to the UN Committee on the Rights of the Child regarding other countries in the region. For example, Oman and Lebanon established child helplines one to two years after the recommendation in the Concluding Observations (Secretariat General of the League of Arab States, 2013).

In 2009, the first workshop on child helplines in conflict zones was held in Jordan. This was the start of Child Helpline International's engagement in providing support for children on the move, and subsequent years Child Helpline International had a working relationship with the UN special representative for children in armed conflict and launched a manual for child helplines in emergencies. In 2013, Child Helpline International supported the member helpline in Iraqi Kurdistan to reach out to Syrian refugees to provide information about child-friendly spaces and child protection centers in refugee camps. An additional goal was to provide information to parents and to offer psychosocial support to parents and children. In 2015, Child Helpline International obtained observer status at the International Organization for Migration, which enables further international advocacy efforts in supporting children and parents on the move.

Child Helpline International's work in the MENA region was also recognized in the Comparative Arab Report on Implementing the Recommendations of the UNVAC (United Nations Office of the High Commissioner on Human Rights, n.d.), in which an entire chapter was dedicated to the status and benefits of child helplines in the region. This report notes that child protection systems in most of the Arab states are incomplete and poorly supported financially, in addition to suffering a lack of standardized responses to rights violations. Raising the level of reporting of violence by children and adults is a key strategy in an attempt to raise the efficacy of protection (Secretariat General of the League of Arab States, 2013). The work of strengthening child helplines in the MENA region continues, in particular with a focus on running child helplines in conflict areas.

Development of Child Helplines in Europe

In Europe, several child helplines were already established at the time Child Helpline International first launched. More than half of the original child helpline members were European. Rather than establishing new child helplines, the European challenge was to improve the scope and capacity of existing ones and ensure that children's voices were included in European policy. To do this, it was essential to join networks that advocated for the inclusion of children in European Union policy and to gain access to the European Parliament to advocate for these issues. In 2004, Child Helpline International joined the European Children's Network EURONET to work for the inclusion of children in EU policy. In 2005, Child Helpline International met with Member of European Parliament (MEP) Lissy Gröner to advocate for the support of child helplines. The same year, MEP Gröner tabled a declaration in support of child helplines (European Parliament, 2005). The declaration urged the European Union to support toll-free child helplines as an essential part of child protection systems and to involve children's rights organizations in the development of EU policy. With support from Child Helpline International, the European child helplines mobilized and contacted their local MEPs to urge them to sign the declaration. The declaration was subsequently accepted, forming a building block for many of the developments that followed. Child Helpline International gained a grant from the European Commission to create a European identity for child helplines in the European Union.

The Implementation of the 116 111 Number

Social work values encourage practitioners to regularly monitor and evaluate policies, implementation of programs, and interventions (NASW, 2017). At the 2006 International Consultation of Child Helplines in Stockholm, Sweden, European child helplines decided to apply for a uniform number for all child helplines: 116 111. This was agreed to by the European Parliament and was also reiterated by the ITU. Between 2006 and 2016, almost all members of the European Union started using the 116 111 number. In 2017, Suffolk University conducted a study commissioned by Child Helpline International (2017) to explore awareness of child helplines and the 116 111 number among children, general population, national stakeholders, and European stakeholders. The study indicated that just over half of children and young people were aware of the existence of child helplines, but that the 116 111 number was less known. However, there had been an increase in awareness of the services provided by 116 111 between 2015 and 2017. One may infer a correlation between increased awareness and the awareness-raising campaign coordinated by Child Helpline International through the member child helplines. In addition, the results of the study suggested that child helplines are a safe entry point into child protection systems. Furthermore, the results suggested that the function of child helplines is to refer children to other services, guide children through child protection systems, inform children of their rights, highlight gaps in child protection, and support policy making through data on children's needs

Conclusion

Child helplines were not a noteworthy item on the global children's rights agenda before Child Helpline International. The social entrepreneurial model of Childline India was successfully scaled and applied to an international context. What is remarkable is that the director of TISS and the founder of

Childline India are both social workers who used the entire repertoire of social work competencies—micro, mezzo, and macro—to create a safe environment for street children and continue advocating on their behalf from local to international levels. They were true to the principles of community organizing, in that they engaged the street children actively and regularly to understand their challenges and also to help design the sustainable innovative solution of Childline India. Subsequently, Child Helpline International was created to address the needs and concerns of employees and volunteers at child helplines. From this case of social entrepreneurship venture, it is unmistakably evident that for a successful and sustainable venture, beneficiaries and target groups should be actively engaged in formulating the issue and shaping the solution(s). Further, for the venture to continue its relevance, their participation must be continuous. Finally, beneficiaries must be included in the supervision structure of the organization. These significant principles underlying the success of social entrepreneurship ventures also align with community organizing, planning, and development principles in social work (Nandan, London, & Blum, 2014).

The focus of Child Helpline International was to build a network and engage relevant stakeholders—such as the United Nations, Facebook, Google, and the telecom sector—that could legitimize the practice of child helplines as part of a multisectoral child protection system. It is through these partnerships with the private and public sectors that capacity is being built for child helplines, and helplines are now on global children's rights agendas.

Measuring the impact of social entrepreneurships is difficult, and measuring the impact of global advocacy and brokered partnerships is even more so. However, by recording the chronological events in the form of meetings, conferences, campaigns, and collaborations, a picture will emerge. There are more child helplines today than ever before, more child helplines have toll-free numbers, and child helplines have more extended opening times to be available to more children. As mentioned, eradicating violence against children is a top priority for the global collective of child helplines, but there is still a long way to go as there are large gaps in data. As a social work entrepreneur, I will unceasingly use all the social work competencies, values, and social entrepreneurship processes for perpetually expanding the scope of Child Helpline International.

References

Acs, Z. J., Boardman, M. C., & McNeely, C. L. (2011). *The social value of productive entrepreneurship* (GMU School of Public Policy Research Paper No. 2011-08). Retrieved from https://papers.ssrn.com/sol3/papers.cfm?abstract_id=1725947

Auerswald, P. (2009, Spring). *Nonprofits: Creating social value.* Retrieved from https://ssir.org/articles/entry/creating_social_value

Bahar, O. S. (2017). A promising partnership: Uncovering the middle ground between social innovation and social work: Response to Dr. Marylin L. Flynn's remarks. *Research on Social Work Practice, 27,* 131–133. doi:10.1177/1049731516658769

Cajaiba-Santana, G. (2010). Socially constructed opportunities in social entrepreneurship: A structuration model. In A. Fayolle & H. Matlay (Eds.), *Handbook of research on social entrepreneurship* (pp. 88–106). Northampton, MA: Edward Elgar.

Child Helpline International. (2004). *Connecting to children: A compilation of child helpline data* (3rd ed.). Retrieved from http://www.childrenatrisk.eu/blog/connecting-to-children-a-compilation-of-child-helpline-data-third-edition-2004-data/

Child Helpline International. (2014a). *Child Helpline International and the Committee on the Rights of the Child.* Retrieved from https://www.childhelplineinternational.org/child-helplines/tools/child-helpline-international-committee-rights-child/

Child Helpline International. (2014b). *Rewind: Voices of children and young people 2003–2013.* Retrieved from https://resourcecentre.savethechildren.net/sites/default/files/documents/chi_global_web_final1.pdf

Child Helpline International. (2016). *Annual report 2015.* Retrieved from https://www.childhelplineinternational.org/wp-content/uploads/2017/04/child_helpline_international-annual-report-2015.pdf

Child Helpline International. (2017). *Awareness of the 116 111 Child Helpline number: A report on the findings of an evaluation in five European countries.* Retrieved from https://www.childhelplineinternational.org/data-overview/publications/awareness-116-111-child-helpline-number/

Childline India Foundation. (2001). *Listening to children: An overview to Childline.* Retrieved from https://childlineindia.org.in/pdf/Listening-To-Children.pdf

Childline India Foundation. (2002). *Cross connections: The partnership model of Childline India.* Retrieved from https://www.childlineindia.org.in/pdf/Cross-Connections.pdf

Committee on the Rights of the Child. (2006). *Concluding observations: Oman.* Retrieved from http://tbinternet.ohchr.org/_layouts/treatybodyexternal/Download.aspx?symbolno=CRC%2fC%2fOMN%2fCO%2f2&Lang=en

Council on Social Work Education. (2015). *Educational policy and accreditation standards for baccalaureate and master's social work programs.* Retrieved from https://www.cswe.org/getattachment/Accreditation/Accreditation-Process/2015-EPAS/2015EPAS_Web_FINAL.pdf.aspx

de Benitez, S. T. (Ed.) (2007). *State of the world's street children: Violence.* London: Consortium for Street Children. Retrieved from https://www.streetchildren.org/resources/state-of-the-worlds-street-children-violence/

Dressler, A. (2007). Foreword. In S. T. de Benitez (Ed.), *State of the world's street children: Violence* (pp. vi–ix). London: Consortium for Street Children.

European Parliament. *Written Declaration 0050/2005 on Child Helplines in Europe.* (2005). Retrieved from http://www.europarl.europa.eu/sides/getDoc.do? pubRef=%2f%2fEP%2f%2fNONSGML%2bWDECL%2bP6-DCL-2005-00 50%2b0%2bDOC%2bPDF%2bV0%2f%2fEN

Glauser, B. (2015). Street children: Deconstructing a construct. In J. Allison & A. Prout (Eds.), *Constructing and reconstructing childhood: Contemporary issues in the sociological study of childhood* (pp. 141–157). New York: Routledge.

Gittell, R., & Vidal, A. (1998). *Community organizing: Building social capital as a development strategy.* Thousand Oaks, CA: Sage Publications.

Global System Mobile Association. (2015). *Child Helpline and mobile operators: Working together to protect children's rights: A practical guide.* Retrieved from https://www.gsma.com/publicpolicy/child-helplines-mobile-operators-working-together-protect-childrens-rights

Hassan, A., & Wimpfheimer, S. (2015). *Human services management competencies: Guidebook for human services professionals.* Retrieved from https://socialwork manager.org/wp-content/uploads/2016/01/Competency-Brochure-4-19-15-With-Forms.pdf

Hervieux, C., & Turcotte, M. B. (2010) Social entrepreneurs' actions in networks. In A. Fayolle & H. Matlay (Eds.), *Handbook of research on social entrepreneurship* (pp. 182–200). Northampton, MA: Edward Elgar.

International Telecommunication Union. (2016, May). [Press release]. Retrieved from http://www.itu.int/net/pressoffice/pressreleases/2016/CM06.aspx#.Wc F1TmCzIU

Leadbeater, C. (1997). *The rise of the social entrepreneur.* London: Demos.

Mathur, M., Rathore, P., & Mathur, M. (2009). Incidence, type and intensity of abuse in street children in India. *Child Abuse and Neglect, 33,* 907–913. doi:10.1016/j.chiabu.2009.01.003

McKendall, M. A., & Wagner, J. A. (1997). Motive, opportunity, choice and corporate illegality. *Organization Science, 8,* 624–647.

Mintrom, M., & Norman, P. (2009). Policy entrepreneurship and policy change. *Policy Studies Journal, 37,* 649–667. doi:10.1111/j.1541-0072.2009.00329.x

Mizrahi, T. (2014). Community organizing principles and practice guidelines. In K. Corcoran & A. R. Roberts (Eds.), *Social workers' desk reference* (3rd ed., pp. 894–906). New York: Oxford University Press.

Nandan, M., London, M., & Blum, T. (2014). Community practice social entrepreneurship: An interdisciplinary approach to graduate education. *International Journal of Social Entrepreneurship and Innovation, 3*(1), 51–70.

National Association of Social Workers. (2017). *Code of ethics of the National Association of Social Workers.* Washington, DC: Author.

National Association of Social Workers. (n.d.). *Social work & child abuse and neglect*. Retrieved from https://www.socialworkers.org/LinkClick.aspx?file ticket=W13Tn7j7O1A%3d&portalid=0

Nicholls, A. (Ed.). (2006). *Social entrepreneurship: New models of sustainable change*. New York: Oxford University Press.

Pais, M. S. (2010, November 7). Marta Santos País greets participants of fifth CHI International Consultation [Video file]. Retrieved from https://www .youtube.com/watch?v=h56u1y8HzoI

Rao-Nicholson, R., Vorley, T., & Khan, Z. (2017). Social innovation in emerging economies: A national systems of innovation-based approach. *Technological Forecasting & Social Change, 121*, 228–237. doi:10.1016/j.techfore.2017.03.013

Robbins, S. P. (2013). From the editor: Navigating change, transitions, and uncertainty. *Journal of Social Work Education, 49*, 1–3. doi:10.1080/10437797.2013. 761094

Secretariat General of the League of Arab States. (2013). *The comparative report on implementing the recommendations of the UN Secretary General's study on violence against children*. Retrieved from http://srsg.violenceagainstchildren .org/document/_934

Tan, N. T. (2012). Social entrepreneurship: Challenge for social work in a changing world. *Asia Pacific Journal of Social Work and Development, 14*, 87–98. doi:10.1080/21650993.2004.9755956

United Nations Development Programme. (2016). *Human development report 2016*. Retrieved from http://hdr.undp.org/en/2016-report

United Nations Office for Drug Control and Crime Prevention. (n.d.). *Rapid situation assessment of street children in Cairo & Alexandria*. Retrieved from https:// www.unodc.org/documents/egypt/egypt_street_children_report.pdf

United Nations Office of the High Commissioner on Human Rights. (n.d.). *United Nations Study on Violence Against Children*. Retrieved from http:// srsg.violenceagainstchildren.org/un_study

World Health Organization. (2014). *Global status report on violence prevention*. Retrieved from http://www.who.int/violence_injury_prevention/violence/ status_report/2014/en/

Żur, A. (2015). Social problems as sources of opportunity: Antecedents of social entrepreneurship opportunities. *Entrepreneurial Business and Economics Review, 3*(4), 73–87. doi:10.15678/EBER.2015.030405

7

Community Development, Empowerment, and Social Entrepreneurship by "Thankyou": An Australian Example

Manohar Pawar

This chapter is about Thankyou, a social entrepreneurship organization founded by Daniel Flynn, Jarryd Burns, and Justine Flynn in 2008. First, the chapter describes the social problem of global poverty and associated issues, such as water crises and child and maternal health, that the Thankyou social entrepreneurship venture (SEV) is addressing, as well as the rationale behind its work. Second, the chapter details approaches followed by Thankyou to address the issue of global poverty. Third, I delineate how this SEV relates to social work practice at the micro, mezzo, and macro levels. Finally, in the concluding section, I discuss Thankyou's social impact and value creation, some of the challenges experienced by the organization, and opportunities for scaling up. This chapter argues that social work has a great potential to contribute to the practice of social entrepreneurship.

Global Poverty, Water, and Food Insecurity

The main aim of Thankyou is to address the issue of global poverty, though it started with the agenda of contributing to reducing the world water crisis. Despite the significant global decline in the poverty rate, poverty still persists in various forms and degrees in almost all countries (Pawar, 2017). It is a complex and challenging issue, but many individuals and organizations demonstrate optimism that poverty can be made history. It is exciting to note that efforts are being made across the globe to address such endemic issues.

Poverty is defined and understood from several perspectives in terms of degree, ranging from absolute to relative; income; calorie intake; material consumption; rural or urban location; basic needs; capability; and overall standard of living or quality of life (Cox & Pawar, 2013). Poverty is multidimensional in nature, and these perspectives are interconnected. For example, the World Bank, in its review of global poverty, stated that people

> often lack adequate food and shelter, education and health, these deprivations that keep them from leading the kind of life that everyone values. They also face extreme vulnerability to ill health, economic dislocation, and natural disasters. Moreover, they are often exposed to ill treatment by institutions of the state and society and are powerless to influence key decisions affecting their lives. (World Bank, 2000–2001, p. 1)

From the income perspective, "A person is poor if, and only if, [their] income level is below the defined poverty line. . . . Often the cut-off poverty line is defined in terms of having enough income for a specified amount of food" (United Nations Development Programme [UNDP], 1997, p. 16). According to the UNDP, the most common way of defining poverty is the concept of a basket of food required for survival and the cost of that basket in a specific context measured against prevailing income levels. People require more than food in a relative sense, but food is the basic requirement for everyone, and people should have a necessary income or resources to meet such basic need. Perhaps, that is why poverty has to have a human rights connotation. Based on income and using 2011 purchasing power parity, the international poverty line is currently defined as $1.90 per person per day.

From the capability perspective, the UNDP stated that

> poverty represents the absence of some basic capabilities to function—a person lacking the opportunity to achieve some minimally acceptable levels of these functionings. . . . The capability approach reconciles the notions of absolute and relative poverty, since relative deprivation in incomes and commodities can lead to an absolute deprivation in minimum capacities. (1997, p. 16; see also Sen, 2001)

The minimum capacity to earn an income and access healthy food, education, and health services to lead a self-reliant life is essential for everyone, but most people living in poverty lack such capacity. From this perspective, being employed does not make a person financially self-sufficient.

Using the aforementioned international poverty line as its benchmark, the United Nations Statistical Division (UNSD) reported that an estimated 767 million people lived in poverty in 2013, down from 1.7 billion people in 1999. These figures demonstrate that the global poverty rate has declined from 28 percent in 1999 to 11 percent in 2013. Although this is significant and encouraging progress, poverty levels sharply differ from one region to another and one country to another. For example, in 2013, only 3 percent of people lived in extreme poverty in Eastern and Southeastern Asia, which is a huge reduction from 35 percent in 1999 (UNSD, 2017). In contrast, in 2013, more than 42 percent of the population continued to live in conditions of extreme poverty in sub-Saharan Africa, where poverty was reduced by only about 15 percent; it was nearly 58 percent in 1999. About half of the world's people living in poverty are in sub-Saharan Africa, nearly one-third in South Asia, and approximately one-fifth in the rest of the world (UNSD, 2017).

Although the "working poor" figure has been reduced by more than half since 2000, unfortunately, about 10 percent of the working poor and their family members lived below the poverty line in 2016 (UNSD, 2017). Young people between the ages of 15 and 24 years are most likely to be included in the working poor category. The highest level of working poor and their families (34 percent) were in sub-Saharan Africa (UNSD, 2017). Several factors can account for and are related to this phenomenon: labor productivity in sub-Saharan Africa is one of the lowest in the world (2.9 percent in 2015); there is a high unemployment rate of women (almost double) compared with men in North Africa; food insecurity is most prevalent in sub-Saharan Africa; more than half of the world's population is not covered by any social protection scheme, and in sub-Saharan Africa this was true of 87 percent of the population. Hence, on most of the Sustainable Development Goals (SDGs), sub-Saharan Africa did not fare well (UNSD, 2017). Without social protection and supports such as quality education, affordable quality health care, and clean water and sanitation, for instance, it is very difficult to fight poverty, particularly for vulnerable groups such as women, children, mothers with newborn babies, people with disabilities, and the elderly.

Closely connected to the poverty issue is a lack of access to safe drinking water and the global water crisis. According to the World Bank Water and Sanitation Program and the International Finance Corporation (2013), about 780 million people lack access to safe water. Neglecting the water needs of the poor costs nations dearly. About 1.8 million children die each year from diarrhea; there is a loss of 443 million school days each year from water-related illnesses; about half of developing countries' populations suffer from ill health caused by water and sanitation deficits; and women often spend several hours daily collecting water (Pawar, 2014). Lack of access to clean and safe water and the scarcity of water are connected to poverty, lower education levels (particularly of girls), child mortality, poor health and sanitation practices and related problems, and natural catastrophes (UNDP, 2006; United Nations Educational, Scientific and Cultural Organization [UNESCO], 2009, 2012).

Another consequence of poverty is food insecurity and malnutrition, which appears to have caused stunted growth (that is, low height for their age) of 155 million children under the age of five in 2016 (UNSD, 2017). Of these, Southern Asia and sub-Saharan Africa accounted for 75 percent of the stunted growth. In 2016, an estimated 52 million children under the age of five worldwide suffered from wasting (that is, low weight for their height). The global wasting rate in 2016 was 7.7 percent, with the highest rate (14.9 percent) in Central and Southern Asia. In 2015, the mortality rate for children under the age of five worldwide was 43 deaths per 1,000 live births, whereas in sub-Saharan Africa, it was 84 deaths per 1,000 live births. The neonatal mortality rate (death in first 28 days of life) in Central and Southern Asia and in sub-Saharan Africa was 29 deaths per 1,000 live births in 2015. It is estimated that about two-fifths of neonatal deaths could be prevented by providing appropriate care for both mother and baby around the time of birth. In 2015, the global maternal mortality ratio was 216 deaths per 100,000 live births (UNSD, 2017).

Global poverty is caused by a combination of several factors. For some, it may be resource-deprived geographic locations, including remote inaccessible areas. For others, these factors may include prevailing economic and market conditions and policies, deep-rooted cultural practices, politics or governance, and a lack of anti-poverty policies and programs. In addition, natural and human-made disasters, conflict and war, and climatic conditions do contribute to poverty. Some population groups are more affected by poverty than others, particularly, women, children, and the elderly; and some minority groups, such as refugees and migrants (Cox & Pawar, 2013), are disproportionately affected by these issues.

Poverty-affected individuals, families, and communities need to be empowered by introducing and implementing effective policies and programs at both global and local levels. Efforts to address the poverty issue have increased globally, particularly since the Social Development Summit in 1995, the United Nations Millennium Development Goals (MDGs) implemented from 2000 to 2015, and the declaration of the SDGs in 2015 (Midgley & Pawar, 2017). Although significant progress was made against some aspects of the MDGs (Pawar, 2017), SDG 1 recommits to ending poverty in all its forms. The fact that 192 countries have endorsed the SDGs suggests that there is a global commitment to seriously addressing the issue of poverty. The recent review (United Nations Department of Economic and Social Affairs [UNDESA], 2017) of SDGs pointed out that the work toward implementing and achieving SDGs is not consistent across the countries and different regions of the world and is also insufficient in many areas. The SDG Business Forum has vowed to step up action to tackle the world's most pressing social, economic, and environmental challenges (UNDESA, 2017).

Against this backdrop and following a brief overview of social entrepreneurship ventures in Australia, the relevance of the Thankyou SEV in addressing certain SDGs—ending poverty and hunger, ensuring healthy lives, combating inequalities within and among countries, and healing and securing the planet—will become apparent.

SEVs in Australia

SEVs have been in existence for a long time, but recently they have been gaining increasing traction, both in the developed and developing worlds. According to Barraket, Mason, and Blain (2016),

> social entrepreneurship ventures are organisations that: are led by an economic, social, cultural, or environmental mission consistent with a public or community benefit; trade to fulfil their mission; derive a substantial portion of their income from trade; and reinvest the majority of their profit/surplus in the fulfilment of their mission. (p. 3)

A recent study (Barraket et al., 2016) estimated that there are at least 20,000 Australian entrepreneurship ventures, and about one-third of them were two to three years old. There are great opportunities as well as constraints for the operation of entrepreneurship ventures. Most of them focus on creating employment opportunities for specific groups and developing innovative solutions to a range of problems; many are local in nature, though some reach out internationally. The majority of SEVs are small, though some are large. Their economic production activities include retail, wholesale, and manufacturing, but about two-thirds of them provide service for a fee. An analysis of the turnover of 189 entrepreneurship ventures showed monetary values ranging from zero to AU$199 million. For SEVs to realize their full potential, new public policy initiatives are needed (Barraket et al., 2016).

Thankyou: A Case Study

Of the many SEVs, I purposively and subjectively selected Thankyou as the subject of this chapter because of its mission and vision of addressing the global issue of poverty, its use of innovative approaches, its cofounders' passion, easy access to data on its Web site and in the publication *Chapter One* (Flynn, 2016), its international outreach and impact, its consistent communication with supporters and customers, and its alliance with social work practice and values as exemplified in the social entrepreneurship process. The chapter is based on a review of data from Flynn (2016) and the Thankyou Web site, and I have identified relevant themes as they pertain to social work practice (Pawar, 2004).

Thankyou's Approaches and Efforts

The genesis of Thankyou can be traced to informal discussions by a small group of friends to start an organization that "would challenge the very fabric of the capitalist global business model" (Flynn, 2016, p. 12). Initially launching from a family garage, Thankyou began its journey in 2008 with a bottled water product in the market to address the world water crisis (Pawar, 2014) by directing 100 percent of its profit to safe drinking projects in developing countries. One of the cofounders, Daniel Flynn (2016), stated:

> Many years ago, I had an idea. What if there was a brand, a collection of consumer goods that could empower consumers and give them a choice between the big multinationals, who exist to profit shareholders, and brand that existed 100 per cent to fund life-changing aid and development programs for people living in extreme poverty? I had never heard of a social entrepreneurship venture that existed 100 per cent for impact (no share holder interest) that had achieved a market leading position. (p. 15)

Later in July 2013, this project was rebranded as Thankyou. At the time of writing, Thankyou had over 50 products available in 5,500 outlets in Australia (including 7-Eleven, Coles, and Woolworths, Australian grocery supermarkets). After excluding expenses, it uses 100 percent of its profits to fund projects that combat poverty and related issues, such as improving access to safe water, food, and hygiene and sanitation services around the world.

The Thankyou Web site (https://Thankyou.co/about) lists 50 staff members on its team, consisting of directors, board members, and the other personnel covering the following areas: finance, accounting, business, marketing, sales, creative design, impact, customer experience, public relations and communications, quality assurance, taste, operations, supply chain and procurement, growth hunting, community building, product development, innovation, and information technology.

It is apparent from Thankyou's (2017) Web site (https://Thankyou.co) and its financial statements (https://Thankyou.co/structure) that its efforts are based on five core impact values. First, it is open for learning and evidence. Admitting to not knowing everything, per the Web site, the SEV is "committed to ongoing learning and development through intentionally collecting evidence that demonstrates long-lasting impact." Second, it believes in empowering communities. It believes that "the communities it serves are the solutions to the issues they face. Its role is to come alongside them, and back their dreams for their own communities. Education and the transfer of skills are therefore at the core of every program it funds." Third, it values people as a "skilled, dedicated and passionate team, which is the greatest determinant of an organization's success. Its impact partners both foster and retain incredible people who live and breathe what they say." Fourth, it believes in the value of the capacity of people and its partners, which have "the internal structure, systems, and capacity to meet its funding requirements." Finally, it believes in complete transparency and trust. It states that to make the impact together, "transparency and trust are fundamental" (Thankyou, 2017).

As a registered charitable trust, Thankyou owns the business. After deducting all the expenses, net profits are deposited with the trust, and a large portion is later distributed to partners for funding projects that are addressing issues of food, water, health, and sanitation around the world. A portion of the net profits are directed toward growth activities of the organization. The organization also receives donations for copies of the book *Chapter One*, which was authored by the cofounder Daniel Flynn (2016). Two additional funding sources include access to social finance with low interest to meet capital costs, as well as direct donations to fund high-risk, high-return new products.

To empower communities and to bring lasting change, Thankyou follows a project-based model that requires partnerships with organizations focusing on the five core impact values stated earlier. In other words, through such non-exclusive partnerships, Thankyou funds specific projects proposed by partners, provided they meet the impact values and criteria. Partners take responsibility for implementing projects on the ground and submit progress reports, which are shared with Thankyou customers through Track Your Impact—an online feature. Each Thankyou product has a unique tracker ID, and customers can use that ID on the Thankyou Web site to identify the projects funded through their purchases (https://Thankyou.co/projects/).

Thankyou's Outreach to Communities

The current project partners listed on the Thankyou Web site include Care, One Heart Worldwide, Oxfam, Splash, the United Nations Children's Fund (UNICEF), and World Vision. Through these partners, Thankyou is reaching seven countries in Africa and 12 countries in Asia and the Pacific Rim (see Table 7.1). As of February 2017, Thankyou had distributed AU$5.5 million and helped to get food to 132,664 people, safe water and sanitation services to 545,360 people, and maternal and child health services to 77,314 people around the world (see Table 7.1).

These projects have been implemented by Thankyou's partners through engagement with local communities across the two continents, to enable empowerment and local development by mobilizing local strengths and assets.

TABLE 7.1 Thankyou Partnered Projects in Different Countries

Number	Country	Nature of Contribution
1	Sudan	In 2015 food assistance to over 56,000 people
2	Ethiopia	Access and availability of safe water, sanitation and hygiene hardware and training
3	Kenya	Since 2011, access to safe water; since 2015, food to prevent malnutrition
4	Uganda	2010–2011, water, sanitation and hygiene
5	Burundi	2013, gravity-fed rainwater harvesting systems
6	Tanzania	Water access, hygiene and sanitation training
7	Zimbabwe	Since 2014, installed and fixed wells, toilets, and hand-washing facilities; focus on improved child and maternal health
8	Bangladesh	Since 2014, water, sanitation and hygiene training
9	India	Since 2013, disaster-resilient solutions in rural areas, water, and sanitation
10	Myanmar	2014–2015, water, sanitation and hygiene training
11	Nepal	2016, child and maternal health in rural areas
12	Sri Lanka	2012, safe water access, hygiene and sanitation training
13	Cambodia	Since 2010, safe water, hygiene education, food security
14	Laos	2014, safe water, sanitation and hygiene training
15	Vietnam	Safe water, sanitation and hygiene training
16	Timor-Leste	Since 2013, gravity-fed water systems, community ownership
17	Papua New Guinea	Safe water, sanitation and hygiene training
18	Vanuatu	2014–2015, safe water storage, repair of affected water catchments
19	Australia	2014, daily meal service to vulnerable groups in Melbourne, youth services

Source: https://Thankyou.co/projects/

SEVs and Social Work Practice

I propose that when an SEV operates according to its vision and mission, it helps to achieve meaningful social and economic objectives for people and their communities, ensuring dignity and respect, without any connotations of charity, sympathy, and dependency. Such a venture's conscientious methods of making, redistributing, and reinvesting profits are in stark contrast with organizations that concentrate capital in the hands of a few. It is important to note that the efforts of such ventures often contribute to social cohesion and strong informal networks, by liberating people from poverty, oppression, and hopelessness. Within the current context of diminishing resources or unwillingness to direct resources to empower people in poverty, an SEV is an innovative pathway and orientation for meeting basic human needs, improving lives, and empowering vulnerable communities.

The conceptualization of social work has four important elements. First, social work is a practice-based profession as well as an academic discipline, which aims to achieve social change, social development, social cohesion, and empowerment and liberation of people. Second, it pursues those goals by following certain values and principles such as social justice, human rights, collective responsibility, and respect for diversity. Third, to achieve these goals by committing to the values and principles, it draws its knowledge from social work theories, a range of social sciences and humanities, and indigenous knowledge sources. Finally, focusing on the values-oriented goals and applying the knowledge from various sources, social work works with people and (their) institutions and structures to meet their needs and rights or to address issues and enhance their overall well-being (International Federation of Social Workers & International Association of Schools of Social Work, 2014).

The comparative analysis of SEV and social work's conceptualization clearly demonstrates how both complement each other for enhancing well-being of people, particularly the most disadvantaged, needy, and neglected. Using issue and context, social work practitioners and managers can draw on social entrepreneurship knowledge and skills to create interventions and institute strategies that address endemic social issues. Social work manager competencies that relate to social entrepreneurship include facilitating innovative changes, fundraising, advocating for social justice, maintaining stakeholder relationships, managing risks, designing effective programs, and collaborating with various community partners to create change (Hassan & Wimpfheimer, 2015).

A small number of social work programs are offering electives in social entrepreneurship and social innovation. However, there is great potential and need to incorporate more of this content into social work curricula (Berzin & Camarena, 2018; Nandan, London, & Bent-Goodley, 2015; Nandan, London, & Blum, 2014) for achieving social work objectives. In fact, if social work construes SEV as one type of intervention to enhance human and community well-being, I can demonstrate how Thankyou's efforts dovetail with the ecosystem's perspective and social work competencies at micro, mezzo, and macro levels.

The ecosystem perspective focuses on both person and environment in a balanced way, with a view to understanding interconnections, linkages, and mutual dependencies between the two. These two influence each other in a circular fashion, sometimes in positive ways and sometimes in negative ways. Within this person-in-environment framework, individuals, families, groups, and communities contribute to, or draw from, various subsystems or parts through interactions and transactions within the environment, to enhance social functioning of individuals and institutions. For the purpose of understanding and practice, these complex person-in-environment interactions and transactions have been delineated at the micro, mezzo, and macro levels (Compton & Galaway, 2005; Payne, 2014).

At the micro level, an individual directly interacts with systems such as family, schools, and work sites. At the mezzo level, interwoven relationships exist among groups, organizations, and institutions—systems that individuals interact with at the micro level. The macro level involves the physical, social, cultural, economic, and political structures of larger society, including technology, language, housing, laws, customs, and regulations (Compton & Galaway, 2005; Magnusson & Allen, 1983). At each level, social work competencies of applying ethical principles to guide practice, critical thinking to inform professional judgment, advancing human rights and social and economic justice, applying knowledge of human behavior in different environments, applying policy practice skills, and engaging, assessing, and evaluating practice with individuals, families, groups, organizations, and communities are relevant (Council on Social Work Education, 2015).

As evident in Figure 7.1, the conceptualization of Thankyou as a social entrepreneurship venture essentially began at the micro level, when Daniel Flynn discussed his ideas with his close friends, Jarryd Burns and Justine Flynn. Daniel's worldview, perceptions, experiences, and interactions with influential stakeholders influenced how he chose to approach global poverty and human suffering (global macro issues). More specifically, his experiences with, and knowledge about, various production systems, market mechanisms, and consumers (both at mezzo and macro levels) influenced his thinking about ways for generating resources for people and communities living in poverty. His resourcefulness was evident when he began using his parents' garage for storing and distributing packaged water bottles. In addition, he gained support for the cause from peers and significant stakeholders, demonstrating his ability to influence. He appeared to use several social work management competencies, including initiating innovative change, generating resources, and maintaining relationships with various stakeholders. He also exhibited social work competencies of critical thinking; advancing human rights; working toward social and economic justice; engaging with individuals at the micro, mezzo, and macro levels; assessing Thankyou's work; and building trust.

Forming Thankyou as an SEV organization, establishing a product brand, and reaching out to market outlets all constitute mezzo-level activities. Now, Thankyou is a well-established SEV with approximately 50 employees. These employees are regularly involved in innovating new products, processes, and

FIGURE 7.1 Understanding Thankyou through an Ecosystems Perspective

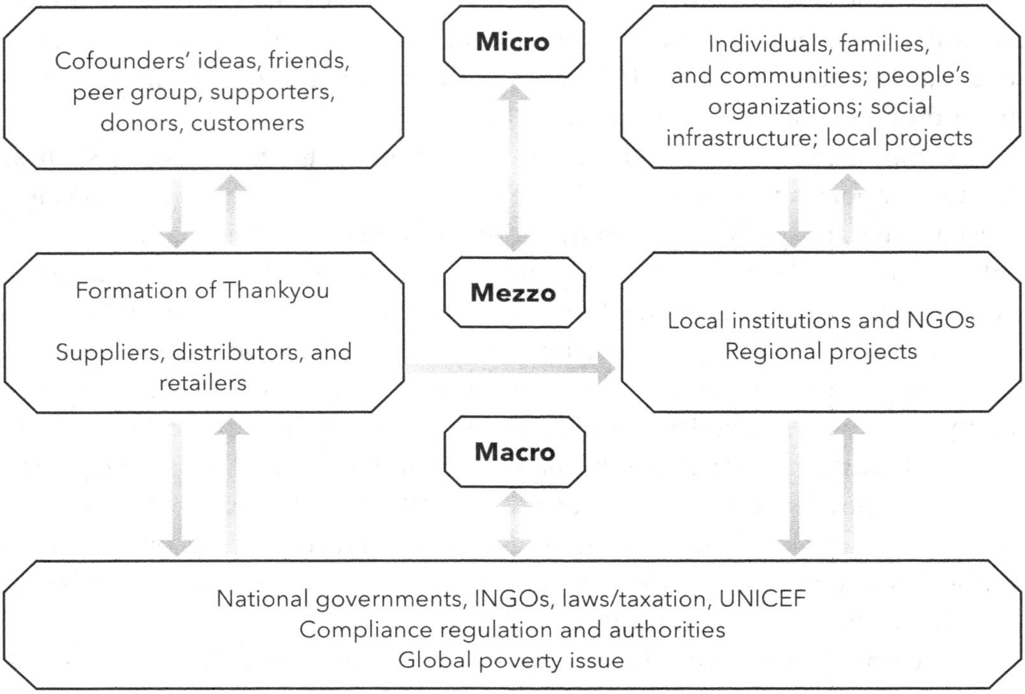

Notes: NGO = nongovernmental organization; INGO = international nongovernmental organization.

services and in enhancing the quality of what they do. For efficient functioning, the organization has separate subsystems for finance, accounting, marketing, design, and so forth. Thankyou interacts with various systems such as schools, sport organizations, and over 5,000 retail outlets and supermarkets to promote and market its products—a mezzo-level activity. The consumption of its products by individual consumers occurs at a micro level. Several activities performed by the organization—through the employees and cofounders—appeared to align with social work community organizing, mobilizing, and administration efforts and competencies.

These micro- and mezzo-level activities must occur within macro national and global systems. Thankyou is a registered trust adhering to national laws, and its business operations adhere to the national taxation system. Its production, distribution, and marketing efforts are subjected to macroeconomic, social, and cultural factors. Its Web site is available for viewing and receiving contributions from across the globe.

To achieve its core vision and mission, Thankyou partners with several macro-level organizations—international nongovernment organizations (INGOs)—including Care, One Heart Worldwide, Oxfam, Splash, UNICEF, and World Vision. Through these partnerships, it identifies specific projects of INGOs for funding and support. These projects have to relate to water and sanitation, food distribution, and child and maternal health. Most of these macro-level INGOs implement their efforts through mezzo-level local government or non-government organizations. By using local knowledge and skills and INGOs' support, these mezzo-level organizations or systems engage with individuals, families, and groups for creating infrastructure, such as wells, water tanks, and toilets. Such engagement and infrastructure construction, as well as training locals with skills for self enhancement, enhances community empowerment.

Impact and Challenges

It appears, given the available evidence, that Thankyou is making an impact at several levels. First, it is fulfilling its mission and vision of generating profits by selling products in the open competitive market and investing the same for growth and to promote human well-being across the globe. Second, the size of the SEV continues to grow, as do the number of product lines and retail outlets. Third, its expansion suggests that Thankyou has been able to convince thousands of customers to buy its products, which in turn supports its cause of alleviating global poverty. Fourth, by adhering to its values and principles, Thankyou has successfully developed partnerships with the INGOs and distributed its profit in 18 developing countries in Africa and Asia and the Pacific Rim, reaching more than 755,000 people. As stated earlier, thus far, Thankyou has distributed AU$5.5 million to enhance access to safe drinking water, sanitation, and food (see Table 7.1). In addition, over 96,000 copies of Daniel Flynn's (2016) book titled *Chapter One: You Have the Power to Change Stuff* have been sold, generating over AU$1.7 million in profits. In 2014, Thankyou received an estimated 50 million media impressions. The organization and its founder also has received a number of awards: 2013 and 2014 Social Traders Social Enterprise Award; 2015 Employer of the Year Award from *Food Magazine*; 2015 Entrepreneur of the Year; and 2014 Victorian Young Australian of the Year.

Specifically, Thankyou has created social value through partnerships with organizations in different parts of the world, to address the need for food, water, health, and sanitation among vulnerable populations. As Auerswald (2009) highlighted, this SEV was innovatively creating solutions to address social problems in a more effective, efficient, and sustainable manner, with the value created by this venture accruing primarily to society as a whole rather than just to private individuals. Put more simply, Thankyou has been instrumental in creating social value by addressing social problems, alleviating poverty, and empowering vulnerable populations throughout the world (Acs, Boardman, & McNeely, 2013) through its sustainable SEV.

To make such a remarkable impact in so many countries in such a short time is not easy. It is natural to encounter challenges while attempting new ideas. The three cofounders had innovative ideas but were young, inexperienced, and learned by doing and making mistakes—an important lesson for social workers as they innovate. Mobilizing resources was a significant challenge, particularly because the organization was working on a shoestring budget at the outset (Flynn, 2016, p. 130), and funds were tight for scaling up the business as well. Fundraising or financial resource mobilization is an important strategic management competency for social work managers (Hassan & Wimpfheimer, 2015). The ability to take risks, deal with the fear of failure, and cope with the fear of losing hard-earned respect and reputation are challenging in any business, and Thankyou was not an exception. Managing risks is an important social work manager's competency (Hassan & Wimpfheimer, 2015). Although Thankyou had innovative ideas, convincing stakeholders, suppliers, retail outlets, and big grocery supermarkets to stock and sell Thankyou products was far from easy. Furthermore, meeting legal requirements relating to marketing the products was complex and challenging. Strategic management competencies focusing on marketing and maintaining public relations and the executive leadership competency of maintaining stakeholder relationships are significant for social work managers (Hassan & Wimpfheimer, 2015).

With new products, facing competition in an open market is a challenge even for experienced businesspeople. Market competitors, whom Flynn (2016) called "haters," create obstacles for entry of new businesses—for their own survival. It appears that Thankyou and its customers faced this challenge confidently and boldly. Flynn stated,

> When you have spent [a] good part of your life building something for the sole purpose of helping others, it can be discouraging to watch people rip into it. But, we had to mentally prepare . . . we could not let the uninformed and irrational haters bring us down. (2016, p. 156)

Technological glitches, particularly at crucial hours, had caused anxiety among some concerned staff members. Similarly, effectively dealing with other unexpected issues in the course of Thankyou's operations was a challenge. Consciously and continuously learning from all sources, supporters, and opposition, and from positive and negative feedback, was humbling. Finally, Thankyou went to great lengths to ensure that its net profits distributed to partners for special projects ultimately reached vulnerable populations across the communities.

Because this case is based on information obtained from the book authored by Daniel Flynn (2016) and Thankyou's Web site, readers should understand the scope of subjectivity in this account. In the future, the case study may be expanded by undertaking systematic research, directly interviewing staff members and customers, and undertaking field visits to places where partners are implementing the projects.

Conclusion

This chapter briefly illuminated global poverty and water and food insecurity — which the Thankyou SEV is committed to addressing. I described the efforts and approaches used by Thankyou for generating funds and distributing the profits through partners to empower people living in poverty, to develop access to safe water and sanitation, and to provide food in several countries in Africa, Asia, and the Pacific Rim. It demonstrated how SEV and social work practice and values complement each other and how Thankyou's strategies align with social work managers' competencies and the ecosystems model of social work practice. This Australian example of an SEV shows how the ecosystems model is useful and applicable at both local and global levels, to reach out not only to people in need of basic sustenance in many developing countries but also to people who are homeless in the midst of affluent Melbourne. Notwithstanding the challenges, Thankyou is clearly making an impact in many countries. Its efforts address SDGs related to poverty, clean water, and child and maternal health. From a very humble and hard beginning, its cofounders have scaled up the organization's activities with courage and determination. Apparently, there are opportunities to scale up even further in the future, as new products are introduced and new projects are implemented through INGOs. Thankyou's case is an inspiration for social workers addressing complex needs of vulnerable populations across the globe.

Many students join social work with radical ideas of changing the world, but by the time they complete their degree and begin social work practice, most of them seem to get caught up in routines of micro practice only, forgetting their original intent for social action and social change. This SEV example demonstrates the importance of pursuing social work ideals of creating change through innovative means. On the basis of his experiential knowledge, cofounder Flynn argues that the path one follows does not matter, as the power to create change lies within. The Thankyou SEV and its cofounders are an inspiration to social workers traveling the path to create social change while promoting social justice.

References

Acs, Z., Boardman, M., & McNeely, C. (2013). The social value of productive entrepreneurship. *Small Business Economics, 40,* 785–796. doi:10.1007/s11187-011-9396-6

Auerswald, P. (2009). Creating social value. *Stanford Social Innovation Review, 7*(2), 51–55.

Barraket, J., Mason, C., & Blain, B. (2016, June). *Finding Australia's social enterprise sector 2016: Final report.* Melbourne, Australia: Social Traders and the Centre for Social Impact Swinburne Melbourne. Retrieved from http://apo.org.au/system/files/64444/apo-nid64444-48516.pdf

Berzin, S. C., & Camarena, H. (2018). *Innovation from within: Redefining how non-profits solve problems.* New York: Oxford University Press.

Compton, B. R., & Galaway, B. (2005). *Social work processes.* Belmont, CA: Brooks/Cole.

Council on Social Work Education. (2015). *2015 educational policy and accreditation standards for baccalaureate and master's social work programs.* Retrieved from https://www.cswe.org/getattachment/Accreditation/Accreditation-Process/2015-EPAS/2015EPAS_Web_FINAL.pdf.aspx

Cox, D., & Pawar, M. (2013). *International social work: Issues, strategies and programs.* Thousand Oaks, CA: Sage Publications.

Flynn, D. (2016). *Chapter one: You have the power to change stuff.* Sydney, Australia: Messenger Group.

Hassan, A., & Wimpfheimer, R. S. (2015). *Guidebook for human service professionals: Human services management competencies.* Retrieved from https://socialworkmanager.org/wp-content/uploads/2016/01/Competency-Brochure-4-19-15-With-Forms.pdf.

International Federation of Social Workers & International Association of Schools of Social Work. (2014). *Global definition of social work.* Retrieved from http://ifsw.org/get-involved/global-definition-of-social-work/

Magnusson, D., & Allen, V. L. (1983). An interactional perspective for human development. In D. Magnusson & V. L. Allen (Eds.), *Human development: An interactional perspective* (pp. 3–34). New York: Academic Press.

Midgley, J., & Pawar, M. (2017). Social development forging ahead. In J. Midgley & M. Pawar (Eds.), *Future directions in social development* (pp. 3–19). Basingstoke, UK: Palgrave Macmillan.

Nandan, M., London, M., & Bent-Goodley, T. (2015). Social workers as social change agents: Social innovation, social intrapreneurship, and social entrepreneurship. *Human Service Organizations Management, 39*(1), 38–56. doi:10.1080/23303131.2014.955236

Nandan, M., London, M., & Blum, T. C. (2014). Community practice social entrepreneurship: An interdisciplinary approach to graduate education. *International Journal of Social Entrepreneurship and Innovation, 3*(1), 51–70. doi:10.1504/IJSEI.2014.06410

Pawar, M. (2004). *Data collecting methods and experiences: A guide to social researchers.* Chicago: New Dawn Press.

Pawar, M. (2014). *Water and social policy.* Basingstoke, UK: Palgrave Macmillan.

Pawar, M. (2017). Social development: Progress so far. In J. Midgley & M. Pawar (Eds.), *Future directions in social development* (pp. 41–57). Basingstoke, UK: Palgrave Macmillan.

Payne, M. (2014). *Modern social theory.* Basingstoke, UK: Palgrave Macmillan.

Sen, A. (2001). *Development as freedom.* Oxford, UK: Oxford University Press.

Thankyou. (2017). *Our core impact values.* Retrieved from https://Thankyou.co/impact/how-projects-work

United Nations Department of Economic and Social Affairs. (2017, August). More than 40 countries report progress on SDGs but stronger partnerships still needed. *Voice, 21*(8). Retrieved from https://www.un.org/development/desa/undesavoice/in-case-you-missed-it/2017/08#34817

United Nations Development Programme. (1997). *Human development to eradicate poverty* [Human Development Report]. New York: Oxford University Press.

United Nations Development Programme. (2006). *Beyond scarcity: Power, poverty and the global water crisis* [Human Development Report]. New York: Oxford University Press.

United Nations Educational, Scientific and Cultural Organization. (2009). *Water in a changing world: United Nations World Water Development, Report 3.* Paris/London: UNESCO/Earthscan.

United Nations Educational, Scientific and Cultural Organization. (2012). *Managing water under uncertainty and risk: The UN World Water Development Report 4.* Paris: Author.

United Nations Statistical Division. (2017). *The sustainable development goals report 2017.* Retrieved from https://unstats.un.org/sdgs/report/2017/overview/

World Bank. (2000–2001). *World development reports: Attacking poverty.* New York: Oxford University Press.

World Bank Water and Sanitation Program & International Finance Corporation. (2013). *Tapping the market: Opportunities for domestic investments in water for the poor.* Retrieved from https://www.wsp.org/sites/wsp.org/files/publications/DPSP-Water-Report-Conference-Edition-WSP-August-2013.pdf

Acknowledgments

I would like to thank my well-meaning and generous friend Dr. Alok Sharma, a well-known eye surgeon, who introduced me to the book *Chapter One: You Have the Power to Change Stuff*, written by Daniel Flynn, cofounder of Thankyou, without which I would not have thought of writing a chapter on Thankyou. I also would like to thank the editors for inviting me to write this chapter.

8

Innovation in a Chinese Social Work Context

Louise Brown and Jie Lei

Much has been written about the process of diffusion and adoption of innovation in relation to ideas and practices spanning both the public and private sector (Brown & Osborne, 2013; Kelly, 2012; Larson, Dearing, & Backer, 2017; Mulgan, 2014). Although there is a belief that the private sector is the real home of innovation, significant financial investment continues to occur in a vast array of pilots, programs, and proof-of-concept projects within the public sector.

Despite being very discipline specific, an expanding literature exists covering the whole and specific parts of the innovation process or innovation journey. By examining the literature covering the many individual case studies that have been reported on, it is possible to begin to draw lessons regarding the implementation of models transferring to new sites and the factors that help or hinder their adoption. However, one gap that remains in the literature is an understanding of this process as innovations move between countries. In a global economy, where boundaries between countries have become more permeable and the potential to network and seek out new ideas to solve common problems has increased, so has the need to better understand how to support this process. This desire to learn and borrow social work models from other countries is actively encouraged within the field of social services. For example, the Global Agenda for Social Work and Social Development encourages shared learning between countries (International Federation of Social Workers [IFSW], 2012). This agenda aims to "promote the development, dissemination and exchange of knowledge between all social professionals through established and innovative channels of communications" (IFSW, 2012, p. 5). Furthermore, the United Nations Millennium Development Goals and subsequent Sustainable Development Goals have created a framework for mobilizing global policy making and generating innovative partnerships (United Nations [UN], 2015). The United Nations sees innovation as crucial to the implementation of the post-2015 agenda demanding "renewed efforts to mobilize innovation, science and technology for sustainable development" (UN, 2015, p. 68). Therefore, understanding how best to support the movement of innovative models of practice internationally has never been more important.

This chapter examines the transfer of an innovative social work model, namely, family group conferencing (FGC), from the United Kingdom to China. It details the implementation process and findings from the initial process evaluation in China of FGC—a practice-based social work intervention that has transferred across many international boundaries (Rauktis, Bishop-Patrick, Jung, & Pennell, 2013). FGC is a social work model that originates from and out of traditional practices in Maori communities in New Zealand. It is a method for resolving concerns about the welfare of children through working with families to help them arrive at their own solutions. It is an approach to social work decision-making processes that aims to empower families to make plans about keeping their own children safe. FGC is viewed here as a service innovation, which was defined by West and Farr (1990) as "the intentional introduction and application within a role, group or organisation of ideas, processes and products or procedures, new to the relevant unit of adoption, designed to significantly benefit the individual, the group, organisation or wider society" (p. 3).

In recent years, we have seen the emergence in the literature of the term "social innovation." Amid the many definitions that exist, *social innovation*, as opposed to simply innovation, tends to refer to "new ideas that work in meeting social goals" and is "motivated by the goal of meeting a social need" (Mulgan, Tucker, Rushanara, & Sanders 2007, p. 8). The context in which this term has emerged is that of environmental and social problems, such as climate change or the aging population. The term refers to ideas, processes, or products, but the discourse tends toward more practical examples of new products, services, or programs that have some impact on social needs.

Viewing the FGC model as an example of social innovation, this case study explores the implementation process of the model in southern China. It draws on the theory of innovation literature and existing frameworks to examine the process, challenges faced, and lessons learned (Greenhalgh, Robert, Macfarlane, Bate, & Kyriakidou, 2004; Rogers, 2003; Walker, 2014). Together these frameworks form a conceptual model derived from a synthesis of relevant theoretical and empirical findings. This aids in assessing the impact of the case and provides an overview of the multiple-level factors, determinants, and antecedents that we might expect to see influence the implementation of this social work example, such as system readiness, fidelity, adaptation, and the "external environment and influences" (Greenhalgh et al., 2004, p. 608). The literature indicates that the decisions to adopt, and the factors affecting implementation, depend on many external influences.

Family Group Conferencing: A Response to Child Welfare Concerns

The development of the FGC model for use in mainstream social work practice arose out of a unique situation in New Zealand during the 1980s. It developed from a growing awareness that the overrepresentation of indigenous Maori children in the state care system was a result of institutional racism arising out of an inherently white European professional discourse (Connolly, 2004). A government inquiry into these concerns resulted in the Children and Young Person's Act of 1989, which promoted the use of family conferences to redress the power imbalance, by using practices that more closely reflected Maori cultures, values, and traditions. Family group conferences were made mandatory in child welfare cases in which children were at risk of entering the public care system. The model was designed to reflect how Maori communities viewed the responsibility for the welfare of their children in the context of their extended family and community. It promoted greater partnership with families and communities to ensure that decision making was shared and represented a cultural perspective. The FGC model rejected the notion that professionals know best, keeping central the principles that families know their children best and that the best place for children to be brought up is within their own family. In an endeavor to achieve this, the model used a participatory approach and series of stages incorporating "private family time" through which families addressed professionals' concerns and developed a plan to safeguard the welfare of their children.

The principles of the FGC model and the promotion of family empowerment reflected the ongoing debate surrounding the correct balance between state intervention and private family life. The model quickly caught the attention of international professionals concerned about the extent to which "professional expertise" was disempowering families and resulting in poor decision making and poor outcomes for children in state care. Despite a weak evidence base, the model quickly transferred from New Zealand to Australia, to the United States, and by 1996 to the United Kingdom. Family group conferences are now used in over 20 different countries across the world, with recent trials taking place in Guatemala, again in response to a disproportionate number of indigenous children being placed outside their families (Roby, Pennell, Rotabi, Bunkers, & deUcles, 2015).

The current state of play in relation to the evidence base for the FGC model is helpfully summarized in two articles by Frost, Abram, and Burgess (2014a, 2014b). They acknowledged that the evidence base for the FGC model regarding outcomes remained weak, despite it being almost 30 years since the inception of the model. Evaluators have come up against numerous difficulties with producing outcome evidence about the FGC model, including variance in the models being tested, lack of longitudinal studies, lack of control groups, and lack of any statutory obligation in most countries to use the model. Likewise, within the implementation process, the same barriers repeatedly arise, such as resistance from social workers to change their practice (Adams & Chandler, 2004; Brown, 2003). However, "the process evidence is overwhelmingly positive suggesting a clear role" for family group conferences (Frost et al., 2014b, p. 506). Despite the difficulties in proving that the model has positive outcomes, it is regarded as a potential solution to increasing concerns about how professionals manage "at risk" children who come to the attention of formal services. Its core principles and values appear to resonate with practitioners, and this has resulted in it being received in a positive manner.

China: A New Context

Growing media coverage in China toward child maltreatment and an almost zero-tolerance policy adopted around child sexual abuse have over the last decade initiated a public debate about child maltreatment and the ways it might be best tackled. Although the exact prevalence and rates of child maltreatment remained unclear as there is no official reporting system in China, studies indicated that the rates were comparable to those of Western countries. Relying largely on self-report studies, Chen, Dunne, and Han (2004) estimated that the prevalence for child sexual abuse in the central provinces—Henan, Hubei, Hebei, and Beijing—was 10.5 percent for boys and 16.7 percent for girls. From a comparative perspective, most of these figures fell within the international range as identified by Finkelhor (1994): 3 percent to 29 percent for men and 7 percent to 36 percent for women. A more recent study, a systematic review of the prevalence of child maltreatment in China, concluded that "maltreatment is a common experience for Chinese children," which in turn "underscores the need to steer resources towards child protection and to strengthening the knowledge base regarding the scale and consequences of child maltreatment at national level" (Fang et al., 2015, p. 10).

Furthermore, the scale of migration within China has resulted in vast numbers of children living in conditions that potentially leave them more vulnerable. In 2010, the number of migrant children and "left-behind" children reached 35.81 million and 69.73 million, respectively (United Nations Children's Emergency Fund [UNICEF], 2014, p. 112). Guangdong was the most preferred destination province for internal migrants in China, with 13 percent of China's temporary migrants choosing this province to settle in during the 1990s (UNICEF, 2014). Despite the vast numbers migrating from rural China to cities and contributing to China's economic growth, migrants remained marginalized. Some of these children were left behind in villages and separated from their parents. Others moved province and lost *hukuo*—the official registration enabling access to public benefits. This left them with no or limited access to education and health care.

Alongside this growing awareness of the risks posed to children, opportunities arose to develop services as investment in welfare provision in China started to increase. In 2002, the Communist Party of China changed its focus from economic reform to social development, particularly in terms of strengthening its role with regard to welfare provision. Despite studies proving and reinforcing the significant prevalence of child maltreatment, the institutional framework currently remains underdeveloped and too fragmented to fully carry out the function of protecting children. Although the United Nations' Convention on Rights of the Child came into effect in China in 1992, China continues to lack a comprehensive system for managing child protection. There remains an absence of statutory agencies, reporting systems, or alternative institutional care arrangements for children identified at risk of harm (Shang, 2012). The formal liability falls to several different authorities; however, their coverage and duties remain limited. Public security departments are intended to be the major authorities that have been given the legal power for tackling crime against children, but they often do not intervene until serious physical harm has been caused. The police rarely take precautions to ensure child protection, as they share the general public's perception that "child maltreatment" is "child discipline" and the family is a private sphere (Qiao & Chan, 2005). At the time of developing this case in China, there was an absence of any formal child protection system. Children are still seen as the responsibility of their parents or the wider family and community, with minimum intervention by any professional or central state agencies.

Although social work training programs in Chinese universities exist, social work graduates rarely have an opportunity to go into practice as limited employment opportunities exist. Social work is truly in its infancy, with few agencies, services, or resources for practitioners to draw on. Nationally, the Ministry of Civil Affairs (2014) has begun to grow its child welfare system. It has established the Department of Social Welfare and Social Affairs, whose work has so far tended to focus on abandoned children, orphans, and street children (Katz, Shang, & Zhang, 2010). With a lack of resources and continuing "cultural reluctance" to intervene, a gap in the institutional framework existed for meeting the needs of children (Katz et al., 2010, p. 94). However, conditions are changing and opportunities opening for the development of services to work with and support at-risk children. Within this context, funding for the development of social work services for children is flowing at a rapid rate from local government sources via the hands of Chinese academicians directly into the formation of local nongovernmental organizations (NGOs). However, with social work as a profession still in its infancy in China, Chinese academicians have been keen to explore what services might be appropriate to import and test out in their local context. It was into this gap and against a backdrop of increasing awareness of child maltreatment that an FGC pilot project was proposed. With formal, professionally dominated systems in their infancy, it was thought that the FGC model might lend itself to a Chinese context, in which Confucian principles dominate family life and great weight is placed on informal support and family and community networks.

Social Innovation Case Study: Implementing FGC in China

Nationally, there was a growing appetite among practitioners working with children in local NGOs to start tackling some of the more complex cases in their community. A dialogue had already begun between a university-based social work department and two local NGOs regarding future service developments.

The social workers based in the local integrated family service centers reported that they were identifying children in the community who were at risk of, or were experiencing, emotional and physical abuse and neglect. These social workers were concerned about not having the skills to respond effectively to these situations. A project team was composed of a Chinese academician, a UK academician who had a background in child protection practice, and members from two NGOs in Guangzhou, who were already working with the Chinese academician.

The UK academician had already been in China providing basic safeguarding training to practitioners in the local area, incorporating a range of methods for working with families. In the absence of any formal service provision, methods were required that built on existing community resources and mobilized informal support networks. The FGC model appeared to offer practitioners with additional approaches to the standard casework, individual, and family counseling services being offered. There was sufficient interest for the project team to seek funding to pilot the development of an FGC project in Guangzhou. Small-scale funding was subsequently secured through a local professional social work organization and a university start-up and alumni fund. Guangzhou is renowned for being open to experimentation. Its social work workforce had already grown to 8,435 by 2014 and was identified as an appropriate site for the pilot (Lei & Walker, 2013).

There were two key stages in the preparation phase of the project: first, securing permission to pilot a social work project in the area; and second, exploring the appropriateness of the FGC model for the Chinese context. At a very practical level, to establish an FGC pilot, permission was required from a number of key agencies, including the Youth League. The FGC China project team began by seeking official political and local support at a regional level. Public consultation events were held alongside closed meetings involving stakeholders from the area. An outline of the FGC model was presented and publicly debated. Local NGOs and international organizations already working in China, such as Save the Children and UNICEF, were also consulted. Networking with a broad range of stakeholders at this early stage of implementation is known to facilitate successful adoption of innovations. A complex innovation relies on "other actors in the organizational environment" (Walker, 2014, p. 23). Therefore, this was an important stage in preparing the ground for adoption.

The early consultation led to a number of concerns being raised about the FGC model: whether Chinese families had large enough networks; whether Chinese families would engage and be prepared to discuss their problems with a wider network of family and friends; whether the absence of a legal mandate for social workers to intervene in family life would prevent engagement with families; whether social workers had the skills and capacity required to deliver the model; and whether it was it too early in the development of social work systems in China to introduce the FGC model.

The second phase of preparation concerned assessing the FGC model itself and considering the context in which it was going to be piloted. The project team invited an experienced FGC trainer from the United Kingdom to China to present the model and explore with local practitioners how it might need to be adapted. The project team acknowledged that importing an idea used in Western practice into a country in the initial stages of developing its social work system could constitute "professional imperialism." The team members were conscious about, and sensitive to, this potential phenomenon (Gray, Coates, & Yellow Bird, 2008). The project team was committed to developing the FGC model in China through a process of information exchange, which took account of local knowledge and allowed for cultural adaptation. Internationally, the FGC model is used with children in need who are also at risk of child maltreatment (Brown, 2003). However, in many of these countries, such as the United Kingdom, the FGC model sits alongside or acts as an alternative to formal statutory services. The Chinese context was unusual in that no other formal services existed. This meant that when social workers identified children at risk, they were responsible (although not legally) for ensuring some action was taken. The project team wanted to avoid social workers going into families, raising expectations, and potentially leaving children further exposed or vulnerable.

A series of development meetings were held with the FGC trainer present to explore the model and consider how it might be used and adapted for the local context. Eight social workers and two managers attended. Up until this time, the social workers' interactions with families had consisted of outreach work in the community, responding to concerns raised by schools (often about absenteeism), and offering general counseling skills. Additional service in the form of homework clubs catered to children whose parents worked long hours.

During the development meetings, the social workers presented examples of typical cases. They described cases that covered all aspects of physical abuse, emotional abuse, and neglect. They did not identify any suspected cases of child sexual abuse. They presented cases involving children living with aging relatives, disabled grandparents unable to provide adequate care, children who were left alone for long periods, parents who were misusing alcohol or drugs, and children who had been subject to severe beatings by family members. There was also a growing awareness of mental health issues among young adults, some of which were attributed to the importance placed on education and pressure to excel at school. Poverty was a significant factor in many of the reported cases. Employees from the two NGOs were concerned about the well-being and safety of children and young adults in over 100 families in their area.

A response was needed that would fit with local values, cultural norms, and family practices. The Chinese social workers believed that the FGC model, with its roots in community decision-making forums and its emphasis on empowering families to mobilize informal support networks, would fit well within the community context. It would offer a potential mechanism through which families might be able to leverage additional support in a way that would not conflict with local family values and traditions.

Developing and Adapting the FGC Model

As already stated, the project team approached the introduction of the FGC model to China from a position of facilitating local practitioners to adapt the model to fit the local context. The end goal was to redesign an FGC model that the NGOs could accept and own, would support their practice, and address their concerns regarding the level of support they could currently offer children and families living in their area. This development process presented particular challenges as the Chinese practitioners struggled to know how best to adapt the model. A study by Yuen-Tsang and Ku (2008) in China had reported that practitioners experienced difficulty reconceptualizing and reconstructing models from other countries. With social work at fledgling and early stages of development in China, practitioners "lacked the creative ability to reconceptualize Western social work theories and to experiment with innovative culturally appropriate approaches" (Yuen-Tsang & Ku, 2008, p. 184). The team, including mainland Chinese academicians, were careful about avoiding a "West is best" message. Unfortunately, the Chinese project-based practitioners had little practical experience to draw on and naturally found it difficult suggesting adaptations to the model.

A range of frameworks exist that are designed to assist with the process of cultural adaptation of evidence-based innovations internationally (Castro, Barrerra, & Steiker, 2010; Parra-Cordona, Domenech-Rodriguez, & Bernal, 2012). The project team drew on these and tried to identify the core components of the FGC model that could be put into a different operational system if required (Nadkarni et al., 2015). The development meetings focused on the core components of the FGC model and investigated the parts that may require adaptation to fit Chinese values and principles. A key question pertained to defining the social worker's role in relation to family issues. For example, in the United Kingdom, a social worker's role and duty to intervene in family issues is clearly defined by legislation, which is absent in the Chinese context.

Given that social workers had no legal mandate to intervene in family life, even where concerns about a child were identified, they had to be very careful in how they questioned families about the care families were providing for their children. Now the FGC model required the two NGOs to redefine the relationship between social workers and families and design a new approach to working in their community. This change meant that social workers were entering completely new territory and were unsure about managing their role as an FGC facilitator; in addition, they were unsure about the extent to which families would accept this shift in their role. The issues related to this shift are described later in the chapter.

Following the development meetings, the social workers and managers decided to test the FGC model in its original form with the provision and understanding that it could be adapted over time. The only change suggested by the group during the initial stage was to change the name from "family group conference" to "family group decision making" (FGDM). The word "conference" (*huiyi*) was considered too formal, and they thought it might deter family involvement. The trainer from the United Kingdom trained two managers and eight social workers in traditional FGDM "coordinator" roles.

A considerable amount of time was spent developing a set of referral criteria for the FGDM project. It was finally agreed that the service would be offered to children between 8 and 18 years of age in families where parental mental health illness or parental addiction (drugs, alcohol, gambling) affected parenting capacity. The NGO employees were confident that a large number of families and children would qualify for the services and would also choose to participate in the project. Children younger than 8 years of age were deliberately not included in the project. The criteria emphasized parenting issues and did not blame children for problems that existed in the family. Guidance was given to avoid referrals by schools or parents for cases involving school absences or the educational ability of child. FGC training, including delivering knowledge and skills related to a child-centered approach, was central to the solution. The full involvement of children and young adults in the FGDM process was encouraged, and the social workers were trained in how to support their attendance at the FGDM.

Although risk is inherent in all innovative activities, it is particularly heightened when experimenting with new approaches with vulnerable populations. Writers have identified risk as an issue in implementing innovation and have recommended that organizations need to be explicit in advance about the risks the innovation poses to both individuals and the organization (Brown & Osborne, 2013). The risks in this pilot were identified during the training and openly discussed, and measures were put in place to mitigate them.

First, and of utmost importance, was the potential risk to the children and families receiving the service. The project team was concerned that families might be encouraged to open up about the difficulties they were experiencing and place the blame for these on their children. This had the potential for the FGDM process to expose children to further risk, leaving them unsupported in a setting where social workers had no legal right to intervene. Consequently, referral criteria prevented the involvement of very young children. All children invited to take part were asked to give consent in their own right, as were all family members. Child-friendly information leaflets were designed, and any family members participating were made aware that they could withdraw at any time. The responsibility for the quality of the social work practice within the pilot rested with the two NGOs. The two managers attended the FGC training and offered regular supervision to the social workers. They were responsible for safeguarding the well-being of children and young adults referred to the service and for ensuring that children were not left unsupported. In addition, the project team commissioned a qualified and experienced social work consultant based in Hong Kong to provide additional supervision to the social workers in the FGDM project on the cases, and the consultant attended the FGC training.

Second, the two NGOs experienced both organizational (financial and human) and reputational risks. Expectations were high, and politically the pilot had attracted considerable attention. It was possible that the pilot could fail if the teams did not refer families to the project or the families chose not to participate. The trained social workers went back to their teams to educate their colleagues about the services and to encourage continuous referrals. During project implementation, social workers started using the model with families with whom they had relationships. The pilot aimed to facilitate 10 to 12 FGDM meetings within the first year.

Evaluation

The two universities on the project team designed an evaluation framework that was implemented concurrently with the project. The two types of evaluation planned were (1) a process evaluation to examine the factors influencing the implementation and (2) an outcome evaluation. The process evaluation consisted of individual interviews with the eight social workers, conducted at 6- and 12-month intervals after the project launch.

The UK university's institutional review board approved the project, and the evaluators ensured that the NASW (2017) *Code of Ethics* was followed for conducting evaluation research. A research protocol was established by the project team, and a Chinese research assistant was trained in the use of the protocol. Confidentiality was assured to all participants, and steps were taken to ensure that any information recorded and stored was in accordance with the UK Data Protection Act. For process evaluation, face-to-face interviews were conducted by the UK academician with the assistance of a translator. Secondary data in the form of family plans were also reviewed. For the outcome evaluation of FGDM, the focus was on the family members' perception of change and improvement. In addition, the size of their support networks was assessed for measuring change. The family members who granted informed consent were interviewed (providing qualitative data) before the implementation of the FGDM project and again three months after the project implementation. Eco-maps and other child-friendly tools were used to measure impact on young adults. In other words, age-appropriate research tools were used to ensure the children and young adults understood the questions and what they were consenting to.

By employing an experienced FGC trainer from the United Kingdom, the project team ensured that the social workers were competent to pilot the model in their community. The trainer ensured that the social workers had developed the skills to facilitate FGDM and had suitable supervision in place. The NGOs involved were committed to ensuring the well-being of the families and that of the children and young adults. By restricting the age of the children, it was possible to ensure that they had the capacity to give informed consent. Participating families completed two consent forms, one to consent to participate in the FGDM pilot project and the other to participate in the evaluation study. Family members were assured that services would continue to be provided even if they declined to participate in the evaluation.

Implementation of Social Innovation: Challenges and Opportunities

During the first 12 months of the pilot, the two NGOs held a total of five FGDM meetings with families in the area. The referral rate was considerably lower than the numbers projected by the NGOs. Only five cases, composed of family members and young adults or children, attended the meetings. In one case the family left without making a plan. In reviewing transcripts and data about these five families, it became clear that the FGDM model worked well with families dealing with physical neglect. For example, a 10-year-old girl, whose parents had divorced and left the city, was being raised by her grandparents and two uncles. The person making the referral was concerned that the girl was suffering neglect because she was arriving to school unkempt, dirty, and with head lice. Moreover, the child was struggling to form friendships and was becoming socially isolated. Another case involved a boy with learning difficulties who lived with his grandparents, both of whom had dementia. The school was concerned about these caregivers' capacity to sufficiently care for the boy. He, too, was becoming socially isolated. A third case involved a family in which the father had committed suicide and the mother was struggling to care for her 12- and three-year-old daughters when she went to work. The mother took the younger child to her place of work and tied her to a table to ensure her safety. In all three cases, a family plan was developed and relatives stepped in to help. In one of the cases, the social worker invited three volunteers to attend, and they subsequently provided additional support to the family and to the child. In all five cases, poverty was a significant factor contributing to the family's situation.

With a relatively small number of participants during the first year of the project, conducting process evaluation made the most sense. However, interviews were conducted with four families for preliminary initial feedback. Family members were asked to assess the level of concern they had about their child on a scale of 1 to 10 pre- and post-FGDM. Data indicated that in all four cases, family members' concern levels were a little appeased after FGDM meetings. However, with the small sample size and the nature of the data collected, it is difficult and premature to comment on the effectiveness of the project.

The process evaluation took place throughout the 12-month period and findings were shared with the NGO employees. The following factors contributed to the slow adoption and participation of families in the FGDM project:

- Reluctance by family members to take part and accept the offer of a family meeting;
- Reluctance on the part of colleagues in the NGOs to refer cases to the pilot because of a lack of knowledge about the model, how it works, its potential benefits, how to sell it to families, and the types of cases to refer;
- Social workers not feeling competent to facilitate FGDM;
- Limited resource capacity (human and financial) for the pilot, that is, the NGOs were unable to give priority to the FGDM project vis-à-vis other programs, and social workers felt too burdened with other work to be able to devote sufficient time to the FGDM pilot.

Despite the slow start and lower-than-expected FGDM meetings held, there were a number of factors that participants felt were working well and were important for the future success of the pilot:

- The families were more inclined to try a FGDM approach when they had strong, trusting relationships with the social workers.
- Appointing additional social workers who were dedicating a portion of their time to the FGDM project helped with resource issues.
- Having initial success with the small number of cases demonstrated that the model could work and led to a more positive response among team members.

What was very noticeable throughout the initial 12 months was that both NGOs started to adapt the model to fit their local context. Both NGOs chose to widen the referral criteria, including families who they were already working with and who they thought would benefit from holding a FGDM meeting. The existing relationship they had with the family assisted family members to trust the new process and participate.

A key adaptation to the model was the role of a coordinator. In the United Kingdom, as in other countries using the traditional FGC model, the person who convenes and facilitates the meeting—the coordinator—is always different from the family social worker. This difference is important in a place where social work services are mandated by law. However, in China, where no formal system exists, distinguishing between social workers and coordinator was not necessary; one person fulfilled both roles in the pilot.

A second adaptation was opting to introduce and invite volunteers and family sponsors to the FGDM meetings. In the United States and United Kingdom, where the FGC model has been implemented in its purest form, no one apart from family attended the private family time. However, in China, volunteers were invited into this space. They were considered to have something valuable to offer the family through their support. Volunteers are an important part of Chinese culture, and their presence—in the absence of formal professional support service—assisted the family. Following the initial 12 months of the pilot, a third NGO (another community-based social work organization) joined the project, and additional social workers were trained in the FGDM model. Further adaptations made to the model at this site included using volunteers and not social workers to facilitate the family meetings. Although the NGOs initially had difficulty identifying ideas for adaptations, they were able to suggest relevant changes and modification for their contexts after gaining experience with the model.

Implications for Social Work Practice

This case illustrates how the project team experimented with new ideas and models, joined forces with local partners (for example, volunteers, support networks), attempted to change some of the existing systems, and explored how to scale by inviting other NGOs to the table. These efforts were directed toward adding social value within the province of China. The application of an international FGC model innovatively tailored to address the problem of child maltreatment in a different culture highlights the creation of social value in terms of the sustainable positive effects on children and empowerment of families in Chinese society (Acs, Boardman, & McNeely, 2013). Specifically, the FGC model created social value by increasing awareness and knowledge about child abuse among families in Guangdong Province and by reducing the potential for child abuse (Auerswald, 2009). Such impact on families would strengthen the social fabric of Guangdong Province and also enhance the growth and development of the children.

    This case example of piloting FGDM in China represents a process of implementing a complex practice-based social innovation in a new country. This effort reflects the process of social value creation as outlined by Singh's (2016) definition, in that an innovative adaptation of a Western-origin child welfare intervention with families to suit the Chinese cultural context was successfully implemented to address child maltreatment problems and hold families accountable for child welfare. It has highlighted a number of lessons that point to the need for systemic change at macro, mezzo, and micro levels of practice. First, the case questions how countries might borrow models to support their development and how the social work profession can support the transfer process so that appropriate models move safely and effectively. Globally, the social work profession has embraced the notion of learning and borrowing models from other countries. In this example of a country in the throes of developing new services, the case study has raised a number of issues, such as whether the timing was right; whether fidelity or adaptation should be promoted to ensure a fit for the local context; and how to manage the process of cultural adaptation effectively.

This case demonstrated that the social work profession needs to carefully consider the external context within which new models are being adopted. Introducing new forms of practice requires consideration of the existing political, social, and economic context and an assessment of the degree to which the values enshrined within the model will be a good fit. Piloting new approaches that require systemic changes may run the risk of failure during implementation if the environment is not ready or open to change or if the model is not culturally appropriate. For this pilot, despite having political support for its trial in its purest form, the model challenged and questioned the existing role of social workers in private family life. In China, where filial piety remains a central value within Confucian family life, the subordination, respect, and support by children for their parents and elders remains strong. Such values continue to form the basis of political governance in China (Wang, Xu, Sun, & Zhou, 2014).

The FGC model originates from a country where the state has mandated that social workers intervene in family life once concerns are identified. In contrast, the social workers in China had no formal obligation to intervene with families, despite concerns about children's unmet needs. Therefore, local practitioners adapted the model to fit their context. They engaged the community and volunteers in a supportive network around the child—an important step in cultural adaptation. They advocated a process through which both families and practitioners could strike the right balance of intervention and support—where the model's fidelity was trumped by the need for adaptation. As China begins developing and delivering new services, practice models need to fit within deep-rooted family and political values. If the system is not ready, the model risks failure. From Rogers's (2003) seminal work on the diffusion of innovation, it is clear that compatibility with, in this case, traditional cultural values and norms is a critical consideration.

Academicians have questioned the appropriateness of importing an intervention model from another country and also questioned whether new service development should occur from existing local practices. Osei-Hwedie and Rankopo (2012) have argued that developing culturally appropriate indigenous services is "a complex undertaking given the lack of resources in developing countries, which makes it difficult to depart from dominant modernist Western models" (p. 723). This case example reinforced the difficulty in deviating from the original model during the early stages of implementation. However, with time, as confidence grew among practitioners, cultural adaptation became possible. The project team realized that piloting of this nature—where the model was implemented alongside local values and practices—would take a number of years to go through the development stages. Because the model had to be adapted during the development phase, it was possible to implement only process evaluation with a cursory review of the outcome. Only after the model is completely and appropriately adapted and has the necessary resources would a meaningful outcome evaluation be possible.

A significant challenge to social workers in this context was the impact of poverty on families. Unlike families in the West, Chinese families do not have access to services related to financial support. In addition, family members often felt ashamed, isolated, and powerless to help themselves. It also became clear that other individuals in the support network who were drawn into the FGDM meetings were also experiencing similar levels of hardship and felt that they had little to offer. Therefore, the social workers had to be creative, drawing sponsors into the family network who could offer practical or occasionally financial support. Such adaptation to the original FGC model had not occurred in other countries where it had been implemented. At a macro level, such piloting can allow social workers to see connections between the wider economic and social context and outcomes for children living in poverty.

At a mezzo level, the case exposes challenges experienced by neighborhoods and local NGOs participating in a pilot. Greenhalgh et al.'s (2004) model highlighted the importance of adopters having continuing access to information about the innovation (p. 600). In this case, it was necessary to continue the cycle of educating referral sources about the FGDM model. The case also identified many of the internal antecedents described in the innovation literature. According to Walker (2014), the size of the organization is significant, as both large and small organizations can present barriers and opportunities in different ways. In this case, the two NGOs were small organizations, consisting of fewer than 150 staff members each. This meant that they had little capacity, if any, to deploy staff and administrators to a new project. Social workers did not always have the capacity to lead, coordinate, or support the innovation. In addition, the nature of their funding was such that they had few "slack resources" (Walker, 2014, p. 25). Furthermore, the funding that they received from local government was ring-fenced for particular activities and future funding was highly dependent on reaching targets. Thus, a key consideration in piloting innovation is to balance keeping existing programs intact while diverting resources to new services. The NGOs had not given this sufficient thought, yet once they allocated one member of the team to the pilot project, progress was made. The project required additional resources, training, and staff time.

At a micro level, the lessons drawn from the pilot relate to the capacity and competency of social workers to engage with families and deliver the appropriate intervention. Process evaluation identified that the social workers did not feel competent or that they had the technical capacity to run the FGDM model (Greenhalgh et al., 2004, p. 605). The social workers were previously trained predominantly in casework methods, whereas the FGDM approach was founded more on community development methods. Though community development methods are not unusual in China, work with families is casework driven. Hence, additional skills training was needed before and during implementation of the pilot.

This case involving the piloting of FGC in China has demonstrated the challenges and difficulties associated with implementing a complex social innovation in a new context. It raised issues at the macro, mezzo, and micro level of practice, all of which were intrinsically interlinked. It demonstrated that all three levels need to be considered if systemic change is to be achieved, albeit slowly. The most difficult of these to achieve was at a macro level, particularly in a country like China, with its geographical vastness, social diversity, and a single centralized political system of power. However, with some provinces such as Guangdong receiving greater levels of autonomy, particularly in relation to specific areas of policy, and a growing awareness of issues affecting children, it was a valuable learning experience in adapting a model of practice to fit a local cultural context. Finding sites that are open to experimentation is important.

To conclude, it is still too early to say whether the FGDM model is an appropriate social work method to meet the needs of children and families in China. The FGDM approach in its adapted format has shown potential, particularly with cases involving child neglect. The innovations literature highlights that innovations can take up to 20 years to diffuse and reach critical mass; therefore, this case may represent the first part of a long journey (Balas & Boren, 2000). Given the infancy of social work services in China and the little time the profession has had to develop localized services, it is likely that they will continue to borrow from other countries. However, they simultaneously need to develop conceptual frameworks and services that are appropriate for the unique sociocultural context of mainland China. The key message from this pilot is that although paying attention to all three levels of practice is important, adaptation to the local cultural context is critical. Cultural adaptation processes remain underresearched in the social innovation literature and form the basis for a fertile future research agenda, not least within the social work context.

References

Acs, Z. J., Boardman, M. C., & McNeely, C. L. (2013). The social value of productive entrepreneurship. *Small Business Economics, 40*, 785–796.

Adams, P., & Chandler, S. (2004). Responsive regulation in child welfare: Systemic challenges to mainstreaming the family group conference. *Journal of Sociology and Social Welfare, 31*, 93–116.

Auerswald, P. E. (2009, Spring). Creating social value. *Stanford Social Innovation Review*. Retrieved from https://ssrn.com/abstract=1376425

Balas, E. A., & Boren, S. A. (2000). Managing clinical knowledge for health care improvement. *Yearbook of medical informatics*: *Patient-centered systems* (pp. 65–70). Retrieved from http://hdl.handle.net/10675.2/617990

Brown, L. (2003). Mainstream or margin? The current use of family group conferences in child welfare practice in the UK. *Child and Family Social Work, 8,* 331–340. doi:10.1046/j.1365-2206.2003.00293.x

Brown, L., & Osborne, S. P. (2013). Risk and innovation: Towards a framework for risk governance in public services. *Public Management Review, 15,* 186–209.

Castro, F. G., Barrerra, M., & Steiker, L.K.H. (2010). Issues and challenges in the design of culturally adapted evidence-based interventions. *Annual Review of Clinical Psychology, 6,* 213–239.

Chen, J., Dunne, M. P., & Han, P. (2004). Child sexual abuse in China: A study of adolescents in four provinces. *Child Abuse and Neglect: The International Journal, 28,* 1171–1186.

Connolly, M. (2004, January). *A perspective on the origins of family group conferencing* [American Humane FGDM Issues in Brief]. AHA Publications.

Fang, X., Fry, D. A., Ji, K., Finklehor, D., Chen, J., Lannen, P., & Dunne, M. P. (2015). The burden of child maltreatment in China: A systematic review. *Bulletin of the World Health Organization, 93,* 176C–185C.

Finkelhor, D. (1994). The international epidemiology of child sexual abuse. *Child Abuse and Neglect: The International Journal, 18,* 409–417.

Frost, N., Abram, F., & Burgess, H. (2014a). Family group conferences: Context, process and ways forward. *Child & Family Social Work, 19,* 480–490.

Frost, N., Abram, F., & Burgess, H. (2014b). Family group conferences: Evidence, outcomes and future research. *Child & Family Social Work, 19,* 501–507.

Gray, M., Coates, J., & Yellow Bird, M. (2008). *Indigenous social work around the world.* London: Routledge.

Greenhalgh, T., Robert, G., Macfarlane, F., Bate, P., & Kyriakidou, O. (2004). Diffusion of innovations in service organizations: Systematic review and recommendations. *Milbank Quarterly, 82,* 581–629.

International Federation of Social Workers. (2012). *The global agenda for social work and social development commitment to action.* Retrieved from http://ifsw.org/get-involved/agenda-for-social-work/

Katz, I., Shang, X., & Zhang, Y. (2010). Missing elements of a child protection system in China: The case of LX. *Social Policy & Society, 10*(1), 93–102.

Kelly, S. (2012, July). *Literature review on the diffusion of innovations and best practice for technology transfer.* Retrieved from https://pdfs.semanticscholar.org/4dc2/ed1768b3b3f774cc2c8cc7564b8813d5ab5e.pdf

Larson, R. S., Dearing, J. W., & Backer, T. E. (2017). *Strategies to scale up social programs: Pathways, partnerships and fidelity.* Retrieved from http://www.diffusionassociates.com/pdfs/strategies.pdf

Lei, J., & Walker, A. (2013). The big society in China: A failed experiment. *Social Policy and Society, 12*(1), 17–30.

Ministry of Civil Affairs. (2014). *Notice about further developing the pilots of moderately universal child welfare* [in Chinese]. Retrieved from http://www.mca.gov.cn/article /zwgk/fvfg/shflhshsw/201404/20140400627373.shtml

Mulgan, G. (2014). *Innovation in the public sector: How can public organisations better create, improve and adapt?* London: Nesta.

Mulgan, G., Tucker, S., Rushanara, A., & Sanders, B. (2007). *Social innovation: What it is, why it matters and how it can be accelerated* [Working paper]. Retrieved from http://eureka.sbs.ox.ac.uk/761/

Nadkarni, A., Velleman, R., Dabholkar, H., Shinde, S., Bhat, B., McCambridge, J., et al. (2015). The systematic development and pilot randomized evaluation of counselling for alcohol problems, a lay counselor-delivered psychological treatment for harmful drinking in primary care in India: The PREMIUM study. *Alcoholism: Clinical and Experimental Research, 39,* 391–574.

National Association of Social Workers. (2017). *Code of ethics of the National Association of Social Workers.* Washington, DC: Author.

Osei-Hwedie, K., & Rankopo, M. (2012). Social work in developing countries. In M. Gray, J. Midgley, & S. A. Webb (Eds.), *The Sage handbook of social work* (pp. 723–739). London: Sage Publications.

Parra-Cordona, J. R., Domenech-Rodriguez, M., & Bernal, G. (2012). Culturally adapting an evidence-based parenting intervention for Latino immigrants: The need to integrate fidelity and cultural relevance. *Family Processes, 51*(1), 56–72.

Qiao, D.-P., & Chan, Y.-C. (2005). Child abuse in China: A yet to be acknowledged "social problem" in the Chinese mainland. *Child and Family Social Work, 10*(1), 21–27.

Rauktis, M. E., Bishop-Patrick, L., Jung, N., & Pennell, J. (2013). Family group decision-making: Measuring fidelity to practice principles in public child welfare. *Children and Youth Services Review, 35,* 287–295.

Roby, J. L., Pennell, J., Rotabi, K., Bunkers, K. M., & deUcles, S. (2015). Contextual adaptation of family group conferencing model: Early evidence from Guatemala. *British Journal of Social Work, 45,* 2281–2297.

Rogers, E. M. (2003). *Diffusion of innovations.* New York: Free Press.

Shang, X.-Y. (2012). Looking for best practice in caring for disabled children: A case of socialized foster care in China. *Asia Pacific Journal of Social Work and Development, 22*(1–2), 127–138.

Singh, A. (2016). *The process of social value creation: A multiple-case study on social entrepreneurship in India.* New York: Springer.

United Nations. (2015). *The millennium development goals report.* New York: Author.

United Nations Children's Emergency Fund. (2014). *Children in China: An atlas of social indicators.* Beijing: Author.

Walker, R. (2014). Internal and external antecedents of process innovation: A review and extension. *Public Management Review, 16,* 21–44.

Wang, F., Xu, Z., Sun, Y., & Zhou, L. (2014). The filial piety mind of contemporary Chinese and its transition. *Psychological Exploration, 34,* 529–535.

West, M. A., & Farr, J. L. (1990). Innovation at work. In M. A. West & J. L. Farr (Eds.), *Innovation and creativity at work: Psychological and organizational strategies* (pp. 3–13). Chichester, UK: Wiley.

Yuen-Tsang, A., & Ku, B. (2008). A journey through a thousand miles begins with one step: The development of culturally relevant social work education and fieldwork practice in China. In J. Coates, M. Gray, & M. Yellowbird (Eds.), *Indigenous social work around the world. Towards culturally relevant education and practice* (pp. 177–190). Aldershot, UK: Ashgate.

Acknowledgments

The FGC research was supported by the University of Bath Alumni Fund and the Social Work Association of Baiyun District. The project team would like to acknowledge the support that they have received from Family Rights Group in the United Kingdom, the Torbay FGC Project, the Qichuang Social Work Service Center, the Baiyun Hengfu Social Work Service Association, Brenda Yao, the brave social workers, and the children and families who went first.

9

Innovative Practices in Financial Inclusion and Asset Building: Relevance for Social Work Practice

Mathieu R. Despard

Despite a modest economic recovery from the Great Recession, many U.S. households are struggling financially. Just over half of households could use cash on hand to pay for an unexpected $400 expense (Larrimore, Dodini, & Thomas, 2016), and less than half of households have enough money saved to cover expenses for three months in the event of a job loss or other major event (Financial Industry Regulatory Authority Investor Education Foundation, 2016). Low- and moderate-income (LMI) households are especially vulnerable. Over half have difficulty paying bills because of volatile income and expenses, and only 34 percent could cover an emergency expense (Larrimore et al., 2016). LMI households are also much more likely than higher-income households to lack a bank account and turn to money stores, payday loans, and other alternative financial services (Federal Deposit Insurance Corporation [FDIC], 2016), especially in communities with a concentration of these services (Friedline & Kepple, 2017).

The financial struggles of LMI households call for innovative solutions that promote financial inclusion—ensuring that all households have access to the financial products and services that meet their needs throughout the life course (World Bank, 2017). This extends beyond simply having a bank account; households also need opportunities and incentives to build assets (Sherraden, Frey, & Birkenmaier, 2016).

Social work plays an important role in promoting financial inclusion. Financial social work has emerged as a recognized practice field in recent years (Despard & Chowa, 2010; Despard, Chowa, & Hart, 2012; Sherraden et al., 2015), rekindling social workers' historic efforts in addressing the financial needs of individuals and households (Stuart, 2013). Social workers aim to help individuals become financially capable—able to meet basic needs, cope with unexpected events, and build assets. This means individuals need financial knowledge and skills (ability) and access to safe and affordable financial products and services (Sherraden, 2013).

Social workers can help promote financial inclusion because they understand the daily struggles of LMI households and have an ethical obligation to promote social and economic justice. Adopting a person-in-environment perspective, social workers also can develop an understanding of how LMI households access and interact with financial institutions and their products and services. Because cross-sector approaches are endemic to social innovation, social workers can play important roles as organizers and facilitators of such approaches for community change that promote financial inclusion and asset building.

The purpose of this chapter is to describe an array of social innovations that promote financial inclusion and asset building among LMI and other underserved households. Phills, Deiglmeier, and Miller (2008) defined "social innovation" as "a novel solution to a social problem that is more effective, efficient, sustainable, or just than existing solutions and for which the value created accrues primarily to society as a whole rather than private individuals" (p. 36). Financial exclusion—lack of access to and use of safe and affordable financial products and services to help LMI and other economically vulnerable households meet their needs across the life course (Baradaran, 2015; Barr, 2010; FDIC, 2016)—is a major social problem that calls for innovative solutions.

The innovations described in this chapter address the multiple needs of LMI households to be financially secure and include transaction and credit products and services, saving and asset-building opportunities, and tax assistance. Key themes include the role of technology, partnerships, integration of financial inclusion and asset building in nonfinancial settings, and the role of intermediary organizations.

Some of the innovations described in this chapter have been developed and are being implemented by social workers, whereas others have emanated from other professions. Innovative solutions transcend the usual roles of the social sector, for-profit business, and government and require cultivating cross-disciplinary perspectives (Nandan, London, & Bent-Goodley, 2015; Nandan & Scott, 2013). An important goal of this chapter is to invite social workers both to join our profession's financial inclusion efforts and to learn from the ideas and efforts of other professions, corporations, and organizations that typically identified with social work. Therefore, following a description of innovative solutions, I discuss implications for social work education and practice to identify the roles social workers can play in social innovations that promote financial inclusion and asset building.

Financial Product and Service and Asset-Building Innovations

Financial inclusion means ensuring that everyone—especially the economically marginalized—has access to safe and affordable financial products and services to meet a variety of needs (World Bank, 2017). Individuals and households need financial products and services to conduct day-to-day transactions, manage finances, borrow, and save (Birkenmaier, 2012), yet serving LMI households is typically not profitable for banks (Cohen et al., 2015). Thus, efforts to promote financial inclusion and asset building are an important expression of social entrepreneurship, particularly in the face of market failure.

Transaction Products and Services

A lack of finances to open, or justify owning, an account and bank fees are prominent reasons why millions of LMI households in the United States are unbanked (FDIC, 2016). To address these barriers, key strategies include low- or no-fee basic accounts, gateway products and services, general-purpose reloadable prepaid cards, and "second chance" accounts for individuals "bounced" out of the banking system because of a history of overdrafting (Haynes-Bordas, Kiss, & Yilmazer, 2008; Rengert & Rhine, 2016). The FDIC's Model Safe Accounts template and pilot project (FDIC, 2012) and Bank On national account standards (Cities for Financial Empowerment Fund [CFEF], 2017b) offer a set of account features advocates can promote. These features include

- debit or prepaid card for point-of-sale capability
- minimum opening deposit of $25 or less
- monthly maintenance fees of no more than $5 (not waivable) to $10 (waivable with at least two options)
- no possibility of incurring overdraft or nonsufficient fund fees
- free online and telephone banking, in-network ATM transactions, bill pay, check cashing, and monthly statements

Additional recommendations include denying accounts for new customers only in cases of past fraud (versus overdrafting), acceptance of alternative forms of identification to open accounts, and free savings accounts and account transfers (CFEF, 2017b).

Acceptance of alternative forms of identification such as consular identification cards are especially important for immigrants and refugees who wish to open accounts (Bair, 2003). In addition, local governments such as Washtenaw County and Detroit, Michigan, offer identification cards for individuals in need of bank accounts yet for whom obtaining state or federal government-issued identification is difficult. Advocates can also encourage financial institutions to offer remote deposit capture, enabling customers to deposit paychecks when they cannot get to a bank or credit union branch (for example, individuals who work seasonal jobs far away from home).

Prepaid debt cards offer consumers a checkless option for conducting and managing transactions. An important feature of prepaid cards is that an individual cannot make a purchase for an amount that exceeds the card's balance, thus avoiding expensive insufficient funds and overdraft fees (Fusaro, 2008). Prepaid cards should offer easy loading and unloading, person-to-person payments, one-step cash reloads, clear fee schedules, fee waivers (for example, for using direct deposit of paychecks), alerts, budgeting notifications and tools, and a savings feature (Garon & Latta, 2016). Electronic benefits transfer (EBT) cards provide a similar function as prepaid cards for recipients of public assistance programs such as Temporary Assistance for Needy Families (TANF); recipients use their cards to make retail purchases. Yet the EBT system also represents an opportunity to set up bank accounts for public assistance recipients as a default (Gill, Mills, & McKenna, 2015).

Financial Technology: Cash Flow and Financial Management Apps

A range of mobile apps and online programs developed by financial technology (FinTech) start-up firms and larger financial service firms help consumers better track their spending, manage cash flow, and ensure that bills are paid on time. Whereas online banking allows consumers to monitor account activity, these apps and programs help consumers analyze their spending habits and patterns and determine the best way to pay bills given the timing of inflows. Popular apps and programs include Mint, a free program offered by Intuit, which links to consumers' bank accounts. Mint features bill tracking and payment, budgeting, credit score, alerts and tips, and information about financial product and service offers.

Some apps and programs have been designed in response to the specific needs of LMI households. Neighborhood Trust Financial Partners (NTFP), a community development financial institution (CDFI) serving the Washington Heights neighborhood of upper Manhattan, offers the workplace-based PayGoal app coupled with financial advising for LMI employees. PayGoal helps employees allocate their earnings to help pay bills on time and better manage their finances to meet other financial goals (Dorrance & Gorham, 2016). Fresh EBT is an app to allow Supplemental Nutrition Assistance Program (SNAP) participants to locate grocers that accept SNAP, check the monthly benefit balances on their EBT cards, and track household spending.

Credit Products and Services

Access to affordable credit is important, particularly for LMI households that struggle with income and expense volatility that makes household finances unstable and unpredictable (Morduch & Schneider, 2017). Access to credit, including the ubiquitous credit card, has increased in the United States over the last several years. Short-term credit can help households manage cash flow and access funds in an emergency. However, LMI and racial minority households have less access to credit cards and short-term loans and face higher interest rates and fees (Birkenmaier & Curley, 2009; Larrimore et al., 2016; Weller, 2007).

Though some banks offer unsecured personal loans, credit checks are customary, and many LMI households likely have damaged credit because of difficulty paying bills on time and managing debt with limited income (Birkenmaier & Curley, 2009). These households are more likely to use payday and similar consumer loans (FDIC, 2016), which do not require credit checks. Yet these loans carry triple-digit interest rates and are structured in a way that makes repayment difficult, trapping borrowers in cycles of debt (Birkenmaier & Curley, 2009; Consumer Financial Protection Bureau, 2013; Pew Charitable Trusts, 2012). Thus, innovation is sorely needed to help LMI households access safe and affordable short-term credit. High-cost and predatory credit is a matter of social and economic justice social workers must help address (Karger, 2007).

Wage and salary advances and loans through employers or financial institutions provide households with a working member an alternative to payday loans for dealing with financial emergencies. NTFP partners with FlexWage Solutions, a small for-profit firm, to offer WageGoal. When financial emergencies arise or an important payment such as rent is due, WageGoal allows employees of participating companies to access a portion of their earned wages before payday for a $5 fee (http://www.wagegoal.com). For example, if an employee has an $800 rent payment due on the 15th of the month but is $300 short, WageGoal allows the employee to use $300 in accrued wages to make this rent payment, rather than having to wait until payday, at which point rent would be overdue. In partnership with Sunrise Banks, a CDFI in Minnesota, Employee Loan Solutions offers TrueConnect, a 12-month loan of up to $3,000 with an interest rate like those charged for credit lines and consumer loans. Monthly loan payments are automatically deducted from employees' pay, and borrowers also have access to financial counseling. Employers pay nothing to offer TrueConnect to their employees (Frank-Miller, Covington, Despard, Hannon, & Grinstein-Weiss, 2017).

Many credit unions such as State Employees' Credit Union in North Carolina offer salary advance loans, with incentives for borrowers to save for future expenses. Many credit products offered by credit unions have savings features, such as the Federation of Community Development Credit Unions' Borrow and Save program, part of the Filene Research Institute's incubator project. Loans of up to $3,000 are offered, with 10 to 50 percent of the loan placed in a restricted savings account for the loan term. Some banks offer similar products, such as the CreditPlus loan from Mississippi-based BankPlus, which requires a portion of the loan to be deposited into a savings account. Borrowers also must complete a financial literacy seminar and are encouraged to use their loans to pay off more expensive payday or similar loans. BankPlus offers CreditPlus explicitly to offer customers an alternative to payday loans, which are unrestricted in Mississippi.

Nonprofit organizations other than credit unions and CDFIs offer short-term loans. Jewish federations and loan associations (http://www.iajfl.org) offer interest-free loans for emergencies, small businesses, education, and other household needs. The Kansas Loan Pool Project is specifically designed to offer low-interest loans to help individuals refinance expensive payday loans (Catholic Charities of Northeast Kansas, n.d.).

Alternative credit reporting and scoring is an additional area of innovation with the potential to disrupt lenders' application and underwriting processes. Credit reports and scoring greatly affect households' access to credit and the interest rates and fees they pay to use credit (Birkenmaier & Curley, 2009). Yet, roughly 45 million—of whom LMI households and minority, young, and old adults make up a disproportionate share and do not have credit records or are "unscoreable"—have credit files that are too thin to produce a credit score (Brevoort, Grimm, & Kambara, 2016).

Alternative scoring models, such as L2C, LexisNexis, and FICO, are leveraging "big data" to incorporate data not included in a traditional FICO score, such as utility payments, employment, and alternative lending activity (for example, payday loans, rent-to-own contracts). These models have the potential to extend access to credit among these "unscoreable" consumers while managing lenders' risk (Schneider & Schutte, 2007). However, many individuals without credit histories or with unscoreable records may not have sufficient data, such as housing leases and utility accounts in their names, for alternative models either. Moreover, it is unclear how accurately these alternative scoring models assess creditworthiness to help expand access to credit (Brevoort et al., 2016).

The examples offered here illustrate efforts to respond to credit market failure. The lack of access to safe and affordable credit among LMI households motivated these product innovations and disrupted the alternative financial services industry, which relegates LMI households to a fringe economy (Karger, 2007). The credit innovations described here also aim to help

LMI households improve their credit scores, which determine interest rates and access to other forms of credit (Birkenmaier & Curley, 2009). Many credit innovations also help households save for future emergencies to help break the cycle of incurring debt to cover income shortfalls. Yet credit innovations offered through credit unions and employers lack the broad reach of innovations offered by banks. Nonetheless, regulatory changes are needed to scale up safe and affordable short-term bank loans.

Social workers assist with meeting the needs of marginalized individuals and families by helping them find the necessary resources. This includes ensuring access to safe and affordable credit products when income and public assistance fall short, especially when households experience financial shocks, such as a job loss or hospitalization and other emergencies. Fairly priced credit is also a matter of economic justice that social workers ought to promote. As credit innovations are developed, social workers should critically examine whether these innovations really are affordable and meet the needs of LMI and other marginalized households.

Savings and Asset-Building Innovations

Michael Sherraden's 1991 book, *Assets and the Poor*, challenged key assumptions about poverty and strategies to alleviate it. Assets promote financial security and other important outcomes in ways that income alone cannot, Sherraden argued. Individual development accounts (IDAs) were launched in the late 1990s as the first major expression of asset-based practice and policy through the American Dream Demonstration (ADD). IDA participants are expected to make monthly deposits toward a long-term savings goal, which are matched usually on a 2:1 or 3:1 basis. Upon achieving their savings goal, participants are eligible to use matched funds for certain purposes, typically buying a home, paying for postsecondary education, or starting a business. IDA participants usually also receive financial education and services related to their savings goal, such as business planning assistance or homeownership counseling. Accounts held at local banks or credit unions typically name the host nonprofit organization as the custodian, limiting withdrawals prior to achieving savings goals to emergencies. Evidence from the ADD indicates that LMI individuals can and will save when offered incentives, facilitation, and support (Sherraden, Schreiner, & Beverly, 2003).

The matched savings concept in IDAs has inspired similar innovations. Child development or savings accounts (CDAs) were originally suggested by Sherraden (1991) and materialized in 2004 through the Saving for Education, Entrepreneurship, and Downpayment–Oklahoma (SEED-OK) demonstration. Through CDAs, parents and other family members make deposits in accounts that are held in a child's name and are matched with public or private dollars. These accounts are meant to grow over several years and to be used by beneficiaries to pay for postsecondary education, to buy a home, or to establish a retirement account. A common configuration demonstrated by SEED-OK is for state 529 college savings plan accounts to serve as the CDA. Research has demonstrated that parents can and will save for their children's future education by using CDAs (Nam, Kim, Clancy, Zager, & Sherraden, 2013; Shanks, 2014). Furthermore, assets are positively associated with children's educational outcomes (Elliott, Destin, & Friedline, 2011; Shanks & Destin, 2009).

Early work on CDAs through SEED-OK has inspired several local and state CDA initiatives. Maine's Harold Alfond College Challenge automatically enrolls all newborns in Maine and provides a $500 seed grant, which is deposited into a state 529 plan account (Clancy & Sherraden, 2014). San Francisco's Kindergarten to College program automatically enrolls every child entering kindergarten in a college savings account with a $50 seed deposit and an additional $50 deposit for children receiving free or reduced school meals. Subsequent family contributions are matched on a 1:1 basis for the first $100 in contributions and an additional $100 is granted if at least $10 is deposited for six consecutive months (Bevans, 2013). Other college savings–focused CDA initiatives have been launched or are in development in Lansing, Michigan; Cuyahoga County, Ohio; New York City; Colorado; Connecticut; Utah; and Rhode Island. Also, the 1:1 Fund is a national platform launched by Prosperity Now (formerly Corporation for Enterprise Development) to facilitate deposits to CDAs by directing supporters and donors to local CDA programs.

A limitation of IDAs and CDAs is that savings and matches are restricted for long-term purposes. Rothwell and Han (2010) found that having children, negative net worth, and not owning a car predicted applying to but not enrolling in an IDA program. Many LMI households may be unable to save for long-term goals and may have more immediate financial needs (Adams & West, 2015; West, Banerjee, Phipps, & Friedline, 2017). Accordingly, the focus of savings programs has shifted toward shorter-term savings goals and horizons, such as having an emergency savings fund to cover three months of usual household expenses in the event of a job loss or other major financial shock. Yet less than half of all U.S. households and less than a quarter of households with income under $25,000 have such a "rainy day" fund (Financial Industry Regulatory Authority Investor Education Foundation, 2016). Among LMI households, having emergency savings lessens risk of material hardship (Gjertson, 2016) and makes these households less likely to turn to payday or similar loans in the event of an unexpected large expense.

Adams and West (2015) described a program offered by a CDFI in California to help LMI households build emergency savings. Participants had up to $500 of savings deposits matched on a 2:1 basis with philanthropic dollars over a two-year period, for a total possible balance of $1,500. Before opening an account, participants were required to attend 10 to 12 hours of financial education classes. The basic structure of this program was like an IDA, yet with the goal of saving for emergencies. San Francisco–based EARN also uses a savings match through its Starter Savings program for individuals who have an online savings account with a bank or credit union. Participants use a mobile app linked to their savings account to choose a savings goal, including building an emergency fund, and receive a $10 reward for saving at least $20 each month.

Savings accelerator accounts (SAAs) are an example of how incentives can be structured and delivered to encourage asset accumulation. SAA savings account incentives include sign-up bonuses, deposit matches to incentivize a regular pattern of saving, and interest. Also, incentives are distributed exponentially to discourage early withdrawals. That is, the distribution schedule acts as an implied time restriction (Khashadourian, 2015).

Prize-linked savings is an innovation capitalizing on the thrill of winning. Save-to-Win was launched in 2009 by Commonwealth, the Filene Research Institute, and the Michigan Credit Union League. Credit union members earned an entry into a monthly lottery drawing for every deposit made (with restrictions). By 2017, this program was being implemented in credit unions in 11 states. Commonwealth has expanded prize-linked savings to general-purpose reloadable prepaid card with a savings feature. Every savings deposit made using an app or Web site linked to these prepaid cards earns an entry to a monthly national lottery drawing.

Finally, interventions that incorporate knowledge from behavioral science can encourage saving. MAGIC Mojo is an impulse saving program that addresses lack of willpower and planning and capitalizes on impulsivity. When participants forgo an impulse purchase or save money from a prepaid card purchase, they text the amount they saved, which is subsequently transferred to the savings side of the card. Participants also receive text message savings reminders in relation to their stated savings goals (Manturuk, Dorrance, & Halladay, 2015).

As Sherraden (1991) argued, practices and policies aimed only at income are insufficient. Households also need assets to have resources to draw on during times of need and to invest in new opportunities such as homeownership and postsecondary education. Asset building also promotes self-determination, as households have resources they fully control and with which they can exercise choices concerning a range of financial needs and goals. Thus, social workers' commitments and efforts to meet client needs and promote economic justice should include a focus on assets, not just helping clients access and receive public assistance.

Tax Assistance

Helping LMI households claim tax credits—especially the earned income tax credit—and file tax returns for free is an important strategy to promote financial security. Annual tax refunds are the single largest lump sum payment many LMI households receive (Halpern-Meekin, Edin, Tach, & Sykes, 2015). Consequently, exploring different ways that refunds can be used to better promote a household's financial security is another opportunity to innovate. For example, research has found an association between refund saving and lessened risk for material hardship (Grinstein-Weiss et al., 2016). Thus, many tax assistance programs encourage filers to set aside at least part of their tax refunds in savings. The Extra Credit Savings program helped tax filers in Chicago open savings accounts with a preferential interest rate (Beverly, Tescher, & Romich, 2004) whereas filers in New York City received a 50 percent match for initial savings account deposits made with their refunds (Key, Tucker, Grinstein-Weiss, & Comer, 2015). In addition to prized-linked savings campaigns and help in opening bank accounts, the Center for Economic Progress in Chicago and Prepare and Prosper in Minneapolis–St. Paul offer financial coaching through their Volunteer Income Tax Assistance (VITA) sites.

Yet not all LMI individuals go to VITA sites to file their taxes. To reach online tax filers, the Center for Social Development at Washington University in St. Louis partnered with Intuit Corporation and the Duke University Center for Advanced Hindsight to offer Refund-to-Saving (R2S). LMI individuals who qualify for, and use, Intuit's free TurboTax Freedom Edition (TTFE) receive savings prompts and messages informed by behavioral science and embedded in TTFE software. Each year, these prompts and messages change to test new ideas for encouraging refund saving. Results of R2S studies indicate effectiveness in encouraging refund saving (Grinstein-Weiss et al., 2015; Grinstein-Weiss, Russell, Gale, Key, & Ariely, 2017) and savings account openings in the months after filing taxes. However, online tax-time saving is limited by the inability for filers to open savings accounts when they file their taxes, a functionality the Internal Revenue Service could establish through its Free File Alliance in partnership with federal bank regulators and financial institutions.

Lessons for the Field of Financial Inclusion and Asset Building

Key insights and lessons concerning how to promote financial inclusion and asset building can be inferred from the innovations described here, which represent new practices that disrupt the status quo of a financial services industry that fails to meet the needs of all households. First, an array of products and services are needed to fulfill multiple household financial needs. Second, products and services can be enhanced with technology. Third, financial inclusion and asset-building efforts should be brought into nonfinancial settings with a specific focus on empowerment of vulnerable population groups.

Addressing Multiple Household Financial Needs. Households have multiple needs to be addressed with financial products and services. It does little good to offer only tax assistance or offer only a savings program and not also offer transaction services and access to credit. Integrating credit and savings through products like Borrow and Save (described earlier) is especially important. Other examples include Local Support Initiatives Corporation (LISC) Twin Accounts, Innovations for Poverty Action's Pay Yourself Back, and Ideas 42 and Oliver Wyman's Financial Stabilizer (Commonwealth, 2016). Also, the Prosperity SmartSave card links a credit card to savings incentives (Henderson, 2015). Savings can also be incorporated into debt management plans (Heisler & Lutter, 2015) and into mortgage payments so LMI homeowners have a fund for home repairs and other emergencies (Moulton, Samek, & Loibl, 2015).

It is important to note that access to safe and affordable financial products and services alone may be insufficient; individuals can also benefit from financial education and counseling. For instance, through the Pathways to Financial Empowerment initiative, participating credit unions offer credit counseling in branches (National Federation of Community Development Credit Unions & Neighborhood Trust Financial Partners, 2015).

Integrating Technology. As illustrated with many of the examples already provided, mobile and online technologies can be integrated with and enhance financial products and services to offer households more tools to effectively manage resources. Mobile banking itself may offer an alternative to access financial products and services through physical bank or credit union branches. As described in Chapter 4, the M-PESA mobile banking platform in Kenya serves as an illustration of how technology can dramatically promote financial inclusion. However, mobile banking is less likely to affect communities that lack sufficient cellular and broadband coverage or households that are concerned about the security of sensitive data, have a strong preference to conduct cash transactions (Bennett, Conover, O'Brien, & Advincula, 2014), or do not own smartphones or computers (Burhouse, Homer, Osaki, & Bachman, 2014). Also, financial management apps—despite claims of solving cash flow problems—are unlikely to supplant households' needs for access to affordable credit and savings incentives and support.

Integrating Financial Inclusion and Asset-Building Efforts in Nonfinancial Settings. A promising strategy for lowering barriers to financial products and services and asset-building opportunities for LMI and other underserved households is to bring these resources into nonfinancial settings, such as the workplace (Frank-Miller et al., 2017). Examples include AutoSave, employer-facilitated automatic contributions to unrestricted savings accounts (Lopez-Fernandini & Schultz, 2010); NTFP's Employer Solution program, which offers financial coaching in the workplace for LMI employees; and TrueConnect, described previously. Other employee financial wellness benefits include financial coaching, financial education classes, credit counseling, and debt management (Frank-Miller et al., 2017).

Social welfare programs and human service systems are also amenable to integrating financial inclusion strategies. Fresh EBT and TANF bank accounts are examples of integration in social welfare programs. Regarding human service systems, the Opportunity Passport is a program sponsored by the Jim Casey Youth Opportunities Initiative to help youths in foster care build assets through matched savings (Annie E. Casey Foundation, 2009). Services integrated in the public workforce development system for persons living with disabilities include financial coaching, credit and debt management, and assistance in opening bank accounts (Morris & Goodman, 2015). A growing number of county and municipal Offices of Financial Empowerment are integrating financial services in city and county social work and other human services and launching financial empowerment centers to serve the public. Mental health services are another social work practice setting through which financial inclusion and asset-building efforts can better meet the needs of clients (Cuddeback, Blank-Wilson, Despard, Tomar, & Chowa, 2017).

Youth development programs and schools are other social work practice settings through which financial inclusion and asset-building interventions can be implemented. MyPath is a savings program in San Francisco to reach youths receiving their first paycheck through summer youth employment programs (Loke, Choi, & Libby, 2015). School-based savings programs have a long history in the United States (Cruce, 2002) and have garnered renewed interest in communities. Hillside High School in Durham, North Carolina, was reportedly the first high school to open a bank branch when it brought Wood-forest National Bank on campus in 2014. Many youth development programs such as Alternative for Girls in Detroit, Michigan, host matched savings programs for participants. Bank account ownership during teen and young adult years is important because it predicts ownership of a diversity of assets during adulthood (Friedline, Despard, & Chowa, 2016).

Role of Community Change Initiatives

In addition to the innovations already described, promoting financial inclusion and asset building takes coordinated, community-wide effort. Bank On coalitions are local partnerships among nonprofit organizations, financial institutions, and governmental agencies to increase the number of residents who have access to and use affordable financial products and services. Financial institutions are encouraged to adopt national account standards and receive validation through the National Consumer Law Center (Cities for Financial Empowerment Fund, 2017a). Yet only 9 percent of banks meet the full set of Bank On national account standards (Friedline, Despard, Eastlund, & Schuetz, 2017), illustrating the need for these local partnerships.

America Saves is a project of the Consumer Federation of America to support local, regional, and statewide savings campaigns. These campaigns recruit individuals to make savings pledges, hold awareness-raising events during America Saves Week, and conduct savings competitions. Other coalition approaches to promote financial inclusion and asset building include Money Smart Kansas City and Money Smart Nebraska. Outreach and engagement strategies are supported by a broad section of the community: banks, credit unions, local and state government agencies, nonprofit organizations, housing providers, neighborhood groups, advocacy groups, and faith communities.

Another approach to financial inclusion is to target groups of residents who are less likely to own a bank account, such as racial and ethnic minorities and immigrants. The Banking in Color project found that LMI communities of color have unique needs and require different approaches to financial inclusion and asset building (National Council of La Raza, 2014). The Latino Community Credit Union (LCCU) in Durham, North Carolina, formed in 2000 from a partnership among El Centro Hispano, the Support Center, Self-Help Credit Union, and the North Carolina State Employees Credit Union (LCCU, 2017). LCCU formed largely out of concern that recently arrived Spanish-speaking immigrants were getting robbed of the cash they held at home and were missing asset-building opportunities through small business development and homeownership. These new residents were reluctant to visit banks because of bad experiences with or distrust of financial institutions in their home countries or because they could not meet legal documentation requirements. Currently, most banks and credit unions will accept forms of identification other than driver's license and social security cards, such as the Mexican Consular Identification Card.

Nuestro Barrio is an example of an innovative media-based intervention aimed at financial inclusion and empowerment of Latino immigrants. This Spanish-language telenovela, designed and distributed by the Community Reinvestment Association of North Carolina, includes plot lines and characters to convey important information about financial products and services (Spader, 2009). Similar to findings from Zhan, Anderson, and Scott (2009) regarding financial education outcomes for immigrants, *Nuestro Barrio* had a positive impact on financial knowledge, homeownership preparedness, and bank account ownership (Spader, Ratcliffe, Montoya, & Skillern, 2009).

Bank development districts use a supply-side strategy to promote financial inclusion by focusing on banking deserts—neighborhoods where there is no bank branch within a reasonable distance of residents. In New York, state government agrees to deposit state funds in banks that agree to expand their services in underserved communities. Local governments can provide additional incentives, such as property tax abatement (Calderon, 2009). Similarly, post office banking is a proposed solution to provide basic financial services to communities without a bank or credit union branch (Baradaran, 2015).

The examples of community change initiatives to promote financial inclusion and asset building outlined here are opportunities for social workers to apply a host of community practice roles and skills (Weil, Gamble, & Ohmer, 2013). Social workers can help organize local coalitions of banks, credit unions, nonprofit organizations, advocacy groups, neighborhood associations, and local government to envision and implement new collaborative strategies for promoting financial inclusion and asset building. These initiatives can promote social work values, and the changes that result add to the social value generated in the community.

Role of Intermediaries

Intermediary organizations facilitate financial inclusion and asset-building innovation by pooling financial resources; launching pilot, demonstration, and incubator programs; and offering technical assistance to local organizations. These organizations are important resources for social workers who want to launch, strengthen, or expand local efforts.

The Center for Financial Services Innovation (CFSI) pools philanthropic resources to host programs such as the Financial Capability Innovations Fund. CFSI received $30 million over five years from JPMorgan Chase and Company for the Financial Solutions Lab, which provides funding, technical assistance, mentoring, networking, and peer learning to nonprofit and entrepreneurial FinTech providers. CFEF supports local Bank On coalitions, financial inclusion efforts among municipal summer youth employment programs, and replication of municipal financial empowerment centers. Filene Research Institute offers incubator programs to develop small-dollar loans, non–prime auto loans, integrated credit and savings, and savings innovations through credit unions. Similarly, the Federation of Community Development Credit Unions provides support to member credit unions implementing pilot projects. The Aspen Institute sponsors Nonprofit Leaders in Financial Technology—organizations dedicated to promoting financial inclusion through technology. Prosperity Now (formerly Corporation for Enterprise Development) promotes the development of financial inclusion and asset-building initiatives, shared learning, and advocacy campaigns among networks of local organizations.

Think tanks and academic research centers also play an important role as research, evaluation, and policy development partners. These include the Center for Community Capital at the University of North Carolina at Chapel Hill; the Center for Social Development at Washington University in St. Louis; the Center for Financial Security at the University of Wisconsin; Center for Assets, Education, and Inclusion at the University of Michigan; the Aspen Institute; and New America.

Implications for Social Work Education and Practice

Social workers can, and should, play significant roles in the numerous examples of financial inclusion and asset-building innovations described in this chapter. Ensuring that all individuals and families have access to financial products and services that meet their needs throughout the life course, that they have opportunities to build assets to cope with life's uncertainties, and that they can unlock new opportunities is a matter of social and economic justice consistent with the National Association of Social Workers (2017) *Code of Ethics*. Financial inclusion and asset building should also be embraced as an intervention strategy by social workers because it promotes self-determination. The more individuals and families can participate in, and enjoy, the benefits of the economy, the greater their control over resources to meet basic needs and realize goals.

How can social workers promote financial inclusion and asset building? At the micro practice level, social workers can expand their assessments beyond income and receipt of public assistance to include assets, debt, and use of financial services. This information can be used to make referrals to local community development credit unions, credit counseling and debt management services, and asset-building programs. This information may also be used to inform treatment and service plans, such as helping survivors of intimate partner violence gain economic independence (Sanders, 2013), persons living with serious mental illness avoid predatory financial services (Cuddeback et al., 2017), or youth aging out of the of the foster care system to gain financial independence.

At the mezzo practice level, social workers can also advocate for their agencies to form partnerships with organizations mentioned earlier, to make it easier for clients to access safe and affordable financial products and services. For example, while working in a Head Start program, I arranged for a local bank representative to introduce parents to a free checking account program and formed a partnership with a credit counseling agency to help improve IDA applicants' credit before taking steps toward homeownership.

Social workers can also help form, organize, and facilitate community coalitions and partnerships to promote financial inclusion and asset building. For example, I formed and facilitated an IDA partnership among financial institutions, affordable housing groups, local government, United Way, and nonprofit organizations. Consistent with a social innovation framework (Phills et al., 2008), this cross-sector partnership made it possible to envision innovative strategies that no single organization could implement on its own. Social workers can also play a role in organizing local efforts to combat predatory lending that harms LMI households (Caplan, 2014).

Promoting financial inclusion and asset-building innovation requires a willingness of social workers to work with financial institutions. These initiatives may be well aligned with banks' corporate social responsibility strategies (Anderson, 2014) and Community Reinvestment Act portfolio needs. Most banks recognize that they are not reaching all households, which opens the door for social workers to guide and help banks' efforts. With larger banks, it is helpful for social workers to identify and develop a relationship with a community development officer or a program officer with the bank's corporate foundation. These and other foundations provide funding to support many of the innovations described in this chapter.

Social workers can also consider working within financial institutions, particularly community development credit unions and financial institutions whose missions align with social work values. Social workers can also work for Council on Accreditation accredited consumer credit counseling agencies, community action agencies, and community development corporations. For example, LISC supports a national network of financial opportunity centers. Through their work within these alternative institutions, social workers can add to the social value created—by influencing the level and extent of impact created.

By working in these types of organizations, social workers can promote innovation in financial products and services on the basis of their understanding of, and concern for, economically vulnerable households. For example, social workers can help credit unions design new credit products that offer LMI households an alternative to payday and auto title loans. Social workers can also help infuse a social and economic justice perspective in these organizations by acknowledging and responding to economic challenges facing LMI households that are beyond their control (Feldman, 2017). For example, in a community action agency, I developed a money management guide that helped inform LMI clients of predatory lending and acknowledged the difficulty of managing household budgets with low incomes.

At the macro practice level, social workers can also play an important role in advancing policy innovations that promote financial inclusion and asset building. ADD of the Center for Social Development, located at the George Warren Brown School of Social Work at Washington University in St. Louis, helped pave the way for the proliferation of IDAs supported by the Assets for Independence Act (Sherraden, 2000). ADD and its research on IDAs inspired and laid the groundwork for additional policy innovations championed and shepherded by social workers, such as CDAs (Elliott, 2009) and tax-time savings (Grinstein-Weiss et al., 2017). ADD has also informed policy innovations to reach vulnerable populations. The Achieving a Better Life Experience (ABLE) Act was passed in 2014, permitting tax-free savings accounts for people living with disabilities. Account holders can accrue savings up to $100,000 before Supplemental Security Income cash benefits are affected, while Medicaid eligibility is unaffected. The ABLE Act was an important policy breakthrough for the disability community. Through such policy entrepreneurship, social workers added social value within different communities.

Through the Grand Challenges initiative of the American Academy of Social Work and Social Welfare, the directive to "build financial capability for all" challenges existing policy solutions (Sherraden et al., 2015). These include initiating stronger consumer protections, CDAs, and a financial capability gateway supported by the federal government to provide individuals with electronic tools to better access financial services and manage household finances (Sherraden et al., 2015). The Build Financial Capability for All network has a policy task force that is currently developing policy briefs that address various financial inclusion issues.

In different contexts, by participating in the process of financial inclusion and asset building for different beneficiaries of human service organizations, social workers create social value. From the perspective of end users and beneficiaries, the value can be in the extent and level of usefulness of these products and services (Bowman & Ambrosini, 2000). Social value can also be in the form of total social impact on beneficiaries and other stakeholders that these products and services generate (Polonsky & Grau, 2008). Clearly, through their social innovation and entrepreneurial efforts in the financial dimensions described in this chapter, social workers have generated social value in different communities.

Notwithstanding the aforementioned initiatives by social workers, more policy innovation work is still outstanding. The redistributive scale of asset-building policies intended to benefit LMI households is quite limited. The most recent federal appropriation for IDAs was a mere $19 million, in contrast to the $326 billion in tax expenditures to promote homeownership and retirement savings that disproportionately benefit upper-income households (Cramer &

Schreur, 2013). Thus, social workers should advocate for redistributive changes in the tax code to free up tax dollars that can finance large-scale financial inclusion and asset-building policy innovations. For instance, reducing the size of mortgages covered by the mortgage interest deduction to $500,000 could free up $213 billion over 10 years (National Low-Income Housing Coalition, 2016).

To enable social workers to support social innovation in financial inclusion and asset building, personal finance instruction is needed in social work education programs (Birkenmaier, Loke, & Hageman, 2016; Despard & Chowa, 2013; Kindle, 2013; Loke, Birkenmaier, & Hageman, 2017) and via continuing education to help social workers better address clients' financial problems (Frey et al., 2015). Social workers need to better understand how individuals and families are exploited by alternative financial service providers, such as payday lenders that offer expensive and predatory products to economically vulnerable people (Karger, 2015). Social workers might consider earning an additional credential, such as accredited financial counselor, to fulfill these professional roles (Despard & Chowa, 2010). Such a credential may offer social workers a deeper and fuller understanding of financial concepts needed to promote innovative financial inclusion and asset-building practices, especially if they work within financial institutions or credit counseling agencies.

Limited, though important, efforts to integrate financial and economic literacy in social work education have emerged in recent years. These include the Financial Capability and Asset Building Initiative of the Center for Social Development at Washington University in St. Louis, the Financial Social Work Initiative of the University of Maryland, the Council on Social Work Education's Clearinghouse for Economic Well-Being in social work education, and the Economic Literacy in Human Services course developed by the New York City Region of Schools of Social Work Economic Literacy Consortium (Frey, Sherraden, Birkenmaier, & Callahan, 2017; Horwitz & Briar-Lawson, 2017).

Yet personal finance knowledge and skills are not enough to promote financial inclusion and asset building. Social workers—especially in mezzo practice roles—may also need a deeper understanding of social entrepreneurship methods, such as taking risks in dynamic political and economic climates, creatively using scarce resources, forming strategic partnerships, and working collaboratively and proactively (Germak & Singh, 2009; Nandan et al., 2015). Many, if not most, of the social innovation examples provided in this chapter were developed using such methods. Social workers can also benefit from more exposure to transdisciplinary perspectives (Nandan & Scott, 2013), such as business school courses on corporate social responsibility and impact investing.

Conclusion

Financial inclusion and asset building are promising strategies for promoting financial security among LMI households and building social value within communities. Several examples of efforts that leverage technology, lower barriers to financial inclusion, and aim to meet LMI households' transaction, financial management, credit, and savings needs have been described in this chapter. Collectively, these efforts reflect social innovation—cross-sector and interdisciplinary initiatives to disrupt the status quo that excludes LMI and other economically vulnerable households from the financial mainstream. Social workers do, and can, play micro, mezzo, and macro practice roles in these efforts, but not without being trained differently, both in terms of financial and economic literacy and in understanding the process of social innovation and entrepreneurship. A hope for readers of this chapter is that they are inspired to discover the next innovation that brings LMI households into the economic mainstream and promotes greater financial security.

References

Adams, D., & West, S. (2015). Asset building among low income adults: An exploratory study with participants in an emergency savings program. *Journal of Community Practice, 23*, 436–461. doi:10.1080/10705422.2015.1091421

Anderson, S. (2014). *New strategies for social innovation.* New York: Columbia University Press.

Annie E. Casey Foundation. (2009). *The Opportunity Passport™: Building assets for youth aging out of foster care.* Retrieved from http://www.aecf.org/m/resourcedoc/JCYOI-TheOpportunityPassport-2009.pdf

Bair, S. (2003). *Improving access to the U.S. banking system among recent Latin American immigrants.* Washington, DC: Inter-American Development Bank. Retrieved from https://publications.iadb.org/bitstream/handle/11319/6263/Improving%20access%20to%20the%20U.S.%20banking%20system%20among%20recent%20Latin%20American%20immigrants.pdf?sequence=1

Baradaran, M. (2015). *How the other half banks: Exclusion, exploitation, and the threat to democracy.* Cambridge, MA: Harvard University Press.

Barr, M. S. (2010). *And banking for all?* Darby, PA: Diane Publishing.

Bennett, B., Conover, D., O'Brien, S., & Advincula, R. (2014). *Cash continues to play a key role in consumer spending: Evidence from the Diary of Consumer Payment Choice.* San Francisco: Federal Reserve Bank of San Francisco. Retrieved from http://www.frbsf.org/cash/files/FedNotes_Evidence_from_DCPC.pdf

Bevans, J. S. (2013). *Children's education savings accounts: A case study of San Francisco's Kindergarten to College program.* San Francisco: EARN Research

Institute. Retrieved from https://www.earn.org/wp-content/uploads/2015/03/130619-K2C-Practitioners-Report-Final.pdf

Beverly, S. G., Tescher, J., & Romich, J. L. (2004). Linking tax refunds and low-cost bank accounts: Early lessons for program design and evaluation. *Journal of Consumer Affairs, 38*, 332–341. doi:10.1111/j.1745-6606.2004.tb00872.x

Birkenmaier, J. (2012). Promoting bank accounts to low-income households: Implications for social work practice. *Journal of Community Practice, 20*, 414–431. doi:10.1080/10705422.2012.732004

Birkenmaier, J., & Curley, J. (2009). Financial credit: Social work's role in empowering low-income families. *Journal of Community Practice, 17*, 251–268.

Birkenmaier, J. M., Loke, V., & Hageman, S. A. (2016). Are graduating students ready for financial aspects of social work practice? *Journal of Teaching in Social Work, 36*, 519–536.

Bowman, C., & Ambrosini, V. (2000). Value creation versus value capture: Towards a coherent definition of value in strategy. *British Journal of Management, 11*, 1–15.

Brevoort, K. P., Grimm, P., & Kambara, M. (2016). Credit invisibles and the unscored. *Cityscape: A Journal of Policy Development and Research, 18*, 9–33. Retrieved from https://www.huduser.gov/portal/periodicals/cityscpe/vol18num2/ch1.pdf

Burhouse, S., Homer, M., Osaki, Y., & Bachman, M. (2014). *Assessing the economic inclusion potential of mobile financial services.* Washington, DC: Federal Deposit Insurance Corporation. Retrieved from https://www.fdic.gov/consumers/community/mobile/mobile-financial-services.pdf

Calderon, O. (2009). *Banking development districts: Promoting local economic development through enhanced banking services in underserved communities.* Washington, DC: New America Foundation. Retrieved from https://www.newamerica.org/documents/184/banking-development-districts

Caplan, M. A. (2014). Communities respond to predatory lending. *Social Work, 59*, 149–156.

Catholic Charities of Northeast Kansas. (n.d.). *Kansas Loan Pool Project.* Retrieved from https://catholiccharitiesks.org/wp-content/uploads/klpp-sheet-v4.pdf

Cities for Financial Empowerment Fund. (2017a). *Bank On coalition playbook.* Retrieved from http://cfefund.org/bank-on-playbook/

Cities for Financial Empowerment Fund. (2017b). *Bank On national account standards (2017–2018).* Retrieved from http://joinbankon.org/wp-content/uploads/2017/05/Bank-On-National-Account-Standards-2017-2018-final.pdf

Clancy, M., & Sherraden, M. (2014). *Automatic deposits for all at birth: Maine's Harold Alfond College Challenge* (CSD Policy Report 14-05). St. Louis: Center for Social Development, Washington University in St. Louis. Retrieved from https://csd.wustl.edu/publications/documents/pr14-05.pdf

Cohen, N., Davis, K., Tantia, P., Wright, J., Chandrasekhar, C., & Spence, T. (2015). *Reimagining financial inclusion* [Report by Oliver Wyman and Ideas42]. Retrieved from http://www.ideas42.org/wp-content/uploads/2015/11/Reimagining-Financial-Inclusion-Final-Web-1.pdf

Commonwealth. (2016). *Building financial security through integrated financial solutions: Combining savings and credit.* Retrieved from https://www.jpmorganchase.com/corporate/Corporate-Responsibility/document/Commonwealth-Building-Financial-Security-Savings-and-credit.pdf

Consumer Financial Protection Bureau. (2013). *Payday loans and deposit advance products: A white paper of initial data findings* (White paper). Washington, DC: Author. Retrieved from http://files.consumerfinance.gov/f/201304_cfpb_payday-dap-whitepaper.pdf

Cramer, R., & Schreur, E. (2013). *Personal savings and tax reform: Principles and policy proposals for reforming the tax code* [New America Foundation Policy Brief]. Retrieved from http://community-wealth.org/content/personal-savings-and-tax-reform-principles-and-policy-proposals-reforming-tax-code

Cruce, A. (2002). *School-based savings programs, 1930–2002* (Working Paper No. 02-7). St. Louis: Center for Social Development, Washington University in St. Louis. Retrieved from https://csd.wustl.edu/publications/documents/wp02-7.pdf

Cuddeback, G. S., Blank-Wilson, A., Despard, M. R., Tomar, N., & Chowa, G. (2017). Financial insecurity and risk experiences of justice involved persons with severe mental illness. *Social Work in Mental Health, 15,* 615–631.

Despard, M., & Chowa, G.A.N. (2010). Social workers' interest in building individuals' financial capabilities. *Journal of Financial Therapy, 1*(1), 23–41. doi:10.4148/jft.v1i1.257

Despard, M. & Chowa, G.A.N. (2013). Training social workers in personal finance: An exploratory study. *Journal of Social Work Education, 49,* 689–700. doi:10.1080/10437797.2013.812895

Despard, M. R., Chowa, G. A., & Hart, L. J. (2012). Personal financial problems: Opportunities for social work interventions? *Journal of Social Service Research, 38,* 342–350.

Dorrance, J., & Gorham, L. (2016). *Iteration to impact: Insights from the PayGoal product journey* [Research report]. Chapel Hill: Center for Community Capital, University of North Carolina at Chapel Hill. Retrieved from http://communitycapital.unc.edu/files/2016/03/Paygoal-March-2016.pdf

Elliott, W. (2009). Children's college aspirations and expectations: The potential role of children's development accounts (CDAs). *Children and Youth Services Review, 31,* 274–283.

Elliott, W., Destin, M., & Friedline, T. (2011). Taking stock of ten years of research on the relationship between assets and children's educational outcomes:

Implications for theory, policy and intervention. *Children and Youth Services Review, 33*, 2312–2328.

Federal Deposit Insurance Corporation. (2012). *FDIC Model Safe Accounts Pilot: Final report.* Washington, DC: Author. Retrieved from https://www.fdic .gov/consumers/template/SafeAccountsFinalReport.pdf

Federal Deposit Insurance Corporation. (2016). *2015 FDIC National Survey of Unbanked and Underbanked Households.* Washington, DC: Author. Retrieved from https://www.fdic.gov/householdsurvey/2015/2015report.pdf

Feldman, G. (2017). Contradictory logics in asset-building discourse: Habits, identities and discipline. *Social Policy & Administration.* Advance online publication. doi:10.1111/spol.12326

Financial Industry Regulatory Authority Investor Education Foundation. (2016). *Financial capability in the United States 2016.* Retrieved from http:// www.usfinancialcapability.org/downloads/NFCS_2015_Report_Natl_ Findings.pdf

Frank-Miller, E., Covington, M., Despard, M. R., Hannon, G., & Grinstein-Weiss, M. (2017). *Employee Financial Wellness Programs Project: Comprehensive report of findings* (CSD Research Report No. 17-31). St. Louis: Center for Social Development, Washington University in St. Louis. Retrieved from https://csd.wustl.edu/Publications/Documents/RR17-31.pdf

Frey, J. J., Sherraden, M., Birkenmaier, J., & Callahan, C. (2017). Financial capability and asset building in social work education. *Journal of Social Work Education, 53*(1), 79–83. doi:10.1080/10437797.2016.1256170

Frey, J. J., Svoboda, D., Sander, R. L., Osteen, P. J., Callahan, C., & Elkinson, A. (2015). Evaluation of a continuing education training on client financial capability. *Journal of Social Work Education, 51*, 439–456.

Friedline, T., Despard, M., & Chowa, G. A. (2016). Preventive policy strategy for banking the unbanked: Savings accounts for teenagers? *Journal of Poverty, 20*(1), 2–33.

Friedline, T., Despard, M., Eastlund, R., & Schuetz, N. (2017). *Are banks' entry-level checking accounts safe and affordable? Comparing a stratified random sample of banks to safety and affordability guidelines.* Lawrence: University of Kansas, Center on Assets, Education, & Inclusion.

Friedline, T., & Kepple, N. (2017). Does community access to alternative financial services relate to individuals' use of these services? Beyond individual explanations. *Journal of Consumer Policy, 40*(1), 51–79.

Fusaro, M. A. (2008). Hidden consumer loans: An analysis of implicit interest rates on bounced checks. *Journal of Family and Economic Issues, 29*, 251–263.

Garon, T., & Latta, J. (2016). *2016 prepaid industry scorecard: Assessing quality in the prepaid industry with CFSI's Compass Principles.* Chicago: Center for Financial Services Innovation. Retrieved from https://s3.amazonaws.com/

cfsi-innovation-files/wp-content/uploads/2017/01/19204903/Prepaid-Score card-FINAL.pdf

Germak, A. J., & Singh, K. K. (2009). Social entrepreneurship: Changing the way social workers do business. *Administration in Social Work, 34*(1), 79–95.

Gill, K., Mills, D., & McKenna, M. (2015). Enhancing financial capability: TANF bank accounts. In J. Michael Collins (Ed.), *A fragile balance* (pp. 107–123). New York: Palgrave Macmillan.

Gjertson, L. (2016). Emergency saving and household hardship. *Journal of Family and Economic Issues, 37*, 1–17. doi:10.1007/s10834-014-9434-z

Grinstein-Weiss, M., Despard, M., Guo, S., Russell, B., Key, C., & Raghavan, R. (2016). Do tax-time savings deposits improve financial outcomes and reduce hardship among low-income filers? A propensity score analysis. *Journal of the Society for Social Work and Research, 7*, 707–728. doi:10.1086/689357

Grinstein-Weiss, M., Perantie, D. C., Russell, B. D., Comer, K., Taylor, S. H., Luo, L., et al.(2015). *Refund to Savings 2013: Comprehensive report on a large-scale tax-time saving program* (CSD Research Report 15-06). St. Louis: Center for Social Development, Washington University in St. Louis. Retrieved from http://csd.wustl.edu/Publications/Documents/RR15-06.pdf

Grinstein-Weiss, M., Russell, B. D., Gale, W. G., Key, C., & Ariely, D. (2017). Behavioral interventions to increase tax-time saving: Evidence from a national randomized trial. *Journal of Consumer Affairs, 51*(1), 3–26.

Halpern-Meekin, S., Edin, K., Tach, L., & Sykes, J. (2015). *It's not like I'm poor: How working families make ends meet in a post-welfare world*. Oakland: University of California Press.

Haynes-Bordas, R., Kiss, D. E., & Yilmazer, T. (2008). Effectiveness of financial education on financial management behavior and account usage: Evidence from a "second chance" program. *Journal of Family and Economic Issues, 29*, 362.

Heisler, K., & Lutter, S. (2015). Incorporating savings into the debt management plan. In J. Michael Collins (Ed.), *A fragile balance* (pp. 193–200). New York: Palgrave Macmillan.

Henderson, S. (2015). Prosperity SmartSave Card: An incentivized emergency savings strategy. In J. Michael Collins (Ed.), *A fragile balance* (pp. 141–152). New York: Palgrave Macmillan.

Horwitz, S., & Briar-Lawson, K. (2017). A multi-university economic capability-building collaboration. *Journal of Social Work Education, 53*, 149–158. doi: 10.1080/10437797.2016.1212750

Karger, H. J. (2007). The "poverty tax" and America's low-income households. *Families in Society: The Journal of Contemporary Social Services, 88*, 413–417.

Karger, H. (2015). Curbing the financial exploitation of the poor: Financial literacy and social work education. *Journal of Social Work Education, 51*, 425–438.

Key, C., Tucker, J. N., Grinstein-Weiss, M., & Comer, K. (2015). Tax-time savings among low-income households in the $aveNYC Program. *Journal of Consumer Affairs, 49,* 489–518.

Khashadourian, E. (2015). Accelerating savings among low-income households. In J. Michael Collins (Ed.), *A fragile balance* (pp. 153–174). New York: Palgrave Macmillan.

Kindle, P. A. (2013). The financial literacy of social work students. *Journal of Social Work Education, 49,* 397–407.

Larrimore, J., Dodini, S., & Thomas, L. (2016). *Report on the economic well-being of U.S. households in 2015* [Board of Governors of the Federal Reserve System Report]. Retrieved from https://www.federalreserve.gov/2015-report-economic-well-being-us-households-201605.pdf

Latino Community Credit Union. (2017). *Our history.* Retrieved from https://latinoccu.org/about-us/our-history/

Loke, V., Birkenmaier, J., & Hageman, S. A. (2017). Financial capability and asset building in the curricula: Student perceptions. *Journal of Social Work Education, 53,* 84–98.

Loke, V., Choi, L., & Libby, M. (2015). Increasing youth financial capability: An evaluation of the MyPath Savings Initiative. *Journal of Consumer Affairs, 49,* 97–126.

Lopez-Fernandini, A., & Schultz, C. (2010). *Automatic savings in the workplace: Insights from the AutoSave Pilot* [Asset Building Program Brief]. Washington, DC: New America Foundation. Retrieved from https://www.newamerica.org/asset-building/policy-papers/automating-savings-in-the-workplace/

Manturuk, K., Dorrance, J., & Halladay, J. (2015). Building emergency savings through "impulse saving." In J. Michael Collins (Ed.), *A fragile balance* (pp. 125–140). New York: Palgrave Macmillan.

Morduch, J., & Schneider, R. (2017). *The financial diaries: How Americans cope in a world of uncertainty.* Princeton, NJ: Princeton University Press.

Morris, M., & Goodman, N. (2015). *Integrating financial capability and asset building strategies into the public workforce development system* [National Center on Leadership for the Employment and Economic Advancement of People with Disabilities Report]. Berkeley, CA: National Disability Institute. Retrieved from http://www.leadcenter.org/system/files/resource/downloadable_version/integrating_fin_cap_asset_dev.pdf

Moulton, S., Samek, A., & Loibl, C. (2015). Save at home: Building emergency savings one mortgage payment at a time. In J. Michael Collins (Ed.), *A fragile balance* (pp. 39–54). New York: Palgrave Macmillan.

Nam, Y., Kim, Y., Clancy, M., Zager, R., & Sherraden, M. (2013). Do child development accounts promote account holding, saving, and asset accumulation for children's future? Evidence from a statewide randomized experiment. *Journal of Policy Analysis and Management, 32*(1), 6–33.

Nandan, M., London, M., & Bent-Goodley, T. (2015). Social workers as social change agents: Social innovation, social intrapreneurship, and social entrepreneurship. *Human Service Organizations: Management, Leadership & Governance, 39*(1), 38–56.

Nandan, M., & Scott, P. A. (2013). Social entrepreneurship and social work: The need for a transdisciplinary educational model. *Administration in Social Work, 37,* 257–271.

National Association of Social Workers. (2017). *Code of ethics of the National Association of Social Workers.* Washington, DC: Author.

National Council of La Raza. (2014). *Banking in color: New findings on financial access for low- and moderate-income communities.* Retrieved from http://pub lications.nclr.org/bitstream/handle/123456789/1203/bankingincolor_web .pdf?sequence=1&isAllowed=y

National Federation of Community Development Credit Unions & Neighborhood Trust Financial Partners. (2015). *Financial counseling in credit unions: A survey of the field* [Issue brief]. Retrieved from http://www.cdcu.coop/ wp-content/uploads/2015/04/Financial-Counseling-in-Credit-Unions-Issue-Brief-April-2015.pdf

National Low-Income Housing Coalition. (2016). *The mortgage interest deduction: Frequently asked questions.* Retrieved from http://nlihc.org/sites/default/ files/UFH_MID-FAQ.pdf

Pew Charitable Trusts. (2012). *Payday lending in America: Who borrows, where they borrow, and why.* Washington DC: Author. Retrieved from http://www .pewtrusts.org/~/media/legacy/uploadedfiles/pcs_assets/2012/PewPayday LendingReportpdf.pdf

Phills, J. A., Deiglmeier, K., & Miller, D. T. (2008). Rediscovering social innovation. *Stanford Social Innovation Review, 6*(4), 34–43.

Polonsky, M. J., & Grau, S. L. (2008). Evaluating the social value of charitable organizations: A conceptual foundation. *Journal of Macromarketing, 28,* 130–140. doi:10.1177/0276146708314585

Rengert, K. M., & Rhine, S. L. W. (2016). *Bank efforts to serve unbanked and underbanked consumers: Qualitative research.* Washington, DC: Federal Deposit Insurance Corporation. Retrieved from https://www.fdic.gov/consumers/ community/research/QualitativeResearch_May2016.pdf

Rothwell, D. W., & Han, C. K. (2010). Second thoughts: Who almost participates in an IDA program? *Journal of Social Service Research, 36,* 107–117.

Sanders, C. K. (2013). Financial capability among survivors of domestic violence. In J. Birkenmaier, M. Sherraden, & J. Curley (Eds.), *Financial capability and asset development: Research, education, policy, and practice* (pp. 85–107). New York: Oxford University Press.

Schneider, R., & Schutte, A. (2007). *The predictive value of alternative credit scores.* Chicago: Center for Financial Services Innovation. Retrieved from https://s3.amazonaws.com/cfsi-innovation-files/wp-content/uploads/2017/02/05053225/The-Predictive-Value-of-Alternative-Credit-Scores.pdf

Shanks, T. (2014). The promise of child development accounts: Current evidence and future directions. *Community Investments, 26,* 12–15. Retrieved from http://www.frbsf.org/community-development/files/ci_vol26no2-Promise-of-Child-Development-Accounts.pdf

Shanks, T. R. W., & Destin, M. (2009). Parental expectations and educational outcomes for young African American adults: Do household assets matter? *Race and Social Problems, 1*(1), 27–35.

Sherraden, M. (1991). *Assets and the poor: A new American welfare policy.* Armonk, NY: M. E. Sharpe.

Sherraden, M. (2000). From research to policy: Lessons from individual development accounts. *Journal of Consumer Affairs, 34,* 159–181.

Sherraden, M. (2013). Building blocks of financial capability. In J. Birkenmaier, M. Sherraden, & J. Curley & (Eds.), *Financial education and capability: Research, education, policy, and practice* (pp. 3–43). New York: Oxford University Press.

Sherraden, M. S., Frey, J. J., & Birkenmaier, J. (2016). Financial social work. In *Handbook of consumer finance research* (pp. 115–127). New York: Springer.

Sherraden, M. S., Huang, J., Frey, J. J., Birkenmaier, J., Callahan, C., Clancy, M. M., & Sherraden, M. (2015). *Financial capability and asset building for all* (Working Paper No. 13). Retrieved from http://aaswsw.org/wp-content/uploads/2016/01/WP13-with-cover.pdf

Sherraden, M., Schreiner, M., & Beverly, S. (2003). Income, institutions, and saving performance in individual development accounts. *Economic Development Quarterly, 17*(1), 95–112.

Spader, J. (2009). *The bold and the bankable: Nuestro Barrio telenovela and financial education.* Chapel Hill: Center for Community Capital, University of North Carolina at Chapel Hill. Retrieved from http://communitycapital.unc.edu/files/2009/06/BoldandBankable.pdf

Spader, J., Ratcliffe, J., Montoya, J., & Skillern, P. (2009). The bold and the bankable: How the *Nuestro Barrio* telenovela reaches Latino immigrants with financial education. *Journal of Consumer Affairs, 43,* 56–79.

Stuart, P. H. (2013). Social workers and financial capability in the profession's first half-century. In J. Birkenmaier, M. Sherraden, & J. Curley (Eds.), *Financial capability and asset development: Research, education, policy, and practice* (pp. 44–61). New York: Oxford University Press.

Weil, M., Gamble, D. N., & Ohmer, M. L. (2013). Evolution, models, and the changing context of community practice. In M. Weil, M. Reisch, & M. L.

Ohmer (Eds.), *The handbook of community practice* (2nd ed., pp. 117–149). Los Angeles: Sage Publications.

Weller, C. (2007). *Access denied: Low-income and minority families face more credit constraints and higher borrowing costs.* Washington, DC: Center for American Progress. Retrieved from https://www.americanprogress.org/wp-content/uploads/issues/2007/08/pdf/credit_access.pdf

West, S., Banerjee, M., Phipps, B., & Friedline, T. (2017). Coming up short: Family composition, income, and household savings. *Journal of the Society for Social Work and Research.* Advance online publication. doi:10.1086/693047

World Bank. (2017, April 5). *Financial inclusion: Overview.* Retrieved from http://www.worldbank.org/en/topic/financialinclusion/overview

Zhan, M., Anderson, S., & Scott, J. (2009). Banking knowledge and attitudes of immigrants: Effects of a financial education program. *Social Development Issues, 31*(3), 15–32.

10

Social Entrepreneurship: Case of Livelihoods and Economic Development in an Urban Environment in India

Archana Singh

Financial exclusion affects economic development. Financial services and an effective banking industry are vital components of a nation's economic growth (Solo, 2008). In addition, poverty is a major challenge in many countries, especially when daily income is less than $2 per person (Collins, Morduch, Rutherford, & Ruthven, 2009). Consequently, financial inclusion has become a policy priority in many countries in recent years (Sarma & Pais, 2011) and more so in developing countries (Arora, 2012).

In developed countries, the unbanked (that is, those not served by banks or similar financial institutions) are in a minority and are often unemployed, whereas in developing countries, many employed individuals are unbanked (Cnaan, Moodithaya, & Handy, 2012). They have no savings accounts and insurance policies, and they do not receive credit from formal financial institutions. In addition, deeply rooted differentiations based on caste, class, religion, and gender in Indian societies have resulted in social exclusion of certain classes of people. Financial exclusion is indeed a manifestation or reflection of social exclusion (Sarma & Pais, 2011). Financial inclusion is very important not only for improving the living conditions of poor farmers and other vulnerable groups (Dev, 2006) but also for poverty reduction, social cohesion, empowerment of vulnerable groups, and inclusive growth (National Bank for Agriculture and Rural Development, 2008). Thus, financial inclusion has increasingly attracted the attention of several scholars as a tool for inclusive growth of the country. This chapter presents a case study of the SammaaN Foundation, a social entrepreneurial venture that creates an empowering environment for cycle rickshaw pullers (CRPs) who are poor, vulnerable, marginalized, and disadvantaged (PVMD) residents in the slums of Patna, Bihar (an eastern state in India). This chapter describes the journey traveled by the social entrepreneur and the innovative processes and products he cocreated to enhance the ability of CRPs to experience financial inclusion and independence. This chapter also aligns the social entrepreneurial activities implemented by the founder of the SammaaN Foundation with social work practice and values.

Social Entrepreneurship (SE) and Social Entrepreneurs

SE is considered as a response to market failure, state failure, or both, in meeting social needs (Nicholls, 2006; Yujuico, 2008). SE refers to the process of solving social problems and creating social value and can emerge in all three sectors: not-for-profit, public and for-profit, and cross-sector partnerships (Johnson, 2000; Mair & Noboa, 2003; Neck, Brush, & Allen, 2008; Nicholls, 2006). Most scholars perceive social entrepreneurs as individuals who identify and exploit opportunities, combine resources, and act innovatively to solve social problems, create social value, and bring about social change. They are recognized as "change agents" in the social sector (Nicholls, 2006). "For social entrepreneurs, the social mission is explicit and central" (Dees, 1998, p. 3).

Financial Inclusion

The concept of financial inclusion has various definitions in the literature (Arora, 2012). Financial exclusion occurs mainly among people who are marginalized in society (Sarma & Pais, 2011). Most important, it does not include credit alone, but it refers to the limited access of low-income groups to the full range of financial services, that is, to deposit and savings accounts and to payment systems (Solo, 2008). Financial inclusion contributes to the empowerment of individuals and communities. Empowerment and social justice advocacy are important components of the National Association of Social Workers (NASW) *Code of Ethics* (NASW, 2017; Voorhis & Hostetter, 2006), and social workers have the responsibility to create empowering environments for clients, which can influence all aspects of their lives (Huff & Johnson, 1998). The International Labor Office (2017) also has emphasized empowering rural communities through financial inclusion.

Financial Inclusion as a Priority in India

The Indian government has identified financial inclusion as a priority. The review of literature reflects some interesting contradictions regarding financial inclusion in India. On the one hand, micro-credit schemes are viewed as an integral part of financial inclusion, as these bring savings and borrowing opportunities to marginalized groups, and credit is needed for economic development (Ray, 1998). On the other hand, these schemes are criticized because they do not cover all the aspects of financial inclusion. Whereas micro-credit focuses on loans and saving, financial inclusion includes all banking products alongside saving and loans (Cnaan et al., 2012). In addition, micro-credit also leaves the poor in debt (Solo, 2008). The effectiveness of micro-credit programs, in this context, is seriously questioned by scholars (Government of India Planning Commission, 2008; Solo, 2008). Thus, it is time to think beyond micro-credit as a means for financial inclusion of PVMD populations.

Enough information is available on the services provided by financial institutions and nodal agencies (Laeven & Valencia, 2013). However, supply-side-focused literature completely ignores the demand side of financial inclusion, providing an incomplete view of financial inclusion. There are only a few studies (for example, Arora, 2012; Bapat, 2010; Bhanot, Bapat, & Bera, 2012; Sarma & Pais, 2011) available on the demand side of financial inclusion. In addition, most of these studies (Arora, 2012; Sarma & Pais, 2011) are quantitative cross-country studies based on secondary data only. Few demand-side studies in the Indian context (Bapat, 2010; Bhanot et al., 2012) are based on primary data, but in these studies, too, information is collected quantitatively, primarily through structured interview schedules, during which strict closed-ended questions are used. The findings from these sources reveals that factors such as sustainable income and financial information play important roles in financial inclusion of the PVMD populations. However, there appears to be an absence of rich, qualitative, and wholistic data on financial inclusion.

Despite efforts made by the government, Reserve Bank of India, and other financial institutions, a significant percentage of the population still does not have access to financial services. At the same time, there are SE models available in India that have resulted in the financial inclusion of poor and vulnerable people. It is important to understand how social entrepreneurs are contributing to financial inclusion and solving social problems. This chapter explores one SE model, the SammaaN Foundation, which engaged in empowerment and financial inclusion of a particular segment of the PVMD population, that is, CRPs in India. The case study fulfills the following objectives:

- to understand the motivation of social entrepreneurs to address the problems of the PVMD population segment
- to explore the entrepreneurial process of financial inclusion of the PVMD population segment, for the purpose of understanding the intervention strategies used and competencies required for providing sustainable solutions to a social problem

- to explore the relevance of social work methods, social work values, social work code of ethics, and networks and partnerships in the social entrepreneurial process
- to describe a model of financial inclusion of the PVMD population

Methodology

Recognizing the contextual nature of social entrepreneurship and the exploratory nature of the research, single case study research strategy was adopted (Meyer, 2001; Yin, 2003), facilitating an inductive approach for testing, constructing, or generating theory (Eisenhardt, 1989; Flick, 2006). SammaaN Foundation, founded by Irfan Alam, a social entrepreneur, was selected as a case. Primary data were collected from the founder, six employees, and five beneficiaries through in-depth interviews. Observation was also used to see the interventions and impact. Information was also collected from secondary sources such as SammaaN's Web site, brochure, documents, articles, and audiovisual data sources such as a documentary film on SammaaN. All the data were collected from January 23 through May 24, 2012.

All the voice-recorded data were transcribed first and then coded to develop various subthemes, themes, and categories (Miles & Huberman, 1984; Strauss & Corbin, 1998). Audiovisual data were analyzed using content analysis method. All the data collected from observation were summarized for the analysis. Finally, data collected from different sources were triangulated in the final level of analysis to develop the model.

Case Description: SammaaN Foundation

SammaaN Foundation (http://sammaan.org/) is registered under Section 25 of the Companies Act of 1956 as a not-for-profit organization, and it operates in the Indian states of Bihar and Uttar Pradesh. Alam had aimed to organize the micro-public transport sector of cycle rickshaw pulling; the primary goals for organizing were to enable CRPs to earn a sustainable income and to enhance the standard of living of their families. Thus, the foundation is dedicated to the empowerment of CRPs and their financial inclusion by linking them to the mainstream economy. CRPs make up a large segment of the public transportation system; however, they are unorganized and often marginalized.

SammaaN Foundation began its work by financing 100 rickshaws in Patna (Bihar) in 2007. SammaaN Foundation provides rickshaws, uniforms, bank accounts, and identity cards; health care services to CRPs; and accident insurance to rickshaw pullers and their passengers. SammaaN Foundation has generated a profit since the first year of its operation. Irfan Alam has won several awards, such as the World Bank Innovation Award and Ashoka and Ford fellowships. He was also celebrated by U.S. president Barack Obama in an entrepreneurial summit held in Washington in April 2011. At the time of data collection, SammaaN Foundation's main office was in Patna (Bihar) and had fifteen employees.

SammaaN Foundation's Relationship to Social Work Practice and Values

This section describes the findings from an analysis of the interviews conducted with the founder and five CRP beneficiaries, as well as from secondary data sources as they relate to the SE process and qualities of the entrepreneur. The section also describes the relevance of the process and qualities to social work practice and values.

Context, Social Entrepreneur Qualities, and Their Relationship with Social Work Practice and Values

The kernel of Irfan Alam's innovative idea was born in a simple incident during a cycle rickshaw journey on a hot summer day. During that short journey, Alam's interaction with the rickshaw puller gave him insight into the market and the power of the unorganized sector. However, the driving force behind him initiating the whole process of financial inclusion of members of the PVMD population was a result of two important factors: (1) the strong social and moral values inculcated by his parents throughout his upbringing; and (2) his intellectual capacity complemented with empathy. Irfan Alam reminisced,

> My parents always throughout the upbringing, they kept telling that if you give somebody a motor bike, who already has one motor bike, it may not create much of difference in his life, but if you give a bicycle to somebody who doesn't have a bicycle, it may revolutionize his whole life. They understand its value. And the second thing was that they always said that . . . you know . . . despite everything, you are still fortunate. You go and see outside that there are people who are forced to sleep without having two meals. If you can do something to change that scenario, God will take care of you. That was something that I believe in. And I am blessed. These are the learning, the upbringing, values and circumstances [that] actually groomed me to opt for entrepreneurship with [a] social mission.

Clearly, his family background (financial condition, upbringing) and life experiences (rickshaw incident, his observation of his social surroundings) played important roles in his pursuit of the SE process. Though Irfan Alam was not a formally trained social worker, his family upbringing instilled in him strong social and moral values—reflecting the core of social work values. Professionally trained social workers are guided by six core principles of the NASW (2017) *Code of Ethics*. These are service, social justice, dignity and worth of the person, human relationships, integrity, and competence (NASW, 2017). From this case example, it is evident that with the aim of creating social justice, Alam identified key challenges experienced by CRPs and followed the entrepreneurship process to create an empowering environment for them and address several other challenges they faced. His efforts to create social change that promotes human dignity and social justice and that serves humanity are in sync with social work values (Bisman, 2004).

The second factor of his intellect and empathy appeared to provide him with the confidence for innovation. He was ready to take calculated risks and always wanted to be a trendsetter, not a trend follower. Apart from being passionate about, and obsessed with, his ideas, he described patience and perseverance with the implementation process of his ideas.

His contextual experience, strong social and moral values, and entrepreneurial qualities motivated him to use the SE process for addressing some of the major challenges experienced by CRPs. Human service practitioners also display innate personal characteristics while delivering professional services. Their own moral character becomes an essential feature of their professional practice, and without it their interpersonal engagement would become merely a mechanical transaction that voids the core purposes of the profession (Clark, 2006). Therefore, Haynes (1999) emphasized incorporating personal, social, political, and professional values into social work education.

Problem Identification as an "Opportunity"

Irfan Alam explored, identified, and assessed the challenges experienced by CRPs and discovered that they (1) were financially excluded from the banking industry, (2) were exploited by rickshaw fleet owners, and (3) did not have sustainable sources of livelihood. A *livelihood* is understood as the capabilities, assets, and activities required for a means of living (Serrat, 2008), and *sustainable livelihood* is a living that is adequate for the satisfaction of basic needs and that is secure against anticipated shocks and stresses (Chambers, 1995). Because of the migrant nature of their work, CRPs were often separated from their families; they lacked access to proper health care for themselves and their families and quality education for their children. These problems, in addition to financial exclusion, reflected their *social exclusion*. An individual can become socially excluded if her or his condition of deprivation is persistent or worsens over time (Bossert, D'Ambrosio, & Peragine, 2007). Irfan Alam discovered that lack of sustainable sources of livelihood was one of the primary reasons for some of the aforementioned challenges related to social exclusion and financial exploitation. Alam discovered that though the rickshaw pulling sector was large, very few agencies and organizations worked with or on behalf of this sector—whether private, government, or nongovernmental organizations (NGOs). He perceived and assessed these challenges as potential opportunity for sustainable change.

Mair and Marti (2006) explained that opportunities are embedded within social contexts, as is apparent in the present case. The level of embeddedness in the local environment is determined by the network, ties, and relationship of the entrepreneurs through which they gain credibility and their knowledge and experience (Jack & Anderson, 2002). The opportunity already existed in the context, though Alam identified the same because of his knowledge and life experiences, that is, his entrepreneurial experiences, education, and familial and social background. This opportunity identification parallels the needs assessment process used in social work practice. Social workers are committed to remedying situations of personal injustice and hardship experienced by clients after a thorough assessment of clients' situations (Hopkins, 1978). Social workers also understand that needs are embedded within contexts. To identify these needs as opportunities, social workers need to immerse themselves in the client's local environment. Social workers have the necessary skills, knowledge, experiences, and expertise to build rapport with clients and to gain an understanding of the local context. Though social work education teaches students the importance of immersing themselves in the client's or population's context for thorough assessment, in practice such efforts are limited.

Profit-Making Market Creation Approach

After identifying the opportunity, Alam developed a business model, initially around advertisement and product sales to generate revenues. He thought that if he could help this population segment with earning a little more than what they were currently earning, he could assist them with generating additional revenue through investing in the stock market, where he would serve as the fund management entity. This way he could add value to their lives. Alam believed that there were enough opportunities in the market to generate profit, to pass on some of this revenue directly to the rickshaw pullers, and to provide other social benefits in the form of health care services, accident insurance, affordable housing, and so on, to the CRPs and their families. Essentially, he created customer loyalty by providing beneficiaries, that is, CRPs and their families, with social benefits. He also believed in, and emphasized, market creation and enhancement for generating additional revenue and financial sustainability. This way, he continued to create new markets and penetrate existing ones, thereby positively influencing the bottom line. He elaborated:

> I think, the sole or the main value of the whole enterprise is that ultimately I want to empower market, I want to create market, I want to strengthen market. I mean, in corporate terms. In social term[s], I want to empower my rickshaw operators.

His method reflects the bottom-of-the-pyramid approach that argues for the simultaneous pursuit of financial and social well-being by creating markets for PVMD population segments (Ansari, Munir, & Gregg, 2012). He was able to create markets and generate profits by providing social benefits to his customers or beneficiaries through his nonfinancial initiatives. Basically, he identified several other opportunities in the process of financial inclusion of CRPs (discussed later). This profit-making market creation approach may seem unethical and contradictory to the social work profession, and social work practitioners who face dilemmas may hesitate to use this kind of an approach. However, if social work practitioners reflect on social work values and clearly identify how such an approach creates benefits for clients while reducing financial and social injustices, they may be more willing to embrace such an approach.

The NASW (2017) *Code of Ethics* emphasizes that social workers must keep current with emerging knowledge relevant to social work and that they should promote the general welfare of society—from local to national and global—and development of people, communities, and their environments. The *Code of Ethics* also emphasizes that social workers should advocate for and work toward ensuring conducive living conditions for people to meet their basic human needs. The ethical responsibilities speak to the need for social workers to examine different and new intervention models and strategies and to learn from indigenous populations about approaches that may work well within that context.

Organization Creation

Irfan Alam created a self-sustainable business model and registered his organization as a company in the not-for-profit sector, under Section 25 of the Companies Act of 1956, which is now known as a Section 8 company under the Companies Act of 2013. He did not want to run his organization like an NGO and hence never accepted a single donation. Over time he identified more opportunities in the process of financial inclusion of the PVMD rickshaw pullers and operators and started other for-profit organizations. He revealed:

> What I am doing is, basically, trying to empower them. I am trying to link them with the main market. That's the reason, after this NPO [not-for-profit organization], we have incorporated another company called SammaaN Ventures Limited, which is a for-profit company. . . . It's very much different from SammaaN Foundation. It is an absolutely public limited company, for-profit, in which majority shares are with the promoters like me and the rickshaw pullers. And why I did so, because I strongly believe that, you know, that . . . every life is an equal value of life and money empowers life.

Alam created these organizations to generate more funds for the beneficiaries, that is, the CRPs, to make them financially independent and create a sense of empowerment for them; he linked them with the mainstream economy and markets and contributed to the economic development in their communities. His initiatives and innovative strategies were contributing not only to positive micro-level impact on the rickshaw pullers (in terms of financial inclusion and empowerment) but also toward macro-level development. Irfan Alam's endeavor is an example of how social workers can creatively use their micro, mezzo, and macro skills to provide sustainable livelihood opportunities for empowering vulnerable population groups.

The two social work professional organizations, Council on Social Work Education and NASW, have been emphasizing more macro orientation within the profession and the curriculum. In addition, the Association for Community Organization and Social Administration established a "20 in 2020" goal to enhance the enrollment in macro practice concentrations or methods within MSW programs nationwide by 2020 (http://www.acosa.org/joomla/pdf/Flyer-United-for-Macro-Practice-NEW.pdf). Despite these aspirations, the contemporary composition of U.S.-based social work is preponderantly weighted toward clinical practice (Rothman & Mizrahi, 2014). It is important for social workers to understand and internalize the reciprocal relationship between macro- and micro-level development and impact. It is not an either–or situation or approach; both are needed for promoting social justice and creating equitable access and equal opportunities for all population segments.

Resource Mobilization

Irfan Alam faced severe resource constraints. He mobilized financial capital through his social and personal network, in particular, family members. He said,

> My mother gave me first finance, Rs. 25,000. Then my father gave me Rs. 500,000 or something. My elder brother has given me some Rs. 180,000 or something. Then my sister, my brother has given me Rs. 15,000. In this way I arranged some 1,000,000 rupees.

He raised the balance through bank loans. His personal network provided not only financial capital but also human resources. During the initial years of implementation, one of his best friends worked without drawing any remuneration. Using his entrepreneurial skills and knowledge, such as creative and innovative thinking and risk taking, he mobilized different kinds of resources, operated the venture, and created social impact. From the outset, his venture generated profits and was self-sustaining in the not-for-profit sector.

For social workers, this case presents the importance of entrepreneurial approaches and processes for service development and delivery. Social workers are continuously facing resource challenges, including personnel, finances, space, and technology. Using creativity and innovative thinking, they can locate and access resources that they do not possess. An entrepreneurial approach in mobilizing resources is very important for social work interventions to create sustainable social change. Social workers in private practice may use some elements of these approaches without fully aligning them to an entrepreneurial approach. As SE grows within social work practice, social workers' ability to consciously make these connections will further the work in this area.

Sustainable Livelihood Approach

"The sustainable livelihoods approach is a way of thinking about the objectives, scope, and priorities for development activities" (Serrat, 2008, p. 1). It facilitates the identification of priorities for actions important to people who are poor and vulnerable. This approach focuses on inherent potential of people in terms of their skills, social networks, access to physical and financial resources, and ability to influence core institutions. This approach makes connections between people and the overall enabling environment that influence the outcomes of livelihood strategies.

Irfan Alam focused on addressing the prioritized needs of CRPs. In setting priorities, he first focused on providing CRPs with opportunities to develop sustainable means of earning their livelihood by making them owners of their own rickshaws and thereby improving their income. Subsequently, he focused on other components of their lives, such as health, education of their children, and basic dignity to improve their sense of empowerment. Joshi et al. (2006) recognized the livelihood improvement process as an appropriate tool for reaching people who live in poverty, as it helps to sensitize and inform all providers about the need of pro-poor and inclusive development processes.

At the initial stage, Alam appeared to draw on micro-practice strategies used by social work practitioners by engaging with CRPs and their families individually to assess issues and address them. Through the assessment process, he attempted to have a comprehensive understanding of the multidimensional nature of their challenges. Subsequently, he deployed some mezzo- and macro-level social work practice strategies by organizing the whole community of PVMD CRPs to create institutional change within this transportation sector. Ultimately, his efforts contributed to economic development within several communities of Bihar, one of the poorest states in India. In essence, the sustainable livelihood approach used by Alam combined micro-, mezzo-, and macro-level skills and practices often used by social workers, for improving the well-being of PVMD rickshaw pulling communities and for economic development in Bihar.

Unfortunately, the bifurcated structure of social work education—micro versus macro—is often very restrictive and unwarranted (Vodde & Gallant, 2002). The present case suggests that social work education and practice should seamlessly integrate micro, mezzo, and macro knowledge, skills, strategies, and approaches for preparing graduates to create sustainable social change—the mission of social entrepreneurs—as suggested by Vodde and Gallant (2002). "The time to recalibrate the imbalance between micro and macro social work is now" (Rothman & Mizrahi, 2014, p. 91). The approach used by Irfan Alam, a social entrepreneur, reflects and reinforces the understanding that social problems require complex and sustained intervention simultaneously at all levels of social work practice.

Innovation

Innovation played an important role in the process of financial inclusion of the PVMD rickshaw pullers. Starting with developing an innovative idea by using a sustainable livelihood approach for the financial inclusion of the rickshaw pullers, Alam introduced various product innovations related to different components of the approach. For example, he improved the design model of the cycle rickshaw, which was easier to drive for rickshaw pullers as well as comfortable for passengers. More recently, he designed a battery-operated cycle rickshaw. In his business model, manufacturing rickshaws emerged as the most important element of his innovative idea. For this reason, he started SammaaN Ventures Limited, a for-profit company for the manufacturing of cycle rickshaws, and he made CRPs co-owners of this company. Ifran employed experienced, retired, and old rickshaw pullers as the rickshaw designers in his company instead of traditional engineers. He said,

> They [that is, the rickshaw pullers] are co-owners. They are also the best designers. We don't have engineers in our team. We don't have an engineer by degree, by qualification, but we have people who have been pulling rickshaw for 25 years. We have people who have been assembling rickshaws for 40 years. They are the best people. So, we created a for-profit company, and we are dreaming to go public with this company.

Social workers trust in the abilities of their clients and involve their clients in product and service innovation or in designing new solutions. Through these efforts, Alam created empowering environments for rickshaw pullers, promoted their self-determination, trusted their knowledge, and used their strengths to redesign the rickshaws. He went a step ahead and shared the ownership and profits with them and created an environment of economic empowerment.

To address the health care needs of CRPs and their families, Alam innovatively created SammaaN Swasthya Vertical, a mobile bus equipped with a small operating room, X-ray machine, small pathology lab, medicines, and a doctor. *Swasthya* is a Hindi word that translates as "health" in English. This initiative was self-sustainable because he carefully managed the costs in the supply chain. With this initiative and vertical approach, Alam exemplified the social work value of creating services where none existed.

To address CRPs' financial needs, Alam was involved in process innovation. He developed close relationships with banks, encouraging them to provide micro-credit to the rickshaw pullers in addition to savings bank accounts. Through his relationships, he changed the whole process of borrowing for the CRPs, moving from informal sources to formal banking for buying assets and for meeting emergency financial needs. Consequently, a population segment that was financially exploited and marginalized was able to participate fairly and equitably in the banking industry—exemplifying a value that should resonate with social workers.

Finally, Alam also used an innovative method to market products and generate additional revenue. Rickshaws were used not only for transporting passengers but also for advertising the products and consumables that the CRPs sold and delivered to consumers, such as water, soda drinks, and fruit juices. Shaw (2004) has suggested that social enterprises must adopt entrepreneurial and creative approaches to their marketing if they are to resolve social problems, which they are established to address. Alam received commission for the sales, which he shared with the rickshaw pullers.

Alam initiated organizational, product, process, and marketing method innovations to create social change (Organization of Economic Cooperation and Development, 2005). For social workers practicing as social change agents, innovation processes must be an integral part of their intervention strategies, and they must learn to think beyond the traditional intervention strategies currently used within the field.

Partnerships

To create financial inclusion of the CRPs, Alam developed multiple partnerships with government and private-sector organizations, which greatly assisted with the innovations—product, process, and marketing methods—that positively affected and created value for rickshaw pullers and their families. Specifically, his partnerships with the state government of Bihar resulted in accessible and affordable health care for the CRPs and their families; partnerships with government insurance companies resulted in the provision of accident insurance; and partnerships with government sector banks resulted in access to loans and other banking services not otherwise available to the CRPs. He was also in the process of building partnerships with private builders for constructing low-cost shelter for the rickshaw pullers. Thus, cross-sector social partnerships can produce benefits at individual, organizational, sectoral, and societal levels (Selsky & Parker, 2010). The social skills of this social entrepreneur helped him in developing networks and partnerships. Fligstein (1997) defined social skill of entrepreneurs as an ability to motivate cooperation of other actors by providing them with common meaning and identities. Social workers are adept at these skills.

Owing to the complex and interrelatedness of social problems, Mayhew (2012) determined that no single organization is in the position to successfully address the multifaceted dimensions of these problems. Through collaborations with partners, human service organizations can design seamless service delivery systems for addressing needs more comprehensively (Mayhew, 2012). Consequently, collaborations and cross-sector partnerships are essential strategies for social workers, social entrepreneurs, and social work entrepreneurs.

Financial and Social Inclusion

Alam's sustainable livelihood approach resulted in financial inclusion of PVMD rickshaw pullers. With Alam's partnership and innovative strategies, CRPs were linked to the formal banking system, where they had their own savings accounts and could access and use various financial services. Many CRPs borrowed funds to upgrade from battery-operated cycle to auto-rickshaw and get out of the clutches of cycle rickshaw fleet owners; the latter often exploited the CRPs when providing them with emergency funds. Clearly, these efforts by Alam empowered the rickshaw pullers and connected them with the formal economy, which resulted in their financial inclusion.

In addition to the strategies described earlier, CRPs' incomes increased, and they felt more capable in meeting family obligations, such as providing quality education for their children and savings for emergencies. As a result, their standard of living improved significantly. One of the beneficiaries mentioned, "My earlier income was barely sufficient to survive. With improved income, I am able to give [my children] better education, and we lead a better life, thanks to SammaaN."

Essentially, the CRP beneficiaries obtained health care services, insurance opportunities, and identity because of connection with SammaaN; now, they also had hope for their own shelter. By getting these services and opportunities, financial benefits, social benefits, and security of food and shelter, they improved their capabilities, which resulted in their improved self-esteem, self-confidence, and dignity. They experienced social inclusion—an important social work value. These changes demonstrate that financial and social inclusion are interrelated. Innovation and entrepreneurship have deep effects on social and economic change and thus are important drivers for inclusive growth (Hall, Matos, Sheehan, & Silvestre, 2012). In this entire process of financial inclusion of CRPs, Alam created value for all his partners while also generating profits for organizational sustainability.

Like SE, the primary mission of the social work profession is to meet basic human needs, with particular attention to the needs and empowerment of people who are vulnerable, oppressed, and living in poverty (NASW, 2017). Social workers seek to enhance the capacity of people to address their own needs. Social workers strive to end discrimination, oppression, poverty, and other forms of social injustice. The mission of the social work profession is rooted in a set of core values, which includes service, social justice, dignity and worth of the person, importance of human relationships, integrity, and competence (NASW, 2017). Alam displayed these values. An SE perspective and approach can be a relevant strategy that social workers can use to create social and financial empowerment of vulnerable populations, beyond the provision of social welfare services, which may appease but not eliminate social and financial exclusion. The model of financial inclusion of PVMD CRPs based on innovation and a sustainable livelihood approach is presented in Figure 10.1.

The model in Figure 10.1 demonstrates that, driven by his strong moral and social values, Alam identified problems in the cycle rickshaw sector that

FIGURE 10.1 The Model of Financial Inclusion of the Poor (Cycle Rickshaw Pullers) through Innovation and Sustainable Livelihood Approaches

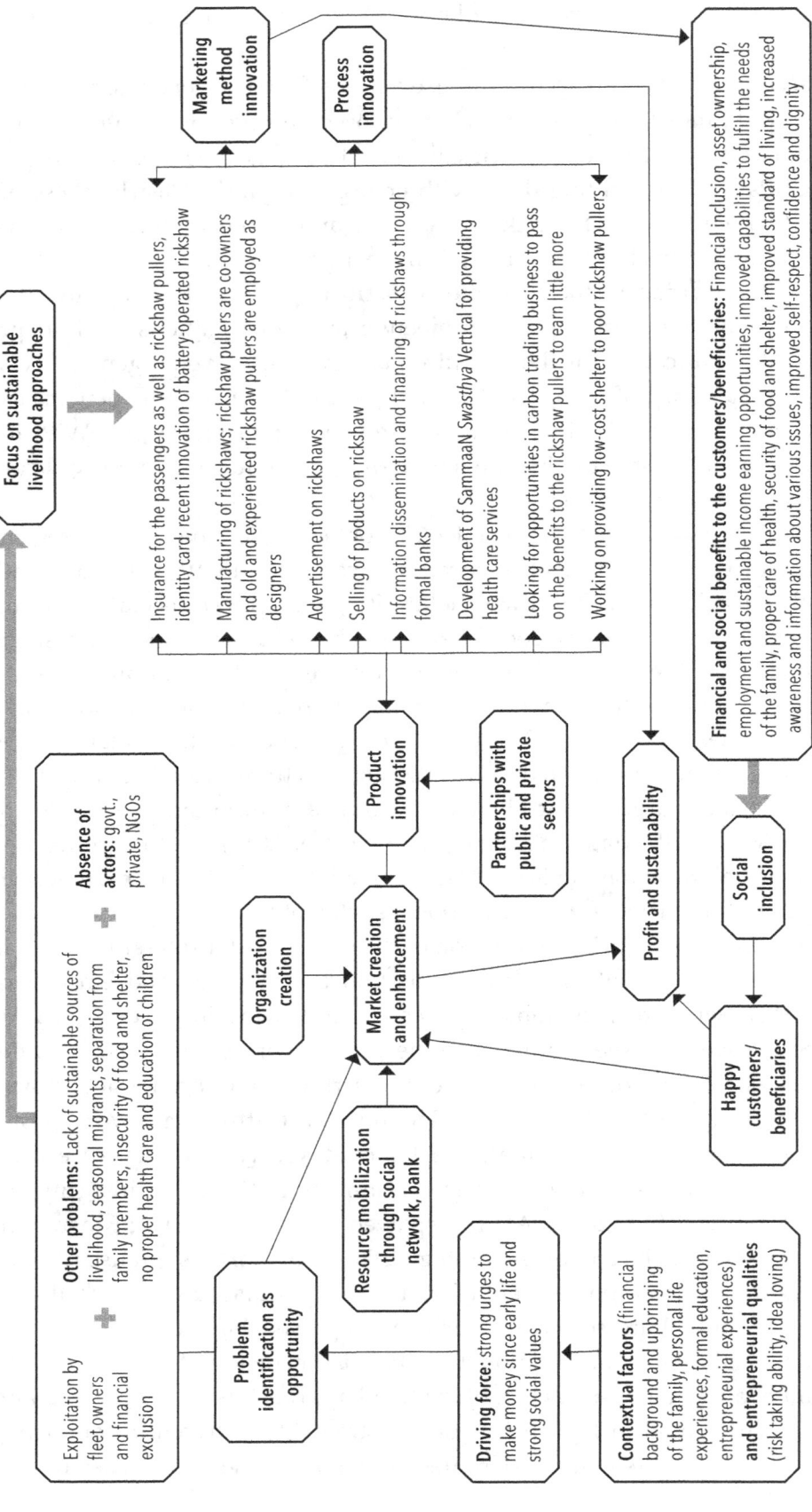

he perceived as an opportunity grounded in the context. He observed CRPs' exploitation and their financial exclusion as well as the absence of professionals, resources, and stakeholders working within and for this sector. His background and his context influenced his social and moral values, urging him to start his own enterprise for innovatively solving the aforementioned challenges in the sector. Following an entrepreneurial approach, he mobilized resources through his personal network and bank. In this process, he used his innovative idea; combined products, processes, and marketing innovations; and created a sustainable business model by using the sustainable livelihood approach. These efforts resulted not only in financial inclusion of PVMD rickshaw pullers but also in their social inclusion and inclusive development within the state. Within social work practice, "inclusion" is emphasized for micro, mezzo, and macro development, which was clearly evident in this case (Pless & Appel, 2012).

Conclusion

Poverty is a major social problem in India, and absence of sustainable livelihood opportunities was identified as a major contributor to the conditions of PVMD rickshaw pullers. Incorporating each of the components of a sustainable livelihood approach and profit-making market creation into the innovative business model of SammaaN Foundation, Irfan Alam not only succeeded in creating financial and social inclusion for PVMD rickshaw pullers but also contributed to economic development. This case describes nine categories of the SE process:

1. context, social and moral values, and entrepreneurial qualities of the social entrepreneur
2. problem identification as an opportunity
3. profit-making market creation and an enhancement approach for sustainability
4. organization creation
5. resource mobilization
6. a sustainable livelihood approach
7. innovation
8. partnerships with private and public sectors
9. financial inclusion and social inclusion

The case shows that a successful strategy for financial or social inclusion of the PVMD population segment must go through the profit-making sustainable livelihood approach and innovation, simply because absence of sustainable sources of livelihood and opportunities are the root causes of the financial and social exploitation and exclusion of this population. This case study has significant implications for social work practice because social workers promote social justice and social change. Social workers continually strive to develop and enhance their professional knowledge, expertise, and skills and to apply them in practice to create change (NASW, 2017). Social workers naturally and intuitively network, collaborate, and build partnerships. These skills can enhance their SE predisposition and ability to learn, embrace, and practice these strategies. The strategies used in this case particularly parallel social work community development and social work mangers' competencies and practices; hence, learning how to use entrepreneurial decision making and actions for achieving social mission, while operating within the boundaries of core social work values, is important.

References

Ansari, S., Munir, K., & Gregg, T. (2012). Impact at the bottom of the pyramid: The role of social capital in capability development and community empowerment. *Journal of Management Studies, 49*, 813–842.

Arora, R. U. (2012). Financial inclusion and human capital in developing Asia: The Australian connection. *Third World Quarterly, 33*(1), 177–197.

Bapat, D. (2010). Perceptions on banking service in rural India: An empirical study. *International Journal of Rural Management, 6*, 303–321.

Bhanot, D., Bapat, V., & Bera, S. (2012). Studying financial inclusion in northeast India. *International Journal of Bank Marketing, 30*, 465–484.

Bisman, C. (2004). Social work values: The moral core of the profession. *British Journal of Social Work, 34*, 109–123.

Bossert, W., D'Ambrosio, C., & Peragine, V. (2007). Deprivation and social exclusion. *Economica, 74*, 777–803.

Chambers, R. (1995). Poverty and livelihoods: Whose reality counts? *Environment and Urbanization, 7*(1), 173–204.

Clark, C. (2006). Moral characters in social work. *British Journal of Social Work, 36*, 75–89.

Cnaan, R. A., Moodithaya, M. S., & Handy, F. (2012). Financial inclusion: Lessons from rural south India. *Journal of Social Policy, 41*(1), 183–205.

Collins, D., Morduch, J., Rutherford, S., & Ruthven, O. (2009). *Portfolios of the poor: How the world's poor live on $2 a day.* Princeton, NJ: Princeton University Press.

Dees, J. G. (1998). *The meaning of social entrepreneurship.* Retrieved from http://www.redalmarza.cl/ing/pdf/TheMeaningofsocialEntrepreneurship.pdf

Dev, S. M. (2006). Financial inclusion: Issues and challenges. *Economic and Political Weekly, 14*, 4310–4313.

Eisenhardt, K. M. (1989). Building theories from case study research. *Academy of Management Review, 14*, 532–551.

Flick, U. (2006). *An introduction to qualitative research.* London: Sage Publications.

Fligstein, N. (1997). Social skill and institutional theory. *American Behavioral Scientist, 40*, 397–405.

Government of India Planning Commission. (2008). *A hundred small steps: Report of the committee on financial sector reforms.* New Delhi, India: Sage Publications. Retrieved from http://planningcommission.nic.in/reports/genrep/rep_fr/cfsr_all.pdf

Hall, J., Matos, S., Sheehan, L., & Silvestre, B. (2012). Entrepreneurship and innovation at the base of the pyramid: A recipe for inclusive growth or social exclusion? *Journal of Management Studies, 49*, 785–812.

Haynes, D. T. (1999). A theoretical integrative framework for teaching professional social work values. *Journal of Social Work Education, 35*(1), 39–50.

Hopkins, J. (1978). Models of assessment in social work. *British Journal of Social Work, 8*, 465–475.

Huff, M. T., & Johnson, M. M. (1998). Empowering students in a graduate-level social work course. *Journal of Social Work Education, 34*, 375–385.

International Labor Office. (2017). *Empowering rural communities through financial inclusion.* Retrieved from http://www.ilo.org/wcmsp5/groups/public/@ed_emp/documents/publication/wcms_159004.pdf

Jack, S. L., & Anderson, A. R. (2002). The effects of embeddedness on the entrepreneurial process. *Journal of Business Venturing, 17*, 467–487.

Johnson, S. (2000). *Literature review on social entrepreneurship.* Retrieved from http://www.business.ualberta.ca/ccse/Publications/Publications/Lit.%20Review%20SE%20November%202000.rtf

Joshi, M., Dhakal, L., Paudel, G., Shrestha, R., Paudel, A., Chand, P. B., & Timsina, N. P. (2006). The livelihood improvement process: An inclusive and pro-poor approach to community forestry-experiences from Kabhrepalanchok and Sindhupalchok districts of Nepal. *Journal of Forest and Livelihood, 5*(1), 46–52.

Laeven, L., & Valencia, F. (2013). The real effects of financial sector interventions during crises. *Journal of Money, Credit and Banking, 45*(1), 147–177.

Mair, J., & Marti, I. (2006). Social entrepreneurship research: A source of explanation, prediction and delight. *Journal of World Business, 41*, 36–44.

Mair, J., & Noboa, E. (2003). *The emergence of social enterprises and their place in the new organizational landscape* (Working Paper No. 523). Retrieved from www.iese.edu/research/pdfs/DI-0523-E.pdf

Mayhew, F. (2012). Human service delivery in a multi-tier system: The subtleties of collaboration among partners. *Journal of Health and Human Services Administration, 35*(1), 109–135.

Meyer, C. B. (2001). A case in case study methodology. *Field Methods, 13,* 329–352.

Miles, M. B., & Huberman, A. M. (1984). *Qualitative data analysis: A sourcebook of new methods.* New Delhi: Sage Publications.

National Association of Social Workers. (2017). *Code of ethics of the National Association of Social Workers.* Washington, DC: Author.

National Bank for Agriculture and Rural Development. (2008, January). *Report of the Committee on Financial Inclusion in India.* Retrieved from http://www .nabard.org/pdf/report_financial/Full%20Report.pdf

Neck, H., Brush, C., & Allen, E. (2008). The landscape of social entrepreneurship. *Business Horizons, 52,* 13–19.

Nicholls, A. (2006). Introduction. In A. Nicholls (Ed.), *Social entrepreneurship: New models of sustainable change* (pp. 1–35). New York: Oxford University Press.

Organization of Economic Cooperation and Development. (2005). *Oslo manual: Guidelines for collecting and interpreting innovation data.* Retrieved from http:// epp.eurostat.ec.europa.eu/cache/ITY_PUBLIC/OSLO/EN/OSLO-EN.PDF

Pless, N. M., & Appel, J. (2012). In pursuit of dignity and social justice: Changing lives through 100% inclusion: How Gram Vikas fosters sustainable rural development. *Journal of Business Ethics, 111,* 389–411.

Ray, D. (1998). *Development economics.* New Delhi, India: Oxford University Press.

Rothman, J., & Mizrahi, T. (2014). Balancing micro and macro practice: A challenge for social work. *Social Work, 59,* 91–93.

Sarma, M., & Pais, J. (2011). Financial inclusion and development. *Journal of International Development, 23,* 613–628.

Selsky, J. W., & Parker, B. (2010). Platforms for cross-sector social partnerships: Prospective sense making devices for social benefit. *Journal of Business Ethics, 94,* 21–37.

Serrat, O. (2008, November). *The sustainable livelihoods approach.* Manila, Philippines: Asian Development Bank. Retrieved from http://digitalcommons.ilr .cornell.edu/cgi/viewcontent.cgi?article=1207&context=intl

Shaw, E. (2004). Marketing in the social enterprise context: Is it entrepreneurial? *Qualitative Market Research: An International Journal, 7,* 194–205.

Solo, T. M. (2008). Financial exclusion in Latin America—or the social costs of not banking the urban. *Environment and Urbanization, 20*(1), 47–66.

Strauss, A., & Corbin, J. (1998). *Basics of qualitative research: Techniques and procedures for developing grounded theory* (2nd ed.). London: Sage Publications.

Vodde, R., & Gallant, J. P. (2002). *Bridging the gap between micro and macro practice.* Retrieved from http://anzasw.nz/wp-content/uploads/Social-Work-Review-Issue-15-Summer-03-Articles-Vodde-and-Gallant.pdf

Voorhis, R. M. V., & Hostetter, C. (2006). The impact of MSW education on social worker empowerment and commitment to client empowerment through social justice advocacy. *Journal of Social Work Education, 42,* 105–121.

Yin, R. (2003). *Case study research: Design and methods* (3rd ed.). Thousand Oaks, CA: Sage Publications.

Yujuico, E. (2008). Connecting the dots in social entrepreneurship through the capabilities approach. *Socio-Economic Review, 6,* 493–513.

11

Social Entrepreneurship: Case Examples in Homelessness and Mental Health in the United States

Carol S. Collard and Irene Searles McClatchey

Starting a new service, expanding existing services, or providing services to a new population are examples of innovative ways to address social concerns that are routinely pursued by social workers (Brooks, 2009). The actions and efforts used when social workers successfully engage in innovative problem solving is often born out of necessity. For many in the field, it may appear that social work practice is a natural breeding ground for social innovation (Nandan, Mandayam, Collard, & Tchouta, 2016). Yet, social innovation and social entrepreneurship are among the least heralded—or examined—courses of action that a social worker takes when working to solve social problems.

This chapter provides two case studies that describe the journeys of distinctly different organizations in Georgia. Although different in size and scope, their process for problem solving uses similar concepts of social entrepreneurship, that is, problem identification, opportunity recognition, risk taking, resource mobilization, and value creation. In addition, as social entrepreneurial ventures, these organizations share a relentless commitment to finding effective solutions for their targeted social problems (Brooks, 2009). Given that their work seeks to address inequities in Georgia's system of care, the organizations also share a common quest for social justice—a shared desire to relieve suffering.

In the pursuit of social justice, social workers often engage in a process of problem solving that drives innovation or requires entrepreneurial action. However, the process of finding those solutions is rarely examined in practice or scholarly research. The chapter also offers recommendations on how to validate and promote the practice of innovation and social entrepreneurship among social work students and practitioners (Nandan et al., 2016; Neal, 2015; Traube, Begun, Okpych, & Choy-Brown, 2017).

Social Entrepreneurs Use Innovative Solutions
for Chronic Homelessness in Georgia

According to the National Alliance to End Homelessness (NAEH, 2017), on any given night in the United States, more than 600,000 persons are without a place to call home. There are a variety of causes—for example, evictions, domestic violence, addiction, or mental illness—but ultimately, homelessness is often directly linked to poverty (Kyle, 2005; NAEH, 2017). The lack of afford-able housing and the inadequate supply of housing assistance programs both exacerbate and perpetuate the homeless problem (NAEH, 2017). The NAEH reports that the majority of those experiencing homelessness do so for short and singular periods; however, approximately 26 percent of those who are homeless are also coping with a behavioral health disorder, such as mental illness or addiction. These individuals are more likely to remain homeless for longer periods and to have multiple episodes of homelessness. Such long-term or repeated episodes are characterized as chronic homelessness (Culhane & Byrne, 2010; NAEH, 2017).

Although they comprise less than one-third of those who are homeless, individuals experiencing chronic homelessness consume more than half the resources devoted to addressing homelessness (Corporation for Supportive Housing [CSH], 2017; Culhane & Byrne, 2010; NAEH, 2017). In addition to access to affordable housing, they need other supports to help stabilize their daily functioning and optimize their ability to live independently (Cohen, Sokolovsky, & Crane, 2001; Kyle, 2005). Housing combined with social ser-vices such as case management and counseling is called *supportive housing* (CSH, 2017). It is a proven, cost-effective solution to ending homelessness and helping individuals manage complex addiction and other health-related conditions (CSH, 2017; Culhane, Metraux, & Hadley, 2002; Kyle, 2005; NAEH, 2017; Rog, 2004). Unfortunately, there is an inadequate supply of supportive housing to meet the demand. Further, the stigma often attached to individuals with such special needs complicates efforts to expand availability. Therefore, the need for more supportive housing persists as a social problem (Bernstein, 2002; CSH, 2017; Hoch, 2000; NAEH, 2017).

The effort to end homelessness has evolved over the last 30 years in tandem with the heightened recognition of the need to create more supportive housing to serve the chronically homeless. This problem posed a unique challenge as few nonprofit organizations had the real estate development and social services expertise needed to successfully build and operate a supportive housing pro-gram. Most important, fewer still had access to the funding needed to ensure that those critical supportive services were made available. Funding for such projects continues to be limited—both the governmental and private resources.

Social Change through Social Entrepreneurship

Solutions to social problems such as homelessness are often the result of efforts led by mission-driven nonprofit organizations. The organizational leaders who can see past the problem, recognize opportunities, be proactive, and use innovation to create change are characterized as social entrepreneurs (Austin, Stevenson, & Wei-Skillern, 2006; Bent-Goodley, 2002). This case describes the journey of two innovators—a housing developer and a social worker—who deployed the social entrepreneurship process by identifying and leveraging opportunities to reduce homelessness in Georgia, creating better services for their clients, and increasing social value within the community.

Residential real estate developers secure land to build new housing or acquire dilapidated properties to renovate. Success in the industry is characterized by matching high risk with high financial reward. Because the financial reward rarely meets the risk, there were and still are few housing developers committed to creating more housing for the homeless. However, in the 1990s, the chief executive officer of one of Georgia's nonprofit housing developers recognized the growing national trend in using supportive housing to help solve the homeless problem. Through his organization, Progressive Redevelopment, Inc. (PRI), this developer social entrepreneur contributed to increased inventory of affordable and supportive housing in the state over a 20-year span. The developer social entrepreneur also inspired a legacy of social innovation and intrapreneurship when he encouraged one of his staff to create a division to deliver supportive services to its residents. This division was so successful that the staff person was encouraged to spin it off and operate it as a separate nonprofit. The second nonprofit organization, CaringWorks, Inc. (CWI), has continued the legacy of social entrepreneurship and has gone on to become one of Georgia's leading supportive housing providers. This case study highlights the legacy of proactive problem solving and innovative practices of these two nonprofit organizations.

Opportunity Identification, Resource Mobilization, and Risk Taking

The developer social entrepreneur demonstrated his prowess for problem solving by engaging in proactive behaviors and innovative practices early on. He seized opportunities presented to grow the organization and later leveraged its reputation to expand its capacity to provide an improved selection of services. This section details the circumstances that led to its growth.

As the host of the 1996 Olympic Games, Atlanta was committed to putting its best face forward. Known as the "city too busy to hate," it began an exerted effort to "end" homelessness. In addition to increasing its law enforcement presence with anti-loitering and trespassing ordinances, local government increased funding to develop affordable housing for the homeless and low-income households. In this climate, the developer social entrepreneur recognized and seized the opportunity to create more affordable housing for low-income and homeless households. Between 1993 and 1996, PRI, leveraging a variety of government and private funding sources, opened six apartment communities, increasing the inventory of affordable housing in Atlanta by nearly 1,000 units, and became one of Georgia's most prolific affordable housing developers.

As the organization was both developer and owner, PRI's staff had ongoing contact with residents who were previously homeless, which heightened its understanding of the unique needs many of them faced, particularly those who had experienced multiple or extended episodes of being unhoused. Having been chronically homeless, their residents had needs that went beyond simply securing a roof over their head. Many were coping with persistent, disabling physical and mental illnesses. Still more were also battling substance addiction. If left unchecked, those would be the very conditions that could put their housing status in jeopardy and perpetuate the cycle of homelessness (CSH, 2017). Success for these clients involved being stable with both their housing and behavioral health status, as well as having access to a reliable, sustaining source of income (Collard, Lewinson, & Watkins, 2015; CSH, 2017; Kyle, 2005; Rog, 2004).

In other parts of the country, nonprofit, faith-based service providers partnered with nonprofit housing developers to create supportive housing. The service providers owned and operated the properties as developers were rarely the owners of such housing developments. In Georgia, PRI was unique in its desire to develop and own supportive housing properties. Initially PRI opted to have services provided by partnering with social services agencies in the community. As there was very limited funding available, the housing developer relied on agencies that were able to secure their own funding to provide the services. The primary service offered was case management. At the time, there were only two supportive housing projects in Atlanta, and service effectiveness proved inconsistent as each service provider operated with different levels of funding. In one program, case management was limited to a part-time staff person, who primarily made referrals to third-party community resources. The other program, which benefited from more funding, had a full-time staff person who provided counseling and emphasized skill building that led to clients' improved daily functioning and household management skills.

To better understand whether services could be more effective, PRI's staff continued research on other supportive housing programs across the country.

In other states, supportive housing programs introduced more on-site services, such as relapse prevention services and programs to develop job readiness skills, in addition to case management. Seeking a way to provide more meaningful and consistent results for residents, the developer social entrepreneur took a risk in 1996, mobilized resources, and created a new division within the organization to provide these services to its residents. Working with the philanthropic community and leveraging targeted government programs, the developer was able to secure funding for this new entrepreneurial initiative. Until then, no known developer in Georgia had started its own program of supportive services. By 2002, the services division had become so successful that it spun off into a separate nonprofit entity, which operated with an approach to care that better aligned with nationally recognized best practices of supportive housing. The developer social entrepreneur, with the help of the social work intrapreneur within his organization, formed the second social entrepreneurship venture, CWI. PRI had earned a local and national reputation for its progressive work in the homeless sector. Although a few nonprofits in other parts of the country had initiated similar projects (Culhane et al., 2002), this was the first time a developer had pursued such a venture in Georgia.

A Social Entrepreneur Inspires Social Intrapreneurs

Indicative of the propensity for innovation within its organizational culture, the developer social entrepreneur inspired his staff to be proactive and creative problem solvers. His egalitarian leadership style encouraged staff input and involvement in decision making (Hassan & Wimpfheimer, 2015). He encouraged and supported open communication and gave staff the freedom to seek and take advantage of new opportunities to improve the client experience. In doing so, he created a rich climate for nurturing staff to become social intrapreneurs (Berzin & Pitts-Catsouphes, 2015; Nandan et al., 2016). Social intrapreneurs are employees of organizations who leverage the existing infrastructure and assets of their employer to create and engage in innovative approaches to problem solving (Nandan et al., 2016). Over a decade ago, one of those social intrapreneurs on the developer's staff recognized the opportunity to turn the supportive services division into a separate venture. This social intrapreneur, as the founder and chief executive officer of CWI, is now a social work entrepreneur (SWE). The agency has evolved since its inception from being solely a service provider to providing housing and comprehensive behavioral health services. This case study will further detail how CWI's staff continued the legacy of engaging in innovative practices to help reduce homelessness and how the organization has emerged as one of metropolitan Atlanta's leading nonprofit supportive housing providers.

Continuing a Legacy of Social Innovation

The mission of CWI is to "reduce homelessness and empower the marginalized by providing access to housing and services that foster dignity, self-sufficiency and well-being" (http://www.caringworksinc.org/). CWI is led by a senior management team that includes two social work professionals who believe that the ultimate mission of their work is to increase access to social justice for their clients. They assert that access to decent housing and health care should be the right of all citizens, not a privilege. CWI also operates in a manner that is consistent with the social work values of integrity, competence, and respecting the dignity and worth of the person. Like PRI, CWI adheres to the human services management competencies endorsed by the Network for Social Work Management (Hassan & Wimpfheimer, 2015). Its leadership initiates and encourages innovation.

Further, as members of both management and direct service staff have histories of homelessness and recovery from behavioral health conditions, they also serve as role models for their clients. Although this is not uncommon among service providers, many of those same staff members can also proudly point to relevant educational and professional credentials that do distinguish them from many of their peers. That mix of peer credibility and professionalism is not typically found in similar programs, yet it is a crucial example to clients of what can be achieved after recovery. Also like the developer social entrepreneur who encouraged her, the SWE who leads CWI is a keen observer of the environment in which clients must function, recognizing that context can be an influence on the plausibility and effectiveness of innovation.

Consistent with a continuous quality improvement model (McLaughlin & Kaluzny, 2004), CWI also relies on data to improve its service delivery protocols and emphasizes building fidelity with relevant evidence-based practices. For example, as the work addressing chronic homelessness evolved in the first years of the 21st century, a new approach to care called Housing First drew increasing attention across the country (Tsemberis, Gulcur, & Nakae, 2004). Housing First emphasized getting chronically homeless adults off the street earlier and bringing more intensive psychiatric and behavioral health services to them rather than waiting for clients to visit a clinic. This innovative, evidence-based practice is undergirded by a harm reduction philosophy that embraces the idea that a client's pursuit of recovery should be a choice that he or she can make after securing a roof overhead and should not be a condition for housing (Tsemberis et al., 2004).

Initially benefiting from a federal grant from the Substance Abuse and Mental Health Services Administration in 2009, CWI was among the first supportive housing providers in Georgia to embrace this approach to care. This was a significant departure from the traditional method of care in supportive housing, which offered primarily case management and wraparound supports. Housing First also ended the need for rigid admission requirements that made clients wait months to prove sobriety or stability to secure housing. If a housing unit was available, clients could be placed in days.

In the Housing First model, the shortened time before access to housing is an undeniable benefit to the client. However, it poses extra challenges to service providers. To optimize the client's chances of remaining successfully housed, a cadre of workers can be deployed to the client's apartment to deliver services. Psychiatrists, nurses, therapists, case managers, addiction counselors, and other paraprofessionals make routine visits to each client based on his or her level of functioning. By contrast, in the traditional supportive housing model, case management and relapse prevention services were offered within the housing environment, but clients were referred to third-party providers in the community for psychiatric and intensive behavioral health services.

The intensity and consistency of the services using the Housing First approach demonstrate an improved process of service delivery and—consistent with social work values—heightened respect for clients. However, the Housing First model is significantly more expensive than the traditional model, which is staffed primarily by case managers and addiction counselors. As the majority of the residents in supportive housing in most states are Medicaid recipients, Medicaid-funded behavioral health providers are engaged to implement the program. However, in states like Georgia, which has not expanded its Medicaid program, fewer than 50 percent of its supportive housing residents receive Medicaid. Services here continue to be funded through an amalgam of grants, private donations, and contracts.

Ironically, as the Housing First approach became more popular across the country and more providers were leveraging Medicaid resources to pay for services, this led to policy changes that reduced existing funding for services. Those reductions made it much more difficult to provide services in states that did not embrace the expansion of Medicaid. These changes underscored the need for CWI to diversify its funding sources as it was overly dependent on government grants.

Problem Mapping and Opportunity Recognition

CWI realized there were two problems to resolve. While CWI was seeking ways to cope with the changes in funding opportunities, the agency also became more aware of challenges clients were having when trying to access their psychiatric and related health services. Many clients would complain of having to wait three months or more to be seen by a psychiatrist, which often negatively affected medication management. Clients also expressed frustration with having to see a different doctor or therapist for each visit, which further affected quality of care. The disruptions to care continuity created adverse effects on clients' daily functioning and their ability to live independently. In mapping out these seemingly incongruent problems, the SWE recognized the opportunities to create value in community while overcoming funding challenges. After much deliberation with staff, board, clients, and other stakeholders, the SWE decided that CWI would continue the legacy of entrepreneurship inspired by PRI by starting a new division that would offer comprehensive psychiatric and behavioral health services. Funded by Medicaid, this expansion of services provided an innovative method of revenue generation for the organization. This initiative enabled CWI to offer an expanded array of services to its clients as well as to any Medicaid-eligible persons in the general population. This would provide a benefit to the community as it would increase service capacity for Medicaid-eligible citizens. Importantly, the new venture also afforded CWI the opportunity to reduce its dependency on grants by diversifying its revenue sources. Anticipating that funding resources would continue to diminish and become harder to access, the SWE saw the initiative as a win–win for the community and the agency.

Risks and Rewards of Implementation

The SWE did not take the decision to become a Medicaid-funded provider lightly. There were many hurdles that had to be overcome, not the least of which was overcoming the concern about how it might change the organizational culture. There was a risk that the goal of furthering the organization could overshadow the goal of helping clients (Austin et al., 2006). In starting this venture, CWI's staff put emphasis on perfecting its service model. Given the funding structure of Medicaid, which imposes limits on how much billable time is allowed for each client session, the new emphasis on billable time risked a diminishment of the client–provider experience. CWI has historically always placed value on a client-first approach, so it was crucial that staff continue to place emphasis on actual client need rather than revenue potential. Although staff did adhere to Medicaid requirements regarding billing their time, staff training also reinforced attending to client need even if the time spent did not generate income. The SWE, like other social entrepreneurs, sought to emphasize the social value earned from the venture rather than the financial gain (Martin & Osberg, 2007).

The social entrepreneur also recognized that this initiative had a twofold benefit. One was to create social value by attending to unmet community demand for behavioral health services (Lepak, Smith, & Taylor, 2007; Singh, 2016); the other was the significant potential for generating unrestricted earned income. Again, consistent with human services management competencies, both staff and board were encouraged to participate in the design, development, and implementation of the initiative.

CWI was also cognizant of the resulting change in management issues that would emerge from the inevitable growth of the organization. Austin et al. (2006) warned of the risk of failing to be mindful of organizational alignment. As there are so many needs in the community, particularly for those experiencing homelessness and vulnerability, CWI could find itself trying to respond beyond its capacity. To address that risk, the organization formed a change management committee that is composed of board and staff members who monitor the effects of growth and change on organizational culture.

Value of Social Entrepreneurship Ventures

Early on, the venture proved valuable for Medicaid-eligible clients as they were able to access care within two weeks of choosing CWI for behavioral health services. In addition, they were able to progress in their care by seeing the same team of practitioners each time. Meeting this need was consistent with state regulations and was also a way of attending to a social work value of preserving the dignity and worth of the client. Moreover, improving access to services speaks to social justice values of the profession.

Pursuit of Innovation: A Matter of Ethics

Starting a new venture poses numerous challenges, including effectively addressing the risks inherent in introducing a new program to your client. There are many factors that must be considered. Is the proposed program or service appropriate for the client? Are the workers competent? Is the social entrepreneur equipped to make an unbiased assessment of the program's efficacy? As with any ethical dilemma, risks must be weighed and prioritized.

In the case of this SWE, although those questions did require answers, the larger ethical dilemma was the prospect of doing nothing. As mentioned, CWI's senior staff includes social work professionals, and the agency is guided by the ethical principles and guidelines of the profession. Senior staff felt it was an ethical responsibility to provide access to services where they were either nonexistent or inadequate. The social work profession embraces the value of social justice, and the equitable availability of health care to all who need it, regardless of ability to pay, is indeed a social justice issue.

Further, CWI adheres to all state and federal regulations and considers it consistent with its ethical obligation to the community and the profession to ensure that all direct service staff receive appropriate training to ensure competency and adherence to relevant cutting-edge practices.

Social Impact and Social Value

According to Lisetchi and Brancu (2014), "the goal of innovation is to bring a positive change" (p. 88). The SWE's risky decision to become a Medicaid-funded behavioral health provider brought about significant positive change for the client and for the larger community's effort to reduce chronic homelessness. The SWE successfully bridged service and profit goals (Dorado, 2006) to grow an organization that is now positioned to integrate a full spectrum of services, including psychiatric care, addiction recovery services, peer support programming, and individual and group counseling. These services, as needed, are layered on top of already existing case management support and life skills training, enabling comprehensive care. By offering a comprehensive array of services to clients in its supportive housing programs, CWI is favorably affecting the community by helping to close the treatment gap for those with behavioral health challenges. During the two years that services have been offered, health outcomes of clients have improved, and CWI's revenue has increased by more than 20 percent. Also of note, CWI has successfully undergone the rigorous scrutiny of state and national regulating bodies, achieving a standing in the community that few providers have achieved (Georgia Collaborative Administrative Services Organization, 2016).

In addition, CWI's focus on data collection and evaluation brings social value to the community by acting as a model for the metropolitan Atlanta provider community. Its success is grounded in effectively and innovatively addressing the social problem (Dorado, 2006). Thus, the venture is a major contributor of data on service effectiveness among its supportive housing clients. These regular evaluations will contribute to the community's ability to examine whether the addition of these services is truly moving the needle toward enhanced self-sufficiency among those hardest to serve. The evaluation orientation is critically important as federal agencies such as the Department of Housing and Urban Development and other federal funders have already moved toward this new model for structuring their funding.

Implications for Social Work Practice

As previously stated, social work professionals form the leadership of CWI. They have promoted a culture of intrapreneurship, particularly encouraging proactiveness and innovation in problem solving among staff. They have exhibited management, resource development, and community engagement skills when interacting with the larger community to develop and promote the venture (Hassan & Wimpfheimer, 2015).

Whether or not it is accurately articulated, the social work profession routinely engages in ventures of social enterprise (Neal, 2015). By default or design, creative business strategies and innovation are frequently used in environments where social problems must be solved with limited resources. In today's environment, government and philanthropic resources are shrinking, while social problems, like homelessness, remain a constant. Those in the field must not be afraid to identify creative solutions to meet needs (Berzin & Pitts-Catsouphes, 2015; Neal, 2015). This could include creating new ventures (macro practice) or engaging in ethically sound development of new best practices that can be used directly with the client (micro practice).

Using creativity and responsible experimentation should be encouraged through schools of social work, professional associations, and employers (Neal, 2015; Traube et al., 2017). Social work professionals with agencies that have successfully engaged in social entrepreneurial ventures should avail themselves as mentors to those seeking to pursue such opportunities and to student interns, who could be inspired by them. Social work students should be trained to embrace innovation, risk taking, and proactiveness as part of their professional social work practice for the grand societal challenges of this century (Nandan et al., 2016).

How an SWE Created a Bereavement Camp for Kids

Losing a parent at a young age is unfortunately common. Worldwide, there were 140 million orphans under the age of 18 in 2014 (U.S. Government, 2016). Of these, approximately 10 percent had lost both mother and father. Close to 2 million children under the age of 18 received Social Security death benefits in the United States that same year (Social Security Administration [SSA], n.d.). It is likely that the number of children in the United States who have lost a parent is higher than that, as the SSA number does not include parents who were unemployed or undocumented. In the state of Georgia, the SSA number for children under 18 receiving death benefits was 44,846 in 2014.

A loss of a loved one is difficult for most people, but for children and adolescents, the death of a parent is particularly difficult. Researchers have shown several detrimental effects, both short-term and long-term, on children after the death of a parent. These include higher rates of substance abuse, deviance, posttraumatic stress disorder symptoms, developmental delays, and many psychological issues (Dopp & Cain, 2012; Ellis, Dowrick, & Lloyd-Williams, 2013; Li et al., 2014; McClatchey, Vonk, & Palardy, 2009).

This section describes how an SWE recognized a problem that needed a response, came up with an innovative idea for a solution, mobilized resources, and took the risk of implementing the innovative idea. The outline is based on Perrini, Vurro, and Costanzo's (2010) social entrepreneurship process.

Individual and Contextual Dimensions

As a person who had experienced the traumatic loss of a parent as an adolescent and who was now working in hospice, where young children and teens were struck by parental death quite frequently, the SWE strived to find resources for youths to help them process their grief. The SWE called schools for resources, searched the Yellow Pages for bereavement resources for youths, and contacted other hospices. She found that grief counseling was delegated to school counselors who have very little training in childhood or teenage grief and in addition have very little time to assist their students because of heavy caseloads. When the SWE could not find the resources she was looking for from this informal needs assessment, she knew that her social work ethics called on her to create a resource for these children in need of bereavement services.

Opportunity Identification

In an effort to assist the bereaved youths she encountered in hospice, the SWE organized "closed" bereavement groups for grieving children and teens whose parents had died on hospice. It was a semi-successful endeavor. The participants were thrown together for an hour a week for six weeks and did not appear comfortable sharing openly with each other. She knew, through her work and professional network, that there were no other resources for bereaved children in the community. Her social work values told her that as a vulnerable population, these children deserved help that worked. Social work ethics also informed her that because she had the skills and training to work with bereaved populations, she was ethically obligated to advocate for or create such a resource as no other existed. The SWE brainstormed ideas of how to serve bereaved youths in a meaningful way. This is when a vision of bringing bereaved children and teens together in a camp setting was conceived. But how would it work? Would parents or guardians bring them to camp? How would she get funding for such a prospect? How much would it cost? Would she be able to get people to assist?

The SWE knew it would be a big risk to undertake something so different even if she could raise funds and mobilize other resources. A new approach, such as a camp setting where the participants could engage in "fun" activities to release grief and also attend bereavement counseling sessions, might work. Children cannot tolerate strong feelings for long periods, so this mixture of fun and seriousness seemed like a perfect solution. It would be a challenge, but it was also an opportunity to reach bereaved children and provide them with guidance through their bereavement process. She seized the opportunity for this social innovation (Kury, 2012).

The SWE was heavily involved in the community through her hospice work. She used her network to mobilize stakeholders. She contacted other members of the hospice community but also school social workers and counselors to get feedback on her ideas and to invite involvement (Hamby, Pierce, & Brinberg, 2010). She was reminded by the identified stakeholders that the camp setting is popular in the community for recreation for children and teens and that a bereavement camp enterprise held promise. Thus, the SWE was a *bricoleur*, trying to solve a small-scale social issue within the community (Zahra, Rawhouser, Bhawe, Neubaum, & Hayton, 2008).

Opportunity Evaluation and Mobilization of Resources

The SWE proceeded to look at possible resources available to create the social enterprise. Her social work values dictated that those in need should be able to access resources regardless of ability to pay. The families she served in hospice lived in underserved areas with limited resources. Therefore, she definitely wanted the program to be free of charge to participating youths. She talked to the owners of the hospice where she worked to see if this innovative idea was something they would support. The executive director of the hospice responded that the enterprise could fall under the hospice's mission statement of grief education. But the SWE needed to mobilize other funding as well. Local Kiwanis and Rotary clubs were willing to share the expenses. State and federal grants were not an option, because the SWE wanted to work independently of public regulations.

Other community resources were explored and mobilized. Knowing that using various art forms with grieving children and teens can have a great impact, the SWE contacted various art institutions in the community. One educational theater group, a subsidiary of a national health insurance company, presented plays in the community as a form of prevention. This group was interested in working with the prospective social enterprise. However, it did not have any plays related to grief. Together the SWE and the art director of the theater group created one puppetry show, *Uncle Gherkin's Magical Show*, for the younger campers, and a play, *Fragments of Grief*, for the older campers. Professional actors from the theater group would perform both for free.

The SWE also looked to her network of key informants for referrals. School counselors and school social workers were immediately eager to participate as referral sources. They had enough bereaved students from just their own schools to fill a camp. Social workers from local hospitals also stated that they had several children and teens to refer should such a program come into existence.

Opportunity Formalization

The SWE had a clear vision of what she wanted to create (Perrini et al., 2010). The social enterprise would use an already existing physical camp structure where children and teens would meet for a weekend to process their grief under the supervision of clinical social workers but also get the chance to participate in regular camp activities, such as canoeing, a ropes course, archery, hiking, hayrides, and talent show. Counseling in a traditional group setting had not worked—the youths did not appear to feel safe and comfortable enough to share in that setting. They needed an environment where they could bond with each other in a unique way to facilitate processing of their grief experiences.

A mission statement was created—"Where bereaved children begin to heal in a safe and nurturing environment"—and goals were established based on the mission statement. This formalization of principles and values created legitimacy for the birth of a social enterprise that would launch the social innovation intervention (Sundin & Tillmar, 2008). A small board was formed, again by networking. Fellow social workers acted as board members. An attorney, who the SWE had met at a Kiwanis meeting when speaking about her dreams for the camp, also joined. This attorney in turn recruited an accountant to join the board.

The SWE made a formal request for grant money from the hospice foundation at the hospice where she was employed. Once the grant request was approved, a camp site located close to the city was reserved and paid for. Other resources were mobilized. The social entrepreneur contacted social workers from her network in various local hospices and hospitals and recruited them to serve as grief counselors. The incentive to work for the weekend included the opportunity to serve as volunteers to a vulnerable population and a small reimbursement for conducting counseling sessions. The SWE felt that with these initial resources, such as a small grant, the support of fellow social workers and school counselors in the community, and other community resources, the socially innovative enterprise would be able to produce changes and become independent (Austin et al., 2006; Chell, 2007).

Opportunity Exploitation

The SWE carefully outlined the business plans for the social enterprise and steps for reaching the realization of the program. After securing funds for the first camp session, creating a name and mission statement, and securing a convenient location for the bereaved campers, a curriculum that met the needs of grieving children and adolescents was needed. It was imperative that the intervention model for bereaved children and teens was not just a recreational time away from home but also provided counseling based on grief theory and evidence-based practice (Perrini et al., 2010). An enterprise that combined typical camp activities with additional healing interventions was the social innovation that was needed in the community. It was important that the recruited grief counselors were paid for their professional work, which ensured that only the most qualified individuals were hired by the social enterprise. Individuals to serve as co-counselors were mobilized among school counselors, hospice, and hospital volunteers. Later, once the SWE became a social work professor, co-counselors were recruited among master's-level social work students who gained critical clinical social work experience and training from the camp. This became a win–win situation. Over time, campers have returned as resources, serving as co-counselors. Some parents of former campers are also involved in camp, volunteering as co-counselors or lead counselors, depending on education and training.

Other volunteers were recruited, too. The SWE served as the unpaid director of the social enterprise but needed assistance from others to prepare, plan, and implement the innovative intervention. Many of the lead and co-counselors were willing to step into these roles—the rationale for volunteering was often a love for the program and for witnessing the change in the campers over the course of the weekend. In many cases, volunteers' own background of parental loss added to their passion to serve in leadership roles. Altruistic motives together with satisfaction with their own performance are two common reasons that people have for volunteering (Randle & Dolnicar, 2009).

The use of a curriculum based on theory and evidence-based practice would provide long-lasting positive effects for campers and prevent many serious negative effects of childhood bereavement (Austin et al., 2006). In addition to providing a social enterprise that was free to participants, there was another important principle guiding the SWE (Sundin & Tillmar, 2008). Children live within some type of family system, and that family system influences the grieving process. In addition, social work values dictate that social workers approach each person in his or her environment. Therefore, it was important to the SWE to offer education and assistance to the adults in the children's lives. The SWE created a one-day workshop a couple of years after launching the camp following numerous requests from participating families. To accommodate the new service, the mission statement was expanded to read, "Where bereaved children *and their caregivers* begin to heal in a safe and nurturing environment." The parent workshop is held the last day of the children's camp. It addresses differences between how children and adults grieve and how adults in the children's lives can help them navigate through the grieving process. Some years later, again based on multiple requests from family members, a weekend retreat for parents and guardians who were experiencing their own grief was established to run parallel to, but separate from, that of the youth campers. This became a form of social intrapreneurship as the workshop and retreat, although offered free of charge, brought many unexpected donations from participants (Mair & Marti, 2006).

Opportunity Scaling Up

As the success of the bereavement camp became evident, the SWE was able to hold more camp sessions in various parts of the state. To share the success of the camp nationally and internationally and thereby maximize its impact on bereaved children and youths (Chell, 2007), she was also able to secure speaking engagements at local, state, national, and international conferences. At these engagements, she spoke about the innovation and principles to guide similar efforts in other areas. Outcome studies of the innovation were published in various peer-reviewed journals. The SWE received, and continues to receive, several requests for advice and input from individuals and organizations who are planning to replicate the social enterprise in their communities. She recently authored a book on how to plan and evaluate bereavement camps and details the curriculum for the camp in her book.

Challenges in Planning and Implementation

The main challenge for the SWE was to create an effective curriculum. Most interventions with bereaved children and adolescents found in the literature were based on traditional grief theory for adults. Outcome studies that were available using adult grief theory on children were inconclusive. To learn more and to research children and grief herself, the SWE decided to go back to school to learn how to do research. With her doctorate in hand, she conducted outcome studies on various interventions at camp and designed a trauma-focused, trauma-informed grief intervention. This effective curriculum has been used for the past 19 years.

Another challenge when planning the program was tied to finding staff and volunteers to match the population the social innovation served. One-third to one-half of participants were from nonwhite ethnicities, mostly blacks. Typically, only a little over a quarter of the staff and volunteers were black. Studies show that similarities between camper and counselor, such as ethnicity, are important to a good camp outcome (Schafer, 2007). Therefore, recruitment of a diverse volunteer group continues and is slowly increasing the number of black and Latino volunteers.

Yet another challenge has been and continues to be to find enough volunteers and other resources, such as funding, to serve the number of children and adolescents on the waiting list. The social enterprise offers three camp sessions a year, each serving 75 to 80 bereaved campers. For optimal outcome and quality, each clinical social worker and the co-counselors are assigned six to eight campers. However, this scaling leaves another 40 to 45 bereaved children and adolescents on the waiting list for each camp session. Ethically, social workers serve those in need or refer those they cannot serve to other resources. The dilemma for the SWE is that there are limited resources available in the community. The SWE continues to work hard to secure more funding and more volunteers to be able to serve everyone who asks for the services.

Empirical Evidence of Program Effectiveness

Several outcome studies have been performed on the program. Two controlled outcome studies have shown the social innovation to reduce complicated grief and posttraumatic stress disorder symptoms among the campers (McClatchey et al., 2009) and to increase emotional and cognitive growth (McClatchey & Raven, 2017). Pre-experimental outcome studies (pre- and posttests) showed that acting-out behavior decreased among campers after camp (McClatchey & Peters, 2015). In addition, qualitative studies have shown the social innovation to benefit participants. Campers have stated that it also helped alleviate guilt associated with their losses and helped them with depression and suicidal ideations. Others claimed that they learned valuable positive coping skills at camp (McClatchey & Wimmer, 2012, 2014). A group of fathers of campers were interviewed after camp and stated that the social innovation was a valuable resource for them and their families (McClatchey, 2017).

On the basis of Dietz and Porter's (2012) definition of social value as something that has value to society, and Acs, Boardman, and McNeely's (2013) definition of productive entrepreneurship as one that has social value, it is clear from these evaluations that the social innovation and the venture created social value for children, caregivers, and the community at large.

Relation to Social Work Practice

The SWE's skills used to create and keep the social innovation active include micro-, mezzo-, and macro-level social work skills (Hepworth, Rooney, Rooney, & Strom-Gottfried, 2013). The SWE communicated with her network of key informants while doing the needs assessment for the social innovation and when recruiting campers (mezzo-level social work skills). The SWE also talked extensively with families, both parents and prospective campers, to do a thorough assessment of each camper planning to attend the social enterprise (micro-level social work skills). The bereavement enterprise also relates to social work micro practice skills when professional social work counselors work and interact directly with bereaved children and teens and families during the weekends. In addition, the SWE and other program volunteers speak at school functions to educate other professionals and the public about children and grief, raising awareness of the consequences of childhood bereavement and the social innovation (mezzo-level social work skills). On a macro level, the SWE and other volunteer staff also advocate on both state and national levels to decrease the stigma around drug-related and suicidal deaths, educating their audiences about how depression and addiction are mental health disorders (American Psychiatric Association, 2013).

The SWE also practiced social work management skills (Hassan & Wimpfheimer, 2015). The SWE displayed executive leadership skills when using her strong communication skills to network with key informants, referral, and funding sources. She obviously facilitated innovative change in her community by creating the grief camp. She created a mission, goals, and objectives for the social enterprise and reviewed the mission at times to make sure it was relevant and made changes as needed. Resource management skills were obvious in her effective management and oversight of budgets and financial resources and successful fundraising; five years after the first camp session, the SWE instituted a golf fundraiser that allows active military to play golf for free while sponsors donate money for the event and for the camp. Thus, the sponsors are supporting two causes with one donation. Finally, the SWE showed strong community collaboration skills when building relationships with other agencies in her community, such as the school system, hospices, hospitals, theater programs, and churches.

Relation to Social Work Values and Ethics

Relations to social work practice include the social innovation's adherence to several social work values and ethics (NASW, 2017), such as service, importance and centrality of human relationships, dignity and worth of the individual, cultural awareness and social diversity, self-determination, informed consent, and competence. The program is based on service to the vulnerable and underserved, a social work value of utmost importance. The professional social workers who work at the social enterprise also volunteer part of their time at camp, adhering to their professional ethics of serving those in need. The relationship between the counselors and camp participants is of the utmost importance, as is showing dignity and worth toward all campers, both of which are central social work values. The social innovation is stressing the importance of cultural humility among all staff members, volunteers, camp participants, their families, and other stakeholders. Training in cultural diversity is regularly provided. Self-determination of the camp participants is stressed as no camper is forced to participate or share but is allowed to do everything at her or his own pace. Each camper is also asked to sign a form agreeing to come to camp, and each participant's guardian gives informed consent. In addition, the social innovation stresses the importance of using only professional counselors who have training in and experience working with bereaved children and teens. Extra training for the counselors in childhood grief and working with the curriculum is held, and social workers and volunteers are provided with a detailed, scripted curriculum for the weekend to ensure competency. As another example of competence, the SWE, when discovering that there was not much research available on bereaved children and adolescents, returned to school to get a doctorate in social work to learn how to conduct research.

Conclusion

This chapter describes how two SWEs created ventures that addressed complex community needs. One SWE started as a social work intrapreneur and, with spin-off of a division, created a social entrepreneurship venture for the homeless population. The other SWE created an innovative resource, intervention, and venture for bereaved children and adolescents. Although the needs that the two SWEs addressed were very different, they were both driven by a strong desire to create social change with a lasting and transformational impact on society (Martin & Osberg, 2007). According to Singh's (2016) definition of social value, both SWEs added social value in their communities by identifying social problems, solving them through innovative means, and creating social change and impact as demonstrated through outcome studies.

References

Acs, Z. J., Boardman, M. C., & McNeely, C. L. (2013). The social value of productive entrepreneurship. *Small Business Economics, 40,* 785–796. doi:10.1007/s11187-011-9396-6

American Psychiatric Association. (2013). *Diagnostic and statistical manual for mental disorders* (5th ed.). Arlington, VA: Author.

Austin, J., Stevenson, H., & Wei-Skillern, J. (2006, January). Social and commercial entrepreneurship: Same, different or both? *Entrepreneurship, Theory & Practice, 30*(1), 1–22. doi:10.1111/j.1540-6520.2006.00107.x

Bent-Goodley, T. B. (2002). Defining and conceptualizing social entrepreneurship. *Journal of Social Work Education, 38,* 291–302.

Bernstein, N. (2002, June 23). Once again, trying housing as a cure for home-lessness: Mothers with children are getting preference in city assignments for subsidized apartments. *New York Times.* Retrieved from https://www.nytimes.com/2002/06/23/nyregion/once-again-trying-housing-cure-for-homelessness-mothers-with-children-are.html

Berzin, S., & Pitts-Catsouphes, M. (2015). Social innovation from the inside: Considering the "intrapreneurship" path. *Social Work, 60,* 360–362. doi:10.1093/sw/swv026

Brooks, A. (2009). *Social entrepreneurship: A modern approach to social value creation.* Upper Saddle River, NJ: Pearson Prentice Hall.

Chell, E. (2007). Social enterprise and entrepreneurship: Towards a convergent theory of the entrepreneurial process. *International Small Business Journal, 25,* 5–26. doi:10.1177/0266242607071779

Cohen, C., Sokolovsky, J., & Crane, M. (2001). Aging, homelessness and the law. *International Journal of Law Psychiatry, 24,* 167–181.

Collard, C., Lewinson, T., & Watkins, K. (2014). Supportive housing: An evidence-based intervention for reducing relapse among low income adults in addiction recovery. *Journal of Evidence-Based Social Work, 11,* 468–479. doi:10.1080/15433714.2013.765813

Corporation for Supportive Housing. (2017, July). *Supportive housing facts.* Retrieved from http://www.csh.org/supportive-housing-facts/

Culhane, D. P., & Byrne, T. (2010). *Ending chronic homelessness: Cost-effective opportunities for interagency collaboration* [Working paper]. Retrieved from http://works.bepress.com/dennis_culhane/94

Culhane, D. P., Metraux, S., & Hadley, T. (2002). Public service reductions associated with placement of homeless persons with severe mental illness in supportive housing. *Housing Policy Debate, 13,* 107–163. Retrieved from https://shnny.org/uploads/The_Culhane_Report.pdf

Dietz, A. S., & Porter, C. (2012). Making sense of social value creation: Three organizational case studies. *Emergence: Complexity and Organization, 14*(3), 23–43. Retrieved from https://search.proquest.com/docview/1349160103?pq-origsite=gscholar

Dopp, A. R., & Cain, A. C. (2012). The role of peer relationships in parental bereavement during childhood and adolescence. *Death Studies, 36*(1), 41–60. doi:10.1080/07481187.2011.573175

Dorado, S. (2006). Social entrepreneurial ventures: Different values so different processes of creation, no? *Journal of Developmental Entrepreneurship, 11,* 319–343. doi:10.1142/S1084946706000453

Ellis, J., Dowrick, C., & Lloyd-Williams, M. (2013). The long-term impact of early parental death: Lessons from a narrative study. *Journal of the Royal Society of Medicine, 106*(2), 57–67. doi:10.1177/0141076812472623

Georgia Collaborative Administrative Services Organization. (2017, December). *Behavioral health quality review: Final assessment report: CaringWorks, Inc.* Retrieved from http://media.beaconhealthoptions.com/ga-reports/BH/Caring%20Works,%20Inc/Caring%20Works,%20Inc%20Final%20Assessment%20BHQR%2012-2017.pdf

Hamby, A., Pierce, M., & Brinberg, D. (2010). A conceptual framework to structure research in strategic and social entrepreneurship. *Journal of Asia-Pacific Business, 11*(3), 166–178. doi:10.1080/10599231.2010.500571

Hassan, A., & Wimpfheimer, S. (2015). *Human services management competencies.* Retrieved from https://socialworkmanager.org/wp-content/uploads/2016/01/Competency-Brochure-4-19-15-With-Forms.pdf

Hepworth, D. H., Rooney, R. H., Rooney, G. D., & Strom-Gottfried, K. (2013). *Direct social work practice: Theory and skills* (9th ed.). Belmont, CA: Brooks/Cole.

Hoch, C. (2000). Sheltering the homeless in the U.S.: Social improvement and the continuum of care. *Housing Studies, 15*, 865–876. doi:10.1080/02673030020002582

Kury, K. W. (2012). Sustainability meets social entrepreneurship: A path to social change through institutional entrepreneurship. *International Journal of Business Insights & Transformation, 4*(3), 64–71. doi:10.1108/IJEBR-11-2015-0259

Kyle, K. (2005). *Contextualizing homelessness: Critical theory, homelessness, and federal policy addressing the homeless.* New York: Routledge.

Lepak, D., Smith, K., & Taylor, S. (2007). Value creation and value capture: A multilevel perspective. *Academy of Management Review, 32*(1), 180–194. doi:10.5465/AMR.2007.23464011

Li, J., Vestergaard, J., Cnattingius, S., Gissler, M., Bech, B. H., Obel, C., & Olsen, J. (2014). Mortality after parental death in childhood: A nationwide cohort study from three Nordic countries. *PLOS Medicine, 11*(7), 1–13. doi:10.1371/journal.pmed.1001679

Lisetchi, M., & Brancu, L. (2014). The entrepreneurship concept as a subject of social innovation. *Procedia—Social and Behavioral Sciences, 124*, 87–92. doi:10.1016/j.sbspro.2014.02.463

Mair, J., & Marti, I. (2006). Social entrepreneurship research: A source of explanation, prediction, and delight. *Journal of World Business, 41*(1), 36–44. doi:10.1016/j.jwb.2005.09.002

Martin, R. L., & Osberg, S. (2007, Spring). Social entrepreneurship: The case for definition. *Stanford Social Innovation Review,* pp. 29–39. Retrieved from https://www.law.berkeley.edu/php-programs/courses/fileDL.php?fID=7288

McClatchey, I. S. (2017). Fathers raising motherless children: Widowed men give voice to their experiences. *Omega: Journal of Death and Dying.* Advance online publication. doi:10.1177/0030222817693141

McClatchey, I. S., & Peters, A. (2015). Can trauma focused grief education improve acting-out behavior among bereaved youth? A pilot study. *Journal of Human Services, 35*(1), 14–27.

McClatchey, I. S., & Raven, R. F. (2017). Adding trauma-informed care to facilitate posttraumatic growth: A controlled outcome study. *Advances in Social Work, 18*, 349–368. doi:10.18060/21239

McClatchey, I. S., Vonk, M. E., & Palardy, G. (2009). The prevalence of childhood traumatic grief: A comparison of violent/sudden and expected loss. *Omega: Journal of Death and Dying, 59*, 305–323. doi:10.2190/OM.59.4.b

McClatchey, I. S., & Wimmer, J. (2012). Healing components of a bereavement camp: Children and adolescents give voice to their experiences. *Omega: Journal of Death and Dying, 65*, 11–32. doi:10.2190/OM.65.1.b

McClatchey, I. S., & Wimmer, J. (2014). Coping with parental death as seen from the perspective of children who attended a grief camp. *Qualitative Social Work, 13*, 221–236. doi:10.1177/1473325012465104

McLaughlin, C., & Kaluzny, A. (2004). *Continuous quality improvement in healthcare: Theories, implementations and applications* (2nd ed.). Burlington, MA: Jones & Bartlett.

Nandan, M., Mandayam, G., Collard, C., & Tchouta, R. (2016). An examination of community practice social workers as social intrapreneurs or social entrepreneurs. *International Journal of Social Entrepreneurship and Innovation, 4*, 114–133. doi:10.1504/IJSEI.2016.076686

National Alliance to End Homelessness. (2017, July). *What causes homelessness?* Retrieved from https://endhomelessness.org/homelessness-in-america/what -causes-homelessness/

National Association of Social Workers. (2017). *Code of ethics of the National Association of Social Workers.* Washington, DC: Author.

Neal, A. A. (2015). The intersection of social work and social enterprise. *Journal of Social Work Values & Ethics, 12*(2), 1–9. Retrieved from http://jswve.org/ download/2015-2/Fall%202015Full%20issue-JSWVE-12-2.pdf

Perrini, F., Vurro, C., & Costanzo, L. A. (2010). A process-based view of social entrepreneurship: From opportunity identification to scaling-up social change in the case of San Patrignano. *Entrepreneurship and Regional Development, 22*, 515–534. doi:10.1080/08985626.2010.488402

Randle, M., & Dolnicar, S. (2009). Not just any volunteers: Segmenting the market to attract the high contributors. *Journal of Nonprofit & Public Sector Marketing, 21*, 271–282. doi:10.1080/10495140802644513

Rog, D. (2004). The evidence on supported housing. *Psychiatric Rehabilitation Journal, 27*, 334–344. doi:10.2975/27.2004.334.344

Schafer, E. (2007). Training counselors role models: The basics and beyond. *Camping Magazine, 80*(3), 1–4. Retrieved from https://c.ymcdn.com/sites/campties.siteym.com/resource/resmgr/counselor_training/role_models.pdf

Singh, A. (2016). *The process of social value creation: A multiple-case study on social entrepreneurship in India.* Mumbai, India: Springer. doi:10.1007/978-81-322-2827-1

Social Security Administration. (n.d.). *Social Security beneficiary statistics.* Retrieved from http://www.ssa.gov/oact/STATS/SRVbenies

Sundin, E., & Tillmar, M. (2008). A nurse and a civil servant changing institutions: Entrepreneurial processes in different public sector organizations. *Scandinavian Journal of Management, 24*(2), 113–124. doi:10.1016/j.scaman.2008.03.006

Traube, D. E., Begun, S., Okpych, N., & Choy-Brown, M. (2017). Catalyzing innovation in social work practice. *Research on Social Work Practice, 27,* 134. doi:10.1177/1049731516659140.

Tsemberis, S., Gulcur, L., & Nakae, M. (2004). Housing First, consumer choice, and harm reduction for homeless individuals with a dual diagnosis. *American Journal of Public Health, 94,* 651–656. doi:10.2105/AJPH.94.4.651

U.S. Government. (2016). *U.S. Government action plan on children in adversity: 2016 report to Congress.* Retrieved from http://www.usaid.gov/open/children-adversity/2016

Zahra, S. A., Rawhouser, H. N., Bhawe, N., Neubaum, D. O., & Hayton, J. C. (2008). Globalization of social entrepreneurship opportunities. *Strategic Entrepreneurship Journal, 2,* 117–131. doi:10.1002/sej.43

12

Social Entrepreneurship: A Zanzibari Example

Ronya Foy Connor and Tricia B. Bent-Goodley

Social work entrepreneurship is not limited to creating new ventures. Sometimes it focuses on strategically supporting the entrepreneurial ventures of others. Certain indigenous communities have created entrepreneurial ventures as an anti-poverty strategy for decades. These ventures have been used to uplift communities from poverty, promote equity, stimulate opportunity, promote relationship building, and respond to negative policy making and practices from outsiders. They also express and manifest community needs. These entrepreneurial ventures often go unnoticed or unacknowledged by the professional community. In an effort to promote evidence-based practices, social work has often overlooked those systems and structures that communities develop even though they are innovative and responsive to community needs. Social work has a major role to play in supporting these practices, strategies, and initiatives. An entrepreneurial social worker will view such indigenous responses as opportunities for growth and development that promote social justice. This chapter presents the case of a group of Zanzibari women engaged in social entrepreneurship as a form of community building, financial independence, and innovation. Implications for how social workers can engage with communities to develop and sustain social entrepreneurship endeavors are discussed at some length.

Social work entrepreneurship matters. At one time, entrepreneurship was viewed negatively in social work (Bent-Goodley, 2002). It was viewed as social workers taking advantage of clients or capitalizing on the misery of others. However, as business schools began to promote social entrepreneurship within their curricula, it became clear that social workers—who naturally and organically deployed some or all of the social entrepreneurship strategies and practices—needed to reexamine their stance on social work entrepreneurship. Though initially there was some resistance to this strategy, social entrepreneurship and innovation have a history within the profession stemming back to the creation of settlement houses as an innovative response to individual, community, and environmental circumstances (Carlton-LaNey, 2001; Schiele, 2010; Segal, 2012). Essentially, social entrepreneurship and innovation designed to promote social good were historical center points in the profession that are now being better illuminated and highlighted as legitimate forms of practice (Nandan, London, & Bent-Goodley, 2015). The social entrepreneurship process includes being innovative, taking calculated risks, and being proactive in addressing problems (Nandan & Scott, 2013).

Today's social worker is compelled to be entrepreneurial because of decreases in public funding for programs that provide critical supports to individuals, families, and communities (Nandan & Scott, 2013). Increasingly, social work entrepreneurship and innovation are becoming an expected aspect of practice to survive and thrive in this highly competitive and dynamic global environment. Moreover, social workers are experiencing increasing competitiveness within the funding environment and are being challenged to create innovative solutions for endemic social problems. Consequently, the idea that social workers should be engaged in these practices and strategies is more welcomed than in previous decades. Social work entrepreneurship challenges the status quo, seeks creative solutions to problems, and sustains them as a means to transform the lives of individuals within communities.

The social work profession's structure supports and complements social entrepreneurship processes. Social work's knowledge and competencies related to human behavior, building relationships, management, policy, and community and organizational development to advance initiatives that are innovative, and other facets of the social work curriculum, prepare social workers for social entrepreneurship orientation and processes. The goal of social development is to "transform people's own outlooks, capabilities, skills and knowledge, drive and initiative, and institution building to find new solutions to age old economic, health, social and governance problems" (Zewde, 2010, p. vi). Though the profession has not fully embraced this orientation, efforts are in progress to bring attention to this viable aspect of social work practice (Archibald, Muhammad, & Estreet, 2016). Students are becoming increasingly interested in learning about different models of social work entrepreneurship and innovation (Vungkhanching & Black, 2012). Thus, there is a growing need to increase knowledge, skills, and competencies in this area of practice. Social work entrepreneurship practices are relevant at the local level as well as at the international level.

Social workers are stewards of the global community and are, by virtue of the *Code of Ethics* (National Association of Social Workers, 2017), expected to advance social justice. Social entrepreneurship is part of contemporary society and is also encouraged internationally as a transformative force (Fargion, Gevorgianiene, & Lievens, 2011; Martin & Osberg, 2015; Ratten & Welpe, 2011).

Social development must produce social well-being that enhances people's self-efficacy for making their own decisions (Reutlinger & Homfeldt, 2009). Social work intervention strategies, at all levels of practice, build on strengths of individuals and groups to create feelings of self-empowerment and an equitable and just society. The following case describes how social work can interface with social entrepreneurship to promote and further entrepreneurial efforts by women in an international community. The chapter concludes with implications for social work practice and education.

Zanzibari Women's Engagement in Social Entrepreneurship Processes

Zanzibar is one of many islands making up the country of Tanzania. It is located off of the East African coast and is a tourist destination with beautiful beaches and a natural supply of fruits and spices. Zanzibar's fusion culture of ethnicities, languages, religions, and traditions lends itself to social entrepreneurial ventures. Women, in particular, support the island's community growth and social development in diverse ways.

Workforce participation for women, as a population that is often marginalized and vulnerable, is an area of focus globally and especially in sub-Saharan Africa, where there are high proportions of women-headed households (Yahya, 2008). Many Zanzibari women work inside homes, cooking, cleaning, and providing primary care for children and dependents, while also working outside the homes in small businesses to generate family income. With women at the forefront of economic development in urban and rural areas of Zanzibar, fifteen Zanzibari social entrepreneurs were interviewed regarding their experiences in operating social ventures in seaweed farming; dress, jewelry, and handicraft making; jam and preserve making; photography; upholstery; and initiatives to support youth education and health and people with disabilities.

The social entrepreneurs discussed overall themes supporting their entrepreneurial ventures that were organized into four categories: (1) external training, skills development, and education; (2) the intersection of culture and gender; (3) personal motivation, endurance, and inspiration; and (4) financial support and financial challenges. Within these themes, the social entrepreneurs identified their motivation and strategy for entrepreneurial success. Their initiatives and ventures were responsive to issues of poverty, addressing issues of social justice and creatively generating funding to support necessary programs for vulnerable populations which did not have policy-related support and legitimacy.

External Training, Skills Development, and Education

One interviewee named Akila led a youth agency focused on social and political betterment. Her social venture focused on "changing of the youth generation, so young people can have a strong voice for what they want and what they don't want" (Foy Connor, 2014, p. 98). The genesis of the venture was based on the belief that young people could make change within communities on government-related issues. To support this mission, training was needed so that members could develop public speaking skills, learn about voter education, and expand their knowledge in youth advocacy. The major challenge was identifying and recruiting trainers in various fields for the organization.

Another interviewee, Zera, had a background in pastry making and began making jam by using the island's sustainable resources, including locally grown fruit, solar dryers, and recycled glass jars. Though the operation began on a small scale, she was grateful to advisers and trainers from London who assisted her to expand the product offerings and hire more local talent (individuals who were currently unemployed) to assist with the production. The third social entrepreneur, Aaliyah, operated a beach program to collect pearl shells from the sand and reuse them to create one-of-a-kind jewelry pieces. A woman from the United States visited Zanzibar and trained beach program participants in grinding shells, creating specific designs, and fitting them into jewelry. The program participants also received training and development support from other African countries, such as Kenya and Rwanda.

Intersection of Culture and Gender

The 15-interviewee analysis also revealed that gender and culture were closely related in Zanzibar—the traditional roles of women affected the social entrepreneurship process and ventures. Muna, whose venture was in the field of youth education, often addressed controversial topics, such as family planning in a society that has strict cultural and religious norms. She stated that it was difficult to educate the population about gender issues, including challenges facing women at work outside the home and sexual harassment. However, she focused on changing the social climate through education. She noted, "I've gotten confidence. I can stand for the people and I can feel free without worrying. Talking with others, we can get a solution for their problem" (Foy Connor, 2014, p. 101).

Faiza, a dressmaker, owned and operated a training program in sewing. She learned the trade from her mother and started teaching other women through a cooperative venture. Faiza described difficulties in managing a business and executing traditional female roles: "You find yourself in the kitchen and you probably are not feeling well but you have no choice, you must get up and do your tasks as usual. I mean there are days when you simply cannot cope at all. . . . There are times I have to stop . . . until after I give birth" (Foy Connor, 2014, p. 113). Nana, owner of a successful upholstery business, noted that Zanzibar's culture of mutual support was conducive for women-based social entrepreneurship ventures, because the women understand that they are able to accomplish more by working together as opposed to asserting control or competing. Nana stated, "I don't count myself as an owner or boss. I just count myself as a leader, but I'm one of them. . . . If I make mistakes they correct me, if they make mistake, I correct. So we work here like a huge family with a different parent" (Foy Connor, 2014, p. 119).

Personal Motivation, Endurance, and Inspiration

Personal motivation is at the heart of social entrepreneurship and forms the basis for the social entrepreneur's efforts directed toward community betterment and social problem alleviation. Barke ran an organization focused on building educational opportunities for girls and improving the lives of women. She noted, "I dedicate myself everything, every day. I'm designer, also supervisor—so I arrange everything." She continued, "Every time when I see the other women's success, I'm happy. This is my secret. I got many opportunities to go abroad, to have a job but I think if I leave, maybe it will be hard for them, they will collapse or something, so I stay back" (Foy Connor, 2014, p. 121). Barke displayed a commitment to her venture primarily to address the needs of girls and women in her community. Nadhari, another social entrepreneur, worked in the field of business development for persons with disabilities. When asked how long she could envision operating her venture, she replied, "Until I die. I'm going to advocate for the rights of the persons with disabilities until one day we see everything is changed" (Foy Connor, 2014, p. 124).

Financial Support and Financial Challenge

Mobilizing financial resources for social entrepreneurs usually entails seeking and managing grant funds, pursuing personal and business loans, and identifying potential sponsors and donors. However, these women social entrepreneurs focused on sustaining a business in a tough economic environment. Akila discussed operating a drug treatment program: "To run the house is expensive and especially the health payments for drug users. Some are homeless as well. [The staff] uses money from their own pockets to help them with support" (Foy Connor, 2014, p. 127). Endesha, a social entrepreneur in agricultural farming and pottery making, described the rural market economy and the decreasing prices for agricultural goods. She noted that an economic downturn made climate and market so difficult for almost everyone in her field that they had each scaled back their operations. In response to the economic environment, she stated, "Challenges are there, but not many. What is the wealth of a poor person? His wealth is life. That is to say if you are living, then you can do anything" (Foy Connor, 2014, p. 90). Raziya, a seaweed farmer and rope maker in a rural area of Zanzibar, reflected, "Sometimes you think you will sell everything but it doesn't happen like that" (Foy Connor, 2014, p. 133). Many of the women social entrepreneurs interviewed felt that unexpected financial demands were part of the economic ebb and flow of business. In fact, most operated anticipating the highs and lows associated with an economy that was highly dependent on tourism.

From the brief discussions summarized here, it is evident that these social entrepreneurial ventures have resulted in employment creation, educational development, and the promotion of sustainable environments. Zanzibari social entrepreneurs also are advocates and create empowering environments for community residents, program participants, and organizational staff. Their initiatives focus on social change and transformation—creating innovative ventures with tangible impacts on local economic and social development.

Implications for Social Work Practice

Lessons from these illustrations and experiences of social entrepreneurs in Zanzibar can be incorporated in social work practice and also inform future research in social work entrepreneurship. First, the social entrepreneurial ventures created empowerment, involved community members, and developed local assets and strengths within social ventures to create positive social impacts. Within such contexts, social workers can provide training, resources, and mentorship for social entrepreneurs who must identify community assets, and build on local strengths, to alleviate pressing societal issues.

Second, in terms of empowerment, resource support for those initiating and operating social ventures is constantly needed. In most cases, resource support is not just financial in nature but includes assisting social entrepreneurs in developing the strength and endurance to continue serving their communities in the face of obstacles and challenges. Social entrepreneurs endure regular hardships, and social workers can play an important role by providing emotional and social support and creating an environment that encourages perseverance. Resources that develop support networks and mentorship relationships assist in connecting like-minded individuals and in creating potential systems for self and group development.

Third, for social entrepreneurs in the beginning or advanced stages of operations, social workers can assist with disseminating information on investment capital, grant or loan opportunities, or potential tax breaks for business owners bettering society. For rural communities that are often marginalized, this basic information can create a turning point for a venture's success or demise. Failure occurs because of a lack of access to critical information, and social workers can assist by communicating and creating systems that promote opportunity creation.

Fourth, for social work practitioners operating at international levels or outside their areas of expertise, cultural competence is critical. "Culture is fluid and vast: an immeasurable, indescribable and constantly evolving concept" (Foy Connor, 2014, p. 201). An in-depth understanding of a population or community is essential for implementing effective and relevant social work interventions and strategies. Social workers cannot build relationships with local social entrepreneurs in different contexts without a firm understanding of the culture, familiarity with the language, and humility needed to learn from the wisdom and experience of the community. The aforementioned elements can also guide social work research related to social entrepreneurship.

In summary, social work involvement in social entrepreneurship in different contexts should focus on the exercise of agency, inclusiveness, strengths of community residents, advocacy for equal opportunity, and social and economic justice.

Implications for Social Work Education

Supporting community development is an important tenet of the social work profession. Consequently, social work education has an important role to play in supporting social work entrepreneurship as a means for communities to grow, sustain, and strengthen their development. First, providing students with opportunities for understanding social work entrepreneurship processes is crucial, and students should be exposed to various models of social entrepreneurship within practice classes. These opportunities should encourage social work students to view themselves as initiators of creative ideas, programs, and ventures and not just as stewards or operators of the same.

Understanding and embracing diversity is one of the competencies within social work education. Hence, it is important to expose students to different cultural experiences locally, nationally, and globally for understanding and engaging with different cultures and communities around social work entrepreneurship. Teaching students how to respect indigenous practices, understand them, and leverage them within communities is important knowledge and a necessary skill set. It is very important for social work students to refrain from judgment about indigenous communities; otherwise, opportunities for innovation and social change can be lost (Wiley, 2016).

Teaching students about the importance of social value creation is also an important aspect of social work education. Social value creation speaks to both a mind-set and a skill set. It affirms the importance of transformation of social conditions as a goal; other goals include leveraging tangible business skills to address social issues, developing and strengthening infrastructure, working collaboratively with partners and communities to promote social change, and identifying mechanisms of sustainability beyond an entrepreneurial venture (Bellostas, Lopez-Arceiz, & Mateos, 2016; Beugre, 2016; Brooks, 2008; Mein Goh, Gao, & Agarwal, 2016; Munshi, 2010; Singh, 2016). Social value creation includes social, economic, and community development rooted in the values and strengths of the community. Thus, it is important that social work students are exposed to and consciously participate in social value creation.

Increasing field education opportunities in social work entrepreneurship, innovation, and value creation is also imperative. Exposing students to these opportunities can be a demonstration of innovation within the framework of the educational experience. Assisting students with generating or initiating an entrepreneurial venture that can address an important issue in the local community is an example of a potential field experience or assignment that can be rewarding and beneficial. Having students work with social work entrepreneurs in the field and develop competencies that support the educational process can enrich learning and foster social value creation. Social entrepreneurship processes and orientation align with community development and human service management competencies already existing within the curriculum. In essence, social work curriculum and field experiences can become a laboratory for growing, developing, and nurturing social work entrepreneurs by providing them with the knowledge and preparing them with competency for serving populations and communities in novel ways.

Conclusion

Social workers are positioned to support communities through sustainable approaches and infrastructures that can transform communities by creating social value. Social work entrepreneurship presents an opportunity to innovatively tap strengths within communities for addressing recalcitrant social problems. The illustrations of Zanzibari female social entrepreneurs demonstrate that women often are ready and able to create lasting solutions for problems in their communities. The cases also provide evidence of social entrepreneurs using their positions and roles to challenge social norms and change social climate. Social workers promote and support social change. They can promote and support these communities through leveraging resources, aiding in the development of local talent, supporting multiple ventures on the ground, helping ventures to innovate and grow, contributing training, and providing sustained encouragement to local social entrepreneurs for promoting such ventures. In essence, social workers can partner with or promote social entrepreneurship that creates social change and local transformation.

References

Archibald, P., Muhammad, O., & Estreet, A. (2016). Business in social work education: A historically black university's social work entrepreneurship project. *Journal of Social Work Education, 52,* 79–94.

Bellostas, A., Lopez-Arceiz, F. & Mateos, L. (2016). Social value and economic value in social enterprises: Value creation model of Spanish sheltered workshops. *Voluntas: International Journal of Voluntary & Nonprofit Organizations, 27*(1), 367–391.

Bent-Goodley, T. B. (2002). Defining and conceptualizing social work entrepreneurship. *Journal of Social Work Education, 38,* 291–302.

Beugre, C. (2016). *Social entrepreneurship: Managing the creation of social value.* New York: Routledge.

Brooks, A. C. (2008). *Social entrepreneurship: A modern approach to social value creation.* Upper Saddle River, NJ: Pearson Prentice Hall.

Carlton-LaNey, I. (2001). *African American leadership: Empowerment tradition in social welfare history.* Washington, DC: NASW Press.

Fargion, S., Gevorgianiene, V., & Lievens, P. (2011). Developing entrepreneurship in social work through international education: Reflections on a European intensive programme. *Social Work Education, 30,* 964–980.

Foy Connor, R. D. (2014). *Zanzibari women in local social entrepreneurship: A participatory social learning approach to community sustainability* (Doctoral dissertation). Available from ProQuest Dissertations and Theses database. (UMI No. 3641738)

Martin, R. L., & Osberg, S. R. (2015). *Getting beyond better: How social entrepreneurship works.* Cambridge, MA: Harvard Business Review.

Mein Goh, J., Gao, G., & Agarwal, R. (2016). The creation of social value: Can an online health community reduce rural-urban health disparities? *MIS Quarterly, 40*(1), 247–263.

Munshi, N. V. (2010). Value creation, social innovation, and entrepreneurship in global economies. *Journal of Asia-Pacific Business, 11,* 160–165.

Nandan, M., London, M., & Bent-Goodley, T. (2015). Social workers as social change agents: Social innovation, social intrapreneurship, and social entrepreneurship. *Human Service Organizations: Management, Leadership & Governance, 39*(1), 38–56.

Nandan, M., & Scott, P. A. (2013). Social entrepreneurship and social work: The need for a transdisciplinary educational model. *Administration in Social Work, 37*, 257–271.

National Association of Social Workers. (2017). *Code of ethics of the National Association of Social Workers.* Washington, DC: Author.

Ratten, V., & Welpe, I. M. (2011). Special issue: Community-based, social and societal entrepreneurship. *Entrepreneurship & Regional Development, 23*, 283–286.

Reutlinger, C., & Homfeldt, H. G. (2009). Social development. *Social Work & Society, 6*(2). Retrieved from http://www.socwork.net/sws/article/view/70/372

Schiele, J. H. (2010). *Social welfare policy: Regulation and resistance among people of color.* Thousand Oaks, CA: Sage Publications.

Segal, E. A. (2012). *Social work policy and social programs* (3rd ed.). New York: Brooks/Cole.

Singh, A. (2016). *The process of social value creation: A multiple-case study on social entrepreneurship in India.* New York: Springer.

Vungkhanching, M., & Black, M. A. (2012). Social work graduate students' perceived knowledge of social entrepreneurship and sustainable development in human services: An evaluation of enhanced instruction. *International Journal of Interdisciplinary Social Sciences, 6*(11), 35–51.

Wiley, K. A. (2016). Making people bigger: Wedding exchange and the creation of social value in rural Mauritania. *Africa Today, 62*(3), 49–69.

Yahya, S. S. (2008). Financing social infrastructure and addressing poverty through wakf endowments: Experience from Kenya and Tanzania. *Environment and Urbanization, 20*, 427–444.

Zewde, A. (2010). *Sorting Africa's development puzzle: The participatory social learning theory as an alternative approach.* Lanham, MD: University Press of America.

13

Self-Help Groups as Social Enterprises: Citizen-Driven Social Entrepreneurship in India

Mahasweta M. Banerjee

Poverty has been, and continues to be, a persistent problem in India. Although income poverty has declined from 45.3 percent in 1994 to 21.9 percent in 2011, approximately 400 million people still live in poverty in India (World Bank, 2017). Over the years, the Indian government has adopted several programs to address income poverty and its consequences related to poor nutrition, health, housing, and education (Kattumuri & Singh, 2013). One such program, the Swarnajayanti Gram Swarozgar Yojana, also known as the Self-Help Group (SHG) program, has helped many rural families out of poverty (Swain & Varghese, 2013). Ending poverty continues as India's Sustainable Development Goal, with the aim of eradicating extreme poverty, measured as people living on less than $1.25 a day, by 2030 (United Nations Development Program, 2015).

The role of social enterprises, such as SHG programs and micro-credit programs, as mechanisms for poverty alleviation continues to be discussed in India (Goel & Rishi, 2012; Haugh & Talwar, 2016). In this discussion, social entrepreneurs are presented as people with a vision and a mission to challenge society's entrenched problems such as poverty by identifying opportunities and pursuing them to bring about change (Bacq & Janssen, 2011). However, what is absent in the combined SHG and social entrepreneur(ship) literature is the role of ordinary citizens who seize an idea related to poverty reduction developed by leading social entrepreneurs, or through social entrepreneurship, and apply it to change their economic circumstances in their local communities. Without these ordinary individuals, who improvise and implement the big idea to fit local needs, change envisioned by pioneering social entrepreneurs may not bear fruit in local communities or scale in different communities. The purpose of this chapter is to present the story of one such ordinary woman who has changed her own life and the lives of many women and families in an interior rural area of India.

Highlighting the actions of ordinary citizens showcases how social workers strive for community and social development through and with community members. Without community members' buy-in, social work practitioners and social entrepreneurs cannot succeed in bringing about local change. Although it would be desirable to have social workers embedded in all communities with large populations living in poverty, experience shows that there are not enough social workers promoting change in such areas. This case study clearly demonstrates the innovative and social entrepreneurial characteristics of community members and the role of cross-sector partnerships and key employees in organizations (for example, government offices) that can support, nurture, and promote such innovation. It also illuminates opportunities for social workers operating at various levels—individual, family, group, community, and policy advocacy—to support such innovation and entrepreneurship among community residents. Social workers support and promote consumer and client empowerment and participation for their overall well-being. This means that social workers cannot focus on just a microcosm of an issue, such as domestic violence, alcoholism, or an absence of steady household income; they need to focus on interrelated factors that could contribute to varied symptoms and ensure that sustainable solutions can be identified and implemented. This chapter seeks to highlight how community practice social workers as well as social workers engaged in public and nonprofit agencies can support social entrepreneurship by nurturing, partnering, and promoting the work of ordinary citizens leading such efforts to enhance the socioeconomic well-being of communities.

Social Enterprises, Social Entrepreneurship, and Social Entrepreneurs

There are several views and definitions of social enterprises, social entrepreneurship, and social entrepreneurs (Bacq & Janssen, 2011; Nandan, London, & Blum, 2014; Schmitz, 2015). Schmitz (2015) noted that these concepts overlap and are often used interchangeably. Moreover, there are a variety of attributes associated with these concepts, including social and environmental responsibility, innovation, social change, social transformation, social justice, and empowering disadvantaged groups. The common denominator is that each focuses on addressing a social problem or a social need (Schmitz, 2015). As such, a social enterprise addresses any one or a combination of these attributes.

Social entrepreneurship refers to bringing together a wide array of stakeholders and organizational representatives to tackle complex community and social issues (Fawcett & South, 2005). Helm and Anderson (2010) described social entrepreneurship as a set of behaviors that create lasting transformational change in society. Others believe that bringing about transformational change is what sets social entrepreneurship apart from other types of entrepreneurs and practitioners (Martin & Osberg, 2007). Schmitz and Scheuerle (2012) reviewed 30 definitions of social entrepreneurship and found that 27 definitions emphasized creating social value or promoting social good, 17 identified innovation, and 15 highlighted creating social change. Focusing specifically on social entrepreneurship and social entrepreneurs, Bacq and Janssen (2011) identified 29 characteristics, and these increased to 47 when social enterprises were included.

After considerable research, Light (2009) argued that social entrepreneurs, social entrepreneurship, and social enterprises have four distinctive characteristics. First, social entrepreneurs are not like other high achievers. They make deliberate decisions to solve social problems, are persistent, and have unshakeable optimism. Second, socially entrepreneurial ideas are not necessarily big ideas. The greatest ideas often start small but eventually expand to break the social equilibrium. Ultimate impact requires "scaling up, diffusion, sustained pressure, and navigation of . . . the ecosystem of change" (p. 22). Third, opportunities for change come in waves, sometimes when the prevailing wisdom weakens, revealing the failure of the status quo to solve problems such as inequality. Last, social entrepreneurial organizations are built to effect change; they are "relatively flat, singularly focused on the idea of change, and often inexperienced in the administrative procedures" (p. 22). Light observed that although some social entrepreneurs prefer to work by themselves, many work in teams, networks, and communities as "teams of experts can hammer together big breakthroughs" (p. 22), but they need considerable help to succeed. These characteristics appear to fit well with the social enterprise of SHGs, and the social entrepreneurship process, as will be presented in the case study later.

Worsham (2012) interviewed Greg Dees about social entrepreneurship and asked about his experiences. Dees said that after several years of teaching social entrepreneurship at Harvard and Yale Universities, he strived to help low-income people in Appalachia start or grow small businesses. However, he felt rejected by residents because the local sentiment was, "Here's this guy from Harvard that is coming to save us" (p. 447). He believed local people perceived him as different and suspected his motivations because to them an outsider rushing in to help might have been considered as an offensive and demeaning act. Even after trying for two years, Dees was uncertain if he succeeded with poverty alleviation in the area. Dees noted that big and good ideas of social entrepreneurs may not gel well without local leadership and acceptance of the idea.

In the context of social work, Nandan et al. (2014) reported five definitions of social entrepreneurs that align with social work values and practice. These definitions highlight (1) being innovative, seeking out opportunities,

being resourceful, and creating value; (2) valuing local initiative and participation and seeking social justice outcomes in guiding and evaluating social
entrepreneurial activities; (3) seeking large-scale sustainable change through
new avenues; (4) creating and sustaining value without being limited by available resources; and (5) pioneering innovative and systemic changes to meet
the needs of marginalized populations that lack the means of bringing about
change on their own.

In the Indian context, the Ashoka Foundation of India (n.d.) has defined
social entrepreneurs as "individuals with innovative solutions to society's
most pressing social problems. They are ambitious and persistent, tackling
major social issues and offering new ideas for wide-scale change." The Ashoka
Foundation added, "Rather than leaving societal needs to the government
or business sectors, social entrepreneurs find what is not working and solve
the problem by changing the system, spreading the solution, and persuading
entire societies to take new leaps." The Ashoka Foundation identified Vinoba
Bhave, among others, as a social entrepreneur. He was the founding leader of
the Land Gift Movement, which resulted in the redistribution of more than
7 million acres of land to *Dalit* (previously known as untouchable) and land-
less people. With such a remarkable example, ordinary citizens might hesitate
to take the first step toward any social entrepreneurial activity, particularly
poverty alleviation. Nonetheless, poverty alleviation as a social enterprise has
been taken up through the SHG movement in India by concerned individual
social entrepreneurs and the government.

Social Work

Social workers consider Jane Addams as the first social entrepreneur because
of her groundbreaking work with immigrants in the settlement houses (Barendsen & Gardner, 2004). Bent-Goodley (2002) defined entrepreneurship as "a
process of putting new ideas into practice . . . and social work entrepreneurship is the creation of institutions through entrepreneurial thinking that are
guided by social work ethics and based on the integration of social service,
business, and public relations" (p. 291). On the basis of a research project with
82 MSW students and 52 professionals, Bent-Goodley (2002) identified that
social entrepreneurs have entrepreneurial thinking, ability to forecast and take
risks, expert management skills, and expertise in social marketing, public relations, resource acquisition, and alliance building.

Nandan et al. (2014) stated that social entrepreneurship can be folded
into community practice work. They formulated the idea of the community
practice social entrepreneur (CPSE) as innovators, risk takers, and proactive
practitioners. Social workers engaged in community practice may use any of

the four intervention strategies: community organizing, community planning, community development, or policy practice. But CPSEs would implement all four of these strategies as they engage in finding opportunities, acquiring resources to address a social problem, adding value as they address the problem, and taking more risks than others in addressing the problem. However, these are only two models of how social workers can be engaged in the social entrepreneurship process.

Before presenting the case study, this chapter will first review social enterprises related to income generation with emphasis on SHGs as presented in the literature. Then, it will describe SHGs as they are operated in the state of West Bengal in India. Next, it will present Noni Begum's case study of social entrepreneurship. Finally, the chapter will summarize Noni Begum's contributions to the development of her own SHG and another SHG that she helped start through her mentee. Potential lessons for social workers will be drawn.

Social Enterprises in India

In a country with 400 million people living in poverty, inclusive growth is a major challenge. Most remain untouched by the economic benefits of growth in India, with many living below $2 a day (World Bank, 2017). Studies have suggested that inclusive innovation activities with new and creative ideas that promote the social and economic well-being of disenfranchised members of society are increasingly being viewed as creating synergies to generate shared value, which ultimately supports inclusive growth (Organization for Economic Cooperation and Development, 2017).

In resource-poor contexts, such as India, some promote the view of social entrepreneurs as bricoleurs. Azmat, Ferdous, and Couchman (2015) observed, "Bricolage has been viewed as resourcefulness and adaptability of entrepreneurs within resource-poor environments because it involves doing things with few or seemingly no resources or utilizing whatever is at hand to facilitate social value creation" (p. 253). These authors reported that people have tangible (economic and other goods or resources) and intangible (physical, social, or cultural) resources. In resource-poor environments, bricolage allows social entrepreneurs to leverage the resources at hand to create opportunities. According to these authors, the three fundamental constructs of bricolage are making do, refusing to be constrained by limitations, and improvising. Azmat et al. reported that at an individual or micro level, any actor possesses stocks of intangible resources, including the physical (for example, energy, emotion, strength), social (for example, family relationships, community relationships), and cultural (for example, specialized knowledge, imagination). Against this background, organizations and individuals integrate resources to cocreate and determine their own value outcomes. Therefore, an individual actor can be considered a primary resource integrator while pursuing life projects and facilitating or cocreating value in partnership with other stakeholders. The authors believe that bricolage can lead to continuous inclusive innovation and empowerment of disadvantaged people.

Kummitha (2016) suggested that work-integration social enterprises, implying social enterprises geared toward job creation for people who are marginalized, are a way to integrate socially excluded persons in the informal labor market in India. Using a case study, the author demonstrated how members of excluded communities not only found income-generating work but also were empowered as they regained their sense of dignity and transformed their lives by reconnecting to social ties and through active participation in the community. In addition, the four agencies implementing work-integration programs gained the trust of the local people.

In another job creation project, Jain (2012) reported that two prominent citizens of India helped bring *chikkan* work (a specialized embroidery on clothes) to the world stage through their vision and mission and helped local people earn more. In addition to individual and nongovernmental organization (NGO) efforts at job creation, SHGs also create jobs. There are several models of SHGs in India. A prominent model was developed by Ella Bhatt (2006): the Self Employed Women's Association. Bhatt has helped several thousand women become self-employed and is considered to be a social entrepreneur in the field of self-employment.

SHGs as Social Enterprises That Promote Social Entrepreneurs

SHGs are a unique Indian innovation designed to address several social, environmental, or financial challenges experienced by residents in different communities. In a country where almost two-thirds of the population have no access to formal financial services, SHGs are a unique route to eradicating poverty, increasing incomes, and helping build productive assets for people who are poor (Harper, 2002). Generally, SHGs are composed of 10 to 20 registered or unregistered small entrepreneurs who voluntarily pool their tiny savings and use them to provide loans to members for income-generating investments in livestock, seeds, and other goods and services, including trade. The interest on the loans then adds to their savings pool (Harper, 2002).

Although no definitive date has been determined for the actual conception of SHGs, the practice of small groups banding together to form a savings and credit organization is well established in India. In the early stages, private-sector NGOs played a pivotal role in conceptualizing the SHG model. The turning point of the SHG movement was a pilot project by the National Bank for Agricultural Development (NABARD) in the early 1990s. The success of the project ignited the SHG movement in India, and by the late 1990s, SHGs were viewed by state governments and NGOs as not only providing financial intermediation but also serving as a common interest group to address social and political issues (Tankha, 2012).

Goel and Rishi (2012) reported that the SHG movement in India is a tri-sectoral approach involving the government, private sector, and citizens' sector. The government provides institutional, technical, and financial support to develop micro-entrepreneurship among the poor; private-sector social entrepreneurs and citizen-sector NGOs provide microcredit, technical assistance, consulting, job training, and skill development. Such teamwork leads to employment generation and micro-enterprises leading to poverty alleviation.

By 2007, NABARD had served 40.95 million families that are poor, with an average loan disbursement of INR 3,167 per family (Mansuri, 2010). Ninety percent of the loans were given to women. SHG members engaged in a wide variety of micro-enterprises, including vermin composting, running public distribution retail outlets, road construction, and sanitation and hygiene efforts in villages with increased participation of government agencies in community-building efforts. The on-time payment of loans has been about 94 percent (Harper, Berkhof, & Ramakrishna, 2005; Tankha, 2012). The SHG Linkage program of NABARD aims to create self-employment and wage-based employment to eradicate poverty. About 15 percent of SHG members have moved above the poverty line since their participation. In addition to NABARD, several other financial institutions and programs lend to NGOs so they can lend money to SHG participants. Tankha (2012) reported that by 2010, the number of SHGs was about 7.46 million, and savings were nearly INR 62 billion ($1.3 billion).

Swain and Varghese (2013) studied the role of skills training in helping SHG members enhance their income and assets. They found that training was associated with enhanced assets but not income. Enhanced income required infrastructural growth in addition to training. Other scholars examining SHGs reported that the SHG model results in empowering participants (Haugh & Talwar, 2016) and enhancing their financial well-being (Datta & Gailey, 2012).

The literature review suggests that although SHGs as social enterprises are successful in enhancing income, assets, and empowerment, it is the leaders who are identified and written about (for example, Bhatt, 2006; Jain, 2012) or there is an overall assessment of SHGs (for example, Harper et al., 2005; Swain & Varghese, 2013). Although the SHG movement is a team enterprise, not driven by individual change makers (Light, 2009), such ventures require ordinary citizen participation and leadership (Worsham, 2012) to create change at the local level, as will be demonstrated through the subsequent case study.

SHGs in the State of West Bengal, India: Background

I learned about SHGs while conducting a Fulbright research project in West Bengal, a state in eastern India. I interviewed both government and NGO officials to learn about SHGs. At that time, the state was ruled by a Marxist government. The government's Marxist views influenced the SHG program operated by the state government. The literature suggests that SHG programs have a tri-sectoral approach. Although this was true in various parts of India, as well as in some NGO-operated SHGs in West Bengal, it was not true of government-run SHGs in West Bengal. In this state, at best, the government-run SHGs had a bi-sectoral approach as there was a partnership between the government and the banking sector, but government-run banks were favored over private for-profit banks. However, the state government brought together a wide array of staff with expertise to initiate, maintain, and promote the functions of SHGs. This chapter focuses only on government-initiated and government-run SHGs.

I spoke with state government officials at various levels of hierarchy from the top to the bottom, and I visited various sites in the state to get a full picture of SHGs. The director and deputy directors at the state government level informed me how SHGs are formed and operate in West Bengal, as models vary by location. They expressed that an SHG generally has 10 to 15 members, but the number can vary depending on location. For example, in more segregated areas, five to 25 people can participate in an SHG. However, because gender segregation is a norm in India, generally group members are of the same gender, either all female or all male. A large majority of these groups are operated by women in rural areas, as poverty is higher in rural than in urban areas. The SHG program serves various purposes, but its primary goal is to empower women who are disenfranchised and living in poverty. The SHG program assumes that social problems such as inadequate housing, education, health, nutrition, sanitation, and income are interrelated. Although there are government programs for each of these concerns, unless people are aware of these programs, they cannot benefit from them. Thus, one of the main aims is to inform people about these programs and their benefits through meetings at SHGs. However, poor people have little time to attend meetings to learn about health and education programs unless their economic poverty can be addressed.

Thus, a major component of the SHG program is to help people become self-employed through micro-enterprises. Examples of micro-enterprises in the state include livestock rearing; bee keeping; sericulture; making hand-loom textiles; growing fruits, vegetables, or rice on a small scale; preparing and selling edible products consumed locally; making handicrafts of various types, such as via tailoring, embroidering, or batik (a specialized form of cloth printing); manufacturing jute-based products such as table mats, and hand bags; creating leather-based products such as bags; jewelry making; pottery making; and so on. When people start micro-enterprises, they are encouraged to engage in a line of business that is traditional to the family or community so that they already have the necessary skills and some familiarity in the field. In addition, they are encouraged to use local products and sell in local markets to develop a sustainable local economy.

Rural women in India generally do not go out of their homes. Because of a low level of formal education or nonliteracy and lack of connection with the outside world, many remain poor. Thus, the government officials noted that one of the primary objectives of SHGs is to enable rural women to step out of their homes, to meet as a group in a local setting, and to connect with one another. When new SHGs form, aided by government staff known as "facilitators," external presenters are invited to discuss issues related to living, such as health, nutrition, sanitation, education, and income, at these meetings. These facilitators and external presenters can be leaders of more mature SHGs who have learned the process of group formation as well as the subject matter through government training. As comfort with the group grows, SHG members discuss more personal matters, such as domestic violence, alcoholism, dowries, and women's health-related concerns. Also, there is an emphasis on financial literacy focusing on ability to sign one's name and on understanding saving, credit, and interest rates from banks.

A deputy director at the district (county) level of the state reported that an SHG with 10 members is eligible for an INR 25,000 first-time loan, of which INR 10,000 ($250) is a government subsidy (grant) and INR 15,000 ($375) is a bank loan. The bank loan must be repaid with a 12 percent annual interest while the government subsidy has to be repaid without interest and remains as a revolving fund for the group. With INR 25,000 as group loan, each member becomes eligible for a loan of INR 2,500 ($62.50) from this fund to start or expand a micro-business. The loan amount can be repaid within three years, but to ensure payment, groups are required to repay the bank some amount of money each month. If a group member cannot repay from the first month, other members who have more mature businesses or businesses that yield immediate returns pay on behalf of the member who cannot pay initially. However, proper accounting is maintained within the group, so no group member pays more than is her due share. Some businesses, such as raising animals for selling meat or products, have a longer gestation period. Other businesses, such as preparing and selling edible goods, have a much quicker turnaround. Consequently, group members generally engage in businesses that would allow for this variation in return yet allow groups to repay in a timely manner.

Generally, many SHGs repay within a year and ask for a larger loan in the second round. The second-round loan can be for INR 60,000 ($1,500), of which INR 25,000 ($625) is government subsidy. If they succeed in the second round, they can go through a third round of loan for INR 150,000 ($3,750) with a higher government subsidy. The state government assumes that people who are apparently poor need micro-credit for at least three years to turn their business around or to get it started. Though many groups ask for loans many times, not all scale up to request the maximum loan limit.

The deputy director at the state government level explained to me that once there are a sufficient number of stable SHGs in an area, they form a cluster, and a number of different clusters come together as a federation of SHGs at a higher level. The leaders of SHGs are represented at the cluster level, where they elect cluster leaders. The leaders of clusters represent the clusters at the federation level, which again has office bearers. Cluster and federation leaders report to government officials about the need for training in various skill areas to enhance the growth and development of micro-entrepreneurs at SHG levels. They also report issues of marketing, and the government addresses these issues. The cluster and federations help with horizontal and vertical integration of SHGs. Often SHG groups forward their products to cluster leaders, who then take them to the federation for selling at larger markets.

The federal and state governments help SHGs in various ways. In addition to helping with financial subsidies for group loan funds, the government offers basic and enhanced skills training courses to operate micro-enterprises, and it helps with marketing SHG members' products at various venues. It pays members to attend training so that they do not lose generating revenue for the enterprise. It organizes local, state, regional, and national fairs to exhibit products developed by SHG micro-entrepreneurs, and it covers all travel and living costs when SHG members travel to fairs to sell their products. The government hires staff members, including expert SHG leaders, to operate various dimensions of this program.

Although social workers are involved with SHGs in some other Indian states, social work involvement was minimal in West Bengal. When I asked government officials the reason for lack of social work involvement, the director at the state level informed me that social workers were rather expensive to hire, and few wanted to live and work in rural areas. Thus, government hired local people with varying qualifications and trained them to serve people. One of the many livelihood development officers (LDOs) I encountered had values and skills similar to social workers, as will be reported later, but not all trained government staff had social work values.

Case Study: SHGs and One of Its Ordinary Citizen Leaders

Government officials showcased several SHG programs in the districts, and there were several stories of empowerment through SHGs. However, I selected this case study because a government official designated as an LDO identified Noni Begum (pseudonym) as a key player and highly successful leader of an SHG in one area. In addition, a totally unrelated woman who was interviewed at a different place, Zaafira Bibi (pseudonym), confirmed Noni Begum's story and her impact on the community. I interviewed Noni Begum at her home, where I could observe the varied and immense jute work produced and stored by Noni Begum and her SHG team members and staff. It is important to note that jute (a plant whose leaves are processed and converted to fiber and thread) grows abundantly in this part of the state and is available at a relatively cheap price. The LDO's role and function in promoting SHGs and social entrepreneurs will be discussed later in the chapter.

Noni Begum and Her Background

I met Noni Begum at her home in a distant village from the district capital and was accompanied and introduced to her by the district LDO. Noni Begum was a very pleasant woman, in her late 30s. She had a fifth-grade education, was married at age 14, and had three children. According to Noni Begum, a few years back her husband lost his job as an insurance broker, and the sudden loss of income made them economically vulnerable. They experienced such dire income poverty that she would pull straws from their thatched roof to light the cooking fire, and she wore her husband's *lungi* (lower garment for men) as a petticoat. To add to their distress, one day their son got very sick. Noni Begum took the boy to a doctor's office and on her way out saw a tattered jute door mat outside the office. She inquired if she could take it home because she wanted to learn how to weave it. Given their poverty, the doctor permitted her to take the door mat. She washed it and tried to figure out on her own how to make jute mats.

Around the same time, she heard from an SHG facilitator visiting the community about SHGs and trainings offered by the government to learn new skills or advance existing skills. She chose to attend a training camp away from her village. For a Muslim woman, leaving the home alone was a taboo in the small rural community. Consequently, she invited some of her female neighbors to accompany her. According to Noni Begum, the training was not of high quality. Nonetheless, she learned how to process jute and started producing jute goods. Gradually and patiently, she self-taught jute handicraft, formed an SHG, and was chosen to be the group's leader. As the quality of her work improved, her SHG products sold in the market at a profit, and the members started to earn an income, she was given opportunities by the LDO to travel to handicraft fairs in the state and later to large metropolitan cities of India to sell her products and those of other members who were unable to travel. Attendance at the fairs created the opportunity to meet other artisans, observe jute and other products sold at fairs, talk to buyers who visited her stall, and understand how to improve her products so they would sell at higher prices in big cities. Slowly, her SHG members expanded their own work infused with her ideas based on new learning from fairs.

In addition to the 10 SHG members whom she led, she hired 40 women to do varied jute work, which she sold at fairs. From a first-time SHG loan of INR 25,000, her SHG progressed to a larger loan of INR 60,000. In addition, she needed to pay her 40 employees on a daily basis. She paid them about INR 300 to 350 per day (about INR 80 per member, which is the minimum wage). She lamented that because she had crossed over the poverty line, her second SHG loan did not have a government subsidy. Consequently, she and her SHG members had to work even harder now. However, with increased awareness about, and access to, institutions, she procured additional loans from government programs serving the Muslim community; with this additional capital, she was able to hire 40 workers (as previously mentioned). Her average monthly repayment of loans was approximately INR 9,000.

Now, after leading the SHG for seven years, her children have grown; one son is in a doctoral program with a full scholarship; one daughter is completing her master's degree out of state; and one son has completed a computer diploma course and is employed within the state. Her husband is supportive of her work and assists in various ways. After paying for all operating and financing costs, labor, and loan installments, she earns a monthly income of about INR 5,000, which has assisted her and her family to move above the poverty line.

Personal Risks

In a patriarchal society, one of the major challenges Noni Begum faced in starting and expanding her SHG and jute micro-enterprise came from local male community leaders. The community leaders accused her of human trafficking and sex work when she would leave the home to attend trainings or visit cities to sell the products. It must be noted that in the Islamic faith, women accused of such wrongdoings can be publicly humiliated, divorced, or served consequences deemed worthy of the transgression. In the face of such false accusations, the effort and strength displayed by Noni Begum to continue the work is noteworthy. Fortunately, her income from sales of jute products was a factor in appeasing her husband, who later assisted her in clearing her name with the local leaders.

Characteristics of Social Entrepreneurs

A few of the major characteristics that helped Noni Begum start and advance her work include her own "hard work, persistence, determination, and optimism." She said, "My fingers never stop. Even when I am at home cooking a meal, sometimes I have to wait for the food to cook; I make use of that time to weave the jute." She added,

> Others [that is, families working with her, government staff, and buyers] love me. I like working for my country. . . . Most families are doing better than before. Husband–wife fights have stopped. Where is the time to fight? Everyone is using their time to produce a jute good that can be sold, and money can come for the family from that product.

She cautioned that skills training by itself was inadequate because many women had received training but not all were as successful; she confessed that success required determination, effort, hard work, and persistence. Further, she believed that women need family support and access to markets to succeed and rise above the poverty level.

Challenges and Opportunities

Notwithstanding her relative successes, Noni Begum identified some continuing challenges. First, she needed a much higher credit line to buy raw materials, produce jute products, and pay the workers. Second, with higher levels of production, she also needed access to a larger market. Instead of focusing just on the domestic market, she recommended that the government link artisans like her to the global market. Clearly, she had aspirations and a vision.

At the time of the interview, the LDO reported that there were 1,500 SHGs in the *block* (which is the government's demarcation of a large geographic area for voting and resource distribution purposes) and 40 SHGs in the village, with only four SHGs still functional in the village where Noni Begum lived. Distrust of community leaders, as well as lack of leadership, skill, and persistence, led to the demise of the remaining groups. However, many of the women from the nonfunctioning SHGs were hired by Noni Begum, and she continued her work despite local criticism while identifying new opportunities. With her financial and personal success, gradually she gained community members' respect. She reported that other women call her *Didi* (older sister), and she is recognized as a helper. She believed that she was "able to get things done because everyone loves me." Women ranging in age from 15 to 50 years worked for her.

Her desire to continue investing in the community manifested in different forms, particularly when Noni Begum adopted a 15-year-old orphan girl. She treated the teenager as her own, investing in her education, and aspiring to spend money at her wedding. She concluded, "I like to work for the good of my country. Today I am doing well, but we have gone through very hard times. There was a time when we could not feed ourselves. Now I am able to help others and it is extremely satisfying."

Production, Market, and Financial Sustainability

Income for members in Noni Begum's SHG was tied to the sales of their products. Noni Begum reported that not every member was able to travel to fairs to sell the group's products; consequently, she assisted them by selling their products at fairs. She bought jute locally and had learned to color and process it. The government gave a grant to Noni Begum to construct a brick room attached to her home where SHG members could work and stock their products. Her group had bought a special machine to embroider on jute. Gradually, over seven years, she had diversified her products from small items (for example, jute dolls, table mats, coasters, bags of all sizes and shapes, door mats, hats, cell phone covers) to large jute carpets. She was excited about her latest innovation: jute carpets, which cost less than woolen carpets, and were "fashionable."

Profits on products varied. Generally, her average profit was 50 percent, and she earned approximately INR 5,000 a month, though sales varied by months and seasons. "Else what will I eat?" she asked. She proudly showed a huge stock of jute products stored in the brick room. Over seven years, not only had she diversified product lines, but she had also ventured into taking different types of loans—the SHG's second loan and her personal loan. She had invested between INR 100,000 and 150,000 in her enterprise. However, she expanded slowly, and things picked up after three years. She said, "The government has started to help more recently. This LDO is very helpful. We worry what will happen when he gets transferred." It was evident that a good staff member, irrespective of gender, religion, or degree, can make a difference in poor women's lives.

Zaafira Bibi: An SHG Participant and Noni Begum's Mentee

I met Zaafira Bibi accidentally at a handicraft fair in Kolkata, the state capital. Zaafira identified as a Muslim woman, in her early 30s, and was married with three children. She was married at age 17 and had not completed her schooling. Her husband worked as an agricultural laborer and more recently had started assisting her by selling jute products at fairs. Her mentor, Noni Begum, had encouraged her to acquire jute handicrafts training, join her SHG, and complete her 10th-grade exam, all of which she did. She was living below the poverty line when she first met Noni Begum. Zaafira said she knew jute work as a young girl but did not earn enough through the sale of products. After discussing it with her mentor, Zaafira recognized that jute work was the best fit for her, given the proximity to raw materials and also her skill set from her youth.

At first her husband would not let her accompany Noni Begum for training because he worried that she would be trafficked. But she insisted on going, "because it is hard to ask my husband for money." She would leave home between 12 and 2 p.m., when her husband was out, and would not know of her absence. She reiterated Noni Begum's story of training quality and fear of human trafficking, but her enthusiasm and determination helped her forge onward to do better than before. She learned jute work at the skills training sessions, some taught by Noni Begum, and improvised to make her products better. "I discovered my own style of work. [Her husband] did not protest once I started to earn money" (he earned INR 50 per day).

Later Zaafira started her own SHG and was chosen as its leader. She described her progress: "Over time, and through Noni Begum's guidance and assistance, I am doing well now. I have a *pucca* [brick] house with two rooms, a bathroom in the house, and a tube well." Discussing income, she said, "I do not have a fixed monthly income. My income depends on how much I am able to sell at fairs. I have sold about INR 15,000 to 16,000 worth of goods at the fair already." When asked how the income helped her, she answered,

> Income helps to pay off debt and spend on children's education. We spend about INR 3,000 per month and earn about that much per month as well. I save INR 1,000 per month. Also, I am able to help other women. I help 40 women [as employees] earn between 2,000 to 3,000 rupees [INR] per month.

She continued, "I am able to do well because of my own hard work, and I have been able to teach many women to do this work and help them earn too."

Discussing other issues she faced despite economic improvement, she observed, "My house is on a small parcel of land, but it is in my husband's name. I also put in 30,000 to 40,000 rupees [INR] to buy a larger parcel of land for rice farming, but that too is not in my name." The land is in her husband's name, though she has learned through SHG participation about women's rights; clearly, she was unhappy because she had invested her savings in this property, but it was not in her name. She added, "At first my husband was my biggest obstacle. People would taunt him that he was living off his wife's income. But I made him understand that there is nothing wrong with this type of work. Now he trusts me fully." She reported, similar to Noni Begum, that "loans and the opportunity to attend fairs have been most helpful. I tell other women to join SHGs. I take them to training centers, I teach them the ropes. I help them. We help one another."

Discussion

Noni Begum's remarkable contributions toward transforming her own family's conditions, as well as those of several families living below the poverty line in her village, rarely get much attention in academic circles. Yet, if we are to teach social workers to support, partner, and promote social entrepreneurships geared toward poverty alleviation, we need to pay attention to Noni Begum's story and stories of similar community residents. The case clearly indicates that the vision of SHGs designed in partnership with government and for-profit (banking) sectors would not have taken root in Noni Begum's village without the risks that she, a less educated, poor Muslim woman, took. Initially she had to make do with available resources; but later she was able to seek out newer and better opportunities to help her own family and others willing to work hard. Her strengths, including persistence despite not seeing immediate gains, determination to change her circumstances despite barriers and lack of local resources, and the optimism that change is possible, deserve recognition (Azmat et al., 2015; Goel & Rishi, 2012; Light, 2009; Worsham, 2012).

Lessons for Social Workers

Although Noni Begum was not assisted by a social worker, the LDO's role and function in the government-run SHG program was similar to what social workers might do in a community setting—for example, linking program participants to external resources, processing and strategizing next steps related to micro-business development, connecting potential community members and external resources to each other, and advocating for needed changes. In this case, after an SHG facilitator informed community residents about the SHG program and related opportunities available to families, some residents chose to form SHGs. The facilitator continued to support the SHG until it produced saleable goods (about a year to a year and a half after the SHG had started) or developed some maturity. Once an SHG became more mature, the LDO got involved in brokering external relations and connecting SHG leaders with external opportunities. These functions can be performed by social workers or social work student interns.

Furthermore, the LDO reported that he would visit villages several times a year and talk about the same programs over and over again. He believed that because change takes time, and government officials were asking village women to behave in ways contrary to their religious and family values and beliefs—such as leaving their homes to meet group members, leaving the village for training, saving money and taking out a bank loan, and discussing intimate and noninti- mate family matters outside the house—repetition was necessary. He observed,

> Even if one out of 10 group members accept a new idea, it's likely to have a ripple effect in the community because she will go back to her home and talk about it, and before long a few more will try out her ways, and down the road others will join and more changes will come.

Clearly, the LDO's philosophy, assumptions, and approach (borrowed from the SHG visionaries) influenced Noni Begum and had a ripple effect on Zaafira Bibi and many other women in the community. Noni Begum, too, acknowledged the LDO's and government's support, partnership, and promotion of her work to help her and others like her through the creation of enhanced training opportuni- ties, loans, and marketing avenues. The role and functions performed by the LDO can easily be replicated by social workers as they visit communities regularly, plant new ideas, and patiently wait for a few residents to buy in to these new ideas. Once a few people agree, social workers may start a project or program, and slowly others will join the program once the benefits are visible to others.

Both Noni Begum and Zaafira Bibi also identified areas for improvement, such as higher credit lines, new markets, and property rights. In these areas, social workers in partnership with LDOs can advocate for policy changes (Nandan et al., 2014). Noni Begum and Zaafira Bibi had transitioned from starting and leading SHGs to becoming employers by hiring 80 women together. In a country where finding jobs can be challenging given the size of the population, helping women who are poor earn a minimum wage that helps the women supplement their family income deserves recognition. Consequently, bank regulations pertaining to loans and interest rates for such local leaders deserve reconsideration. Zaafira Bibi's complaint about investing in land that was not in her name deserves atten- tion and legal remedy; social workers can partner with legal counsel to advocate for changes to women's property ownership rights in the Muslim community.

Relationship to Social Work Values

It is important to note that despite the absence of any formal social work education, the LDO and the two women—Noni Begum and Zaafira Bibi— exemplified social work values of self-determination, dignity and worth of individuals, competence, integrity, importance of human relationships, service, and socioeconomic justice. For example, neither the LDO nor the two women imposed SHG propositions on the local women. Instead, they valued self-determination and encouraged other women to participate in jute production, per their ability and circumstances. If any village woman was willing to participate, they were inclusive and allowed their employees to work at their own pace and ability because, as Noni Begum said, "everyone is needy" and deserves respect (dignity and worth). Though Noni Begum and Zaafira Bibi were highly competent in jute weaving and marketing, they did not impose or overwhelm other women with their skills. They began where the women were and worked with anyone from age 15 to 50 years, teaching jute weaving skills, suggesting designs and products, and selling on their employees' behalf if these women could not travel outside the village. They also demonstrated integrity and fairness because no one got paid more or less than what the market would pay for their product. Not only did they relate well with their group members and hired workers, but they also recognized the value of human relationships in being able to be heard, in learning new skills, and acquiring opportunities for new loans and markets to sell their products (Bent-Goodley, 2002). Noni Begum and Zaafira Bibi, both successful social entrepreneurs, created social value directly by recognizing the problems and implementing solutions to address them in a sustainable fashion, within their respective communities. As Acs, Boardman, and McNeely (2013) highlighted when discussing the entrepreneurial efforts of leaders, they had an impact on members of their community, especially women, by empowering them with the means to challenge oppressive norms and social structures. Furthermore, according to Acs et al.'s (2013) framework, the opportunities gained by these disenfranchised women to learn, share ideas, build networks of trust and solidarity, and develop strong social capital are all examples of context-based social value creation. The overarching theme of Noni Begum's and Zaafira Bibi's work embodies a social and economic justice framework as the women not only improved their own life circumstances by thinking out of the box and scaling up their own micro-businesses but also helped others in similar situations and circumstances to better themselves. Social workers can certainly embody these skills and values in working with social enterprises such as SHGs in communities.

Conclusion

Community practice social workers, as well as social workers in nonprofits and in government organizations, can draw lessons from this case study. In addition to the lessons relevant to community practice social work that were mentioned earlier, lessons from this case study are important for social workers working in any setting. For example, when social workers witness or are informed of issues ranging from interpersonal matters in families to dire poverty and absence of basic necessities, they can connect clients to SHG social entrepreneurs who emerge from the community as the LDO illustrated. These SHG social entrepreneurs have recognition and status in communities and can suggest acceptable options for clients. In other words, social workers can fuel new SHGs in India, they can partner with existing SHGs to take them to the next level of addressing social issues while maintaining financial sustainability, and they can promote the work of local social entrepreneurs as illustrated in this chapter.

References

Acs, Z. J., Boardman, M. C., & McNeely, C. L. (2013). The social value of productive entrepreneurship. *Small Business Economics, 40*, 785–796.

Ashoka Foundation of India. (n.d.). *Who is a social entrepreneur?* Retrieved from http://india.ashoka.org/print/1290.

Azmat, F., Ferdous, A. S., & Couchman, P. (2015). Understanding the dynamics between social entrepreneurship and inclusive growth in subsistence marketplaces. *Journal of Public Policy & Marketing, 34*, 252–271.

Bacq, S. S., & Janssen, F. F. (2011). The multiple faces of social entrepreneurship: A review of definitional issues based on geographical and thematic criteria. *Entrepreneurship & Regional Development, 23*, 373–403.

Barendsen, L., & Gardner, H. (2004). Is the social entrepreneur a new type of leader? *Leader to Leader, 34*, 43–50. doi:10.1002/ltl.100.

Bent-Goodley, T. B. (2002). Defining and conceptualizing social work entrepreneurship. *Journal of Social Work Education, 38*(, 291–302.

Bhatt, E. (2006). *We are poor but so many: The story of self-employed women in India.* New Delhi, India: Oxford.

Datta, P. B., & Gailey, R. (2012, May). Empowering women through social entrepreneurship: Case study of a women's cooperative in India. *Entrepreneurship Theory and Practice, 36*, 569–587. doi:10.1111/j.1540-6520.2012.00505.x

Fawcett, B., & South, J. (2005). Community involvement and primary care trusts: The case for social entrepreneurship. *Critical Public Health, 15*, 191–204.

Goel, G., & Rishi, M. (2012). Promoting entrepreneurship to alleviate poverty in India: An overview of government schemes, private-sector programs, and initiatives in the citizen's sector. *Thunderbird International Business Review, 54*(1), 45–57. doi:10.1002/tie.21437

Harper, M. (2002, November). *Promotion of self help groups under the SHG bank linkage programme in India.* Paper presented at seminar on the SHG–Bank

Linkage Programme, New Delhi, India. Retrieved from https://www .researchgate.net/publication/23778459_Promotion_of_Self_Help_Groups_ under_the_SHG_Bank_Linkage_Programme_in_India

Harper, M., Berkhof, A., & Ramakrishna, R. V. (2005). SHG–bank linkage: A tool for reforms in cooperatives? *Economic and Political Weekly, 40*, 1720–1725. Retrieved from http://www.jstor.org/stable/4416530

Haugh, H. M., & Talwar, A. (2016). Linking social entrepreneurship and social change: The mediating role of empowerment. *Journal of Business Ethics, 133*, 643–658. doi:10.1007/s10551-014-2449-4

Helm, S. T., & Anderson, F. O. (2010). Beyond taxonomy: An empirical validation of social entrepreneurship in the nonprofit sector. *Nonprofit Management and Leadership, 20*, 259–275. doi:10.1002/nml.253

Jain, M. (2012). Social entrepreneurship using business methods to solve social problems: The case of Kotwara. *Decision, 39*, 168–177.

Kattumuri, R., & Singh, M. (2013). Social protection in India: Current approaches and issues. In J. Midgley & D. Piachaud (Eds.), *Social protection, economic growth and social change* (pp. 102–116). Northampton, MA: Edward Elgar.

Kummitha, R.K.R. (2016). Social entrepreneurship as a tool to remedy social exclusion: A win win scenario? *South Asia Research, 36*(1), 61–79.

Light, P. C. (2009, Summer). Social entrepreneurship revisited. *Stanford Social Innovation Review*, pp. 21–22.

Mansuri, B. B. (2010). Microfinancing through self help groups: A case study of bank linkage programme of NABARD. *Asia Pacific Journal of Research in Business Management, 1*, 141–150. Retrieved from https://www.researchgate .net/profile/Babu_Mansuri/publication/267836298_MICROFINANCING_ THROUGH_SELF_HELP_GROUPS-A_CASE_STUDY_OF_BANK_LINK-AGE PROGRAMME_OF_NABARD/links/56c4c59108ae7fd4625a458c.pdf

Martin, R. L., & Osberg, S. (2007). Social entrepreneurship: The case for definition. *Stanford Social Innovation Review, 5*(2), 30–39.

Nandan, M., London, M., & Blum, T. (2014). Community practice social entrepreneurship: An interdisciplinary approach to graduate education. *International Journal of Social Entrepreneurship and Innovation, 3*(1), 51–70.

Organization for Economic Cooperation and Development. (2017). *Inclusive growth.* Retrieved from http://www.oecd.org/inclusive-growth/

Schmitz, B. (2015). Social entrepreneurship, social innovation, and social mission organizations: Toward a conceptualization. In R. A. Cnaan & D. Vinokur-Kaplan (Eds.), *Cases in Innovative nonprofits* (pp. 17–42). Los Angeles: Sage Publications.

Schmitz, B., & Scheuerle, T. (2012). Founding or transforming? Social intrapreneurship in three German-Christian based NPOs. *ACRN Journal of Entrepreneurial Perspectives, 1*(1), 13–36.

Swain, R. B., & Varghese, A. (2013). Delivery mechanisms and impact of micro-finance training in Indian self-help groups. *Journal of International Development, 25,* 11–21. doi:10.1002/jid.1817

Tankha, A. (2012). *Banking on self-help groups: Twenty years on.* New Delhi, India: Sage Publications.

United Nations Development Program. (2015). *Human development report.* Retrieved from http://www.undp.org/country

World Bank. (2017). *World Bank data: World development indicators.* Retrieved from http://data.worldbank.org/

Worsham, E. (2012). Reflections and insights on teaching social entrepreneurship: An interview with Greg Dees. *Academy of Management Learning and Education, 11,* 442–452.

Epilogue

Social workers from across the globe have provided perspectives and illustrations of social workers as innovators, social entrepreneurs, and intrapreneurs or have identified and analyzed cases from within their fields of research or practice in which they observed social innovation, entrepreneurship, and intrapreneurship processes. All authors have clearly aligned these perspectives and practices with social work values. The editors have had several concluding thoughts in reviewing and editing this volume where these processes were illustrated from social work perspectives.

Social workers have been playing, and can play, the roles of pioneering, promoting, and partnering with social intrapreneurs and social entrepreneurs. As micro, mezzo, and macro practitioners, social workers from across the globe can fulfill these roles with the implied pressure to create sustainable and innovative solutions for the 12 Grand Challenges for Social Work (Uehara et al., 2013) and the United Nations Sustainable Development Goals (United Nations Development Programme, n.d.). Consequently, interest has been growing in innovation and social work entrepreneurship and intrapreneurship at conferences and workshops. In addition, some social work programs have started certificates, concentrations, and institutes on these topics.

Social workers are adept in recognizing community-based social entrepreneurship and organization-based intrapreneurship and also in understanding the different trials and tribulations experienced during these processes. Notwithstanding the opportunities or the challenges, social workers can relate social work values that undergird, and are executed during, the entrepreneurial process. Hence, it has been shown that social entrepreneurship and intrapreneurship are consistent with the social work *Code of Ethics* (National Association of Social Workers [NASW], 2017).

Concentrations of social innovators and social entrepreneurs are found throughout the globe in Asia, Latin America, North America, Africa, and Europe (Elkinton & Hartigan, 2008). In this edited volume, we have provided illustrations from Asia, North America, Africa, and Australia. Thus, the volume recognizes that social entrepreneurship is taking place around the world, and social workers are, and should be, integral to such endeavors for promoting social change and social justice. The social work profession has a natural predisposition to creating social value, and this concept, often used by the corporate sector, is a natural occurrence within social work at the global level. Describing social work as a profession that develops and advances social value is an important next step for fully exposing the profession's commitment and contributions to this area.

Human service organizations (HSOs) need to create a conducive environment to facilitate innovations in-house (Berzin & Camarena, 2018). In fact, the human service management competencies for social workers speak to facilitating innovative changes, assisting staff members with implementing positive change, taking calculated risks, and raising funds and revenue sources to sustain organizations. These competencies lend themselves to social workers being innovative and intrapreneurial. Moreover, collaboratively with the beneficiaries of HSOs, social workers can undoubtedly design new and improved processes, products, and services. Human-oriented design thinking is based on this approach.

Mizrahi (2009) referenced characteristics of community social work practice that align with social entrepreneurship processes. More specifically, community social work practice is "integrative, comprehensive, collaborative, participatory, strengths and asset focused, founded on building capacity, sustainable, empowerment focused, focused on the present with an eye on the future, and inclusive" (Mizrahi, 2009, as paraphrased in NASW, 2018, p. 52). Consequently, we are inferring that social work entrepreneurship and community social work practice are related.

Social workers, as innovators and also as best assessors of community needs and strengths, can serve as partners for corporate social responsibility (CSR) projects and can also be employed within CSR units of companies. Similarly, with clinical, community practice and nonprofit management competencies that social workers possess, they can easily partner with, or be employed by, social ventures, benefit corporations, and low-profit limited liability corporations (L3Cs), all of which focus on creating social impact to varying degrees. It is also vital that, within these roles, social workers identify themselves as such. For instance, being able to work in an interdisciplinary fashion, as part of social responsibility projects while identifying oneself as a social worker, furthers the work and the visibility of the profession in finding transformative solutions for the community and the broader society. It also highlights the integral role that social workers can play in addressing social problems in an innovative, sustained, and effective manner.

Although there is no targeted focus on providing social workers with formal training in taking calculated risks, they are comfortable in recognizing opportunities and facing uncertainty within the professional realm. This statement means that social workers are already engaged in the work of managing uncertain and sometimes volatile situations that require being able to think critically and develop solutions that are not as clearly apparent to others. The ability to do this is part of learning how to take, manage, and assess calculated risks as a social entrepreneur and innovator. As social workers continue to receive education, training, and support in this area, they will develop and refine their skills to take and manage calculated risks in more effective ways during innovation, entrepreneurship, and intrapreneurship processes.

Social innovation, social entrepreneurship and intrapreneurship, and social value creation are not antithetical to social work values and ethics. On the contrary, they very much resonate with the NASW (2017) *Code of Ethics*. When social workers create impact that increases awareness about social issues, support empowering environments for beneficiaries of an HSO, develop changes in the living conditions of families, and grow changes in perceptions, attitudes, and behaviors of specific populations and segments, they are creating social value. Thus, it is time for social work to embrace the aforementioned perspectives and strategies and reexamine ethical principles and values that can be promoted through such efforts.

The irony is that social entrepreneurship, social innovation, and social value creation all have the word "social"; however, social workers have historically not been at the table for discussing, developing, and researching these concepts and processes. Consequently, it is imperative that more research is conducted to document current social work innovation and entrepreneurship and intrapreneurship practices, to contribute to the literature that primarily originates in nonprofit and business literatures. In other words, social work literature is in its very early stages of conceptualizing and researching social entrepreneurship, social innovation, and social value creation. Gradually, more authors and researchers need to incorporate these concepts and principles into their writings and research agenda, respectively.

More social work–authored books, articles, and cases on social entrepreneurship and intrapreneurship, social innovation, and social value creation need to be included in the social work, business, and nonprofit sector literatures. There is a growing necessity to infuse social entrepreneurship, social innovation, and social value creation content within the social work curriculum and across the continuum of social work practice (micro, mezzo, and macro). This knowledge is essential for social workers to have successful partnerships across sectors and disciplines. Thus, the development of core competencies in this area would be helpful to advance the educational experience of social work students. Social work faculty need to provide more opportunities for students to develop social entrepreneurship and intrapreneurship, social innovation, and social value creation competencies through field education. This idea means that schools, programs, and departments of social work need to train existing internship site supervisors in these concepts, where needed, and also identify nontraditional internship sites in social ventures, benefit corporations, L3Cs, and so on.

Social workers in private practice particularly, and most certainly in administration and management of organizations and programs, need to receive more formal training in these processes so that their natural predisposition to "create something from nothing" is well guided and effective. Developing a policy statement (in NASW's [2018] *Social Work Speaks*, for instance) on social work entrepreneurship, intrapreneurship, and innovation would also be helpful in creating a sense of guiding principles bound to social work ethics for future social work entrepreneurs.

Social work entrepreneurship, intrapreneurship, innovation, and value creation perspectives and strategies are integral to social work practice. These perspectives, to varying degrees, are already being taught through community and organizational practice courses, though the lexicon and depth of some of the strategies may differ. Founders of the profession were innovative and entrepreneurial—Jane Addams is touted in the business and nonprofit literature as a social entrepreneur. Hence, we must continue to consciously, systematically, and strategically advance these perspectives within the profession to continue spearheading social justice initiatives that promote social change and transform communities.

References

Berzin, S., & Camarena, H. (2018). *Innovation from within: Redefining how nonprofits solve problems*. New York: Oxford University Press.

Elkinton, J., & Hartigan, P. (2008). *The power of unreasonable people: How social entrepreneurs create markets that change the world*. Boston: Harvard Business Press.

Mizrahi, T. (2009). Community organizing principles and practice guidelines. In A. Roberts (Ed.), *Social workers' desk reference* (2nd ed., pp. 872–881). New York: Oxford University Press.

National Association of Social Workers. (2017). *Code of ethics of the National Association of Social Workers.* Washington, DC: Author.

National Association of Social Workers. (2018). Community development. In *Social work speaks: National Association of Social Workers Policy Statements 2018–2020* (11th ed., pp. 51–55). Washington, DC: NASW Press.

Uehara, E., Flynn, M., Fong, R., Brekke, J., Barth, R. P., Coulton, C., et al. (2013). Grand challenges for social work. *Journal of the Society for Social Work & Research, 4*, 165–170. doi:10.5243/jsswr.2013.11

United Nations Development Programme. (n.d.). *United Nations Sustainable Development Goals.* Retrieved from http://www.undp.org/content/dam/undp/library/corporate/brochure/SDGs_Booklet_Web_En.pdf

About the Editors

Monica Nandan, PhD, MSW, has over 25 years of experience working in communities and serving on nonprofit boards dealing with aging, sustainability of nonprofit programs, homelessness, social welfare, bereavement, and health care. With her finance (MBA), health care administration, and social work academic training, she has taught traditional and nontraditional courses in social work. For example, she has taught courses on social innovation, community organizing and social entrepreneurship, and empowering women through social entrepreneurship. She has served as chairperson of social work programs and as interim dean of a college of health and human services.

For almost 15 years, her scholarship activities were in gerontology and health care. Some of the journals she has published in include *Journal of Gerontological Social Work, Social Work Research, Journal of Cross-Cultural Gerontology,* and *Gerontology & Geriatric Education.* Over the past eight years, her scholarship has pertained to social entrepreneurship and interdisciplinary education. Her more recent publications are in the *Journal of Faculty Development, Journal of College Teaching and Learning, Journal of Interprofessional Care, International Journal of Social Entrepreneurship and Innovation, Education + Training,* and *Administration in Social Work.* She also contributed book chapters in publications like *Occupational Social Work/Employee Assistance Program, Encyclopedia of Human Services and Diversity,* and *Aging Education in a Global Context.* She serves on the editorial board of the *International Management Review.* She has published several pieces in gerontological, social work, and social work managers' newsletters. She has presented at several national conferences, and over past three years she has been invited to present at an internationally recognized institution of higher education in Mumbai, India.

Tricia B. Bent-Goodley, PhD, received her MSW from the University of Pennsylvania and her PhD from Columbia University, and she has over 25 years of experience as a professional social worker. Through sustained federal and foundation funding, she has developed and designed culturally specific interventions rooted in social value creation and entrepreneurial thinking in areas such as healthy relationship education; HIV prevention; faith-based interventions; engaging men and boys; and sexual assault and domestic violence education, prevention, and intervention. Serving in numerous local and national capacities, she has received extensive national, regional, and local awards and demonstrates her commitment to addressing issues of inequity and social justice through her service.

Bent-Goodley is a professor at Howard University School of Social Work. As the editor-in-chief of *Social Work*, the flagship journal of the National Association of Social Workers, she was the second African American woman to serve in this role in the journal's 60+ year history. She served as the founding director of the Howard University Interpersonal Violence Prevention Program—the office dedicated to providing prevention education, advocacy, intervention, policy development, coordination, training, and bystander prevention education in the areas of sexual assault, domestic violence, dating violence, and stalking. She also serves as a founding member and chair of the Prince George's County Domestic Violence Fatality Review Team and is a former national elected board member of the Council on Social Work Education. Bent-Goodley is the author and editor of many publications, including *The Ultimate Betrayal: A Renewed Look at Intimate Partner Violence* and *By Grace: Challenges, Strengths, and Promise of African American Marriage.*

Gokul Mandayam, PhD, joined the faculty of University at Buffalo School of Social Work (UBSSW) in the fall of 2017 and is affiliated with the school's interdisciplinary social innovation and social entrepreneurship initiative. Before joining UBSSW, he taught macro social work practice courses for 12 years at various universities in the United States, the Middle East, and India.

His interdisciplinary research interests include social innovation and entrepreneurship, corporate social responsibility, nonprofit management, program evaluation, and application of spatial analysis technology for human services. Before coming to the United States, he consulted for a variety of social development projects in India on topics ranging from non-land-based income generation and evaluation of fish harvesting practices in coastal communities to government nutrition programs and female infanticide. He has published articles on microfinance and spatial analysis for planning social services and has presented at several national and international conferences.

About the Contributors

Mahasweta M. Banerjee, PhD, is professor at the School of Social Welfare, University of Kansas. She teaches quantitative and qualitative research and coordinates study abroad in India. Her research and scholarship focus on poverty and social justice. She had a Fulbright Research Award to India, where she applied insights from the capability approach to explore capabilities that allow income-poor people to work and earn a living. She serves on the editorial board of the Journal of Social Work Education and Urban Social Work and is a board member of the Council on Social Work Education and the International Consortium for Social Development.

Stephanie Cosner Berzin, PhD, is assistant dean of the Doctoral Program at the Boston College School of Social Work. As codirector of the Center for Social Innovation, she conducts research on organizational capacity-building around innovation and intrapreneurship. Her book *Innovation from Within: Redefining How Nonprofits Solve Problems* (Oxford, 2018) helps social sector leaders develop an innovation skill set and helps build organizational capacity for change. Her complementary research explores services to combat poverty and support vulnerable youths.

Jeroo Billimoria, MSW, is the founder of Child Helpline International, Childline India, and seven other social entrepreneurial organizations. Billimoria grew up in Mumbai, India, where she studied social work. Today, she is considered to be among the world's leading social entrepreneurs. Billimoria is a Skoll awardee and an Ashoka and Schwab fellow. Her latest ventures include Child and Youth Finance International, a movement working to ensure financial inclusion and child finance education, and Aflatoun, which provides social and financial education to children in 83 countries. Several of her organizations have been recognized among the world's top 100 nongovernmental organizations.

Louise Brown, PhD, is an associate professor of social work at the University of Bath, England. She is a qualified social worker with a background in child protection practice. Brown has over 15 years of experience as a social work educator and researcher. She has particular expertise in the incubation and implementation of social innovation. Her research interests focus on the international transfer of innovative practice-based models and the role of risk and evidence in facilitating innovation to improve practice.

Carol S. Collard, PhD, LMSW, is an associate professor of social work at the Department of Human Services, Kennesaw State University. Collard's research interests include the intersectionality of homelessness and behavioral health disorders, chronic poverty, and social entrepreneurship. Her professional background includes social work administration, nonprofit management, program development, community organizing, and leadership development. Collard also operates a nonprofit organization that serves individuals and families that have experienced chronic homelessness.

Mathieu R. Despard, PhD, MSW, is research assistant professor with the George Warren Brown School of Social Work at Washington University in St. Louis and a faculty associate with the Center for Assets, Education, and Inclusion at the University of Michigan. He conducts research on financial inclusion, household financial security, asset building, and nonprofit capacity and has taught graduate courses in financial social work, asset building, nonprofit management, community practice, and social policy.

Ronya Foy Connor, PhD, is currently the director of gender affairs for the country of Anguilla, British West Indies. She is a graduate of Howard University's School of Social Work (PhD and MSW) and Cornell University (MPA and BS). Foy Connor has conducted research in the United States, East Africa, and the Caribbean with interest in international social work, women and youth social entrepreneurship, and cross-cultural studies. She has worked for the U.S. federal government in the areas of intercountry adoption, human rights, and labor and with the New York City government relating to community affairs. Foy Connor's life mission is to help those who feel helpless.

Kristina Jaskyte Bahr, PhD, received her doctorate from the University of Alabama. Her teaching, research, and service focus on the management of nonprofit organizations, with a special attention to the topics of innovation and individual creativity. Her other areas of interest include social entrepreneurship, governance, foundations, and cross-cultural research. Her projects have been funded by the National Science Foundation, the ASAE foundation, and government (Georgia Department of Families and Children Services). She has numerous publications on innovation and creativity, and she has presented her research at many national and international conferences.

Jie Lei, PhD, is associate professor in social work and the deputy director of the Center for Social Work Education and Research at Sun Yat-Sen University,

China. He is also the visiting scholar of the University of Bath (England), Gothenburg University (Sweden), and National Taipei University (Taiwan). Lei's research focuses on professionalization of social work, social assistance, and child protection in China. He has published research articles in the *British Journal of Social Work, Critical Social Policy, International Social Work,* and *Social Policy and Society.*

Joshua P. H. Livingston, MSW, is a doctoral candidate at the City University of New York Graduate Center's doctoral program in social welfare, and a practicing licensed master barber. He has an MSW and certificate in human service management from Boston University. His social work practice experience is in youth-based program development, management, and evaluation. His doctoral research focuses on how social innovation, specifically considering the black American barbershop as a model, can be used by black and Latino young men to develop mission-based enterprise within academic and other institutional environments.

James M. Mandiberg, PhD, MSW, is associate professor and chair of the Organizational Management and Leadership Program at the Silberman School of Social Work at Hunter College, City University of New York (CUNY), and faculty member of the CUNY Graduate Center's Doctoral Program in Social Welfare. He has an MSW from Stony Brook University and a PhD in social work and organizational psychology from the University of Michigan. His research and community work are in social innovation and a community development approach to social enterprise. He has held faculty positions at Shikoku Gakuin University in Japan, the University of Wisconsin–Madison, and Columbia University.

Irene Searles McClatchey, PhD, LCSW, has an undergraduate degree from the University of Lund in Sweden and received her master's and doctoral degrees in social work from the University of Georgia. McClatchey is an associate professor and director of the MSW program at Kennesaw State University. She teaches death, dying, and bereavement, and her research focuses on grief experiences of children and teens. She is the founder of Camp MAGIK, an independent nonprofit organization that provides healing camps for bereaved children and adolescents; first held in 1995, it serves 200+ children and their families each year.

Manohar Pawar, PhD, is professor of social work, School of Humanities and Social Sciences, and a member of the Institute for Land, Water and Society, Charles Sturt University, New South Wales, Australia; he is also the president of the International Consortium for Social Development. His publications include *Empowering Social Workers: Virtuous Practitioners* (coedited, Springer,

2017); *Future Directions in Social Development* (coedited, Palgrave Macmillan, 2017); *Social and Community Development Practice* (Sage Publications, 2014); *Reflective Social Work Practice* (Cambridge University Press, 2015); *Water and Social Policy* (Palgrave Macmillan, 2014); *International Social Work* (2nd edition, Sage Publications, 2013); and *Sage Handbook of International Social Work* (coedited, Sage Publications, 2012).

Joe Silva, MSW, is a Brooklyn-based social entrepreneur focused on using design thinking to develop technology that improves the way clients interact with and experience human services organizations. He has worked with people living in extreme poverty, dealing with co-occurring chronic illnesses and behavioral health conditions since 2009. After earning his MSW in organizational management and leadership at the Silberman School of Social Work at City University of New York–Hunter, he was selected as a policy fellow by the Network for Social Work Management and expert fellow at Blue Ridge Labs through the Robin Hood Foundation.

Archana Singh, PhD, MPhil, is currently working as an assistant professor at the Centre for Social Entrepreneurship, Tata Institute of Social Sciences (TISS) in Mumbai, India. She received her MSW from Agra University and then completed her MPhil and PhD in social work at TISS. The focus of her doctorate was social entrepreneurship. Before her academic career, she worked with multiple developmental organizations on diverse social issues in urban and rural areas in India. She has published several papers in reputed international journals and book chapters. In 2016, she published a book titled *The Process of Social Value Creation: A Multiple-Case Study on Social Entrepreneurship in India.*

Index

In this index, *f* denotes figure.

fact that they trust you and believe in what you say. Therefore, the quality of your relationship with the customer is the competitive advantage that enables you to succeed over rivals who may have similar products and services.

Congratulations on purchasing the new authority on relationship selling that is designed to enhance your knowledge and selling ability. Just as optometrists help improve their patients' vision, this handbook serves as a "prescription" for a superior selling career. No one would expect to enhance their eyesight without the right corrective lenses. So why would anyone expect their sales to improve without having the right tools for success? Consider this handbook as the solution for acquiring your selling focus.

The most fundamental principles of relationship building are the same whether you are in North America or selling across the globe. Therefore, our goal is not only to make this handbook a domestic best seller, but also an international best seller. We want every professional salesperson to have access to a training tool that offers the most comprehensive study of the relationship style of selling. Our objective was to find a way to break the process into its most basic components, in an attempt to simplify the complex buyer-seller interaction that takes place in a selling situation. The result is an eight-step sales cycle model that we explore in depth in over one-half of this handbook.

And because attitude is so important for achieving success in selling, we included verbal and nonverbal communication and social style technology as foundation stones in the relationship model of selling, as well as providing an ethical framework upon which a profitable and lasting sales career can be built.

Throughout this handbook, you will see the "world" of selling through current sales literature, personal experience, and stories of successful, active sales professionals who put the theory contained in this handbook into everyday practice. As one top sales pro relayed to us, "Practice without theory is blind and theory without practice is sterile."

This handbook is divided into five sections. We strongly urge you to read one chapter at a time to fully digest the material. Interact with it. Personalize it. Take plenty of notes in the margin, and at the end of each section, think about the practical applications to your sales career.

Read the following section descriptions so that you understand the sequence and how you can get the most out of the organization of the chapters. Remember, this is your handbook, your own personal prescription for sharpened focus and success in relationship selling.

PART I — Relationship Building and the Sales Cycle Framework

Chapter 1 discusses the consultative nature and problem-solving approach to professional selling and details the characteristics that successful salespeople possess. Relationship selling is interactive, involves two-way communication, encourages prospect participation, employs empathy, and promotes a win-win environment. Today's style of selling favors building close and trusting long-term relationships. Positioning yourself as a consultant creates a partnership with your customers. You are peers working to solve problems together.

You gain a better understanding of the complete selling situation and the problems it generates by breaking the sale into its basic tasks. There are several steps to achieving a successful sale. An eight-step sales cycle is introduced in chapter 2 and explained in detail in chapters 7 to 14. It makes sense that if you understand what the steps are in the Sales Cycle Framework for Relationship Selling, and what is required to make each step a successful endeavor, you will become a professional in selling much quicker than those who are simply stumbling through the process trying to figure it out. The chapters included in this section are:

1. Your Career in Professional Selling
2. Relationship Selling

PART II — Cultivating an Ethical Climate and Developing Communication Skills

Few professions give you more opportunities for rejection on a daily basis than does the field of sales. Chapter 3 discusses the need for a strong ethical and moral character to sustain a sales career. Honest and caring service brings customers back and assures your success.

Success in professional selling also depends upon your ability to have a productive exchange of information with prospects and customers. As detailed in chapter 4, the more you understand about prospects and their decision making process, the more readily you can discover what they need and want. Because success in relationship selling depends on accurately getting your message across to prospects, chapter 4 also describes how to break through communication barriers.

An especially useful tool for gaining insight into how the prospect is thinking is knowledge of the social styles model, presented in chapter 5. A social style is the way a person sends and receives information. It is a method for finding the best way to approach a prospect and to set up a working relationship with that person. The chapters included in this section are:

    3. Ethical Issues in Selling
    4. Purchase Behavior and Communication
    5. Finding Your Selling Style

PART III — Gaining Knowledge, Preparing, and Planning for the Presentation

The information in chapter 6 prepares you for success in a sales career by focusing on gaining product knowledge, developing a plan for self-motivation and goal setting, and introducing the use of sales force automation.

Chapters 7 and 8 discuss the procedures for locating and qualifying prospects and identify the information needed to prepare for an effective presentation. Chapter 7 is a very thorough look at prospecting. As the saying goes, "I'd rather be a master prospector than a wizard of speech and have no one to tell my story to." Chapter 8 discusses the process of gathering preapproach information and presents a six-step telephone track for making appointments for that all-important personal interview. The chapters in this section are:

    6. Preparation For Success in Selling
    7. Becoming a Master Prospector
    8. Preapproach and Telephone Techniques

PART IV — The Face-to-Face Relationship Model of Selling

Chapters 9 to 13 are the very heart of professional selling. This is considered the "how to" portion of the handbook. We refer to this as the face-to-face portion of the sales cycle. It is the valuable time spent in the sales interview – the time when a commitment is obtained and kept.

What happens in the opening minutes is crucial to the overall success of the sales interview, so chapter 9 focuses on the approach. Chapter 10 is devoted to the art of asking questions and listening effectively. Questioning and listening guidelines are presented to carry you through the entire sales interview. We explain the SPIN™ selling technique and dramatize it using a very practical example. Chapter 11 details the techniques to use in the actual presentation. Units of conviction are the building blocks for creating and making a meaningful sales presentation. The five elements that comprise a complete unit of conviction are explained and illustrated.

Chapters 12 and 13 present the psychology behind handling objections and closing the sale. A plan to handle objections is introduced, and a separate section in chapter 12 explains several ways of dealing with the difficult price objection. Chapter 13 stresses that closing the sale is the natural conclusion to a successful sales interview. The chapters in this section are:

9. Approaching the Prospect
10. Identifying Needs by Questioning and Listening
11. Making the Presentation
12. Handling Objections
13. Closing the Sale

PART V — Management Aspects: Personal and Organizational

The service you give the customer after the sale has been completed can be as important, or even more important, than the sale itself. Keeping current customers happy and regaining lost clients is the focus of chapter 14. The customer absolutely defines quality in every transaction. Great salespeople don't just talk customer service – they live perfect service.

Chapter 15 shows you how to get better control of your time and your activities. The chapter really is all about personal organization and self-management. You cannot manage time, but you can manage yourself and your personal activities. Administrative ability on the part of the salesperson is fundamental to success. Statistics indicate that only about 20 percent of a salesperson's time during a typical day is spent in face-to-face interviews with prospects. The chapters in this section are:

14. Service After the Sale
15. Personal, Time, and Territory Management

You only get out of something what you put into it. We challenge you to achieve the maximum benefits of this powerful resource. Remember, there is no substitute for personal relationship selling. Commit to this – for yourself, your customers, and your company.

Good luck in your pursuit of sales success!

ABOUT THE AUTHORS

David J. Lill has a combined 30 years of sales, sales training, and teaching experience. He has taught selling classes at Baylor University, New Mexico State University and Belmont University. He earned his Ph.D. degree in Marketing from the University of Alabama. Dr. Lill is also a business consultant specializing in sales, advertising, and communications skills development.

Dr. Lill has won awards for excellence in teaching. He currently spends his time conducting seminars and training courses on sales and marketing related topics. His relationship selling model is being successfully used by companies throughout the country in a variety of industries including insurance, telecommunications, real estate, publishing, banking, hospitality, chemical, and automotive.

Dr. Lill is the author of the highly acclaimed college textbook, *Selling: The Profession*, now in its 4th edition, and is the co-author of *The Official Handbook for Health Club Sales*. Dr. Lill has published over 85 articles in various academic, trade, and professional publications. These include: *Selling Power, Journal of Advertising, Journal of the Academy of Marketing Science, Sales & Marketing Management, Business Topics, Nashville Business Journal*, and the *Journal of Pharmaceutical Marketing & Management*

Jennifer Lill received her first sales training while still in college as an independent contractor for the Southwestern Company. Ms. Lill also has training in human resources management from her work with Mercedes Benz U.S. International.

She attended the University of Alabama, graduating Summa Cum Laude with honors. While there, Ms. Lill was a research assistant and co-authored a finance textbook with an elite group of students and professors. She is currently a project manager and marketing developer for Synergistic Learning and serves on their Board of Advisors.

In addition, Ms. Lill is the co-author of *The Official Handbook for Health Club Sales.* She also has real estate industry experience and has plans to return to school for her Ph.D., while continuing to write and conduct sales training classes and seminars.

Part I

Relationship Building and the Sales Cycle Framework

Get Focused, and you can . . .

C HANGE is often desirable, frequently necessary, and always inevitable.

R EMEMBER . . . only you can give yourself permission to approve of you. Free your mind from negative thinking.

E NVISION yourself as a success. What you think about, you become.

A TTITUDE does determine your altitude. It is what's inside that makes you rise.

T HE right angle to solve a problem is the try-angle.

E LIMINATE failure as an option, and progress naturally occurs.

T HE best is yet to come. Yesterday's impossibilities are today's possibilities.

H AVE your dreams. They are the stuff great people are made of. Reach for the stars, but keep your feet on the ground.

E XTRAORDINARY desire and persistence drive ordinary people to achieve great things. Achievers are not extraordinary people.

S EVEN days without laughter makes one weak.

A smile is the shortest distance between two people.

L ISTEN twice as much as you talk. You have two ears and one tongue.

E NCOURAGING feedback is a process for learning about your impact on those around you.

S UCCESS is the progressive realization of worthwhile, predetermined, personal goals.

E XCUSES are for losers. Winners have ways. May we all find the way.

D ETERMINE never to give up. It's when things seem worse that you must not quit.

G OALS are dreams with a due date.

E XPECT the best of yourself. Be somebody special. The best never consider success optional.

Chapter 1

Your Career in Professional Selling

FOCAL POINTS

- **The value of salespeople**
- **Becoming a master salesperson**
- **Rewards of a sales career**
- **Opportunity knocks on many doors**
- **Characteristics of highly successful salespeople**

EVERYBODY SELLS

Many interactions between people involve selling. Of course, some are universally recognized as selling: Retail salespeople sell you clothes, furniture, or cameras; a salesperson sells you the car you drive; and your insurance agent sells you a policy. In fact, a company is not in business until somebody makes a sale. However, many other common transactions not usually recognized as selling involve the same skills, goals, and behavior patterns that professional salespeople use:

Waiters attempt to sell you on trying a particular entrée, or adding a dessert to your order; politicians want to convince constituents to vote for them or persuade other politicians to join them in promoting certain projects; trial lawyers sell themselves, their clients, and their interpretation of the law to judges and juries; and family members influence decisions such as where to live, who will use the family car tonight, whether to borrow money for a vacation, and what to cook for dinner.

In other words, you are already selling. *You are selling yourself, your ideas, and your desire for cooperation and companionship to almost everyone you engage in anything more than the most casual conversation.*

THE VALUE OF SALESPEOPLE

Partnerships, maintaining customer relationships, team selling, strategic alliances, and global strategies are more than mere words to a growing number of sales organizations today. They are the tools with which winning strategies are being fashioned. There is a growing competitiveness among the world's major corporations.

Using yesterday's sales strategies is dangerous and increasingly ineffective as global competitors battle each other. The latest and best marketing and sales practices are essential in gaining new markets and defending those you currently serve. The sales profession must rise to the challenge because, as Will Rogers said, "Even if you're on the right track, you'll get run over if you just sit there."

It is crucial to understand the business world today and know what challenges customers face, so you can really become a solutions provider. Sales professionals demonstrate their value to customers by providing productive information and helping solve problems.

Reliance on Salespeople

New and improved products and services are never accepted automatically. Neither individual nor business consumers can keep up with all the innovations that become available. So how do businesses expect to keep up with significant developments just in their own fields? They rely on you!

Your job is to identify customer needs, to determine ways those needs could be met by the products or services you have to offer, and then to provide that information to the customer. You also work in the other direction, by identifying customer needs that cannot be satisfied by your current product line and communicating those needs to your company for consideration in the development of new products. Therefore, you are a facilitator of information that keeps you and your customers competitive. Sales is the most important job in any organization!

Compensation Potential

Because of their vital role in business, salespeople are among the best-paid employees of a company. More salespeople earn above $100,000 annually than persons in any other profession. Exhibit 1.1 is a composite summary of the findings from *Sales & Marketing Management's* Sales Compensation Survey, an exclusive survey of nearly 2,000 sales and marketing executives designed to find out what people in sales are earning. The respondents were asked to provide their pay (base salary plus commissions and bonuses) as well as that of the top, mid-level, and low-level performers in their sales forces. The top performers are walking away with the fattest wallets by far, averaging $139,826 in total compensation. They are even doing better than their bosses. These are just averages. Some salespeople make less, some make considerably more. Salespeople are the catalysts of the economy. They are responsible for keeping goods, services, and ideas flowing.

Exhibit 1.1

Salespeople's Compensation

POSITION	BASE SALARY	BONUS & COMMISSION	TOTAL
Sales Executive	$90,222	$46,181	$136,403
Top Performer	74,122	65,704	139,826
Mid-Level	49,542	33,024	82,566
Low-Level	36,740	19,102	55,842
Average Rep	58,936	38,161	97,097

Importance of Sales Training

In today's extremely competitive selling environment, all kinds of companies provide continuing sales training on a regular basis — and many of these companies spend considerable amounts of money for training. For example, Kodak spends more than $20 million a year sending people through its courses at its Marketing Education Center. The reason is simple: Kodak sees sales training as the basis for winning all future battles.

Companies know that it is essential to spend money on training productive salespeople who will be long-term assets to the organization. In a survey of 250 sales organizations, conducted by the Krannert School of Management at Purdue University, the cost of replacing a single sales representative (including recruitment, training, and lost-opportunity costs) ranges from $50,000 to $75,000. A startling report by Bill Ruch, president of Aptitude Testing for Industry, revealed a survey of 125 manufacturing companies showing that every unsuccessful salesperson hired costs a company between $150,000 and $300,000. As you can see, a well-trained salesperson is indispensable!

Positive Attitudes toward Professional Selling

Today, more accurate information and education are helping to improve attitudes toward sales as a career. Over the past few decades, attitudes toward the selling profession have become more favorable. Individuals responding to recent surveys now support the view that selling requires more creativity, offers career opportunities, fosters integrity, and provides better financial incentives than ever before.

BECOMING A MASTER SALESPERSON

> Personal selling is the process of *seeking out* people who have a particular need, *assisting* them to recognize and define that need, *demonstrating* to them how a particular service or product fills that need, and *persuading* them to make a decision to use that service or product.

This definition is broad enough to include any type of selling you may do. It describes the commercial aspect of selling a product or service, as well as the process used to solicit funds for charitable organizations or enlist leaders for youth organizations. It includes the activities of athletic coaches, political parties, clergy, and personnel officers in all kinds of organizations.

Because every sales situation is unique, your career in sales is an exciting and demanding one in which every day brings opportunities to develop new skills and sales strategies and ways to refine existing ones. The potential for personal and professional growth never ends. Because different prospects have varying needs, interests, ability to pay, and authority to make decisions, selling is different in every situation—and constant change creates new possibilities.

To create and maintain a successful career in professional selling, four areas of your personality are involved:

Personal Integrity. Continued success in sales requires the highest possible ethical standards for dealing with prospects, established customers, and your own company. A salesperson who lies or deceives customers to complete a sale is soon out of a job, because customers do not place repeat orders and prospects soon get the word that this person is not to be trusted. An outstanding salesperson has high values and always operates in the most ethical manner.

Personality Structure. Sales is a demanding career, which is why you must have a confident personality, a positive self-image, and a sense of self-worth. A person who is unable to accept the reality that not every prospect becomes a client will be devastated by failures and feel an overwhelming sense of personal rejection. The persistent myth that salespeople are arrogant, overbearing, and excessively aggressive contradicts reality. Successful salespeople are, instead, highly interested in other people and their needs and eager to be of real service to prospects and clients.

Personal Relationships. Master salespeople are in an excellent position to attain status and recognition in the community. They are recognized as productive, capable professionals. Selling need never be personally degrading. You are not required to pretend, to subjugate your own personality or needs, or to become a doormat for customers. Success in professional selling does not call for assuming an inferior position socially, psychologically, or financially. The most successful salespeople find that their customers become friends with whom they form lasting personal relationships.

Personal Abilities. Success in sales requires high levels of intellect and developed skills. You must be able to understand — sometimes quickly and almost intuitively — a customer's business needs and problems. Salespeople must interpret those needs and suggest viable solutions even if customers themselves do not have a clear picture of their own needs or cannot verbalize those needs clearly. You need a broad knowledge of the field in which you operate, and must understand people and how to relate to them positively. The development of these skills requires not only intelligence but also continuous training.

Salespeople are Made, not Born

Too many people involved in selling have not attempted to learn the basic skills needed for success in the profession. They cop out by saying that they weren't born to be salespeople. They are called "90-day wonders" because after 90 days they wonder why they ever got into the sales business. Professional salespeople read books, take courses, ask questions, study the techniques of successful salespeople, work for their customers, and continually strive to outperform themselves.

Selling requires a working knowledge of psychology, sociology, communication, and persuasion. It is not a natural process to "close" a deal. It is a skill to be learned, just like anything else. Even experienced salespeople can fail if they get to the point where they think they know it all. Success in selling is a constant learning process. You must always be a student of your profession. Successful salespeople are *made, not born*, and they are made with concentrated attention, repeated practice, and goal-directed action.

We are all like computers, in that we are only as good as we have programmed ourselves to be philosophically, emotionally, and intellectually. Becoming a real master salesperson takes a long time. Even the very best salespeople adapt and refine their professional skills throughout their careers.

REWARDS OF A SALES CAREER

The once-popular "Wide World of Sports" television program promised the viewer "the thrill of victory, the agony of defeat." This thrill of victory makes sales an exciting and satisfying career, but the thrill comes not just from earning the monetary rewards or beating out the competition. Those are actually minor parts of the satisfaction of successful selling.

The true victory you will enjoy as a successful salesperson consists of satisfying higher personal needs. Maslow's hierarchy of needs (shown in Figure 1.1) has special significance for you as a professional salesperson.

In the beginning, salespeople concentrate on supplying their lower-order needs: earning a living, providing security for themselves and their families, and being accepted socially by their peers. As they satisfy these basic needs, salespeople can concentrate on the higher-level needs: self-acceptance (a positive self-image), making a contribution to community life, and self-actualization (becoming all one can be; knowledge and achievement for their own sake).

A Sense of Independence and Variety

A sales career frees you from a mundane daily routine. You are likely to work in a variety of places and deal with prospects who have widely different personalities. What works with one prospect may antagonize another. Consequently, you must always be aware of every element of the environment and adjust quickly. Selling is never boring.

You can exercise a greater measure of control over your time and activities than many other professional people. Sales is not a nine-to-five job. The hours are usually flexible, long one day and short another. Because your job is not usually structured just for you, you must be a self-starter and stay motivated.

Figure 1.1

Hierarchy of Personal Needs

Opportunities for Advancement

Effective salespeople are not forced into any one career path. Almost any option for career advancement is open to them. Exhibit 1.2 illustrates a potential career path for a highly motivated salesperson. As you move up the corporate hierarchy, the various options require a different blending of personal skills and character- istics. As a result, there is no guarantee that a successful salesperson will also make a successful manager. In fact, many talented salespeople actually refuse promo- tion to higher managerial positions. They simply love what they do, and can often earn more money selling than they could by moving into a middle-management position.

Entrepreneurship. Sales is an ideal career for those who plan to own and run their own businesses one day. No business can survive without a viable marketing organization. An owner or chief executive who has been involved in sales truly understands this part of the business and is in an excellent position to launch and manage a new enterprise successfully. An entrepreneur can find people who understand manufacturing and finance, but the sales and marketing staff must share the founder's dream if the concept is to reach fruition.

Exhibit 1.2

A Potential Career Path for Professionals in Selling

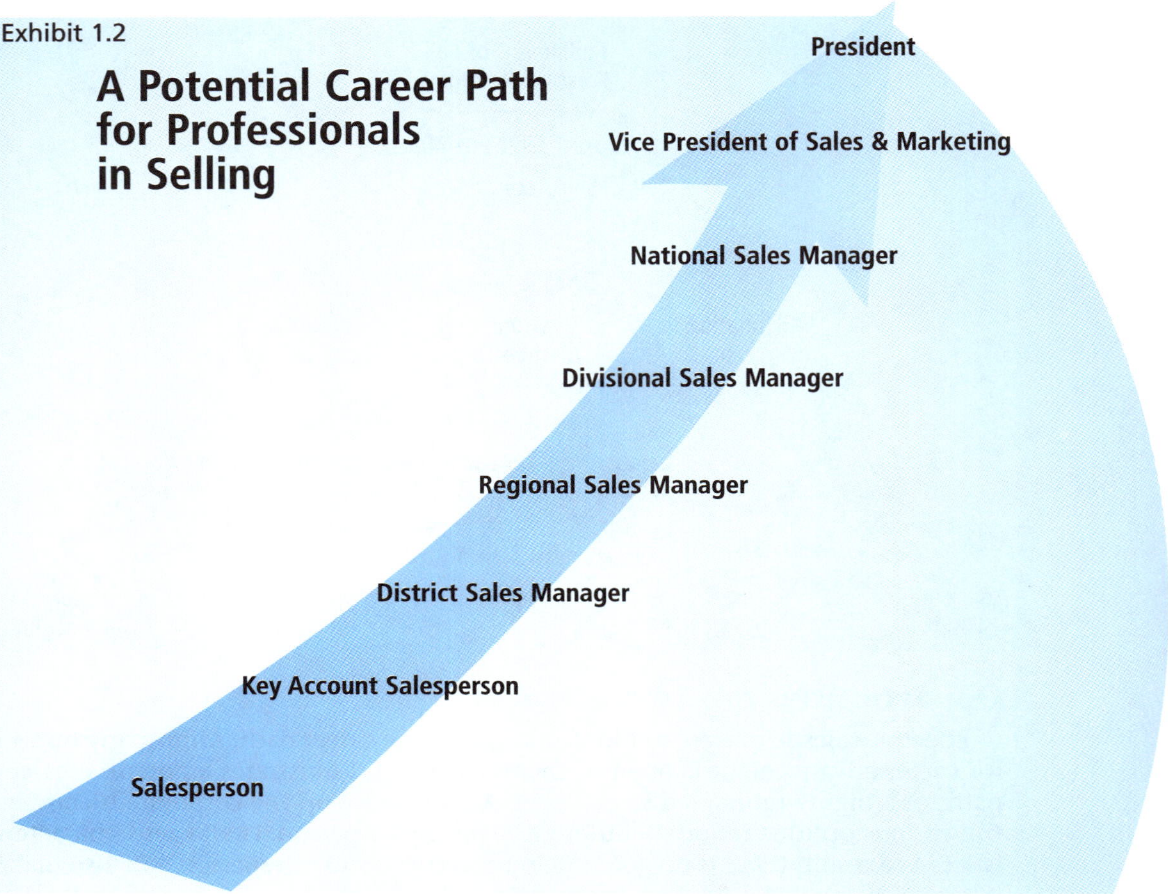

President

Vice President of Sales & Marketing

National Sales Manager

Divisional Sales Manager

Regional Sales Manager

District Sales Manager

Key Account Salesperson

Salesperson

Promotion to Sales Management. A sales manager may have either limited or extremely broad duties. The first step into sales management often consists of supervising two or three other salespeople — monitoring their activities, providing field training through joint sales calls, and/or recruiting additional sales representatives while continuing personal sales activities. More comprehensive sales management positions involve managing an entire local, regional, or nation-wide sales division. Such a position might include budgeting, planning for sales training, sales promotion, and recruiting, in addition to executive duties and status in the company.

Top Management Positions. Sales experience makes an executive a valuable member of the management team. Although chief executive officers (CEOs) have traditionally come from the financial and legal ranks, companies are increasingly tapping into the sales and marketing departments to find their leaders. Organizations are looking for CEOs who are good leaders of people and have good strategic minds. Many skills used in selling closely resemble those needed in top management. Both jobs require great people skills. It is important in both positions to maintain control under stress, to recognize opportunities and threats, and to locate, process, and analyze vast amounts of information. Figure 1.2 profiles one saleswoman who moved into top management by recognizing an opportunity and pursuing it with determination.

Figure 1.2

Saleswoman in the Executive Suite

Carleton (Carly) Fiorina, CEO, Hewlett-Packard Co., has been described as a "selling powerhouse." This selling machine, who started as a sales rep for AT&T, has twice been named the most powerful woman in America by *Fortune* magazine. Perhaps her most impressive sale was selling herself to Hewlett-Packard. Fiorina had no computer industry experience and was in competition with other, more experienced candidates when she decided to turn her weakness into a strength. Fiorina knew her competition for the top position at HP had more computer expertise. This did not stop Fiorina: Instead of offering computer expertise, Fiorina convinced the HP board members that they lacked strategic vision in their company. As a result of her persistence, Fiorina walked away with the job.

Security

Companies will always need salespeople. In fact, the demand appears to be steadily increasing rather than decreasing. Ambitious salespeople are eagerly sought, and most organizations provide excellent rewards and special treatment for their top sales performers. They know that quality salespeople who become dissatisfied can easily go to work for a competitor and possibly take their established customers with them.

Because salespeople are usually paid according to performance, you can directly affect your own income by deciding how much time and effort to invest in the job. Thus, your security comes from your own personal decisions about how hard and how efficiently you want to work. *Work, in many ways, is like money; if you are willing to expend enough of it, you can have almost anything you want.*

OPPORTUNITY KNOCKS ON MANY DOORS

Sales jobs are so diverse that they fit a wide variety of personal needs and interests. Variety exists from industry to industry. The responsibilities of a salesperson who calls on large manufacturing companies to create awareness of computer systems for production-control are vastly different from those of the real estate salesperson who sells homes to families. Sales careers vary within industries as well. For example, the residential real estate salesperson is in a different world from that of the real estate developer who puts together multimillion-dollar projects for shopping centers, office complexes, and industrial parks.

As different as sales jobs may be, they all share some basic similarities:

- The need to understand the prospect's problem.

- The need for appropriate technical and/or product knowledge.

- The need for self-discipline to relentlessly execute a sales plan.

- The ability to translate product features into benefits that resolve the prospect's problem.

Types of Salespeople

The type of person chosen by companies to fill sales positions varies according to the selling task. Other factors in hiring decisions include pricing policies, the extent and complexity of the product line, types of distribution channels, and the type and amount of mass advertising employed. Exhibit 1.3 lists five specific categories of salespeople and describes the content of their jobs.

Exhibit 1.3

Five Types of Salespeople

Account Representative

A salesperson who calls on a large number of already established customers in, for example, the food, textiles, apparel, or wholesaling industries. Much of this selling is low-key, and there is minimal pressure to develop new business.

Detail Salesperson

A salesperson who, instead of soliciting an order, concentrates on performing promotional activities and introducing products. The medical detail salesperson seeks to persuade doctors, the indirect customers, to specify the pharmaceutical company's brand-name product in prescriptions. The company's actual sales are ultimately made through a wholesaler or direct to the pharmacists who fill prescriptions.

Service Salesperson

A salesperson who sells intangibles, such as insurance and advertising. Unlike the four preceding types, those who sell services must be able to sell the benefits of intangibles.

Sales Engineer

A salesperson who sells products for which technical know-how and the ability to discuss technical aspects of the product are extremely important. The salesperson's expertise in identifying, analyzing, and solving customer problems is another critical factor. This type of selling is common in the chemical, machinery, and heavy-equipment industries.

Industrial Products Salesperson, Non-technical

This salesperson sells a tangible product to industrial or commercial purchasers; a high degree of technical knowledge is not required. Industries such as packaging materials or office equipment use this type.

The Order Taker and the Order Getter. The salesperson whose work is described as order-taking responds or reacts to customers' expressed desires. Order getting, or creative selling, requires ingenuity and the ability to generate demand for a product or service among potential buyers. The product may be tangible, such as automobiles, real estate, office equipment, water softeners, or swimming pools; or the product may be intangible, such as a complex telecommunications system, investment services, consulting services, educational or personal development programs, or advertising. Creative selling generally offers the greatest opportrnity for increased income because it requires the highest level of skill, dedication, time, and effort.

CHARACTERISTICS OF HIGHLY SUCCESSFUL SALESPEOPLE

No one list of traits exactly describes every successful salesperson. They are as diverse as members of any other profession. They include both extroverts and introverts — and all the degrees in between: Shy and outspoken, talkative and quiet. However, certain core characteristics seem to be present to some degree in most successful salespeople, despite the numerous ways individuals express those characteristics and adapt them to their own styles and purposes.

Enthusiasm

Ralph Waldo Emerson said, "Nothing great was ever achieved without enthusiasm." One of the most important characteristics in new salespeople is enthusiasm — but a distinction must be made between people who are enthusiastic about their product and those who are merely eager to take the prospect's money. Enthusiasm in salespeople is based on a genuine belief in the product and a conviction that it will serve the needs of the prospect. Such enthusiasm is communicated both verbally and nonverbally to the prospect in terms of your own personality. Enthusiasm may be expressed as calm, quiet confidence or as excited activity. However it is demonstrated, real enthusiasm is highly attractive and reassuring to prospects.

Empathy

Empathy, the ability to understand another person's concerns, opinions, and needs, whether sharing them or not, provides salespeople with the sales edge of being able to think and understand "with" the prospect during a sales call. To accurately understand what a client is saying, you must temporarily set aside your own needs and pride. It is essential, in the initial contact, to uncover the basic problems or requirements your prospect might have *before* you discuss a specific product. By careful listening, effective salespeople absorb prospects' reactions, generate an upbeat environment, and sell themselves to prospects. The combination of sincerity and empathy enables them to tailor the presentation to mesh precisely with the prospect's stated problems.

Goal Direction

Stay focused on your goals and daily activities. A half-dozen things make 80 percent of the difference between success and failure. Ask yourself what things contribute the most to your success. Goal-directed salespeople often respond positively to incentives such as money, prestige, recognition, and pride of accomplishment, which they see as tools they can use to reach their overall goals. When these incentives fit into their overall plan for achieving the goals that represent self-actualization for them, salespeople go all-out to win them.

Ability to Ask Questions

Good salespeople ask questions; poor ones just keep talking. You need to remain in control of the sales interview, and the person who is asking questions is the one in control. When you learn to ask the right kinds of questions, you will gain new prospects, discover valuable qualifying information, uncover prospects' buying motives, and be able to anticipate most objections. Questioning is your best tool for keeping the interview on track and moving toward a successful close, while also giving the prospect the feeling of remaining in control of the situation.

Resourcefulness

Top salespeople are resourceful. On the spur of the moment, they can think of new ways to make an old point, new applications and creative uses for products, and unique reasons for a particular prospect to make a buying decision. They can think on their feet under pressure. For these people, resourcefulness is an automatic response, like a reflex. Resourcefulness comes from an agile and analytical mind and allows you to stay on the right side of the *fine line between being just right and very wrong*. In the sales situation, the right word or phrase clears away the fog and reveals the solutions. The wrong word or phrase is like putting a drop of ink into a glass full of water: It obscures everything. Resourceful salespeople always seem to have at hand a barrelful of ideas, tactics, and strategies. Exhibit 1.4 highlights the thoughts of Tanis Cornell, vice president of sales at Level 3 Communications, Inc., in Dallas. Tanis recognizes the importance of resourcefulness and creativity in a salesperson.

Exhibit 1.4

Tanis Cornell Talks About Success Characteristics for the Sales Professional

Is professional selling a viable career choice for an ambitious person who wants to maximize earning capacity, use unique skills and talents, and enjoy the satisfaction of being personally productive? If you ask Tanis Cornell, her answer is a resounding "yes."

"In today's competitive market," Cornell says, "many products, companies, and even salespeople start to look alike to the prospect. I look for men and women with the creativity to differentiate themselves from their competition. Much more emphasis is directed at keeping current customers happy and providing long-term solutions. Salespeople must not only excel at prospecting and finding that new customer but excel at building long-term relationships with existing customers.

"In my years as a salesperson and as a manager, I noticed one very interesting thing. There are certain individuals, regardless of gender, that excel each and every year. You can change their compensation plan. You can move them to another job or another location. You can throw any number of challenges at them that would disturb the average salesperson. For top performers, it doesn't matter."

Administrative Ability

Efficient self-management, especially the management of time, is essential to success in selling. Your most productive time is spent face-to-face with prospects. However, you are also required to attend meetings, travel, wait, prepare for interviews, read, study, attend to paperwork, and conduct after-sale follow-up and service.

This means that only a small portion of your precious time can be spent in direct contact with prospects and clients. Time and territory management is one of the most critical issues for salespeople today. A typical sales day, according to research done by the *Dartnell Institute of Business* in Chicago, is spent as follows: 24 percent traveling, 21 percent waiting, 19 percent paperwork and administration, and 36 percent on sales-related activities.

Initiative

All great salespeople have a powerful, unrelenting, internal drive to excel. This intrinsic motivation can be shaped and molded, but it cannot be taught. Successful salespeople see the work that must be done and take personal responsibility for doing it. Creative ideas that surface during a presentation must be implemented then and there; you will not have time to ask your sales manager for advice. Salespeople who have self-confidence, supported by solid product knowledge, good judgment, and belief in their own ability to succeed, exercise initiative.

Perseverance

Setbacks often outnumber triumphs, and salespeople must have reserves of strength and resilience to fall back on when this happens. Depending on the type of sales activity and the product or service being marketed, the number of sales closed compared to the number of presentations made usually ranges from five percent to 50 percent or more. Salespeople need perseverance in several areas:

- The ability to keep going to another prospect, no matter how many have refused to buy.
- The ability to make repeated presentations to the same prospect over a period of time.
- The ability to continue asking for an appointment to make a presentation, until one is finally granted.

Pleasant Personality

The way to make a friend is to be one. The salesperson with a pleasant, outgoing disposition is remembered and favored. A key to forming a pleasant personality is to like people and genuinely enjoy knowing as many different kinds of people as possible. People respond to those who like them.

Your Career in Professional Selling

REFOCUS

- Selling is a basic component of all human interaction. It involves discovering needs and providing products or services that satisfy those needs.

- Salespeople are among the highest-paid professionals and make the greatest impact on profitability and success for an organization.

- Partnerships, customer relationship maintenance, team selling, and strategic alliances are the tools with which winning strategies are fashioned today.

- Professional selling offers opportunities that involve a number of different skill levels and a wide diversity of activities.

- All personality types can be successful in sales, but certain characteristics enhance the likelihood of success: enthusiasm, empathy, goal direction, ability to ask questions, resourcefulness, administrative ability, initiative, perseverance, and a pleasant personality.

- Selling is a demanding career that offers substantial rewards and outstanding opportunities for personal achievement.

✱ Continue to improve

Qualities of High Sales Performers

1. **Exchange information. Ask a variety of questions that help the customer to analyze, evaluate, or express feelings and become a valuable information resource to the customer.**

2. **Know when to close. Advocate your products only after you have identified an important need in the customer's mind and involved the customer in developing the solution.**

3. **Sell to people, not organizations, and demonstrate a strong commitment to meeting customer needs. You are helping the customers personally, and the customer's company.**

4. **Be genuinely interested in your prospects' needs, even while actively promoting your company and its products or services.**

5. **Listen to what your customers have to say. If you let them talk, they will reveal their needs. Remember, if the customer says it, he believes it.**

6. **Become a valuable resource for your company. Act as an information feedback source, able to directly provide expertise to your sales manager.**

7. **Regularly establish trust within your own organization by sharing information, encouraging participation in decisions, and recognizing the contributions of the internal staff to your success as a salesperson.**

8. **Engage in behavior such as maintaining eye contact, showing enthusiasm, asking questions about customers' needs, and being prepared with effective responses to buyers' objections.**

Chapter 2

Relationship Selling

FOCAL POINTS

- **The role of relationship selling today**
- **Forget the stereotypes**
- **The steps in relationship selling**
- **The traditional sales model**
- **Build relationships through team selling**

PROFESSIONAL SELLING IN A TECHNOLOGY WORLD

It is impossible to ignore the profound effects the Internet and technology are having on professional selling. Yet the e-commerce revolution is not the most important change that's happening in sales. There is a second revolution occurring. This other revolution is in the relationship selling process where the buyer requires advice and expertise. It is here that face-to-face selling has been the most effective channel to the customer. Even Internet sales companies, such as Charles Schwab and Dell Computer, have created face-to-face sales forces to reach the segments of their markets requiring complex customized products and services. Their "clicks-and-mortar" strategies rely on sales professionals who can create significant customer value by helping clients define their problems and design unique solutions. This new selling is all about value creation: How the selling process itself can be used to create value for the customer.

Relationship selling — in which sales professionals demonstrate not just a product's technical features, but how it can solve a business problem and save money — isn't a new idea. Yet experts estimate that only 20 percent of American companies have adopted the idea. Positioning yourself as consultant and partner creates a more equal relationship with prospects and customers. The willingness and ability to meet each client's needs is the cornerstone of building partnerships. Clients want business partners, not tennis partners.

Build or Break a Relationship

Partnership is a positive word that makes customers feel that you are looking out for their best interests. The partnership formed between the buyer and seller is not a "legal" partnership. Rather it is a part of the continuous quality improvement process companies are implementing. To be successful, take time to get to know the customer's business situation, needs, cash flow problems, decision-making process, and the competitive environment. In sales, a partnership is a living demonstration of the attitudes sales reps have toward their customers. Exhibit 2.1 illustrates the key elements that can build or break this trust-bond relationship between

Exhibit 2.1

How to Build or Break a Relationship

Relationship Builders

- Treat customers like lifelong partners.
- Become a solutions provider.
- Deliver more service than you promise.
- Schedule regular service calls.
- Develop open and honest communication.
- Use the "we can" approach.
- Take responsibility for mistakes made.
- Be an ally for the customer's business.

Relationship Breakers

- Focus only on making the sale.
- Simply wait for a problem to develop.
- Over-promise and under-deliver.
- Wait for customers to call you.
- Lie or make exaggerated claims.
- Use the "us-versus-them" approach.
- Blame somebody else. Knock a competitor.
- Focus on your own personal gain.

buyer and seller. Relationship selling allows you to grasp a company's needs by putting yourself on the customer's side of the desk. You are first a *diagnostician*.

Relationship salespeople create information transfer, support for client goals, and enthusiasm for their success. Mike Hill, business development director at PricewaterhouseCoopers, believes that we need to get away from a selling mentality and let the customer tell us their needs. He states that we should strive to build a relationship, based on a trust in our expertise that can help clients solve problems. When this occurs, Hill says, "We talk about our approach to solving the client's problem and sometimes don't even need to ask for the business. The client often asks us."

> In professional selling, as in medicine, prescription
> before diagnosis is malpractice.

To be a consultant rather than just a salesperson you have to be a creative resource, a value provider, and a friend to clients. The relationship salesperson works hard helping others succeed — not just helping them purchase. Unless you are willing to commit to excellence, *consultation will not occur*. Here are some key characteristics of relationship selling:

- Discover and understand the customers' problems and needs.

- Partner with your customers and become a valuable resource for information.

- Demonstrate to customers how they can achieve their goals with your product or service.

- Have a true conviction that your company, product, and services are the best for your customers.

- Believe in yourself because a positive attitude makes it all work.

RELATIONSHIP SELLING VERSUS TRADITIONAL SELLING

It just makes sense that if you understand what the steps are in the relationship model of selling, and what it takes to make each step a successful endeavor, then you will become a professional in selling much more quickly than those individuals who are simply stumbling through the process trying to figure it out. The sales cycle model in the actual face-to-face meeting between you and the prospect includes these four phases:

1. The Approach
2. Identifying Needs
3. Making the Presentation
4. Handling Objections and Gaining Commitment

Figure 2.1 contrasts the amount of time the relationship salesperson and the traditional salesperson spend in each step. You can see from the figure that the old pyramid model of selling has been turned upside down. The 40 percent of the equation for the traditional model that used to be closing is now building trust in the relationship model. Meanwhile reassuring the customer and closing has shrunk to just 10 percent in the new model.

Figure 2.1

Relationship Selling versus Traditional Selling

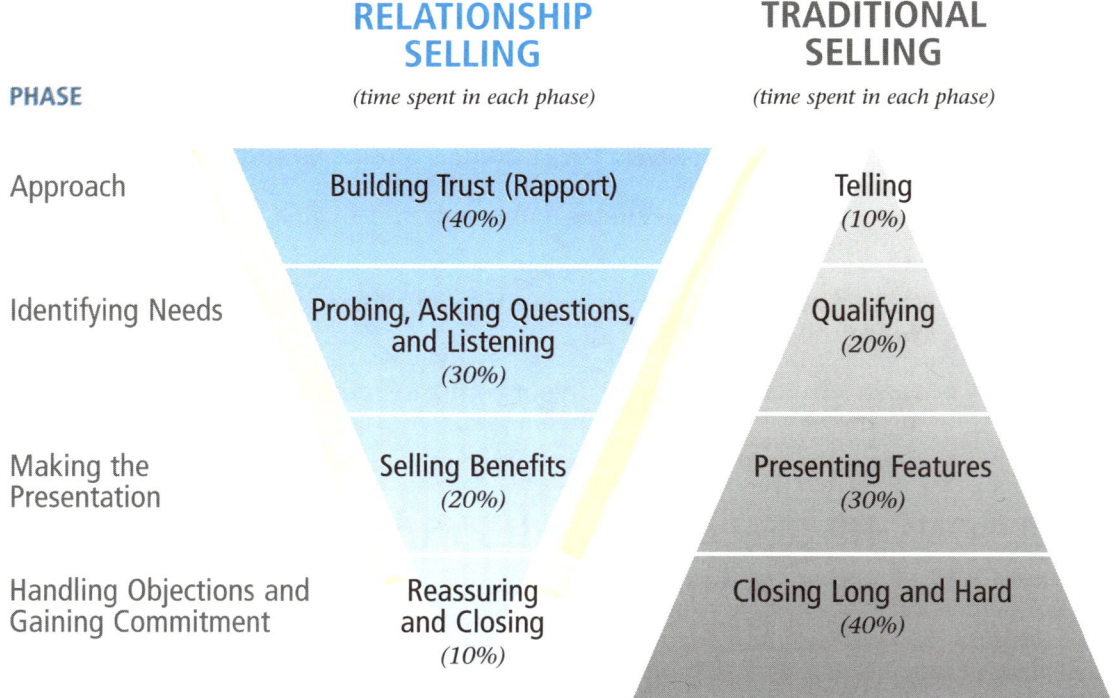

PHASE	RELATIONSHIP SELLING *(time spent in each phase)*	TRADITIONAL SELLING *(time spent in each phase)*
Approach	Building Trust (Rapport) *(40%)*	Telling *(10%)*
Identifying Needs	Probing, Asking Questions, and Listening *(30%)*	Qualifying *(20%)*
Making the Presentation	Selling Benefits *(20%)*	Presenting Features *(30%)*
Handling Objections and Gaining Commitment	Reassuring and Closing *(10%)*	Closing Long and Hard *(40%)*

The relationship salesperson spends the vast majority of time in the first two steps, whereas the traditional salesperson exerts most of the effort and the majority of time on presenting features and trying to close. The goal is to learn how to communicate with your business partners and establish an alliance that is extensive in scope and relevant to the customer's own vision.

You are a solutions provider.

Customers Buy Solutions

Technology helps open new markets, speeds communications between sellers and their prospects and customers, and, frankly, creates a whole new set of problems that you can help clients solve. Customers can now conduct many of their transactions online and have little need for a salesperson that doesn't add value to the transaction. This requires a much more sophisticated and complex set of skills than those possessed by the traditional salesperson.

Low-end selling — essentially transaction processing and order taking — continues to shift away from traditional sales forces into the more efficient, cost-effective, and faster setting provided by the Internet. But this doesn't mean that the Internet will replace the professional salesperson. Selling is simply becoming more strategic. It's moving up the food chain, and the need for relationship selling is increasing. Your company may sell accounting services, office equipment, or design Web sites. However, that's really not what customers are buying — customers are trying to increase their sales and improve efficiency. By demonstrating how you can help customers achieve the goals of their organization, you distinguish yourself from competitors. Selling is still about relationships, and people buy from people they like. Order-takers will vanish, but creative salespeople who know that selling is about building long-term partnerships will flourish.

SALES CYCLE FRAMEWORK FOR RELATIONSHIP SELLING

A better understanding of the complete selling situation and the problems it generates may be gained by breaking the sale into its basic tasks. These steps are presented in a logical sequence, but they are *not necessarily chronological* and the order of the steps will vary. The ebb and flow of a sales interview defies attempts to package it into nice, neat compartments. Every selling situation has a beginning, an end, and a number of identifiable points in between.

Regardless of account size or potential, certain predictable tasks must be performed. These tasks, such as identifying prospects and determining needs, may be called the steps in a sale or the selling cycle. When organized into a prescribed sequence they comprise an overall structure rather than a lock-step approach to selling. The eight basics of successful selling described in Figure 2.2 are the focus of chapters 7 through 14. These steps represent your guide to a rewarding career in sales.

Figure 2.2

A Sales Cycle Framework for Relationship Selling

THE HANDBOOK FOR RELATIONSHIP SELLING

> Your professionalism is defined not by the business you are in,
> but by the way you are in business.
>
> — Dr. Tony Alessandra

Phase One

Identify Qualified Prospects. Prospecting is the process of searching for some-one with a need for the product or service, the ability to pay for it, and the authority to make a buying decision. One of the first steps in the process of finding these qualified prospects is to review your current accounts to see who needs service, who might want to increase the quantity purchased, or who may buy new products for the first time. At the same time, survey your territory to identify new leads and find out information on the businesses in your area that might be interested in your product. The reason for this step is simple: Sales professionals must study the people they want to approach.

Plan Preapproach Activities. After you indentify qualified prospects, establish a definite purpose for each sales call. To accomplish this, you must make an evaluation of your potential customers' needs and determine who the decision-makers are in the companies you have studied. These activities equip you to interact with the customer and then develop an action plan and call schedule to set appointments.

Phase Two

Approach the Prospect. Treat prospects as individuals and not as carbon copies of everyone else. What happens during the opening minutes of the face-to-face encounter affects the success of the whole presentation. Some people do not thaw out immediately, and you must find ice-breakers that help the prospect feel at ease. This is why you should spend time finding the prospect's comfort level. Most first-time meetings between salesperson and prospect produce an *egocentric predicament* arising from your fear of being rejected and the prospect's fear of being sold something that is not really wanted or needed. By redesigning your approach, you can calm the prospect's fear of buying and reduce your own fear of selling.

Discover Needs. During this step of the sales encounter, you and your clients discover whether they need something that you can provide. Because the success of the whole process rests on this basic discovery, the relationship salesperson spends whatever time is necessary and asks questions to get to know the prospect's needs and problems. For this reason, one of your primary goals in every sales situation should be to create an atmosphere within which an act of trust can occur — to make a friend rather than a sale, a customer who has confidence in the integrity and your ability, and confidence in the company and its product or service. You don't talk prospects into a sale; you listen them into a sale.

Make the Presentation. Your evaluation of the prospect's situation should lead you naturally into the presentation of product benefits that fit the needs your client expressed. Every product or service has both features and benefits. A *feature* is any fact about the product or service, tangible or intangible. For example, a feature of a particular automobile is front-wheel drive. However, prospects want to know about benefits rather than features. The front-wheel drive feature is meaningless unless it satisfies some need, solves some problem, or provides some benefit to the prospective customer. The *benefits* of front-wheel drive might be explained in terms of ease of handling, safety, or some other performance quality that promises to satisfy the prospect's need.

Even better than showcasing the value of the product is to allow prospects to assess that value by discovering for themselves the benefits of owning it. The relationship salesperson is customer-oriented. A prospect does not buy without being certain that what you are saying is true. That is why you do not create sales; rather, people buy based on their own expectations. *No one likes to be sold*. They like to see the value of what is being presented, and then they make their own buying decisions based on their own assessment of whether or not your product satisfies their needs. Exhibit 2.2 illustrates how the power of expectation works. The salesperson who holds confident, positive expectations closes far more sales than the one who expects rejection.

Exhibit 2.2

The Power of Expectation

Expectation is powerful. Three mess hall sergeants received large shipments of dried apricots. At first, they were all dismayed because they didn't see how they could use that many apricots. They each dealt with the problem differently.

The first one "knew" no one in his outfit wanted apricots; so he cooked a large pot of stewed apricots, stuck a ladle in the pot, and set it at the end of the serving line. Sure enough, at the end of three days, his negative expectations were fulfilled; he still had most of the apricots.

The second one adopted a more positive approach. He also cooked a large pot of stewed apricots; but he stood in the serving line with a big smile and a ladle in hand. "Let me serve you some apricots," he offered, as people came through the line. He disposed of more apricots than the first sergeant.

The third sergeant decided to create a demand. He put up signs at the beginning and end of the serving line: "Coming Tuesday: Apricots just like your Mother served. Your choice." On Tuesday at breakfast time, a big sign on the front door announced: "It's Tuesday! Mother's apricots are here!" He had prepared stewed apricots and a mix of chopped dried apricots, raisins, and nuts to sprinkle on cereal. For lunch and dinner, he offered apricot fried pies, baked apricot pies, and apricot bread. His shipment of apricots disappeared quickly.

Handle Objections and Gain Commitment. Now is the time to verbally clarify and confirm what both you and the client will do to make the solution work. This part of the overall process helps to avoid misunderstandings by bringing any that exist out into the open so they can be handled. Each clarification and confirmation adds weight to the case in favor of a positive decision. As shown in Figure 2.3, when the scale of decision tips far enough toward the positive side, the prospect can, and does, say yes. When that happens, everyone wins — the client, you, and your company. Relationship selling is a matter of presenting positive benefits that respond to a need, use, and value. Selling in this manner reduces your need to deal with resistance, answer objections, or haggle over price. Since the client has been an active participant throughout, the commitment and close should be the natural conclusion to a successful sales interview.

Figure 2.3

The Scale of Decision

Selling positive benefits tips the scale

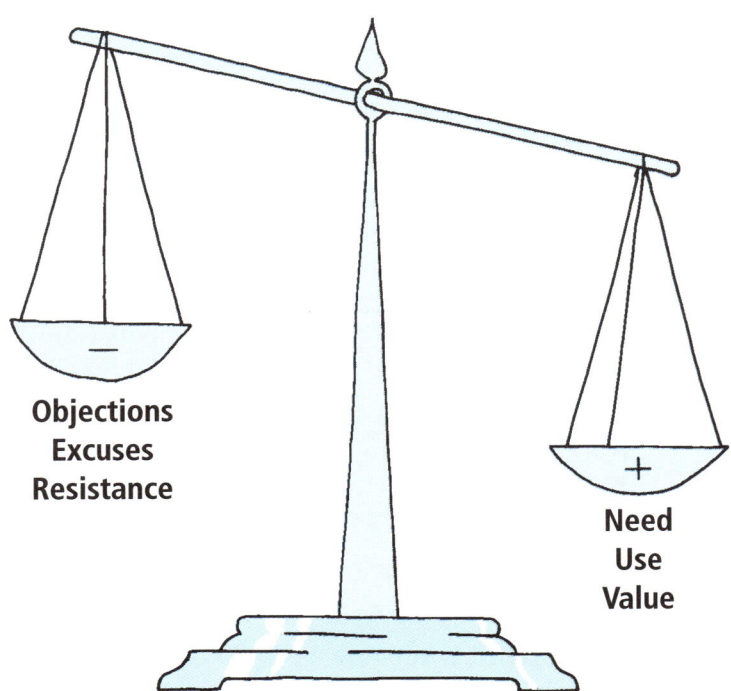

Objections
Excuses
Resistance

Need
Use
Value

Phase Three

Service After the Sale. The final phase of relationship selling is service after the sale. After all, one of the purposes of a business is to create and keep a customer. Service, service, and more service is what counts and gives you a competitive edge. Plenty of satisfied customers do not come back unless you create some kind of trust-bond relationship.

Ultimately, you should look at customer satisfaction as an economic asset just like any other asset of the company. Creating customer satisfaction is an income-producing endeavor. Too many salespeople perform service mechanically, without thinking of the impact their actions have on customers. Clients must sense that you truly care about them. Service after the sale is your way of expressing appreciation for their business. Service makes the difference and is as important as the quality of the product.

CONTINUOUS QUALITY IMPROVEMENT

There has been so much written on Total Quality Management that some have dismissed it as merely a theory that is discussed because it sounds good. But to ignore the underlying principles of TQM would not be sensible. TQM is an essential building block for relationship selling, and the principles have practical implications for you.

How does TQM fit into relationship selling? Total Quality Management has a customer orientation. It is an outside-in approach to business. The center of all discussions is the customer; everyone inside and outside the company is a customer. Continuous quality improvement is a philosophy, an overall style of management that focuses on customer satisfaction. Federal Express Chief Executive Officer Fred Smith states that, "Employee satisfaction is a prerequisite to customer satisfaction." Therefore, TQM not only focuses on fostering healthy relationships with customers, but also on building connections within organizations.

The list below highlights the main points of TQM that deal directly with fostering relationships and building lasting associations. While there are variations in the language and scope of TQM programs, it is possible to target these five principles that are especially relevant in the practice of relationship selling:

1. **Listen and learn** from your customers and your employees.
2. **Continuously improve** the partnership.
3. **Build teamwork** by establishing trust and mutual respect.

4. **Do it right the first time** to ensure customer satisfaction.
5. **Improve communication** in your own company to broaden the utilization of your company's resources. Everybody is involved in the relationship.

Service Quality: A Team Effort

What does an organization have to do to provide exceptional service quality and how does the salesperson fit into the process? First, everyone in your company must think in terms of the whole process rather than their own tasks. The goal is to develop a customer, and that's a process in which the sales rep is only one player. The process includes production people, finance and marketing people, as well as customer service reps. So it's not left to you to solve a customer's problem; the whole organization gets behind the effort. Building customer relationships is everybody's responsibility.

It is important to focus on how you relate to plant and office employees, because this can make a difference in the way they treat your customers. It pays to be liked and appreciated by staff people, especially those in sales support, credit, billing, and shipping. Take a lesson from Mark Twain, who said, "I can live for two months on a good compliment." Take a moment from time to time to compliment and thank the support people in your company for the great job they are doing.

TQM is established today thanks to the pioneering work of W. Edwards Deming. One of Deming's most important lessons is his "85-15" rule. When things go wrong in the field, there is an 85 percent chance the system is at fault. Only about 15 percent of the time can the individual salesperson be blamed. TQM means the organization's culture is defined by and supports the constant attainment of customer satisfaction, through an integrated system of tools, techniques, and training. Prospects and customers notice and think about everyone they come in contact with during the sales encounter. The relationship between perceived effort and customer service is a powerful one. When you and the customer interact, the quality of the interaction itself is an important part of the relationship. Figure 2.4 shows the dynamics of this interaction. Service quality has two dimensions: (1) the process of delivering the service and (2) the actual outcome.

Most business success stories involve taking an old idea or product and doing a better job with it than the next company. Wal-Mart didn't invent discount selling; Sam Walton just did it better. And the executives who now run Wal-Mart are improving the way they buy and stock merchandise to drive their costs and prices even lower. Then there is Starbucks! Coffee shops have been around for a long time, but no one before Starbucks had figured out how to organize and run

Figure 2.4

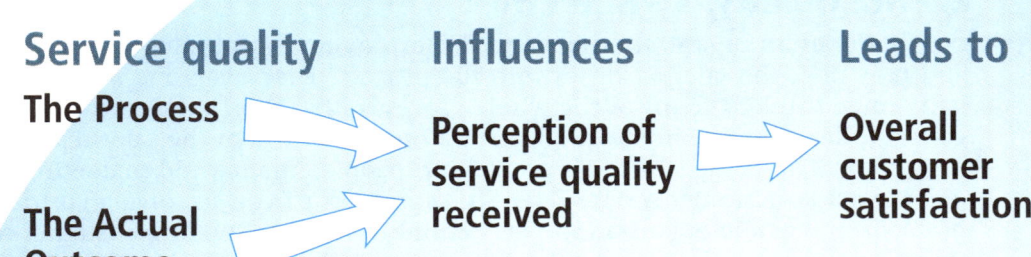

The Service Quality Interaction

Service quality

The Process

The Actual
Outcome

Influences

Perception of
service quality
received

Leads to

Overall
customer
satisfaction

several thousand of them. The overall point is this: You can get a lot out of a current product or service if you change the processes around it, or change the process by which it is delivered. The objective is to change those processes enough that you are delivering more value to your customers or, at the very least, hold on to those customers by offering a fair price.

The $332,000 Customer: Why It Pays to Go the Extra Mile

Tom Peters, author of *A Passion for Excellence*, says, "A customer is not a transaction; a customer is a relationship." The missing link in service often is intense awareness of the customer's point of view. The process of handling the problem is as important to customers as the solution of the problem itself. The logical inference is that every company better organize its service delivery system to answer every customer's implied question: "What are you going to do for me today?"

Peters uses the example of Dallas car dealer Carl Sewell, who has written a book called *The $332,000 Customer* because a loyal lifetime Cadillac customer buys that much from him. Peters goes on to suggest that each lifetime customer generates four or five happy lifetime customers for you. So in fact, one Cadillac customer is roughly a $1,500,000 customer. Two investments Sewell has made illustrate his understanding of the value he places on customer satisfaction. Number one, he bought a street sweeper to keep the front of his dealership extra clean. First impressions count for everything, and people judge his dealership by the cleanliness of everything including the road in front of it. Number two, he convinced an upscale local restaurant to open a branch in his service bay. When it's a simple repair, a lot of his customers come in and enjoy a hot meal while the work is being done.

Figure 2.5 illustrates the kind of behavior wanted in a quality-driven sales organization and the kind that exists in the typical organization. To move from left to right, use the 12 essential elements of TQM and your commitment to customer satisfaction to guide you. Some salespeople will read this and say, "This is nothing new; it is simply common sense." They are right, of course, but it has taken many years for men such as W. Edwards Deming, Philip Crosby, Joseph Juran, and Genichi Taguchi to refine and teach this philosophy.

Figure 2.5

Culture Changes in a Sales Organization

Traditional Mangement Model	Total Quality Management Model
Focus on product	Focus on service
Company knows best	Customer knows best
Transactions	Relationships
Individual performance	Team performance
Firefighting management	Continuous improvement
Blame/punishment	Support/reward
Short-term (year or less)	Long-term (years)
Intolerant of errors	Allows mistakes
Autocratic leadership	Participative leadership
Bureaucratic	Entrepreneurial
Top-down decisions	Consensus decisions
Inward-focused	Outward (customer)-focused

TEAM SELLING

Team Selling is a cooperative action by two or more professionals directed to selling a product or service. The sales team often consists of at least one salesperson, supported by technical specialists, a combination that utilizes the relationship expertise of the salesperson as well as the technical competency of other personnel throughout the organization. Team selling involves not only several people from the seller's company but also a purchasing team from the prospect's company. The concept of team selling balances perfectly with the principles behind TQM because team sales builds lasting relationships, breaks down walls, and opens communication through teamwork. That's why two heads really are better than one.

The team approach gains an advantage over one-on-one selling because it utilizes the strengths of each individual on the team. Some professional salespeople may lack the patience and attention to detail that are required to eventually guide the prospect to commit. Yet, technical support people involved on the team may possess these very characteristics, as they tend to be detail-oriented by nature. Similarly, a personality that appears too abrupt in the eyes of a client may be offset by a conservative personality who can energize the client with a sense of confidence.

Benefits of Team Selling

A healthy team attitude begins with a solid commitment to help team members win. There is no room for prima donnas within the team. The only person who is allowed to be the prima donna is the customer. One of the primary benefits of team selling is that it enables a company to improve its relationship with customers, by allowing direct communication between the buyer and product specialists before the sale is made. Thus, the seller can more accurately define the customer's needs, and the buyer can have questions answered by an individual who has an intimate knowledge of the product. This creates an aura of authority and trustworthiness for the company and the salesperson.

Imagine the technical expertise required to sell satellite time to the telecommunications industry, a service of Satellite Corporation. The needs of each client are unique, and once the sale is made, the relationship has just begun. Buyers not only want to know what the service can do for their company, but also who will be working with them after the sale is made. For these reasons, Satellite Corporation requires that all employees act as informal partners of the sales department and are expected to contribute their expertise in making all sales. Technical people, for instance, frequently accompany salespeople on calls, and the salespeople work closely with their marketing colleagues to produce the brochures, technical guides, and other materials used in setting up and closing a sale.

THE HANDBOOK FOR RELATIONSHIP SELLING